FRENCH WOMEN AND THE FIRST WORLD WAR

FRENCH WOMEN AND THE FIRST WORLD WAR
War Stories of the Home Front

MARGARET H. DARROW

Oxford ● New York

First published in 2000 by
Berg
Editorial offices:
150 Cowley Road, Oxford, OX4 1JJ, UK
838 Broadway, Third Floor, New York, NY 10003-4812, USA

Berg is an imprint of Oxford International Publishers Ltd.

Library of Congress Cataloging-in-Publication Data
A catalogue record for this book is available from the Library of Congress.

British Library Cataloguing-in-Publication Data
A catalogue record for this book is available from the British Library.

ISBN 1 85973 361 1 (Cloth)
1 85973 366 2 (Paper)

Typeset by JS Typesetting, Wellingborough, Northants
Printed in Great Britain by Biddles Ltd
www.biddles.co.uk

Contents

Acknowledgements

The folk tales of my childhood were my mother's war stories. An elementary school teacher in Connecticut, she had helped put two younger brothers through Ivy League colleges while she still lived at home. Pearl Harbor, that day of infamy, was also an act of liberation; she enlisted in the WAVES without telling her principal – or her parents! I heard about the trials of boot camp and the pleasures of her posting in San Francisco, where she lived the high life, bankrolled by sailors looking for a good time before they shipped out. Cocktails at the Top of the Mark. Dancing the night away to the Big Bands. Highjinks on the cable cars. War seemed to me as exciting an adventure for women as it was for men. When I began to absorb the versions of the Second World War in the popular culture of the late 1950s and 1960s, I was surprised that none told my mother's stories. But I soon learned that women did not count except in the home, and that there was an unbridgeable gulf between family tales around the kitchen table and the news of the world. Now, of course, I think otherwise. This book, although about French women and another war, is intended to show, in part, where the bridges are located.

The most pleasant task in publishing a book is acknowledging one's debts and thanking one's friends. For an American, lengthy researches in France require financial assistance, and for this I thank the Whiting Foundation, which funded my initial research, and Dartmouth College for timely grants that allowed me to tie up loose ends. This American in Paris also benefited from the friendship and the guest bedroom of the Susmann-Baudin family and from the stimulating companionship of the BN crowd, especially Danielle Stewart, and Mary Ryan's 1993 women's history seminar. Fortunately I have been able to rely upon suggestions and criticism from many superb scholars of French women's history – Joby Margadant, Judith Wishnia, Linda Clark, Gay Gullickson, Elaine Kruse, Katrin Schultheiss, Steven Hause, Elinor Accampo, Karen Offen and Lou

Acknowledgements

Roberts. Several First World War specialists – Jennifer Keene, Nicole van Os, Laurie Stoff, Angela Woollacott – have helped me see French women's experience in a wider perspective.

Working in a number of libraries and archives has made me very grateful for the friendly, helpful staff at the Bibiliothèque Marguerite Durand, for Kathy Hart and Kathleen O'Malley at the Hood Museum of Art and, as always, the wonderful Patsy Carter and Marianne Hraibi of Dartmouth's Baker Library Interlibrary Loan. Cassie Motz '93 read *Le Petit Parisien* cover-to-cover for the war years, noting every mention of women. The results of her work are in every chapter, and I heartily thank her.

Many of my colleagues at Dartmouth, and especially the members of the Feminist Inquiry Seminar, have contributed to this book with their insights. I am most grateful to Annelise Orleck, Carl Estabrook, Mary Jean Green and Leo Spitzer. Judy Stern, Margot Anderson, Donna Nelson, Joan Hummel, Suzanne Brown, Neil Hochstedtler, Muffin Alexander, Ginny Swain and Susanne Zantop, my skiing, walking, and cappuccino-drinking buddies, have patiently borne with my enthusiasms. Thanks go also to the four-footed crew, who, when not wandering on to the keyboard, have napped by me through thick and thin: Patrick, Alison, Boots and of course, Marlowe. My deepest debt is to my sister, Sarah Darrow, whose support is always just a phone call away.

List of Abbreviations

ADF   Association des Dames françaises, Association of French
       Ladies, one of the French Red Cross organizations
CGT   Confédération générale du travail, General Confederation
       of Labor
CNFF   Conseil national des femmes françaises, National Council of
       French Women
DSA   Direction de Service Automobile, Army Automobile Service
PTT   Postes, Télégraphes et Téléphones, postal service
SSBM   Société de secours aux blessés militaires, Society to Aid
       Wounded Soldiers, one of the French Red Cross organizations
UFF   Union des Femmes de France, Union of French Women, one
       of the French Red Cross organizations
UFSF   Union française pour le suffrage des femmes, French Union
       for Women's Suffrage

1

Woman and War

It seems paradoxical to unite these two words: woman and war.

Women and war . . . if there are two words made not to go together, it is these two: war and women.[1]

The first quotation is from a speech to a women's organization in Paris in 1912; the second, from an article in *L'Opinion Publique*, appeared early in 1940. How little the First World War had done to reconcile French women and war! Even the title of the *L'Opinion Publique* article, "Women and the War," mirrored that of numerous First World War publications.[2] Although a few writers had placed women "during" or, most daringly, "in" the war (such as Gaston Rageot, *The French Woman in the War* (1918)),[3] the most common connection was "and." Women and war could be juxtaposed, but what had the one to do with the other? Although the trenches of the First World War ran through northern France, ensuring that some French women lived in its midst, and although many French women worked to support the war, those who made public opinion in France had difficulty envisioning a relationship between women and the war.[4]

This difficulty did not result from lack of effort. During the war, many French men and women wrote about women's wartime activities. And there were stories, novels and plays about *marraines de guerre* who "adopted" soldiers by correspondence (see Chapter 3), and about battlefield nurses (see Chapter 5) and spies (see Chapter 8). Even the wise fool, Bécassine, had four First World War cartoon adventures.[5] Some French women published diaries or memoirs of their war experiences. But none of these stories "stuck." With the exception of Bécassine's adventures, reissued in 1947 and again recently, French women's stories of the war quickly disappeared. No French counterpart exists to Vera Brittain's war memoir, *Testament of Youth*, a bestseller when it was first published

1

in 1933 and in print almost continuously ever since. Although critics at the time praised some French women's accounts of the war – Maurice Donnay compared Noëlle Roger's nursing sketches, *Carnets d'une infirmière* (1915) to Harriet Beecher Stowe's *Uncle Tom's Cabin*[6] – after the war they soon went out of print. Even the best of women's writing, such as Marguerite Lesage's *Journal de guerre d'une française* (1938), is difficult to find today.

The history of collective memory is a burgeoning field of scholarly interest at the moment, but the meaning of the term is as vague and various as the studies are numerous. By "popular memory" or "public memory" of the First World War, I mean the stories that French people have told to themselves and to each other that helped them make sense of the experience of the war, whether for themselves, personally, or for France. Jay Winter and Emmanuel Sivan remind us that "forgetting and fade-out are usually the rule;" it is remembering that requires explanation.[7] But in the case of French women's experience in the First World War, the lack of stories today, or even in the 1930s, is intriguing considering how many stories there were during the war itself. It has not been individuals' memories that have faded, as ethnographers' interviews with peasant women in the 1970s demonstrated (see Chapter 6). But personal memories did not contribute to a story that had public meaning. Official memorialization in monuments and historic sites ignored French women's role in the war from the first,[8] while popular memory, fed by family stories, school lessons, novels, movies and the like has done little better. Recent fictional evocations of the First World War in Sébastian Japrisot's best-selling novel, *A Very Long Engagement* (1991) and Bertrand Tavernier's film, *Life and Nothing But* (1989) have assigned women the role of attempting, futilely, to understand *men's* war experience; in both, women have no war stories of their own. When I tell French librarians and archivists that I am researching women in France during the First World War, they frequently begin to talk about the Resistance. The Second World War has produced legends of female heroism; the First did not.

Until recently, historians' accounts partially filled the gap. As James McMillan has pointed out, before we began seriously to study women's history, the First World War figured in French history, as it did in British and American history, as a watershed of women's emancipation.[9] Historians mostly repeated as fact contemporary predictions that the war would mark French women's emergence from domestic seclusion and civil inferiority. During the war, feminists and their allies promoted this outcome. Marie de la Hire predicted in 1917 that "after having valiantly replaced men during the war, women will find themselves at men's side in the economy" and "women's suffrage and electoral eligibility will be, tomorrow, the homage rendered to women's recognized and utilized capacities, a mark of confidence from those Frenchmen who defended the fatherland with weapons to their companions who defended it in their hearts."[10] Historians continued to repeat this conclusion long after they knew, as wartime commentators did not, that the vote and full civil rights had not materialized for French women until they had participated in yet another World War.[11]

The story that the First World War emancipated women, French women as well as German, British and American women, has not survived the serious scrutiny of the first generation of scholars of women's history. Gail Braybon for England, Maurine Weiner Greenwald for the United States, Ute Daniel for Germany and James McMillan for France all concluded that emancipation was largely an illusion.[12] In the case of France, the war did not suddenly catapult women into the public arena; they had been there for decades already, as agricultural and industrial workers, as producers of culture, and even as political actors of consequence. The war's impact upon this scene was not revolutionary and probably not even unidirectional. McMillan, who twenty years ago blew the first fresh air at the myth of the First World War as French women's Great Emancipator, argued that the war had little impact upon French women's status except, perhaps, to accelerate trends already well under way. Françoise Thébaud, writing five years later, also minimized the war's effects, but did see them, on the whole, as progressive. By contrast, Michelle Perrot, in her articles about gender relations, Véronique Leroux-Hugon, writing about nurses, and Marie-Monique Huss, examining the pronatalism campaign, suggest the war's impact was regressive.[13] Recently, Mary Louise Roberts has tried to call a halt to the whole proceeding, arguing that it is as important to understand why French people perceived the First World War as a watershed in gender relations as it is to study the actual legal, economic and demographic status of French women in this period.[14] This is an important debate, but it has left French women without any war story at all. French women and the First World War remains the paradoxical juxtaposition predicted in 1912.

At first glance, it might seem obvious that no such story could exist, because women experienced the war in many different ways.

51 le P.

3

Roberts

That there was no unique and unitary feminine war experience in France is the thrust of Françoise Thébaud's book, *La femme au temps de la guerre de 14.* While the chapter titles of the book's first part, "Women at War," remind us that women did many different things to contribute to the war effort – charity work, munitions work, nursing, etc. – the second part, "Women in the Country at War," points out that the war had differing impacts upon single women, married women and mothers, upon working-class women and well-to-do women, upon women in the northern invaded regions and women in the southern protected ones. How could there be one story for all French women, as there was one story for all men, the troglodyte saga of the trenches? But this comparison, in fact, plunges us into the problem that it pretends to elucidate, because although the story of the trench-fighter is indeed the (male) story of the First World War, not all men, nor even all soldiers, were trench-fighters. Besides the air war, whose romance lives on in Snoopy's fantasy, there was also a mostly unsung naval war and the even less storied experience of the military support personnel. By January 1918, 28 per cent of mobilized Frenchmen were non-combatants, performing their military service as clerks, cooks, orderlies, garage mechanics, etc.[15] The trench-fighter's story became *the* story of the First World War, not necessarily because it was the majority story, but because it was the story that made sense out of the war, that installed its meaning – dehumanizing horror but also patriotic sacrifice – in popular conciousness.[16]

Women's wartime experiences that have produced stories in this century, particularly those about the Second World War, make the point clearly. The historians Mary Cadogan and Patricia Craig point out that the possible stories about British women's experience in the two world wars are quite similar, but public memory of them is very different. "The 'war to end wars' is today remembered largely in terms of slaughter and sacrifice. However, when the war of 1939–1945 is recapitulated, its home front activities are frequently evoked."[17] And alongside the perky lassie "doing her bit," there are other heroines of Second World War narratives, such as the American Rosie the Riveter, the British Blitz victim and the French Resistance fighter. And all of these were minority experiences; in the case of female Resistance fighters, a tiny minority. Why didn't French women inscribe such a story of the First World War in the national memory, in memorials and school texts, for example, or in novels and television "docu-dramas"? The First World War had its energetic

4

French girls doing volunteer work, its trouser-wearing munitions workers, its female victims of bombs and even its resistance heroines. Everyone knows Lucie Aubrac; why does no one remember Louise de Bettignies? (See Chapter 8.)

This book explores the stories that could have been and why they were not. These include the experiences of French women in the war, the stories that the women themselves told about these experiences and how French society interpreted them. What did the First World War mean to the Frenchwomen who lived through it? What issues and arguments, what expectations and assumptions competed to shape the feminine meaning of the war? It argues that the project to dictate a French women's war story misfired during the war itself. This was not the case, so familiar to women's history, of memory-loss, a story produced during the war and then erased by the post-war backlash of antifeminism, formidable as the latter was. Instead it was a failure of memory creation. The wartime discourse on "women and the war," in a large measure, prevented the production of a coherent French women's war story.

The masculine story was that of the *petits poilus* who, through suffering and horrific sacrifice, ultimately triumphed in their defense of France. But victory was a long time coming in the First World War. To explain the ups, and especially the downs, of the war, people turned to stories about women. While these stories sometimes cast women in a role similar to that of the heroic soldier – the stories of Invasion Heroines, for example (see Chapter 4) – women were also sometimes villains whose selfish behavior undermined masculine achievement on the battlefield. In 1917, women became scapegoats in stories that explained and predicted French defeat.

While the masculine war story was unitary and unchanging, the feminine story was multiple and shifting, reacting to and explaining the immediate crisis like the German invasion in 1914 or the precipitous rise in the cost of living in 1917. Thus, it was impossible to fix the narrative; now presenting heroines, now villains, the war stories about women undermined any unambiguous relationship between French women and the war and emptied women's wartime experiences of specific meaning. What women did in the war or what was done to them by the war was explained – and explained away – as minor adaptations of a traditional feminine destiny. Thus, the feminine war story became simply the Eternal Feminine, and both the war and the story dropped out. Or, if the war remained front and center, then the story pushed women to the periphery or denied them feminine attributes and thus a feminine experience. War had a story, but women did not; to bring them together into a single narrative threatened both terms: women ceased to be women or war ceased to be war.

The only women's war story that survived is a cautionary one. While the likes of Louise de Bettignies, promoted immediately after the war as emblematic heroines, never entered the public's long-term memory, one woman from the First World War lives on in the popular imagination: Mata Hari. The inspiration of several films, including one in 1964 starring Jeanne Moreau, plays, novels, a wealth of memoirs as well as serious histories, the legend of her treachery continues to imply the dangers in too closely associating women and war.[18]

In Western culture, war is conceptually, although not in practice, an exclusively masculine project, and its relationship to women has been and remains highly problematic. The cultural critics Nancy Huston and Susan Jeffords argue that men, lacking a natural role on the order of motherhood, have seized upon war as naturally masculine. Jeffords writes: "War is described as a biological necessity for the human male; without it, he is somehow only half alive. In the same way, reproduction is portrayed as requisite for the social well-being of the human female, something for which she will feel a nostalgia for having 'missed.'"[19] Like maternity, war functions symbolically, not only as gender's unique marker, but also as its ultimate fulfillment. As femininity supposedly flowers in motherhood, so too masculinity fulfills itself in war. Both, it is claimed, produce an awakening and a transformation, an attainment of full, gendered, adulthood. Reflecting on his experience in Vietnam, William Broyles Jr. writes: "War is for men, at some terrible level, the closest thing to what childbirth is for women: the initiation into the power of life and death."[20] But while Broyles here links life and death, in most formulations the two separate in a dance of gendered polarities, death, destruction and war adhering to the masculine while birth, nurture and peace adhere to the feminine. In our culture's war stories, as the political scientist Jean Bethke Elshtain reminds us, pacific men and bellicose women are forgotten or considered as gender misfits.[21] Those who go to war become men; that is the point of it. Therefore, women have nothing to do with war; the "and" in "women and war" is a false connector.

But although women are to have nothing to do with war, they are nonetheless necessary to it, and not only in peripheral roles. As

Huston and Elshtain argue, woman often appear as the cause of war and as its objective: consider Helen of Troy and the Sabine women.[22] In the nineteenth and twentieth centuries, when war has been depicted as defensive above all, women are what men fight to protect. The cultural historian George Mosse reminds us that marble and bronze women, stately and immobile, raise the flame of Columbia, or carry Britannia's trident, Marianne's staff or Germania's lance in symbolic representation of the nation for whom (male) patriots spill their blood.[23] "Real" women, especially when clutching children in their arms, are made to serve the same purpose. Arguing with the leader of a group of French soldiers deserting the front in May 1917, Capitaine d'Heursel reported: "I tried to reason with him and show him that if he and his comrades gave up, the Germans would profit from it by advancing probably to occupy their own homeland and they certainly must be aware of how the Germans treat women and children in the lands they conquer."[24] Thus, because women embody that which must be defended, they also easily become that which must be despoiled. Huston argues that, in many soldiers' narratives, to rape the enemy's women often seems to be as much the point of war as to kill the enemy himself; for it to be really war, both men's blood and women's tears must flow.[25]

Women also fill a number of peripheral roles in the war story. They are auxiliaries to the warrior – nurses and telephone operators, for example, and providers, willingly or not, of sexual services. They are also the intermittent reminders of the pre-war, non-war life and its values and that this war-forged masculinity should be exported to and wielded in this other context; in contrast and superiority to the woman left behind, the soldier will return as a Man. And most essentially, women are the war's audience, to cheer, to mourn and to listen to its stories. Huston asks, provocatively, "If a war gave rise to no narrative, would it have taken place?"[26] Wars make their meaning in stories, and without an audience, there would be no stories, no meaning and thus no "war" at all.

But although essential to war, women are not central to it. Women may provide war's rationale and its audience, war may be fought over and in front of women, but the people who do the fighting, who make the war and who are made by it, are men. The universal feature of war stories is masculinity. Discussing narratives of the Vietnam War, Susan Jeffords argues: "For such narratives, gender is the assumed category of interpretation, the only one that is not subject to interpretation and variation of point of view, experience, age, race and so on."[27] In fact, war renders race, class, religion and age, insignificant; only gender remains as the one defining "fact," more salient than ever.

Paradoxically, wars, the First World War among them, have often been accused of eroding gender boundaries. The claims that the hippies of the Vietnam War era spelled the total disintegration of American society – "Why you can't tell the boys from the girls!" – repeats the laments of a "civilization without sexes" that French critics feared the First World War had produced. Such rhetoric, Mary Louise Roberts argues, had less to do with actual wartime changes in gender relations than with the new importance attached to radically polarized concepts of masculine and feminine.[28] Margaret and Patrice Higgonet have imagined a double helix to describe wartime gender relations; each gender is always linked in the same status relationship to the other, despite changes in the gender division of labor. Women don't "advance" by their wartime access to previously masculine jobs because men have already moved into the super-masculine job of war itself. The hierarchy of masculine over feminine remains firmly in place. In fact, war exaggerates it by placing the entire job of maintaining the social order upon the shoulders of gender, increasing the pressure upon men to be manly, women to be womanly.[29]

In most war stories, the masculine terrain appears so "natural" that it passes unobserved. It takes a feminist critic like Nancy Huston or Barbara Ehrenreich, already sensitized to gender as an important category of analysis, to use Joan Scott's phrase, to notice the significance of gender in these stories. But some war stories publicly proclaim the central role of masculinity, in particular, those stories that recount or predict national comeback from defeat. Klaus Theweleit argues that a lost war is experienced as lost manhood. After such a defeat, the war is refought – and won – on home ground. "The war of genders is wonderful for re-winning lost wars because of its very certain result: men never lose, women have to."[30] Germany in the aftermath of the First World War and the United States in the aftermath of the Vietnam war blamed their defeats upon feminization and masculine degeneracy. According to Theweleit, in Germany in the 1920s and 1930s, "women were made a strong pillar of the stab-in-the-back legend," and figured as the main enemy to be annihilated in early fascist narratives.[31] In American rhetoric, those who opposed US involvement in Vietnam were "sob sisters" and "wimps." General Norman Schwarzkorpf blamed the military defeat upon "a bunch of military fairies that had never been shot at in anger."[32] The solution, obviously, was, in Susan Jefford's term, to "remasculinize" society in preparation for a future – and final – reckoning.

France after the Franco-Prussian war was unquestionably another society that experienced a humiliating defeat as a failure of masculinity and social change as the collapse of gender polarity. According to a host of commentators at the end of the nineteenth century, the French family, society and nation were all in desperate straits because women were refusing to be feminine and men were not being sufficiently masculine. "Female emancipation" was the leading culprit.[33] By any objective standard, the French feminist movement at this time was small and powerless, particularly in comparison with the contemporary mass movements in Great Britain and the United States. Nonetheless, many French social critics imagined feminism as triumphant in France. French women were refusing to have babies, they were scaling the walls of the Académie Française, having already taken over the Beaux-Arts (with the admission of Rosa Bonheur) and the Academy of Sciences (with the admission of Marie Curie); they were invading the courtrooms and operating rooms. (There were, in fact, by 1900, only eight women admitted to the French bar and approximately a dozen women doctors.) In her study of *fin-de-siècle* literature, Annelise Maugue concludes "that the woman is always represented there as taking to modern society as easily as a fish to water, already free, regardless of her legal status, and always abusing her freedom in order to further subjugate man."[34] For, according to the antifeminists, women were not merely abandoning their own roles in order to claim those of the opposite sex, they were forcing men to do the same. Because women were entering the public arena, critics claimed, men were now forced to stay home darning socks. The antifeminist discourse of the turn of the century always conceived of gender as oppositional and mutually exclusive, interpreting every incidence of women's advancement as evidence of masculine decadence. In this view, gender relations, rather than operating as a double helix, worked a kind of forcible exchange; qualities and status gained by the one gender not only represented a loss to the other, but also forced the losing gender to take on the qualities and status abandoned by the winner. If women became masculine, inevitably men would become – or already had become – feminine.

But feminism was not the only cause of masculine decline. Industrialism, luxury, bourgeois urban culture and modern life all stifled heroic potential. For nationalist writers like Charles Maurras, Paul Deroulède and their ideological descendant, Maurice Barrès, capitalism, urbanization, secularism, democracy and modernism joined emancipated women as well as Jews, Protestants, Freemasons and socialists in the dock, all under indictment as alien "germs" of degeneracy that had undermined the French fighting spirit.[35] A favorite book of young men of the nationalist Right at the turn of the century was Alfred de Vigny's *Servitude et grandeur militaire,* originally published in 1835, which described modern man's lapse into "passive obedience." In the post-Napoleonic world, all chances of heroism and responsible action had disappeared. Military men took as their salient characteristic that most feminine of qualities, abnegation.

France's falling birth rate, another obsession born of the defeat in the Franco-Prussian War, was also laid at the door of the gender crisis. At fault, of course, were unwomanly women who refused their maternal duties, but also the enfeebled condition of men. Coddled in luxury or immobilized in sedentary jobs, men were becoming flabby and impotent according to the phalanx of nationalist Cassandras. Sports appealed to them as a means to revirilize French masculinity; but while Baron de Coubertin saw sports as a way to fight wars "without weapons," the motto of the Union of French Gymnastic Societies was: "Make me men; we'll make them soldiers!"[36] Sport was fine; but the real crucible of masculinity was war.

While waiting for war to reforge the mettle of French masculinity, French men revived dueling in an effort to restore the masculine character of public life. During the Third Republic, professional, middle-class men, especially in politics and journalism, developed an elaborate code of honor and indulged in an orgy of dueling.[37] The rationale was the practical absence of libel law; but the not-very-hidden agenda was to prove masculinity via testing its most fundamental quality: the right to risk and to take life. A second agenda, also perfectly visible, was to exclude women even more surely from public life. The code of honor, in the words of Alfred de Vigny, was "a Male Religion."[38] If the jobs of making public policy and public opinion required the capacity to back up one's words and actions with cold steel, then women were disqualified. Emancipated women were quite aware of the import of this tactic, as the young Madeleine Pelletier discovered when the feminist circle she frequented in the late 1880s discussed whether or not women should

10

demand the right to duel.[39] And one of the issues in the trial of Madame Caillaux that distracted France in the summer of 1914 was whether her murder of *Le Figaro*'s editor, Gaston Calmette, was justified by the fact that her sex prevented her from challenging him "man to man".[40]

Despite the increasingly frequent displays of rampant masculinity in dueling and gymnastics, publications deluged French readers at the turn of the century with lamentations and predictions of the collapse of French civilization, which, of course, meant the end of civilization, *tout court*. A wave of writing, both "scientific" and fictional, argued that the weakness of French gender categories had already brought catastrophic consequences – viz. the birth rate and the defeat by Prussia – and worse would follow unless something was done immediately. Although some works, like Emile Zola's *Nana* (1880), were unmistakably misogynist, much was written by self-proclaimed "friends of women" like Alexandre Dumas *fils* and some by authors who were more worried by masculine degeneracy, in particular by male libertinism and homosexuality, than by feminine virility. How was France to be saved? Some of the most misogynist stories took grim pleasure in the defeat, death and even dismemberment of their female villains;[41] but in general, this literature did not see a solution in forcibly returning women to domesticity and motherhood. Nor did antifeminists in the political arena campaign to roll back the progress women had made, in education, for example.[42] But this does not mean that antifeminists had given up. Although they hoped to convince women to return to their "natural" character and duties, they aimed a more active program at men. Rather than forcing women to be feminine, increasingly they pinned their hopes upon forcing men to be masculine.

Concern, even panic, over gender transformation affected the full political spectrum from right to left; as Maugue points out, antifeminism made strange bedfellows, such as the socialist Proudhon and the monarchist Théodore Joran, who won a prize from the Académie Française in 1905 for his essay, *The Lie of Feminism*.[43] But it was the Right that seized upon the threat of gender disintegration as its comeback bid after the drubbing it had received in the Dreyfus Affair. By identifying the family and the nation, in a rhetoric very familiar to the present-day American Right, the French Right blamed Germany's ascendancy over France upon divorce, female emancipation, the declining birth rate and the degeneration of patriarchal authority in general.[44] But, in an original

Myth → masculinity

twist, the Right saw the remedy for the latter in a rematch with the former. Rather than correct France's social ills so as to be able to take on Germany, increasingly the Right advocated war with Germany as the only way to cure France's social ills. War would rectify the gender order in France by restoring men to their pre-ordained place on top; and it would simultaneously do the same for the international order, by restoring France to its destiny as the premier European power. It was this argument, in its multiple forms, that drummed up the war fever so evident in France after 1905.

In the late nineteenth century, Western Europe and the United States shared a conception of war, that it was chivalric, heroic and regenerative of men and nation. In the rude brotherhood of combat, the vanity of materialism and the plague of social ambition would crumble, and only the true bedrock of national unity would remain. Of this period the American historian J. T. Jackson Lears writes: "The martial ideal emerged as a popular antidote to over civilization."[45] This is what George Mosse has called the Myth of War Experience, first created in Germany in response to defeat by Napoleon's armies and promoted thereafter by every government that had to sell national military service and national wars to its population.[46] Although France indulged fully in this myth throughout the nineteenth century, the shocking defeat by Prussia developed its own particular version that, by emphasizing simplicity, duty, honor – and death – welded together national revival and rampant masculinity.

The picture of army life presented to French readers in the last years before the First World War was one of simple, true-hearted brotherhood. A cluster of novels from these years depicted military service converting pacifists, aesthetes and alienated youth into red-blooded nationalists ready to kill and especially to die for the honor of the regiment.[47] Already in the 1830s, Vigny had mourned the loss of the masculine prerogative of individual glory in war, but had shown individualism's loss to be brotherhood's gain. "In the midst of the soldiers, in camp life, in the mud of the march and the bivouac is the beauty of war."[48] This message resonated with young men after 1900, as this quote from one respondent to Agathon's 1912 survey demonstrates: "It is in camp life and under fire that we will experience the supreme expansion of the French forces within us."[49] Roè's cult novel, *Pingot and Me* was one long disquisition on this idea, as a simple soldier, Pingot, taught the elite narrator about the real men who were the real France.[50]

Besides identifying the redemptive, masculinizing effect of military camp life, Vigny had also called attention – with capital letters – to Abnegation and Duty as the fundamentals of the Passive Grandeur that had replaced derring-do as the true quality of the soldier.[51] To these Maurice Barrès, in his novel *L'Appel au soldat*, added sensibility and enthusiasm. What is striking is that, according to nineteenth-century ideas of gender polarity, all these were peculiarly feminine qualities; but both Vigny and Barrès then added the crucial quality of Honor, which thoroughly masculinized them. As Barrès explained, while femininity is entirely personal, masculinity is *désinteressé*. When poured out in the cause of national honor, abnegation, obedience, devotion, etc. become quintessentially masculine.[52]

What set the French version of the War Myth apart from that of its neighbors was its overriding concern with honor and its closer relationship to death than to victory. The code of honor by which French upper-middle-class men lived put the highest premium upon the combat, the duel itself, not upon a victorious outcome.[53] In Paul Acker's *Soldier Bernard* (1909), the model officer Lieutenant Herbel died from wounds inflicted by striking workers; it was his death that converted Bernard, a socialist pacifist, into a manly militarist. A man proved his superior masculinity by defending Honor even if he died in the effort. And increasingly Frenchmen conceived of a future war with Germany in the same terms. As the historian Edward Berenson argues, material victory was less important than the moral victory of combat itself. Simply to engage in the fight, to risk one's life, would restore the national honor, while to die for the cause would be to achieve a kind of apotheosis of masculinity.[54]

In 1912 Henri Massis and Alfred de Tarde undertook to survey the attitudes of elite French youth for the Parisian paper, *L'Opinion*.[55] They chose as their *nom-de-plume* Agathon, Socrates' disciple, "good, brave in war;" thus it will be no surprise that although their survey was published the following year in book form under the title *Young People of Today*, the people who interested them were young men. So complete was their masculine point of view that although they felt compelled to explain why and how their survey was limited in age, class and education, they never mentioned why they were not interested in the opinions of young women.

This book, which is more manifesto than reportage, welded the war myth to the Right's program of social restoration. Massis and Tarde based their study upon Massis's own circle of friends, whose

13

ideas they presented as representative of those of the best young Frenchmen. They claimed that their generation had been profoundly marked by the defeat in the Franco-Prussian war that had occurred twenty years before their birth: "This poignant and profound feeling of the fatherland humiliated, weakened and whose vital forces are menaced" (p. 118). In response they had taken upon themselves the task of ensuring "the revival and health of the race" (p. 119) by masculinizing themselves. They had adopted a regime of sports and sexual – and intellectual – abstinence, and were hell-bent for action – any action into which they could throw themselves "body and soul," but preferably a war with Germany.

> War: the word has regained a sudden prestige. It is a young word, all new, adorned in that seduction that the eternal bellicose instinct has revived in men's hearts. These young people load it with all the beauty with which they are enamored and of which normal life deprives them. Especially, in their eyes, war is the occasion for the most noble of human virtues, of those that they rank most high: energy, mastery, sacrifice in a cause that surpasses us (pp. 31–2).

And the envisioned outcome was not victory, but honor. The model, according to Massis and Tarde, was a young officer killed during one of the Moroccan campaigns "in full victory, ahead of his men, among the palm trees; there was found in his pack a pair of white gloves and a copy of *Servitude et grandeur militaire*" (p. 33).

Where did women fit into this scheme? In the pro-military novels like *Pingot and Me* and *Soldier Bernard*, women appeared in the plot mainly to mark the hero's heterosexuality, to prevent readers from misinterpreting the nature of masculine fraternity. Otherwise, it was women's role to be renounced in favor of military duty, honor and glory. The "Young People of Today" were remarkably silent about their attitudes towards the opposite sex, especially considering all the brouhaha at the time about the emancipated woman. Massis and Tarde covered gender relations in two short paragraphs, claiming that the current generation of young men was reserved and "a little defensive," a posture they found "suitable with an adversary who is informed and armed." Gender relations, apparently were a war. Although they argued that this was healthier than "that amorous effervescence" that afflicted the older generation, and predicted that "marriage will gain by it, the nation will gain by it, the race will gain by it," (p. 64) it appears that their ideal French youth

preferred to eschew the gender war altogether in order to con-
centrate on the longed-for war of men on men. Perhaps Massis and
Tarde meant that marriage, the nation and the race would gain *after*
a war with Germany had disarmed French women and restored
French masculinity to unquestioned authority.

The War Myth, particularly in its turn-of-the-century French
incarnation, was predicated upon the exclusion of women. The
brotherhood of the camps that would reveal the nation to itself was
male, the national unity that would be forged on the battlefield was
male, national honor was a male religion. The next war, the Right
devoutly hoped, would be, above all, a test and triumph of French
masculinity. For women to have anything to do with it would
obviously vitiate the whole point of the contest. Nancy Huston argues
that women are always perceived as dangerously weakening and
polluting to masculinity in war.[56] This was especially the case in
the French conception of the war that became the First World War.
The war was to occur in a zone of pure masculinity; the feminine
should cease to exist. The shortage of titles placing women "during"
the war and the even fewer that acknowledged women were also
"in" or "of" the war reflects this attitude. Women did not exist
"during" or "in" the war; their place was in another temporal, spatial
dimension, called in English the "home front" but in French the
arrière, i. e. the rear, where, removed from the masculine war, the
feminine hibernated in a state of suspended animation.

Such was the nationalist conception of gender and war in turn-
of-the-century France, the view that became dominant in the decade
of war scares that preceded the actual declaration of war; and it left
French women immobilized, frozen out of the discussion of the
envisioned war experience. The only relationship it admitted
between women and war was a hostile one. Nineteenth-century
conceptions of gender not only dissociated women from war, they
associated women with anti-militarism and pacifism.[57] But it was
also common to associate women and treachery, both the sexual
treachery of the *femme fatale* – as Mireille Dottin-Orsini points out,
Salomé was an icon of the turn-of-the-century[58] – and political
treason. The years before the First World War produced a spate of
French fiction featuring female spies, such as Ernest Daudet's
L'Espionne and Marcel Prévost's *Les anges gardiens*, both published
in 1913. This was the discourse that women and their allies had to
address before and during the war to claim a war experience for
French women.

Notes

1. François de Witt-Guizot, *La femme et la guerre: Comment une femme peut-elle servir la France en temps de guerre?* (Autun: Imprimerie Pernot, 1913); Hélène Français, "Les femmes et la guerre," *L'Opinion publique*, 19 April 1940.

2. Frédéric Masson, *Les femmes et la guerre de 1914* (Paris: Bloud et Gay, 1915); Louise Zeys, "Les femmes et la guerre," *Revue des deux mondes*, 257 (September–October 1916): 175–204; Henry Spont, *La femme et la guerre* (Paris: Perrin, 1916); Henri Robert, "La femme et la guerre," *La Revue mondiale* (May 1917): 243–57.

3. Gaston Rageot, *La française dans la guerre* (Paris: Attinger *frères*, 1918). Also Comtesse Roger de Courson, *La femme française pendant la guerre* (Paris: P. Lethielleux, s.d.); L. L. Klotz, "La femme française pendant la guerre," *La Renaissance politique, économique, littéraire et artistique*, 5 no. 3 (3 February 1917): 2564–6; Marie de la Hire, *La femme française: son activité pendant la guerre* (Paris: Librairie Jules Tallandier, 1917).

4. There have been a few interesting articles about French women in the First World War, such as Steven C. Hause, "More Minerva than Mars: The French Women's Rights Campaign and the First World War," in *Behind the Lines; Gender and the Two World Wars*, ed. Margaret Randolph Higonnet *et al.*, (New Haven, CT: Yale University Press, 1987), pp. 99–113 and a recent book by Laura Lee Downs, *Manufacturing Inequality: Gender Division in the French and British Metalworking Industries, 1914–1939* (Ithaca, NY: Cornell University Press, 1995) that compares women in war industries in the two countries; however, there is only one major study of French women during the First World War, Françoise Thébaud, *La femme au temps de la guerre de 14.* (Paris: Editions Stock, 1986). By contrast, there is a large literature on British and American women in the First World War, including Nosheen Khan, *Women's Poetry of the First World War* (Lexington, KY: University Press of Kentucky, 1988); Sharon Ouditt, *Fighting Forces, Writing Women: Identity and Ideology in the First World War* (London: Routledge, 1994); Maurine Weiner Greenwald, *Women, War, and Work: The Impact of World War I on Women Workers in the United States* (Ithaca, NY: Cornell University Press, 1990); Angela Woollacott, *On Her Their Lives Depend: Munitions Workers in the Great War* (Berkeley, CA: University of California Press, 1994); Eileen Crofton, *The Women of Royaumont: A Scottish Women's Hospital on the Western Front* (East Linton, Scotland: Tuckwell Press, 1996); and Susan Zeiger, *In Uncle Sam's Service* (forthcoming from Cornell University Press). Recently Ute Daniel's 1989 study, *The War From Within: German Working-Class Women in the First World War*, trans. Margaret Ries (Oxford: Berg, 1997) has introduced those of us who do not read German to scholarship on German women during the First World War.

5. Caumery and J. P. Pinchon, *Bécassine pendant la grande guerre*; *Bécassine chez les Alliés*; *Bécassine mobilisée*, *Bécassine chez les Turcs* (Paris: Henry Gautier, 1915, 1917, 1918, 1919).

6. Maurice Donnay, *Lettres à une dame blanche* (Paris: Société littéraire de France, 1917), pp. 72-3.

7. Jay Winter and Emmanuel Sivan, "Setting the Framework," in *War and Remembrance in the Twentieth Century*, ed. Jay Winter and Emmanuel Sivan (Cambridge: Cambridge University Press, 1999), p. 31.

8. Annette Becker, *Les monuments aux morts; Patrimoine et mémoire de la grande guerre* (Paris: Editions Errance, 1989), pp. 80-2; Daniel J. Sherman, "Art, Commerce, and the Production of Memory in France After World War I," in *Commemorations: The Politics of National Identity*, ed. John R. Gillis (Princeton, NJ: Princeton University Press, 1994), pp. 199-202; Antoine Prost, "Verdun," in *Les lieux de mémoire*, ed. Pierre Nora, II, pt. 3 *La nation* (Paris: Gallimard, 1986), pp. 111-47.

9. James F. McMillan, *Housewife or Harlot: The Place of Women in French Society 1870-1940* (New York: St Martin's Press, 1981), pp. 4-5.

10. Marie de la Hire, *La femme française*, pp. 49, 130.

11. For example, see Gabriel Perreux, *La vie quotidienne des civils en France pendant la grande guerre* (Paris: Hachette, 1966), pp. 66-7.

12. McMillan, *Housewife or Harlot*; Greenwald, *Women, War, and Work*; Gail Braybon, *Women Workers in the First World War* (London: Croom Helm, 1981); Daniel, *The War From Within*.

13. McMillan, *Housewife or Harlot*; Thébaud, *La femme au temps de la guerre;* Michelle Perrot, "The New Eve and the Old Adam: French Women's Condition at the Turn of the Century," in Higonnet *et al.* (eds), *Behind the Lines*, pp. 51-60 and "Stepping Out," trans. Arthur Goldhammer, in *A History of Women in the West*, Vol. IV: *Emerging Feminism from Revolution to World War*, ed. Geneviève Fraisse and Michelle Perrot (Cambridge, MA: Belknap Press, 1993), pp. 477-9; Véronique Leroux-Hugon, "L'infirmière au début du XXᵉ siècle: nouveau métier et tâches traditionnelles," *Le Mouvement social* no. 140 (July-September 1987): 55-68; Marie-Monique Huss, "Pronatalism and the Popular Ideology of the Child in Wartime France: The Evidence of the Picture Postcard," in *The Upheaval of War: Family, Work and Welfare in Europe, 1914-1918*, ed. Richard Wall and J. M. Winter (Cambridge: Cambridge University Press, 1988), pp. 329-67.

14. Mary Louise Roberts, *Civilization Without Sexes: Reconstructing Gender in Postwar France, 1917-1927* (Chicago: University of Chicago Press, 1994), pp. 5-6.

15. John Horne, "'L'Impôt du sang': Republican Rhetoric and Industrial Warfare in France, 1914-18," *Social History* 14 no. 2 (May 1989): 203.

16. Leonard V. Smith, "Masculinity, Memory, and the French First World War Novel: Henri Barbusse and Roland Dorgelès," in *Authority, Identity*

and the Social History of the Great War, ed. Marilyn Shevin-Coetzee and Frans Coetzee (Providence, RI: Berghahn Books, 1995), pp. 251-73; Stéphane Audoin-Rouzeau, "Oublis et non-dits de l'histoire de la grande guerre," *Revue du Nord* 78 no. 315 (April–June 1996): 355-65; Paul Fussell, *The Great War in Modern Memory* (New York: Oxford University Press, 1975); Eric J. Leed, *No Man's Land: Combat and Identity in World War I* (London: Cambridge University Press, 1979).

17. Mary Cadogan and Patricia Craig, *Women and Children First: The Fiction of Two World Wars* (London: Victor Gollancz, 1978), p. 287.

18. Léon Schirmann, *L'affaire Mata Hari: Enquête sur une machination* (Paris: Editions Tallandier, 1994), pp. 190-203.

19. Susan Jeffords, *The Remasculinization of America: Gender and the Vietnam War* (Bloomington, IN: Indiana University Press, 1989), p. 89. Nancy Huston, "The Matrix of War: Mothers and Heroes," in *The Female Body in Western Culture*, ed. Susan Rubin Suleiman (Cambridge, MA: Harvard University Press, 1986), p. 131; Barbara Ehrenreich, *Blood Rites: Origins and History of the Passions of War* (New York: Metropolitan Books/ Henry Holt and Company, 1997), pp. 125-9; and V. Spike Peterson, "Gendered Nationalism: Reproducing 'Us' versus 'Them,'" in *The Women and War Reader*, ed. Lois Ann Lorentzen and Jennifer Turpin (New York: New York University Press, 1998), pp. 42-3 make similar arguments.

20. Cited in Jeffords, *The Remasculinization of America*, p. 89.

21. Jean Bethke Elshtain, *Women and War* (New York: Basic Books, 1987).

22. Ibid., p. 58; Nancy Huston, "Tales of War and Tears of Women," *Women's Studies International Forum* 5 no. 3/4 (1982): 274-5.

23. George L. Mosse, *Nationalism and Sexuality: Respectability and Abnormal Sexuality in Modern Europe* (New York: H. Fertig, 1985), pp. 90-100; Peterson, "Gendered Nationalism," pp. 44-5.

24. Service Historique de l'Armée de Terre (hereafter SHAT) 16 N 2405 Permissionnaires, 4 June 1917.

25. Huston, "Tales of War," p. 277.

26. Ibid., p. 271.

27. Jeffords, *The Remasculinization of America*, p. 49.

28. Roberts, *Civilization Without Sexes*; Lynda E. Boose, "Techno-Muscularity and the 'Boy Eternal': From the Quagmire to the Gulf," in *Gendering War Talk,* ed. Miriam Cooke and Angela Woollacott (Princeton, NJ: Princeton University Press, 1993), pp. 67-106.

29. Margaret R. and Patrice L.-R. Higonnet, "The Double Helix" in Higonnet *et al.* (eds), *Behind the Lines*, pp. 31-47; Jennifer Turpin, "Many Faces: Women Confronting War," in Lorentzen and Turpin (eds), *Women and War Reader*, pp. 15-16.

30. Klaus Theweleit, "The Bomb's Womb and the Genders of War (War Goes On Preventing Women from Becoming the Mothers of Invention)," in Cooke and Woollacott (eds), *Gendering War Talk*, p. 285.

31. Ibid., p. 286; and idem, *Male Fantasies*, Vol. 1, trans. Stephan Conway (Minneapolis, MN: University of Minnesota Press, 1987).

32. Cited in Boose, "Techno-Muscularity," pp. 70, 88.

33. Alexandre Dumas *fils, Les femmes qui tuent et les femmes qui votent* (1880); J. Alisson, *Le monde est aux femmes* (1889); Théodore Joran, *Le mensonge du féminisme* (1905); and E. Faguet, *Le féminisme* (1910).

34. Annelise Maugue, *L'identité masculine en crise au tournant du siècle, 1871–1914* (Paris: Editions Rivages, 1987), pp. 70–1.

35. Karen Offen, "Exploring the Sexual Politics of French Republican Nationalism," in *Nationhood and Nationalism in France From Boulangism to the Great War, 1889–1918*, ed. Robert Tombs (London: HarperCollins, 1991), pp. 195–209; Modris Eksteins, *Rites of Spring; The Great War and the Birth of the Modern Age* (Boston: Houghton Mifflin Company, 1989); and Angus McLaren, *The Trials of Masculinity: Policing Sexual Boundaries, 1870–1930* (Chicago: University of Chicago Press, 1997), pp. 31–6.

36. Richard Holt, *Sport and Society in Modern France* (Hamden, CT: Archon Books, 1981), pp. 191–6.

37. Robert A. Nye, *Masculinity and Male Codes of Honor in Modern France* (Oxford: Oxford University Press, 1993).

38. Alfred de Vigny, *Servitude et grandeur militaire,* in *Oeuvres compètes de Alfred de Vigny* (Paris: Louis Conard, 1914), p. 248.

39. Felicia Gordon, *The Integral Feminist: Madeleine Pelletier 1874–1939* (Minneapolis, MN: University of Minnesota Press, 1990), p. 16.

40. Edward Berenson, *The Trial of Madame Caillaux* (Berkeley, CA: University of California Press, 1992), pp. 169–207.

41. Mireille Dottin-Orsini, *Cette femme qu'ils disent fatale: Textes et images de la misogynie fin-de-siècle* (Paris: Bernard Grasset, 1993).

42. Maugue, *L'identité masculine en crise*, pp. 143–64

43. Ibid., pp. 11–16

44. Berenson, *The Trial of Madame Caillaux*, pp. 159–60; Offen, "Exploring the Sexual Politics."

45. J. T. Jackson Lears, *No Place of Grace: Antimodernism and the Transformation of American Culture 1880–1920* (New York: Pantheon Books, 1981), p. 100.

46. George L. Mosse, *Fallen Soldiers: Reshaping the Memory of the World Wars* (Oxford: Oxford University Press, 1990).

47. For example, Paul Acker, *Le soldat Bernard* (1909); Jean Variot, *Hasards de la guerre* (1913); and Ernest Psichari, *L'appel des armes* (1913). Earlier novels on the same theme, such as Art Roè [Patrice Mahon], *Pingot et moi* (1896) were reprinted to new popularity.

48. Vigny, *Servitude et grandeur*, p. 222.

49. Agathon [Henri Massis and Alfred de Tarde], *Les jeunes gens d'aujourd'hui* (Paris: Plon, 1913), p. 32.

50. John Cruickshank, *Variations on Catastrophe: Some French Responses to the Great War* (Oxford: Clarendon Press, 1982), pp. 10–24.

51. Vigny, *Servitude et grandeur*, p. 244.

52. Maurice Barrès, *L'appel au soldat* (Paris: Félix Joven, 1899), p. 27.

53. Nye, *Male Codes of Honor*.

54. Berenson, *The Trial of Madame Caillaux*, pp. 169–207.

55. For an account of the survey and a more general analysis of Massis and Tarde, see Robert Wohl, *The Generation of 1914* (Cambridge, MA: Harvard University Press, 1979), pp. 5–18 and Christophe Prochasson and Anne Rasmussen, *Au nom de la patrie; Les intellectuels et la première guerre mondiale (1910–1919)* (Paris: Editions La Découverte, 1996), pp. 34–48.

56. Huston, "The Matrix of War," pp. 119–21.

57. Joyce Berkman, "Feminism, War, and Peace Politics: The Case of World War I," in *Women, Militarism and War: Essays in History, Politics, and Social Theory*, ed. Jean Bethke Elshtain and Sheila Tobias (Savage, MD: Rowman & Littlefield, 1990), pp. 141–60.

58. Dottin-Orsini, *Cette femme qu'ils disent fatale*, pp. 133–59.

2

Women's War Imagined: 1871–1914

In the drum-beating literature churned out in the years prior to the First World War, French nationalists almost never anticipated a role for women in the conflict they so ardently envisioned. Maurice Barrès, in the novel *L'Appel au soldat*, related women to the national war against Germany in one subordinate phrase: "The sinister cries of death fell poetically like dusk upon the little towns and tore the hearts of women who swore, however, to be worthy of the heroes."[1] An article in the January 1900 issue of *Le Gaulois* depicted women waiting with anticipation for the "intense and magnificent whirl of activity accomplished by men who returned home between two battles to get them with child, only to hasten back to the front having left behind the overpowering image of conquerors."[2] Marius Leblond was one of the few nationalist publicists to devote a chapter to "Woman and the Nation." In it he asserted that passive goodness was not sufficient for modern women, who must embrace a patriotic mission. However, when his rhetoric subsided into practical proposals, his view was the same as that of *Le Gaulois*; for women, patriotism consisted of being "impregnated by her husband."[3]

Women's duty was to the home and family, in a different realm from the masculine war. In contrast to that for boys, who were indoctrinated from primary school in their duty to their country, the girls' curriculum lacked any explicit inculcation of patriotism. As one author of a popular composition manual suggested, feminine patriotism was entirely domestic. It consisted in teaching patriotism to children, influencing husbands and sons to do their civic duties, and "bravery if the country called upon a son or husband to fight."[4] A woman's only connection to war was through her "hero," for whom she was to be the silent support and worthy prize; he was for *Patrie* only, and she for *Patrie* in him.

But Barresian nationalism, though the dominant discourse about patriotism and national identity in turn-of-the-century France, was not the only one. Developing almost in tandem with it was a rhetoric of women's duty to society and nation. According to the historian Sylvie Fayet-Scribe, that French women had a "social mission" rather than merely a private, domestic one was an idea whose time arrived at the turn of the century in an explosion of publications and conferences.[5] Particularly appealing to Catholic women, it was exemplified in the Catholic organization, Woman's Social Action, whose monthly publication of the same name chronicled its almost frenetic activities – conferences, charities, study groups, lectures – throughout the country. But feminine social duty was not the exclusive property of Catholic or conservative women; the idea was popular among Republican and feminist French women as well, to whom it seemed a necessary corollary to women's rights. As members of a Rouen feminist organization, Feminine Action, wrote in 1913: "The word 'service,' whether called military, familial or social, is used frequently today. What is important is that Woman recognizes that if she demands equal rights in society, she must also accept her share of the duties toward society."[6] The big women's and feminist conferences that took place in Paris after 1900 were permeated by this idea, as their proceedings attest.[7] There was agreement that maternity was a social duty as well as a familial charge, and that it was women's highest priority; but beyond this point there was no consensus. If a woman raised children, had she also other duties to society; and if so, what were they? And what of the childless woman? The lack of a clear response kept the question open and guaranteed that people of all political stripes pondered it.

Most advocates of women's social service envisioned social welfare programs, such as public health, education or the alleviation of poverty's miseries. The political climate of the period, fueled by the confrontation of the Catholic Church and the secular Republic and by escalating nationalism, endowed women's philanthropy with a military rhetoric. Reform programs were "campaigns," "struggles," "missions" and "combat" against social and moral enemies. Believing they were engaged in a civil war for France's soul, Catholic women's groups were particularly prone to clothe their activities in military imagery; they waged "the good fight" and "the holy war."[8] Secular feminists used the same kind of rhetoric to describe their efforts to secure women's rights and their activities for social reform. The feminist daily paper, *La Fronde*, for example, published a regular column entitled "The Good War" that discussed efforts to "combat" alcoholism, tuberculosis and sweated labor. When framed in this fashion, discussions of women's duty to society called to mind men's military service and prepared the ground for the question of women's duty to country and their role in war. Several other discussions, each relatively minor in itself, encouraged French women to imagine a role for themselves in the national defense. One of these was the Catholic Church's crusade to canonize Joan of Arc. A second was the French Red Cross campaign for recruits, funds and government recognition and a third was the republican debate over universal (male) conscription. All three achieved the results they desired; in 1905 the legislature enacted universal male military service, in 1909 the Vatican beatified (and in 1920, canonized) Joan of Arc, and a 1910 law incorporated Red Cross volunteers into military mobilization plans. But also, all three, mostly inadvertently, led men and women to formulate and debate feminine versions of patriotism and national service in wartime.

At the turn of the century, however, women's wars were purely metaphoric ones – "the holy war" against anticlericalism, the "good fight" against social ills. The repeated confrontations with Germany, beginning in 1905 and reaching their height in the Second Moroccan crisis of 1911, changed the nature of the discussion. In the decade that preceded the actual outbreak of war, belief that France must soon go to war with Germany spread from traditional *revanchiste* circles – monarchists, military officers – to include a good portion of the political classes. Nationalism became, in Eugen Weber's word, an all-encompassing "atmosphere" shared by the Left as well as the Right, and, although he does not mention this, by women as well as men.[9] A 1913 survey intended to provide a feminine counterpart to Agathon's *Les jeunes gens d'aujourd'hui* reported that, like their brothers, young French women were riding a wave of nationalism. Suzanne Lacouture, age 20, president of an alumni organization of secondary school graduates, wrote: "Like young men, we are going through a crisis of patriotic exaltation. Doubtless, our elders also loved their country. But we are tired of their passive patriotism. We want to devote ourselves, to bring all our young ardor to our country's service."[10] If war broke out, columnist Andrée d'Alix assured her readers, sister would say to brother "with calm courage: 'Your duty is clear, do it. And I, while you fight, I will PRAY AND SERVE ALSO.'"[11] The war against Germany would not be exclusively masculine: French women would have a role to play.

Faced with what looked shortly to be a literal, rather than a metaphoric, mobilization for war, views of women's national missions sharpened. Some of the visions that French women had found most compelling – for example, motherhood – no longer seemed adequate, while others, such as nursing, took on a new urgency. And the terms of the discussion shifted. To some women, claims that they had a duty to the nation had been little more than a *quid pro quo* for the rights the state owed them. Suddenly, the nation's claims upon women loomed much larger than women's claims upon the state. In their own minds, many French women began to mobilize long before 1 August 1914. Grim or exhilarated, many French women faced the prospect of war with Germany convinced that their contributions were essential to defend the nation.

The Joan of Arc Campaigns: A Call to Arms

The rival campaigns to canonize Joan of Arc as a Catholic saint or as a national heroine were almost entirely male affairs. As the bibliographer Nadia Margolis has pointed out, in the late nineteenth century Joan was "appropriated by various male bastions (historiography, theology, politics and law) and their official rhetoric – to say nothing of the world of belles lettres and journalism."[12] In print, in public debate, and even armed with cudgels, the devotees at her shrine, be it Catholic or Republican, were men. As Marina Warner has argued, Joan of Arc's femaleness was essential to all their projects for her; her virginity exemplifying the strength of purity in the face of overwhelming threat signified the strength of Catholic faith confronting a hostile republican regime and/or the strength of the French Nation facing a hostile Germany.[13] But this does not mean that Barrès and his followers saw her as a model for their wives and sisters. Their Joan of Arc was female in the way that Virtue, Liberty and the Republic are female; rather than speaking specifically to women, the femininity of abstract ideals serves to exclude women, by defining the public and the universal as masculine.[14] Like de Vigny's Honor, the Joan of Arc cult, whether Catholic or Republican, was a male religion.

The lack of feminist voices in turn-of-century French discourse about Joan of Arc is striking because such had not always been the case. Joan of Arc was a heroine to earlier advocates of women, such as Christine de Pisan and Madeleine de Scudéry. In the first half of the nineteenth century, the novelists Daniel Stern and Georges Sand had drawn inspiration from her.[15] But while the British and the American women's rights movements adopted Joan of Arc as a standard-bearer,[16] most French feminists held her at a distance. By 1900, Joan of Arc had become the property of the far right wing of the French women's movement, composed of militant Catholic women who opposed the secular Republic. Fighting to revive France as a Catholic state, the two largest French women's organizations, the Patriotic League of Frenchwomen and the League of French Women, brandished Joan of Arc as their patroness and used her legend to authorize their foray into the electoral campaign of 1902.[17] Joan of Arc was also an important figure in the broader arena of Catholic women's social action. For example, her name graced a free clinic in Paris, run by well-to-do Catholic women, to treat blood and skin diseases, an "agronomic institute" to train French girls to be farm wives, hostels for single working women and a host of after-school clubs for girls.[18]

When Joan of Arc appeared in French feminist rhetoric, it was invariably from Catholic feminists led by Marie Maugeret, who used her to cloak their divergence from the Church's opposition to women's emancipation. Maugeret invoked Joan frequently in her monthly publication, *Le Féminisme chrétien*, and organized an annual conference of Catholic women's associations under the title of the Congrès Jeanne d'Arc. Welcomed by the Institut Catholic in Paris, this gathering officially promoted Joan's canonization and condemned the secular Republic; but it also discussed social and moral issues, such as education and alcoholism and, under Maugeret's direction, explored women's rights and working conditions and their responsibility for church and nation. In 1906 it controversially, and briefly, endorsed women's suffrage. However, Maugeret parted company with the larger French feminist movement over the Dreyfus affair. Her Joan of Arc spent more time championing anti-republicanism and anti-semitism than feminism.[19]

It was not only the appropriation of Joan of Arc by anti-republican militants that disturbed most French feminists; there was also her military exploits. Socialist feminists like Dr Madeleine Pelletier equated feminism and pacifism, and republican feminists like Jane Misme proclaimed that feminism was anti-militarist. Joan's militancy posed difficulties for Catholic, nationalist women, too. Saint and martyr, whether to faith or fatherland, Joan of Arc was also an amazon, armor-clad, on horseback with lance at ready. Was this the mission that French women wanted to espouse? Joan's male promoters could ignore this aspect of her legacy because they rarely imagined women as her, or their, audience. *Action française*, for example, proclaimed that Joan's militancy called French *men* to "righteous rebellion" against the regime, but all she asked of her feminine devotees, apparently, was money, and perhaps a few flowers at her memorials.[20] Yet, Joan of Arc's embodiment of a female soldier disturbed French women, whether Catholic or republican. Perhaps she authorized Catholic women to heckle anti-clerical political candidates; perhaps she encouraged suffragists like Pelletier to stone polling places. But did she call French women to take up arms? Even militant nationalists quailed at the prospect. As Mme Duclos protested at the founding meeting of the anti-Dreyfusard Nationalist Union of French Women, "You understand very well, it isn't a matter of transforming each of us into Joan of Arc, and I don't see us in helmets and armor with sword in hand."[21] Across the political spectrum, French women were in general agreement about the unique nature of femininity and what its virtues and strengths could and did bring to society and the polity. The central figure in their belief and their rhetoric was the mother, nurturing, sustaining and compassionate.[22] And motherhood, surely, precluded women from literally wielding swords for their faith or marching forth to do battle for their country. Yet this is what Joan of Arc had done. How, then, were modern French women to read Joan's message to them?

The simplest solution emerged early in the Joan of Arc campaigns, in 1873 in Marie-Edmée Pau's inspirational children's book, *The History of Our Little Sister or The Childhood of Joan of Arc, Dedicated to the Children of Lorraine*.[23] The only significant female voice in late nineteenth-century French literature about Joan of Arc, Pau presented Joan as both a religious and a nationalist heroine, but she cut off her story at the moment when Joan left her home in Lorraine to take up her sword and mount her pyre. Rather than a warrior or a martyr, Pau's Joan is obedient, pious and helpful around the house. She learns her feminine gender role – "Let's leave to men their hard tasks, my child, and try to accomplish our own"[24] – and espouses universal peace through reconciliation and faith. Although Pau's final illustration shows Joan with short hair, no military paraphernalia intrude. To follow in her footsteps, all that French children (and women) must do is their traditional duties. If something more was ultimately required of Joan, nothing more is required of Pau's readers. The patriotic Frenchwoman is simply the good woman, and her duties to *revanchiste* France are those of woman-hood – piety, industry, virtue, obedience.

In the nineteenth century, French women could accept Pau's response to Joan of Arc's challenge. In the nationalist revival after 1900, however, it no longer satisfied even the children for whom it was intended. One terrain of the battle over Joan had been the school; both the Catholic and the state education systems claimed her as their own. But whether textbooks evoked her to awaken infant piety or infant patriotism, they inevitably burnished her militant and military image.[25] The impact upon schoolgirls was somewhat unexpected. One teaching manual from 1909 commented: "The memory of warrior heroism has not lost its force or its prestige. At school, far from rejoicing that their sex allows them to escape military service, the little girls demand to know how they can match the glorious destinies of the boys!"[26]

Some girls, brought up on tales of Joan of Arc, yearned for the glory of combat and patriotic martyrdom that they had been taught had been her mission. Marie Rabut, a Red Cross volunteer during the First World War and a militant Catholic, recalled that as a teenager she was sure it was her vocation to be a soldier for the faith, like Joan; with a friend she had planned to found a female chivalric order. Once the war began, such fantasies became commonplace. Nadine, a columnist for the *Tribune de l'Aube*, recounted a dream in which Joan of Arc gave her weapons and sent her into battle where she fought bravely and died gloriously to be welcomed into heaven by an angelic choir. She awoke in tears, crying: "Why aren't women allowed to die for their country?"[27]

Such forbidden visions troubled adult French women. Nadine answered her own question: women may not die for their country because it is their duty to give life for it. Maternity excluded combat. But Joan *La Pucelle* (The Virgin) obviously did not call French women to maternity; she was no purely domestic incarnation of patriotism. And her stirring story and armored image were ubiquitous in turn-of-the-century France. An outpouring of poems, plays, statues, paintings, sermons, speeches and debates kept her constantly in the public eye,[28] challenging women, Catholic women in particular. After 1911, when war with Germany loomed, French women could not shut their ears to her imperative call to play a role in the defense of France. Like their schoolgirl daughters, they began to ponder how they could equal, or at least contribute to, the sacrifice they believed would soon be required of their men.

The Red Cross Campaigns: A Call to Nurse

France's obsession with Germany began with the disastrous defeat in the Franco-Prussian War in 1870. In this war, some women had volunteered as nurses and helped during the siege. But even their apologists recognized that their efforts had been poorly organized and ineffective, especially when compared with the war work of German women. As publicists for the French Red Cross never tired of pointing out, while the French Red Cross had only three hundred members in 1870, the German organizations had fielded ten times that many volunteers to nurse their wounded.[29]

In the aftermath of the war, the first of the three French Red Cross organizations, the Society to Aid Wounded Soldiers, (Société de Secours aux Blessés Militaires, SSBM), as its name indicates, laid claim to a clear wartime mission. Men dominated the organization, however, and, initially at least, it did not advocate nursing training for female volunteers. Disgruntled members of the SSBM withdrew to form rival Red Cross organizations that would offer women nursing training and opportunities to run the show; the Association of French Ladies (Association des Dames Françaises, ADF) was founded in 1879 and the Union of Women of France (Union des Femmes de France, UFF) in 1881.[30] All three campaigned for membership, for contributions and for official recognition. The directorships, stocked with impressive names, like the Comtesse d'Haussonville, head of the women's committee of the SSBM, and Mme Ernest Carnot, president of the ADF, lobbied the government and made sure the press reported Red Cross exploits.[31] They all disseminated a similar vision of feminine patriotism at their annual conferences and in their publications. Red Cross promoters were the first to pose squarely the question of what French women should do in case of war and to provide an answer.[32]

The image of the nurse, as depicted in Red Cross propaganda, was a new one. Previously, nursing was not considered patriotic – it was not even considered especially feminine. *Infirmiers* (male nurses) were nearly as common as *infirmières* – in fact, much more common in wartime nursing, because, until 1907, all the military nurses were men. Female nurses who worked in municipal or Catholic hospitals were working-class women who did this unpleasant, manual labor for pay – and very low pay at that – or nuns, who labored in self-mortifying service to God.[33] The new ethos of nursing took over the notion of vocation, turned it toward *la patrie* and characterized it as distinctly feminine. According to Red Cross publicist Dr César Legrand, all aspects of nursing were merely femininity and motherhood refined and mobilized in the national cause:

> The cult of the sick: this is her natural tenderness channeled toward a determined goal. The essence of medical cleanliness: this is her need for order and her art of embellishment put to work in the fight against the germ. A special cultivation, a little technical knowledge: this is her original curiosity profitably used. Calm, sangfroid: this is the patience of a mother or a wife . . . Obedience: this is the single acknowledgement of her muscular inferiority and, moreover, it is the law. Military courage, heroism: this is a mother's devotion and incomparable self-abnegation brought to the task of helping the wounded. In truth, what a tiny distance a woman must go to change herself into a nurse![34]

In 1911, the war scare suddenly enlarged and diversified the audience for Red Cross propaganda. Alone among the voices addressing the issue of French women's wartime duty, the Red Cross proposed a mission and had plans and organizations to carry it out. As the lecturers, publicists and newspaper articles explained, women's special duty was to help organize, fund, administer and especially staff auxiliary hospitals to nurse wounded soldiers. For Red Cross recruiters François de Witt-Guizot and Dr Legrand, it was the best – in fact virtually the only – answer to the question: "How can a woman serve France in time of war?" "The medical service, which is the State and, moreover, the Fatherland."[35] The Red Cross slogan became "les hommes au combat, les femmes à l'ambulance." (Men to combat, women to the ambulances.)

This was, of course, bombast. The Red Cross did not envision nor campaign for a wartime mobilization of women comparable to universal male conscription. It did, however, pressure the government to include trained, certified Red Cross personnel in its mobilization plans and to recognize and fund Red Cross hospitals as auxiliaries to the military hospitals. In 1892 the government did agree to make use of Red Cross volunteers, although the first Red Cross military project was a deep disappointment. In 1900 the SSBM outfitted a hospital ship for service in China, but then was not permitted to staff it. It took seven more years of lobbying the government and the army for Red Cross volunteers to be accepted into active military service. In 1907, the government sent teams of Red Cross volunteers to nurse the wounded in the Moroccan war.[36]

29

The success of this experiment led to its expansion when the Second Moroccan campaign opened in 1911 and to the first Red Cross heroine and martyr. Mme Jacques Feuillet of the UFF, a veteran of the 1907 war, died at her post in Meknès in 1912; "A Woman Dead on the Field of Honor" trumpeted *La Française*.[37] In Red Cross publicity, Joan of Arc had traded in her sword and lance for a bandage and a bedpan.

The incessant lobbying and the Moroccan experience finally brought success. The Ministry of War admitted Red Cross volunteers to military hospitals and, in 1910, granted them a defined place within the military medical service.[38] The Red Cross campaign also convinced the French government of the need to reinforce the military medical staff with women; and in 1907 it opened a national school of nursing at Salpetrière to train them.[39] So when men were "called up" to be soldiers, some women would be called to serve as nurses.

The Red Cross publicity and recruitment campaigns, the government's incorporation of women nurses into its military plans, and the Red Cross training courses themselves – by 1914, the SSMB, the largest and most prestigious of the three rival Red Cross organizations, had trained about 10,000 volunteers, mostly women[40] – popularized the idea that nursing was an appropriate way for women to serve their country in wartime. The new role found further confirmation in fiction. Late-nineteenth-century French fiction abounded in *romans de moeurs* that entertained readers with the *risqué* affaires of *mondaines* (society women) who, in the last few pages, usually either died in repentance or retired to convents in order to restore order to society. In 1914 a novel by Georges Clément Lechartier, *La confession d'une femme du monde,* introduced a new, more adventurous moral ending. Its heroine, after enjoying a couple of hundred pages of Parisian high-life, has a moral conversion and – joins the Red Cross! With her husband, another reformed *débauché*, she volunteers for service in Morocco; and the book ends with the two reclaimed souls sailing off into the sunset, having dedicated their future lives to their sacred country – "Sacrifice, devotion to others, to the Fatherland, heroism."[41]

The Conscription Debate: The Women's *Impôt du Sang*

A third impetus to French women's wartime mobilization was a debate launched in the 1870s by the feminist Hubertine Auclert about citizenship rights and conscription. Central to this debate was the catch-phrase *l'impôt du sang*, the blood tax. Opponents of women's rights argued that women did not deserve full rights of citizenship – such as the vote – because they did not pay the "blood tax," i.e. perform military service. In response, advocates of women's rights began to call for feminine national service comparable to military service. Initially, women's claims to rights took precedence over the nation's claims upon women in this discussion. However, after the war scare of 1911, the priorities reversed. Faced with the imminent prospect of war, French women, including many feminists, succumbed to what the historian Rita Thalmann has called the "nationalist temptation."[42] The focus of their interest became the defense of France rather than the acquisition of women's rights.

The context of this discussion was the classical republican connection between citizenship and military service. Part of French republican discourse since the French Revolution, it moved into the forefront of definitions of citizenship in the first decades of the Third Republic – with obvious problems for women. During the Revolution, some French women had responded by demanding the right to bear arms, a move that earned them the epithet of "furies" in popular memory.[43] This was not a hopeful precedent for feminists of the Third Republic, who faced, in the militarization of the notion of citizenship, a formidable obstacle to women's rights.

Radical republicans advocated universal (male) military service in order to extend social and civic equality and to reform the army. Under the conscription system inherited from the Second Empire, the army resembled the armies of the Old Regime much more than a republican force – officers drawn from the Catholic aristocracy, the troops from the rural poor. Radicals began to push for universal (male) conscription as soon as the Republic was founded, but did not succeed in instituting it until 1905.[44] In the meantime, conscription remained an almost constant issue in the legislature.

The catchphrase of the conscription debate was *l'impôt du sang*, the blood tax. It had originated in debates over military levies in the 1820s,[45] but republicans quickly picked it up to express their belief that military service was a basic duty of citizenship, like paying taxes, and that it must be the same for all.[46] That the definition of citizenship that arose from this discourse was exclusively masculine did not trouble turn-of-the-century republicans,[47] but it did trouble women's rights activists, particularly when women's exemption from the *impôt du sang* began to emerge as a main pillar of anti-feminist arguments.

Since women's ejection from the political process during the French Revolution a century earlier, the dominant discourse justified the masculine monopoly on politics by defining citizenship as rational, independent and above all, public, thus excluding women, who were defined as naturally irrational, dependent, private and domestic. In the late nineteenth century, feminists subjected this conclusion to a wide-ranging attack.[48] Among their arguments was one that centered on the gendered nature of citizenship. French law guaranteed civil rights to *tous les français,* but in practice excluded women from the vote while requiring them to pay taxes and obey the law. Feminist Hubertine Auclert argued that the French state imposed all the duties of citizenship on women while withholding all the rights. Antifeminists of a nationalist stripe shot back that although women did pay fiscal taxes, they were indeed exempt from the heaviest tax of all, the *impôt du sang.*[49]

Most feminists had a response ready: women too paid a blood tax, in motherhood, and a far higher one than men. For example, Auclert wrote in her paper, *La Citoyenne,* in 1881: "It is ridiculous to object to women's vote on the basis of their exemption from military service, since so many men vote without ever bearing arms. Furthermore, the maternity tax claims many more victims than the blood tax."[50] At the National Congress of Civil Rights and Women's Suffrage in Paris in 1908, deputy Louis Martin made the same argument with figures to back it up. Death in childbirth, he argued, was for women "to die *au champ d'honneur,* to die for the race," and in the past dozen years, there had been four or five times more female than male casualties in the national cause. "Considering the statistics, a wit who wanted to upset the argument of those who make dying for the race the basis of suffrage could ironically claim that in the name of blood spilled . . . for the nation, it would be necessary to give women several votes!"[51]

Women's rights advocates saw advantages in equating motherhood and military service that resonated with the belief in the oppositional but complementary nature of the genders. As Karen Offen and Anne Cova have shown, the French women's movement across the political spectrum made its case from a position Offen has termed "relative" or "familial" feminism.[52] This argued that women deserve and need rights not because they share identical humanity with men but because of their unique feminine

32

contributions to society. In accord with the science of the time, which emphasized the polarity of male and female, the French women's movement stressed the complementarity of masculine and feminine and the need for the feminine in the public sphere to balance and complete masculine policy. In this argument, motherhood became a civic function; women not only raised the future citizens as individuals, they were also responsible for "mothering" society as a whole, for bringing to social and political issues the instincts and special insights of motherhood. Without the benefit of such insights, feminists argued, France was on the road to disaster, be it secularism, capitalism or social disintegration, depending upon the branch of the women's movement to which one subscribed.

Feminists' focus upon motherhood as a civic duty played into French anxieties about the birth-rate and enlisted the arguments of the pronatalist campaign. France's quick and total defeat in the Franco-Prussian War had shocked and demoralized French nationalists. Their frantic search for a cause and a remedy quickly fixed upon the relative size of France's population compared to Germany's and the low French birth rate. As a result, pronatalism became a prominent nationalist cause. In their efforts to make the birth rate a national priority, pronatalists imbued all their rhetoric with militarism. For them, maternity was a measure of national defense, as in Dr Just Sicard de Plauzeoles's tract, *Maternity and National Defense Against Depopulation* (1909). In order to persuade the French government to fund measures to increase the birth rate, they repeatedly drew parallels between motherhood and military service. For example, Louise Koppe argued for a Ministry of Child Welfare as an equivalent to the Ministry of War, and Dr Blanche Edwards-Pillet campaigned for paid maternity leave as the counterpart to military service. Mothers and soldiers, she argued, were equally national servants, and equally should be exempted from other work and paid for their national service.[53]

Not all feminists were happy with motherhood as an equivalent blood tax, nor with the allies that such an argument attracted. Some were wary of making motherhood a civic duty, recognizing that pronatalism tended to reduce women to their reproductive capacities. Writing in 1908, the feminist and socialist Dr Madeleine Pelletier opposed "the assimilation of maternity to military service." This, she judged, "far from hastening women's emancipation, will only put a spoke in its wheels."[54] So if motherhood was not women's *impôt du sang*, what was? Pelletier and other feminists, notably

Marguerite Durand, began to devise national service schemes for women.

Although Pelletier was a pacifist, she argued that if military service was the price of political rights, then women must be ready to do military service, drill, guns and all. And then she played the flip side of the republicans' claims for universal (male) conscription to argue that military service was essential to making French citizens, female as well as male. In fact, her army would not only be a school of citizenship, it would be training in gender equality.

> For women, the army would also be excellent schooling in the energy that they need so much. If, for the general good of humanity, men need to become more feminine, to lose their coarseness, their brutality and their egotism and to gain some goodness and delicacy, women need even more, for the health of their sex, to become virile, and a few years in a regiment would be salutary in this regard. In the army, they would be trained in physical exercises and as a result gain muscular strength; they would acquire the spirit of discipline, the habit of subordinating their individuality to something larger than themselves. There they would learn to imagine sacrificing their existence as a possible eventuality.[55]

Although she did not advocate that women actually hoist guns, or "become virile," Marguerite Durand argued in the same vein. Editor of the feminist daily, *La Fronde*, Durand was one of the most influential French feminists of the day (see Figure 2.1). In 1910, she decided to organize women candidates to run for legislative office to publicize the cause of women's rights and to challenge election law. In her platform she included a call for "obligatory humanitarian service for all adult women – mothers excepted – as long as there is obligatory military service for men."[56] Although this demand did not figure prominently in Durand's campaign, which was largely concerned with the rights of working women and the legalization of paternity suits, it did provoke a good deal of comment in the press. The commentators understood it as a response to the *impôt du sang* argument against women's political rights. *Le Radical* wrote "The main argument for men is obligatory military service. Now, Mme Marguerite Durand is not hampered by so small a point; she proposes to institute a service for women." *Le Soleil* rightly placed it as a compromise between the two poles of military service, advocated by Pelletier, and the more common feminist claims for motherhood. Although – or because – these journalists understood the import of obligatory service for women, they chose to make it

Figure 2.1 Marguerite Durand, candidate for the Chamber of Deputies in March 1910. © Bibliothèque Nationale de France, Paris.

the target of criticism and belittling humor. Several articles used the parallel with military service to present Durand as an "amazon" mobilizing a "feminist army." Some simply condemned the idea as an attack upon motherhood and family harmony; *Gil Blas* turned it into a dirty joke.

As far as Mme Marguerite Durand is concerned, she wants to do her military service. The candidate declares "Women can serve in the administration or in the ambulances." But why stop there, madame? There are other services you could supply to our soldiers in the solitude and boredom of the distant garrisons. Each serves his country as he can. Mme Marguerite Durand's idea could be fertile. Let's vote for her.

Nonetheless, in another article, *Gil Blas* admitted that many people no longer found the idea of feminine national service ridiculous – it appealed to their sense of equality, if not, the paper maintained, to their good sense. It was an idea "in the air."[57]

Neither Pelletier's proposal nor Durand's resulted in any legislation, but, fortified by the enthusiasm for women's social service, these proposals did prompt French women to look beyond motherhood for a basis of feminine citizenship. And, albeit somewhat unintentionally, by imagining a feminine national service equivalent to military service, they raised the issue of female patriotism and women's wartime duty.

1911 and After: War Imagined

Fed by these sources, a small discursive stream devoted to women's potential role in national defense flowed through the peripheries of nationalist discourse in the first decade of the twentieth century. It was divided into two main currents, one that proposed motherhood, and one that proposed nursing. (Durand's proposal for humanitarian service, when taken seriously, was also interpreted to mean nursing.) Despite the image of Joan of Arc, few even within militant feminist circles were willing to endorse Pelletier's call for women to perform military service. However, except in the case of a few Red Cross volunteers engaged in Morocco, the discussion was theoretical, developed to explore the parameters of feminine nationalism and female citizenship rather than to address the specific situation of women in war. The repeated confrontations with Germany, beginning with the first Moroccan crisis in 1905, and especially the second Moroccan crisis in 1911 changed the terrain and the terms of the discussion.

Eugene Weber, in *The Nationalist Revival in France, 1905–1914*, described the rising war fever in France. "Love of the fatherland stressed in public, generals once more allowed to wave the flag, prize-giving speeches bringing patriotism back into the schools . . .

growing awareness of past dangers, growing acceptance of the possibility of war, growing emphasis on material and moral readiness, were clearly marked in all quarters, especially among the young."[58] Nationalism ceased to be a doctrine, a party, or even a movement; it became a pervasive climate of opinion endorsed by the government; in 1913 Poincaré declared 8 May, Joan of Arc's festival, a national holiday (see Figure 2.2). But while men's reactions were almost programmed, the responses available to women were ambiguous. Weber concluded that in July 1911, when a German warship steamed into Agadir Bay, French men were ready and willing to put on their uniforms and march. But what were French women to do?

Figure 2.2 8 May, the Festival of Joan of Arc, in 1913. Some 25,000 Action française stalwarts paraded in Paris to her statue at the Place des Pyramides. © Bibliothèque Nationale de France, Paris.

The government helped maintain the atmosphere of urgency by campaigning in 1913 to extend military service from two to three years.[59] An unintended consequence of this campaign was to heighten the pressure French women felt to embrace some kind of national duty. If the blood tax on French men was to be raised, surely

French women should contribute something, particularly if they were to continue to make claims to citizenship. Young women of the same age as male conscripts felt a particularly urgent need to demonstrate their willingness to sacrifice for their country. For example, in 1913 Catholic Women's Social Action formed a new Girls' Patriotic Social Club to respond to the crisis. In its first meeting the club declared that young women should become a positive force for patriotism in their families and in society at large. Catholic social action was their model for patriotic action: "We should manage to do for our country what through our charities we do for God; isn't our country a second religion?"[60] In particular they intended to consider the implications of the "harsh, doubtless, but indispensable" Three Year law for their own behavior. At the second meeting, the president of the organization, Mlle Schwérer, enumerated a list of topics the group should discuss:

> (1) What changes will the Three Year law cause in the family? What are your duties towards your parents, and towards your brothers or servants called to the flag? . . .

> (2) What changes will the Three Year law cause in the professions of those around you? How can you soften the consequences? . . .

But from a discussion of cushioning the effects of longer military service, her list moved quickly to contemplating war and encouraging preparation for it.

> (4) Where will your parents take you in case of war? Will you be in the country or the city? What should be your duties in either event? How can you prepare yourself?[61]

Other young women believed that voluntary mobilization was insufficient. Andrée d'Alix, a columnist for the *Revue du foyer*, a conservative women's magazine, was astonished when she began to receive a steady stream of letters demanding that she "specify the kind of services that could be provided in wartime by a young woman." She believed in motherhood as the sum of women's national duty, but not so her young readers: "Our young women *want to serve*, and to serve in the army."[62] Another group of young women petitioned the Ministry of War with the same idea: "Our dearest hope is to be able to offer France a part of our youth and thus to cooperate with our brothers in the national defense . . . [we] wish shortly to obtain from Parliament a law voted in this sense."[63]

And what would constitute women's war service? When the question of women's national duty was posed in this way, motherhood was not an entirely satisfactory response. Dr Legrand put into words the brutality embedded in the notion of motherhood as military service that most of its advocates avoided. He explained that motherhood is patriotic only when it "gives the son when he is twenty years old, without clamor and without tears, to go to be killed by the anonymous bullet of the nation's enemy. Yes, in this manner, but in this manner only, is maternity the patriotism of women."[64] In wartime, the patriotic mother became the Spartan Mother who sent her son off to war with the exhortation, according to Plutarch, to come back with his shield or on it – in other words, victorious or dead! This was disturbing, to say the least, to traditional ideas of motherhood. As Mlle Renkin wrote to the feminist journal *La Suffragiste*: "What woman, if she could oppose it, would let her son or her husband kill the son or husband of another woman?"[65] Responding to a 1913 opinion poll of young women, Hélène Leconte, a Parisian student, admitted her discomfort with patriotic motherhood as a wartime ideal. "Having only one way to serve my country, I would be desolated to fail; that is to say, I hope with all my heart to have children, that they may defend France in time of war, that they may try to elevate her morally in time of peace . . . I add that I would prefer to see them play a pacific role."[66]

The Red Cross stepped into the breach with a ready answer. On to the pedestal beside the patriotic mother, the Red Cross hoisted the volunteer nurse. The Red Cross argued that nursing, unlike the Spartan Mother, truly combined the feminine and the patriotic; it was the civic motherhood that both the Catholic women's movement and the secular women's rights movement had been seeking.

To Catholic women, the Red Cross held out the image of the nun. Red Cross volunteers not only dressed like nuns in long veils and cloaks, they also embodied the nun-like qualities of spirituality, asexuality, compassion, self-sacrifice and complete submission to authority.[67] For Georges Goyau, a Catholic social activist, religious service was more than a metaphor for Red Cross volunteers: he claimed that, deprived by the expulsion of religious orders of the opportunity to dedicate themselves to God, French women had "invented a new set of duties for themselves" by embracing nursing, a vocation that the Red Cross now called them to turn toward the cause of national defense.[68]

To feminists, the Red Cross promised that volunteer nursing was the feminine *impôt du sang*, the distinctive women's contribution to the national defense. Goyau depicted the Red Cross as an alternative kind of national army, "where women will be the fighters," and Louis Lespine called Red Cross nurses "a voluntary reserve of the national army."[69] Rather than offering their sons to German bullets, by volunteering to nurse French women could protect them from harm, perhaps even at the risk of their own lives.

The war fever proved a perfect opportunity for the French Red Cross to take its message to a wider audience. In 1912 the Red Cross promoter François de Witt-Guizot addressed two lectures to Catholic Social Action on the subject "Woman and War: How a Woman May Serve France in Wartime" and another in 1913 on the lessons of the Red Cross in the Balkan wars for French women's preparedness. Also in 1913, the 10th Congrès Jeanne d'Arc included a session entitled "Women and Patriotism" chaired by the president of the SSBM that revisited and elaborated this theme.[70] It was also the subject of a book-length study of the Red Cross by Alix and a how-to manual by Louis Lespine, *French Red Cross Hospitals in Wartime: How to Organize and Register Them*, both published early in 1914.[71] Virtually every speaker and commentator on the issue of feminine patriotism or potential war service evoked the Red Cross, to the extent that a girls' study group, affiliated with Catholic Social Action, reported "the Red Cross is all the rage."[72]

Volunteer nursing was undoubtedly the most popular answer to the question of what women's contribution to the national defense should be. But it was not the only answer. The most controversial proposal came from Mme Jane Dieulafoy, an eccentric member of Parisian salon circles. As a young bride, she had followed her husband to the front in 1871, and ten years later went with him to Persia on archeological expeditions. For both adventures she had dressed as a man; when she and her husband returned to France, she secured permission from the police commissioner to continue to dress in male clothing. Awarded the Legion of Honor in 1886 for her archeological finds – now in the Louvre – she became a well-known figure in Parisian intellectual and literary circles for her archeology and for her novels set in exotic locales, which recounted the exploits of heroines who often, like their creator, disguised themselves as men.[73] In March 1913, when she was over sixty years old, Dieulafoy wrote a public letter to the Minister of War asking him to "reserve for French women the great honor of participating in the national defense" and requesting that she herself be the first woman to be mobilized.

In a series of public letters, interviews and speeches throughout the spring she fleshed out her idea. She was inspired, she said, by a report in the press that the Austrian army was planning to employ women as clerical workers[74] and by the debate over the Three Year Law. If the enemy was going to use women to expand its combat capacity, France must follow suit, or any gains made by the Three Year Law would be erased. She proposed that a reserve corps of women be trained to take over non-combat positions in military administration in the event of mobilization, thus freeing enough officers "to staff two army corps." According to press reports, hundreds of women wrote to her offering their services, and the Minister of War promised to consider the idea.[75]

Dieulafoy was not a feminist;[76] she distanced her proposal from the discussion of a female blood tax that would justify women's suffrage. To distinguish her proposal from Durand's, Dieulafoy underlined that she did not favor compulsory national service for women; her women's army reserve would be an elite, voluntary force. And to distinguish it from Pelletier's call for female military service, she eschewed any participation in combat.[77]

The press response to Dieulafoy's campaign was predictably mixed. The columnists Louis Chevreuse and Marcel Céraud thought that in the context of the proposed extension of male military service, her idea had merit. Writing in *Le Figaro*, Chevreuse cautioned: "If we are going willingly to accept the heavy burden of three years of military service, it seems that the first effort should be to use effectively all those who can be combatants." Just because Dieulafoy's idea was new and perhaps not in accord with accepted habits was no reason to reject it out of hand, he argued, particularly as women were already employed in many branches of government. Céraud framed his commentary with France's falling birth rate and declining pool of military-age men. Dieulafoy's proposal, in his mind, permitted France to stretch the size of the military without further endangering the birth rate [*sacrificer l'avenir de la race*], because married women with children would be barred from serving. He predicted that the idea would catch on. "Don't laugh! The idea will make its rounds and soon we will have our 'reservettes.'"[78]

Other commentators indulged in the laughs. *Le Matin* columnist Clément Vartel asked his readers to decide which woman France really needed, Mme Dieulafoy or the woman who "is a woman without regrets, with the dress and ideas of her sex," the latter beginning in housekeeping and culminating in motherhood – of sons, of course![79] But all in all, journalists treated Dieulafoy's ideas seriously and with surprising respect, especially considering Dieulafoy's eccentric persona. Dieulafoy's proposal articulated in the most dramatic form an idea that was beginning to take shape, that women's wartime duty was to replace men in necessary but non-combattant roles in order to free men to fight and to keep the country running until they returned. This second point was sadly lacking in the government's mobilization plans, as the hardship of the fall of 1914 would show; but it had begun to receive public attention in the context of this discussion.

Andrée d'Alix was one of the few commentators to imagine a long war during which it would be necessary to keep the country going on more than just a temporary, *ad hoc* basis. In her columns in the *Revue du foyer*, she suggested that women should prepare to run the economy and the bureaucracy as well as their own families. Women could replace men in banks, the civil service, factories, and commerce, and especially in agriculture. She recommended that urban school girls use their summer vacations to familiarize themselves with farming in preparation for this essential war work.[80]

The spate of discussions of women's potential contribution to war threw French feminists into confusion. Some were dismayed that their idea of feminine national service was being appropriated for militarist purposes. Others announced their conversion to militant nationalism. The evolution of discussion in Pelletier's *La Suffragiste* is typical. Prior to 1911, *La Suffragiste* equated feminism and pacifism, and was anti-nationalist to the point of declaring: "A woman should put the emancipation of her sex ahead of her country, because, where only men may be citizens, women can know nothing of patriotism."[81] Under the influence of the war scare, however, the paper lost its clear vision on this issue. Caroline Kauffmann, Pelletier's mentor in the feminist movement, recounted in its pages her conversion from "pacifist to the death" to militarist. Mme Remember, another of Pelletier's close associates, although rejecting militarism, called upon feminists to support war in the defense of justice and civilization. Although other contributors, including Pelletier herself, asserted their continued faith in pacifism, judging by responses to Kauffman and Remember many of the journal's readers were trying to reconcile their belief that women were naturally opposed to war with their resolve to help defend France against the German menace.[82]

The women's movement as a whole remained committed to an ideal of feminine citizenship that combined motherhood and national service. But when national service became an auxiliary to, rather than a replacement for, military service, the ideal tore apart. Wrote Jane Misme, editor of *La Française*: "The woman who risks death in order to give life knows the cost of life; she would be a monster if everything in her did not cry out against the fratricidal butchery of those she brings into the world."[83] Debate on the issue of women's patriotic duties disrupted the plenary session of the 10th International Women's Conference in Paris in June 1913 and threatened to overwhelm the Conference of the Moral Education League there in October. Many delegates continued to argue that "the woman who has fulfilled her maternal duties has largely done her duty toward society . . . Motherhood offsets military service," while others protested that women had a "military duty" apart from motherhood, even though motherhood itself was undoubtedly opposed to war.[84]

From Catholic Social Action to the suffragist Misme, the women's movement was uneasy with Dieulafoy's proposal to enroll women in the military. *L'Action sociale de la femme* reported Dieulafoy's proposal without expressing any opinion upon it, simply introducing it as "posing the question" of how women were to do their patriotic duty. Andrée d'Alix similarly praised the intent but dismissed the idea as impractical. Misme reported that many feminists feared it verged upon support for militarism.[85] However, owing to the popularity of calls for women's preparedness and the disagreement within their own ranks over women's response to war, feminists hesitated to condemn the proliferating schemes for women's wartime mobilization. Instead, they tried to transform them into humanitarian, maternal missions. For example, *La Française* described Dieulafoy's goal as being "to attenuate the misery of our soldiers by easing their distress," "to aid, heal and console," thus making war "less cruel." Like *Action sociale*, this republican feminist paper hailed Dieulafoy for demonstrating the "profound and lively feelings of French women for their country," while at the same time it shied away from the commitment to war that lay at the heart of her project.[86]

Jane Misme eventually developed a comprehensive feminist response to the question of women's wartime duties. She argued that modern women increasingly turned against the ideal of the Spartan Mother, sending their men to war with exhortations to do or die, but neither could they endorse the militarization of women. As mothers, women remained pacifists, but until the "pacifist dream" could become a reality, society "must give to women a personal means to participate in the national defense." She called upon her audience to contemplate the steps women had already taken to mobilize themselves: "Women have already entered the army by volunteering for the Red Cross. We all know that at this moment they are asking for a place in the auxiliary administration of the army. We would be wrong to discourage such initiatives." But "if we want women to submit reasonably to the laws of war, women must be permitted to dictate those laws." Women must have a say in the councils of state; they must have the vote.[87]

In this speech to the Moral Education League, Misme tried to return the terms of the debate to their original position, to use women's proven patriotism to claim their civil rights. Two students at the Normal School at Sevres who responded to Amélie Gayraud's opinion survey of young women echoed this argument. For them, feminine patriotism included motherhood, but did not stop there. They argued that French women must condemn royalism and anti-semitism as unpatriotic, endorse a foreign policy that rejected "adventurous politics and war" and reconcile "peace with national honor." Furthermore, they must work toward "a more complete democracy" that included women as full citizens.[88]

Admirable – juggling pacifism, feminism, and patriotism. Comprehensive – combining motherhood, civic service, and political rights. Yet this formulation did not satisfy French women's longings and fears on the eve of the First World War. No true opinion poll exists, but we do have the results of Gayraud's survey, intended as the feminine counterpart to Agathon's, *Les jeunes gens d'aujourd'hui*. Like Agathon's study, it was originally published in *L'Opinion* and, as Gayraud explained in the introduction, she followed their model. Rather than a poll, her text resulted from a series of conversations with educated young women of her acquaintance supplemented by letters from other young women and from experts such as the pacifist Romain Rolland and the antifeminist novelist Colette Yver. Gayraud conscientiously raised most of the same moral and political issues that Agathon had covered in order to complete their survey by adding "a feminine point of view."[89]

Like Agathon's study, *Les jeunes filles d'aujourd'hui* was profoundly skewed by class, education and political outlook – no working-class women or socialists here! Nonetheless, it differed significantly from Agathon's conclusions. Although similarly selective in her respondents, Gayraud could not get her young women to speak in one voice. Like Agathon, Gayraud directly posed the question of patriotism, although she recognized the asymmetry of the issue when gender was taken into account.

When examining universal ideas such as fatherland, religion, etc., that share the same principles as men's ideas, we have tried to disentangle in what ways they create specifically *feminine action* and *will*. For example, to ask: Are men patriotic? is the equivalent of asking, Are men capable of giving their lives for their country? Women do not go to the frontier; what social duty, then, answers the question: Are women patriotic?[90]

She claimed that young women unanimously answered yes, women were as patriotic as men, but when pressed to define their patriotic duty some answered one thing, some another: "They lose themselves in the details and they don't find their way."[91]

But in fact, their responses were not as scattered as her summary would have us believe. A review of the book pointed out that although her young women did not speak in one voice, they did speak in two! First, all endorsed motherhood, yet almost all of them desired to do something more, to embrace a national duty.[92] From the discussion of the proposals that the war scare had provoked, a relatively unified vision of women's war service had begun to coalesce. It was to be patriotic, not opportunistic – no *quid pro quo* of duty for rights. Ideally it would call for devotion and self-sacrifice equivalent to men's. But it was to be feminine – nurturing and non-violent.

For Gayraud's respondents, what best fit the bill was Red Cross nursing. She reported that when young women were asked: "What is women's patriotic duty, *their special duty*", they replied, "in peacetime? – Raise children to love their country." And in wartime? "To be a nurse, a stretcher-bearer."[93] They conceived of volunteer nursing as feminine, maternal devotion, nationalized and combat-ready, but not militarized. Via nursing, women could aid the national defense without making war. Their maternal rejection of killing could remain intact. As George Goyau expressed it, the Red Cross was an alternative army, fighting an alternative war!

Thus [the Red Cross nurses] direct the struggle against death: they are ready . . . for this kind of war in which women will be the combatants, who, from battlefield to battlefield, will track the other war, the homicidal

war. Thanks to these women, the rule of charity will be established . . .
next to the rule of force: separating these two realms, between the plain
where they kill each other and the oasis of human tenderness where the
women labor, is hardly a fold of the landscape. [94]

Hardly a fold of landscape; but a universe of values!

Of all the ideas that had circulated about what women's role in
war should be, volunteer nursing was the only one that French
women found compelling. Although aroused by Joan of Arc's legend,
almost to a woman they rejected a literal interpretation of its
message. Even Mme Dieulafoy denied its relevance, explaining: "Of
course we have seen women excel on the battlefield; in Joan of Arc's
homeland there is no need to be reminded of that. [But] our role is
not in the line of fire."[95] To remain feminine, women's wartime
service could not be warlike. Killing, aiding killing as Dieulafoy's
own proposal seemed to do, even countenancing killing as a Spartan
Mother, could not be women's part. Only nursing embodied French
women's concept of feminine service in the nation's defense.

In the years before the outbreak of the First World War, these
discussions sent some French women into Red Cross classes; but,
for the most part, women's mental mobilization passed unnoticed
and their physical mobilization was ignored. Other than incorp-
orating some Red Cross nurses into the Military Medical Service,
the government had no plans whatsoever for French women.[96] But
two decades of discussion of women's duty to the nation, focused
in the last three years on women's duty in wartime, did have a
profound effect upon French women. Despite the nationalists'
rhetoric of male honor and virility, French women believed that the
next war would not be an exclusively masculine contest. If and when
their men went to war, French women intended to go to war, too.

Notes

1. Barrès, *L'appel au soldat* , p. 50.
2. Cited in Berenson, *The Trial of Madame Caillaux*, p. 115.
3. Marius Ary Leblond, *La France devant l'Europe* (Paris: Bibliothèque-
Charpentier, 1913), pp. 172, 157.

4. Linda L. Clark, *Schooling the Daughters of Marianne: Textbooks and the Socialization of Girls in Modern French Primary Schools* (Albany, NY: SUNY Press, 1984), p. 34; also Jo Burr Margadant, *Madame le Professeur: Women Educators in the Third Republic* (Princeton, NJ: Princeton University Press, 1990), p. 231.

5. Sylvie Fayet-Scribe, *Associations féminines et catholicisme XIXe–XXe siècle* (Paris: Les Editions ouvrières, 1990), pp. 39–55.

6. "Service social des femmes," *L'Action féminine*, 5 (26 February 1913): 466.

7. See for example, *Congrès national des droits civils et du suffrage des femmes, Paris 1908, compte rendu in extenso*, ed. Mme Oddo Deflou (Paris, 1910) and *Le dixième congrès international des femmes, Paris 1913, compte rendu des travaux*, ed. Mme Avril de Sainte-Croix (Paris: V. Girard et E. Brière, 1914).

8. *Le féminisme chrétien* 4 no. 2 (20 January 1899): 51, 55. See Odile Sarti, *The Ligue Patriotique des Françaises 1902–1933* (New York: Garland Publishing, 1992).

9. Eugen Weber, *The Nationalist Revival in France, 1905–1914*, (Berkeley, CA: University of California Press, 1959), pp. 36–7; Prochasson and Rasmussen, *Au nom de la patrie*, pp. 11–37.

10. Amélie Gayraud, *Les jeunes filles d'aujourd'hui* (Paris: Chez G. Oudin, [1914]), pp. 183–4.

11. Andrée d'Alix, *La Croix-rouge française. Le rôle patriotique des femmes* (Paris: Perrin et cie., 1914), pp. 131–2; emphasis in text.

12. Nadia Margolis, *Joan of Arc in History, Literature and Film: A Select, Annotated Bibliography* (New York: Garland Publishing, 1990), p. 372; Michel Winock, "Jeanne d'Arc," in *Les lieux de mémoire* Vol. III pt. 3: *Les France: De l'archive à emblème*, ed. Pierre Nora (Paris: Gallimard, 1992), pp. 675–733.

13. Marina Warner, *Joan of Arc: The Image of Female Heroism* (New York: Alfred A. Knopf, 1981), pp. 255–75.

14. Marina Warner, *Monuments and Maidens: The Allegory of the Female Form* (New York: Atheneum, 1985).

15. Margolis, *Joan of Arc in History*, pp. 377–80.

16. Helen Lefkowitz Horowitz, *The Power and Passion of M. Carey Thomas* (New York: Alfred A. Knopf, 1994), p. 21; Warner, *Joan of Arc*, p. 263.

17. Sarti, *The Ligue Patriotique* and Anne-Marie Sohn, "Les femmes catholiques et la vie publique: L'exemple de la Ligue patriotique des françaises," in *Stratégies des femmes*, ed. Marie-Claire Pasquier *et al.* (Paris: Tierce, 1984), pp. 97–120.

18. *Le Féminisme chrétien*, 2 January 1899; *L'Action sociale de la femme*, 20 March 1900; Marie Maugeret, "L'Institut agronomique Jeanne d'Arc," *Reforme sociale*, 1 December 1909; Sohn, "Les femmes catholiques," p. 118; and Fayet-Scribe, *Associations*, p. 104.

19. For example, *Le Féminisme chrétien*, 20 May 1899. Steven C. Hause with Anne R. Kenney, *Women's Suffrage and Social Politics in the French Third Republic* (Princeton, NJ: Princeton University Press, 1984), pp. 81–6 and Fayet-Scribe, *Associations*, pp. 57–9.

20. Dames de l'Action française collected the "denier de Jeanne d'Arc" to support young male militants: Martha Hanna, "Iconology and Ideology: Images of Joan of Arc in the Idiom of the Action Française 1908–1931," *French Historical Studies* 14 no. 2 (Fall 1985): 220–4. Fund-raisers collected the "sou de Jeanne d'Arc" from girls to support the construction of a basilica at Domrémy: Winock, "Jeanne d'Arc," p. 692. Mgr Dupanlou suggested female devotees of Joan could place flowers at the base of her statue at the Place des Pyramides in Paris: Jacqueline Freyssinet-Dominjon, *Les manuels d'histoire de l'école libre 1882–1959, de la loi Ferry à la loi Debré* (Paris: Armand Colin, 1969), p. 162.

21. *Le Féminisme chrétien*, 20 January 1899.

22. Karen Offen, "Depopulation, Nationalism and Feminism in Fin-de-siècle France," *American Historical Review* 89 no. 3 (June 1984): 648–76; Offen, "Exploring the Sexual Politics," in Tombs (ed.), *Nationhood and Nationalism*, pp. 195–209 and Anne Cova, *Maternité et droits des femmes en France (XIXe–XXe siècles)* (Paris: Ed. Economica, 1997).

23. Marie-Edmée Pau, *Histoire de notre petite soeur Jeanne d'Arc, dédiée aux enfants de la Lorraine* (Paris: E. Plon et cie., 1874). The book was first published in Nancy in 1873 and proved so popular that Plon brought it out the next year. It went through four editions before 1900. See Margolis, *Joan of Arc in History*, p. 377.

24. Pau, *Histoire de notre petite soeur,* Chapter 28.

25. Freyssinet-Dominjon, *Les manuels d'histoire*, pp. 163–5 and Mona Ozouf, *L'école de la France: Essais sur la Révolution, l'utopie et l'enseignement* (Paris: Gallimard, 1984), pp. 189–204.

26. Cited in Ozouf, *L'école de la France*, p. 202. Georgian first-grade teacher Bailey White, *Mama Makes Up Her Mind* (New York: Vintage Books, 1994), pp. 217–19, familiar to National Public Radio listeners, found, to her chagrin, that Joan of Arc has the same impact upon contemporary American children.

27. Nadine, *Rêves de guerre: Une femme de France à ses soeurs françaises* (Ligugé, Vienne: Imprimerie E. Aubin, 1916), pp. 20–2; Marie Rabut, *Les étincelles* (Dijon: Imprimerie Jobard, 1917), pp. 24, 33–4. Also Stéphane Audoin-Rouzeau, *La guerre des enfants 1914–1918* (Paris: Armand Colin, 1993), pp. 174–5.

28. For example, Sarah Bernhardt played Joan of Arc in a drama by Jules Barbier in 1890 and again in 1909 in another play by Emile Moreau. Kevin J. Harty, "Jeanne au cinéma," in *Fresh Verdicts on Joan of Arc*, ed. Bonnie Wheeler and Charles T. Wood (New York: Garland Publishing, 1996), pp. 237–43, cites six films about Joan of Arc prior to the First World War. In 1910 Charles Péguy's *Mystère de la charité de Jeanne d'Arc* set off a literary

quarrel known as the "Bataille de Jeanne d'Arc." In 1908–9 the Thalamas affair produced riots around Joan of Arc's statue in the Place des Pyramides: Warner, *Joan of Arc*, p. 262.

29. Louis Barthou, *L'effort de la femme française* (Paris: Bloud et Gay, 1917), pp. 3–4; Julie Siegfried, *La guerre et la rôle de la femme* (Cahors: Imprimerie Coueslant, 1915), pp. 4–7; Witt-Guizot, *La femme et la guerre:*, p. 22; Alix, *La Croix-rouge française*, pp. 37–8.

30. [L. Ruault,] *Cents ans de Croix-rouge française au service de l'humanité* (Paris: Hachette, 1964), pp. 17–18; 140–3. The exact causes of the schisms remain obscure, but the social exclusivity of the SSBM was probably also a factor.

31. For example, *Le Monde illustré*, 3 December 1898; *La Femme de l'avenir*, 1 October 1899; *Le Petit parisien*, 29 November 1899; and *Le Figaro*, 29 December 1899.

32. Dr César Legrand, *L'assistance féminine en temps de guerre* (Paris: Librairie universelle, 1907).

33. Katrin Schultheiss, *Bodies and Souls: Politics, Gender, and the Professionalization of Nursing in France, 1880–1922* (forthcoming from Harvard University Press) and Véronique Leroux-Hugon, "Emergence de la profession," in Yvonne Knibiehler *et al.*, *Cornettes et blouses blanches: Les infirmières dans la société française (1880–1980)* (Paris: Hachette, 1984), pp. 41–82 and, by the same author, "L'infirmière au début du XXe siècle," pp. 55–68.

34. Legrand, *L'assistance féminine*, pp. 284–5.

35. Witt-Guizot, *La femme et la guerre*, p. 24; also Legrand, *L'assistance féminine*, p. 2.

36. Ruault, *Cent ans de Croix rouge*, pp. 36–7. This effort received favorable comment in the press, for example, *Le Temps*, 27 September 1907.

37. 8 September 1912.

38. Ruault, *Cent ans de Croix rouge*, p. 37 and Leroux-Hugon, "Les dames blanches," in *Cornettes et blouses blanches,* pp. 83–5.

39. By the outbreak of the war in 1914, there were still only 96 of these career military nurses: Leroux-Hugon, "Les dames blanches," pp. 96–107.

40. Ibid., p. 96.

41. Georges-Clément Lechartier, *La confession d'une femme du monde* (Paris: Plon-Nourrit, 1914), p. 287. *La Française*, 14 February 1914, gave this book a very favorable review, claiming it contained "l'accent de la verité."

42. Rita Thalmann (ed.), *La tentation nationaliste: Entre émancipation et nationalisme; la presse féminine d'Europe 1914–1945* (Paris: Editions Deuxtemps Tierce, 1990).

43. See Harriet B. Applewhite and Darline Gay Levy, "Women and Militant Citizenship in Revolutionary Paris," in *Rebel Daughters: Women and the French Revolution*, ed. Sara E. Melzer and Leslie W. Rabine (New York: Oxford University Press, 1992), pp. 79–101; Dominique Godineau, "Masculine and Feminine Political Practice during the French Revolution, 1793–

Year III," in *Women & Politics in the Age of Democratic Revolution*, ed. Harriet B. Applewhite and Darline G. Levy (Ann Arbor, MI: University of Michigan Press, 1990), pp. 61–80; and Laura Strumingher, "Looking Back: Women of 1848 and the Revolutionary Heritage of 1789," also in *Women & Politics*, pp. 259–85.

44. Richard D. Challener, *The French Theory of the Nation in Arms, 1866–1939* (New York: Columbia University Press, 1955), pp. 3–90.

45. Duc d'Aumale, *Les institutions militaires de la France* (Paris: Michel Lévy *frères*, 1867), pp. 157, 185. See Horne, "'L'Impôt du sang,'" p. 202.

46. Challener, *Nation in Arms*, p. 58.

47. Nor has it troubled the historians of this debate, for example Challener, *Nation in Arms*, or recent French politics. As Emmanuel Reynaud, *Les femmes, la violence et l'armée: Essai sur la féminisation des armées* (Paris: Foundation pour les études de défense nationale, 1988), pp. 44–5 points out, the French conscription law passed in 1984 described conscription as "la participation de tous les citoyens à l'effort de défense," despite the fact that it applied only to men.

48. Claire Goldberg Moses, *French Feminism in the 19th Century* (Albany, NY: SUNY Press, 1984) and Hause, *Women's Suffrage*.

49. Steven C. Hause, *Hubertine Auclert, The French Suffragette* (New Haven, CT: Yale University Press, 1987), pp. 68–76. Offen, "Depopulation, Nationalism, and Feminism:" 661 argues that antifeminism was even more central to the turn-of-the-century French nationalist revival than was anti-Semitism.

50. Cited in Moses, *French Feminism*, p. 215.

51. *Congrès national des droits civils et du suffrage des femmes, Paris 1908*, pp. 192–3.

52. Karen Offen, "Defining Feminism: A Comparative Historical Analysis," *Signs* 14 no. 1 (Fall 1988): 119–57; Cova, *Maternité et droits des femmes*.

53. Offen, "Exploring the Sexual Politics," pp. 200–2; Anne Cova, "French Feminism and Maternity: Theories and Policies 1890–1918," in *Maternity and Gender Policy*, ed. Gisela Bock and Pat Thane (London: Routledge, 1991), p. 121; Rachel G. Fuchs, "The Right to Life: Paul Strauss and the Politics of Motherhood," in *Gender and the Politics of Social Reform in France 1870–1914*, ed. Elinor A. Accampo, Rachel G. Fuchs and Mary Lynn Steward (Baltimore, MD: Johns Hopkins University Press, 1995), pp. 83–4, 88.

54. Madeleine Pelletier, *La femme en lutte pour ses droits* (Paris: V. Giard & E. Brière, 1908), p. 41. I thank Steven C. Hause for alerting me to this passage.

55. Ibid. Predictably, press coverage of Pelletier's book was jocular, as in André Tourette, "Aux armes . . . citoyennes: Je veux de la poudre et des balles dit Mme Madeleine Pelletier," *L'Intransigeant*, 30 October 1908.

56. Bibliothèque Marguerite Durand (hereafter BMD) dossier Durand, élections 1910.

57. Ibid., press clippings February–April 1910.

58. Weber, *Nationalist Revival*, pp. 36–7.

59. Gerd Krumeich, *Armaments and Politics in France on the Eve of the First World War: The Introduction of Three-Year Conscription 1913–1914*, trans. Stephen Conn (Dover, NH: Berg Publishers, 1984).

60. "Cercle patriotique social des jeunes filles de l'ASF," *L'Action sociale de la femme* 12 nos. 9–10 (Septembre–Octobre, 1913): 346–7.

61. "Le patriotisme et la femme," *L'Action sociale de la femme* 13 no. 2 (February 1914): 66–70.

62. Alix, *La Croix-rouge française*, p. 11; emphasis in the text.

63. Ibid., p. 5.

64. Legrand, *L'assistance féminine*, p. 16.

65. S. Renkin, "Sur la guerre," *La Suffragiste* 4 no. 29 (June 1912): 11.

66. Gayraud, *Les jeunes filles d'aujourd'hui*, p. 239.

67. Alix, *La Croix-rouge française*, pp. 46–50; Witt-Guizot, *La femme et la guerre*, pp. 33–42; Legrand, *L'assistance féminine*, pp. 247–63.

68. Goyau preface to Alix, *La Croix-rouge française*, p. xii.

69. Ibid., p. vii; Louis Lespine, *Les hôpitaux de la Croix-rouge française en temps de guerre: Comment les organiser et les faire classer* (Paris: Berger-Levrault, éditeurs, 1914), p. v.

70. Witt-Guizot, *La femme et la guerre*; Goyau, preface to Alix, *La Croix-rouge française*, pp. xiv–xv.

71. Alix, *La Croix-rouge française;* Lespine, *Les hôpitaux de la Croix-rouge.*

72. *L'Action sociale de la femme* 12 no. 5 (May 1913): 206–10.

73. Eve and Jean Gran-Aymeric, *Jane Dieulafoy, une vie d'homme* (Paris: Perrin, 1991).

74. *Le Temps*, 12 March 1913 indeed reported the Austrian government's action and, on 22 March, Dieulafoy's response.

75. BMD dos Dieulafoy, press clippings. Most of the clippings, unfortunately, do not include the name of the paper or the date.

76. Jane Misme wrote of Dieulafoy in her obituary: "Mme Dieulafoy ne fut point jusqu'à ces dernières années une militante féministe. Mais elle offrit en sa personne à la cause des femmes un précieux argument" (*La Française*, 3 June 1916).

77. BMD dos Dieulafoy.

78. Ibid.

79. Ibid.

80. Alix, *La Croix-rouge française*, pp. 75–93; also François de Witt-Guizot, "Causerie sur l'organisation de la Croix-Rouge en province et les enseignments de la guerre des Balkans," *L'Action sociale de la femme* 12 no. 2 (February 1913): 47–57.

81. "Les femmes n'ont pas de patrie," *La Suffragiste* 2 no. 18 (September 1910): 13.

82. Caroline Kauffmann, "Paix ou guerre," *La Suffragiste* 4 no. 29 (June 1912): 9–11; Mme Remember, "Aux armes citoyennes," *La Suffragiste* 3 no. 22 (November 1911): 3–10; S. Ispolatof, "Contre la guerre," *La Suffragiste* 5 no. 34 (January 1913): 5–6. S. Renkin, "Sur la guerre," *La Suffragiste* 4 no. 29 (June 1912): 11; Pelletier, "Patriotisme et féminisme," *La Suffragiste* 5 no. 40 (July 1913): 8.

83. Jane Misme, "Les femmes et la guerre," *La Française*, 10 May 1913.

84. Mme Moll-Weiss to the Congrès de la Ligue d'éducation morale, reported in *La Française*, 8 November 1913; Louise Brunet to the 10th International Women's Conference, reported in Avril de Sainte Croix, *Dixième congrès international des femmes*, pp. 430–2.

85. "Cercle d'études." *L'Action social de la femme* 12 no. 5 (May 1913): 207–8; Alix, *La Croix-rouge française*, pp. 12–14; Jane Misme, "Aimer et savoir aimer son pays," *La Française*, 12 July 1913.

86. Marie-Louise Le Verrier, "Les femmes et la défense du pays," *La Française*, 24 May 1913.

87. Jane Misme, "Report sur l'éducation civil des femmes," *La Française*, 8 November 1913.

88. Gayraud, *Les jeunes filles d'aujourd'hui*, pp. 158–65.

89. Ibid., p. 16.

90. Ibid., emphasis in text.

91. Ibid., p. 66.

92. *La Vie* 3 no. 19 (15 July 1914).

93. Gayraud, *Les jeunes filles d'aujourd'hui*, p. 66, emphasis in text.

94. Goyau preface to Alix, *La Croix-rouge française*, pp. vi–vii.

95. BMD dos Dieulafoy, press clippings. Interview with Dieulafoy, early in June 1913.

96. "Si la guerre éclatait," *Le Temps*, 4 January 1913, emphasis in text.

3

The Mobilization of Femininity

By contrast with 1911, France experienced no war fever in the summer of 1914. The assassination of the Austrian archduke provoked little comment; it was simply one more crisis in the crisis-prone Balkans, which had already exploded into war twice in the past three years (1912, 1913) without involving or much interesting France. Although a few memoirs recalled a week or so of heightening tension,[1] typically French women described the mobilization order of 1 August and the declaration of war two days later as totally unexpected. Two stories predominated, both depending upon the season – midsummer – to represent a pastoral peace torn asunder by war, the story of the war bursting on the Parisian bourgeois family on vacation in the country and on the peasant family in the hayfields.

In the first story, the principal actors were the women and children of the Parisian upper middle class, relaxing in the mountains and the countryside and on the seashore. Into this scene, the declaration of war erupted "like a thunderclap."[2] The novelist, Colette described the scene at St Malo, where she was vacationing:

> How would I forget that hour? Four o'clock on a beautiful overcast day of a seaside summer, the golden ramparts of the old city rising up from a sea, green on the beach but blue at the horizon. In search of their afternoon snack, the children in red bathing suits leave the sands and mount the narrow streets . . . And in the middle of the town, all sorts of uproar at once, the alarm bells, the drums, the shouting crowd, the wailing children . . . You press close to the town crier with his drum, who is reading a notice; you don't hear what he reads because you know already. Women leave the group, running, then stop as if shot, then run again as if they have broken an invisible barrier and been launched into another side of life.[3]

The companion scene to this one of sunshine on Parisians at peaceful play was sunshine upon peasants at peaceful work. Emilie Carles recalled the declaration of war in the French Alps:

53

During the first days of August 1914 we were all at Granon, right in the middle of the harvest. When we heard the bells, we all wondered why they were ringing like that . . . It was the local policeman who announced the news. He came all the way up with his bugle, telling everyone he met: "It's war!" "War! What war?" people asked, totally unprepared to hear the news . . . We looked at each other, we were so far away from such a thing. You have to know Granon to understand: it is a plateau on the mountain top, with fields and woods as far as the eye can see, and the sky above. All of us were in the fields in the middle of bundles of hay.[4]

The second act in the drama was the mobilization of the reserves. Unlike the arrival of the news of war, set only in sunlit countryside, memoirists and commentators set mobilization anywhere and everywhere. The significant element in this act was gender; the men marched away and the women remained behind. As the Duchesse de Gramont wrote: "The men go with confident pride – War is an affirmation of virility! – They depart, leaving behind them a troop of women and children."[5] However, as J. Delteil recalled, "on 1 August, France became a train station;" and in most accounts, it was at the train station where the war most dramatically accomplished the triage, both spatially and emotionally. Felix Klein, an army chaplain, idealized the scene in a fashion typical of 1915 when his diary was published. "Heedless of all else, giving no backward glance, leaving unfinished tasks begun, taking no precaution for the future, completely absorbed in the solemn present, [the men] leave family, undertakings, business . . . The astonishing thing is that not one murmurs and many are enthusiastic; but the women weep, and the children they are leaving."[6]

Not everyone agreed that reactions were so completely gendered. The propagandist Berthe M. Bontoux and the novelist Jack de Bussy insisted that "anguish" was universal, but kept in check by similarly universal "patriotic decency;" both men and women hid their fears and kept back their tears until the trains pulled out.[7] However, mobilization figured in all these scenes as the moment of transition from peace to war, a transition made with resolution but also with regret. In some accounts, the population as a whole demonstrated both emotions; in most, men represented one and women (and children) the other. All agreed as to the meaning of gender in this social transformation. The move to war virilized society by valorizing the masculine; the feminine was left behind, subordinated, saddened, silenced.

It was not only the feminine that was to go into abeyance, but all of civilian life. War not only masculinized society, it militarized masculinity. Traditional masculine concerns like politics and business took distant second place to military matters when they did not cease altogether. Gabriel Perreux, who chronicled but also experienced the outbreak of the First World War in Paris, described a city that abruptly shut down. Theaters, restaurants, museums and cafés closed; bus services were suspended, and the metro and tramways ran infrequently. Baronne Jane Michaux reported that many businesses decorated their closed shutters with tricolor bunting and large signs announcing proudly: "The boss is mobilized" or "All the employees have joined up."[8] "Normal" life ground to a halt because of the absence of men, but also to enact patriotism. Fernand Gregh recalled in his memoirs: "In 1914, it was a sudden break with all of life that went before. At first, you lived only by and for the war. A gravity, a sublime austerity fell on the country. In the first days, you hardly dared laugh or sing; to dine out seemed practically a sacrilege." By abandoning work and positively eschewing entertainment, French society dramatically took up its new role as a nation at war. Antoine Delécraz's chronicle of Parisian scenes in August 1914 summed up this reaction in his title: *1914, Paris During Mobilization. Notes of an Immobilized* [un immobilisé].[9]

For most women, and indeed, most civilians, the prescribed role was inaction – waiting, hoping – with all attention fixed upon the battlefield where French virility was deciding France's fate. This meant walking daily or twice daily to the town hall to read the communiqués, buying flags and rosettes, reading the newspapers and studying maps. Many women were at a disadvantage in following war news, never having paid much attention to official news bulletins before and unfamiliar with maps. Louise Weiss recalled that one of her mother's friends who looked at a map of the war zone assumed that the top of the map represented elevation and thus that the Germans were pouring down a slope into France.[10]

By the end of the first week, the communiqués became even more difficult to understand, proclaiming: "Alternating advances and retreats." Newspapers filled their reduced pages with "color" stories with little real information, while in the countryside village criers gave up their rounds entirely.[11] Rumor had free rein: "[E]veryone has a relative, a friend, who knows someone in a Ministry 'intimately,'" explained Michaux. Mme Andrieu, who, as the wife of a Sub-Prefect, really did have inside sources of information, spent her days on the telephone or waiting for telephone calls in search of "a little truth."[12]

The first official word that the French war effort was in trouble was the news, on 23 August, that the Germans had entered Brussels; but the real shocker was the communiqué of 29 August: "Situation unchanged from the Somme to the Vosges." The Somme river is in France. For most of the French population, including many in the government, this was the first news that France was invaded. Michel Corday, an undersecretary in the Ministry of Commerce, at first thought "Somme" was a misprint for Sambre, a river in Belgium.[13] Louise Weiss had walked to the town hall with her cousin Sophie to read the communiqué, as they did every day. She recalled they were at first "flattened" by this news, but then awakened, energized. "I was trembling. To live, yes, but not in isolation. A flood of love swept through me for my country, attacked, wounded, violated. This communiqué? A thunderclap, the first of my young life. I took fire. I also loved France and I wanted to serve her."[14]

The invasion of France shook the gender divide between the war and the *arrière* by intruding the war into the *arrière*, as we shall see in the next chapter. But as Louise Weiss's reaction shows, it also had a significant impact upon the civilian population outside the war zone. The invasion shattered their frozen immobility, creating the desire in both men and women to act. Like Louise Weiss, many women became convinced that they could not simply embody the France that their men were defending. If they were to avoid the fate of France herself – attacked, wounded, violated – they needed to contribute to France's defense. "To serve" – but how? "The problem is an arduous one. Brusquely it is posed to many women . . . Like the author of these pages, they appeal to the mute heavens and cry: 'What to do?'"[15]

The "author of these pages" was teenaged Maïten d'Arguibert, an aspiring writer, and one answer she proposed, realized in the pages themselves, was to keep a journal. This would both record and contribute to France's heroism by keeping up her own morale and that of those around her, she believed. Fortunately for historians, other women reacted similarly. Two of our best chroniclers of French women's lives during the First World War are Marguerite Lesage, the wife of a sugar refiner, and Louise Delétang, a Parisian seamstress; neither had kept a diary prior to the war. The belief that she had witnessed a world-shattering event in the mobilization impelled Delétang to begin writing: "Since this evening I have wanted to preserve the memory for ever," she wrote, and she continued to record her reactions on paper until the armistice. For Lesage, it was not the weight of history but the weight of her responsibilities that drove her to diary-keeping. Left alone by her husband's mobilization with a family and a business to run, she felt unable to share her anxieties with anyone. "I must not, I don't want to complain, so I have no other confidant than this notebook . . . maybe it will help me keep up an external mask of calm, resignation, even courage, all qualities I must acquire because I don't possess them, or enough of them."[16]

But although keeping a record was a response to the war, it hardly qualified as a sufficient contribution to France's war effort. The pre-war discussion of women's civic duty and feminine patriotism reopened suddenly as of the utmost practical concern. What was it that women could and should do to support their nation in war?

This discussion lasted throughout the war. It swamped the pre-war sources of the question, which had been confined fairly narrowly to Red Cross propaganda, the debate over women's suffrage and Joan of Arc's message to modern French women. Now it inspired dozens of books, articles and speeches, engaging the attention of prominent cultural and political leaders such as Louis Barthou, Frédéric Masson, Maurice Barrès and Maurice Donnay, besides the predictably interested circles of feminists, pronatalists and Catholic moralists.[17] It was a serious, often acrimonious debate that recapitulated all the pre-war arguments, but now in a context that gave them immediate relevance to many French women. Nonetheless, it rarely went much beyond the terrain already surveyed by Red Cross recruiters, women's suffragists and Catholic social activists. In the main, French women were left to find their own way to acceptable female war service amid the pitfalls already identified by pre-war commentators. A misstep meant undermining gender by becoming too masculine or undermining the war effort by infusing it with femininity, and the terms of the argument made missteps inevitable. Every action or inaction, every emotion, whether smiles or tears, was suspect.

One of the few issues upon which all commentators agreed was that masculine and feminine duties differed in wartime as they did in peacetime. In this they ratified the message of the train-station scene; war did not disrupt gender categories, it confirmed them. Whatever it was that war required of women, it did not require what it required of men. According to the journalist Marie de la Hire,

Patriotism: . . . a living virtue, as strong in women's hearts as in men's spirits, . . . [has] different sources but a single object: *la patrie*. Feminine patriotism can be translated synthetically by the word, defense, and by extension, preservation, center, birth, giving life and protecting it: while the other, masculine patriotism has always meant conquest, attack, combat, vengeance, blood and death.[18]

As in pre-war rhetoric, commentators repeatedly evoked the example of Joan of Arc to explain that in France, at least, women were not to be totally divorced from war, but as in pre-war writing, they quickly side-stepped the conclusion one could most easily draw from Joan's example by proposing it as an analogy only, removing women from any responsibility for military defense similar to men's.[19] Even those who, in 1915, would argue for the inclusion of women in the French military believed in a natural gender division of activity that must be maintained in order to ensure victory. As Louise Zeys proclaimed: "The war has taught everyone more than one lesson, that it is necessary to apply the principle of division of labor on a grand scale."[20]

Patriotic Motherhood: Spartan or Sorrowful?

The first and most persistent conception of feminine patriotism was maternity – to bear, offer and sacrifice sons for France. Motherhood had figured prominently before the war in feminist arguments for women's full citizenship. Also, the only message from France's militant nationalists to French women had been to bear sons to defend the fatherland. In the first year of the war, however, this emphasis waned, perhaps because maternity could not be imagined as service to the war in progress. Instead, commentators praised French women's past achievements in patriotic childbirth, some-times in rather appalling terms. Dr François Helme, for example, published the following eulogy to French mothers in *Le Temps* in April 1915:

French women! Ah, who will praise them as they merit? We speak endlessly about the progress of our armaments and tactics . . . All that is nothing, however, beside the human armaments that the mothers have known how to supply. Oh! the brave boys, their children, how proud they can be of their work! Speak of them, sing their praises, you can never say enough.[21]

However, baby-making as military service soon returned to the forefront of rhetoric directed at women – and sometimes by women as well. As Marie-Monique Huss has demonstrated in her study of French wartime postcards, the depiction of maternity as military service escaped the confines of small-circulation magazines and pronatalist lectures to invade popular culture. In 1915 and 1916 postcard series depicted infants and children as enrolled in the battalions of the future and called upon French women to "work for France" by becoming pregnant.[22] In the depths of both a manpower crisis and a morale crisis in 1917, commentators argued that maternity was the feminine equivalent of soldiering. The *Revue philanthropique* suddenly devoted its pages once again to exposing the problem of depopulation and prescribing frequent childbearing as women's patriotic duty.[23] Jane Misme's paper, *La Française* agreed; the entire issue of 11 May 1917 exhorted French women to have babies because, otherwise, even if victorious on the battlefield, France would be defeated.[24]

At the beginning of the war, commentators explained that French women who had already experienced the joy of bearing sons for *la patrie* must now embrace the pain of giving them up to her. Initially, this message came from the Catholic Right, drawing upon the exemplar of the Virgin. On 7 August 1914, for example, the *L'Echo de Paris* published an article by Chanoine Bernard Gaudeau that described the train-station scene as a simultaneous re-enactment of Spartan motherhood and Mary's sacrifice.[25] But this discourse quickly slipped its Catholic leash and infused republican rhetoric as well. Louis Barthou asked: "From where do these mothers dredge up their strength? In their sacrifice. They forget themselves in thinking of France . . . It's for France that they give their sons; it's for France that their sons give their lives. In surviving their sons, they give themselves twice over."[26] And in this duty, all French mothers shared: "Duchesses and working women, comfortable bourgeoises and simple peasants, with the same step they mount toward the summit of sacrifice, generously accepted."[27] By offering their sons at the national altar, the women of France joined the *Union sacrée*.

Undoubtedly, this message was designed to facilitate mobilization. The historian Susan Zeiger argues that when the United States entered the First World War, American officials worried that women would oppose conscription. To counter this threat, they warned American women via posters and films that their patriotic duty was to accept their sons' conscription. In England, the goal of propaganda was less passive; in the absence of conscription, British women were to incite their men to enlist.[28] Efforts in France were less coordinated and less controversial in part because mobilization had less resistance to overcome. Unlike Britain, France had already enacted universal male conscription, nor was it, as in the United States, a new measure. In one form or another, conscription in France dated back more than a century, and for the past two decades it had been promoted as the bulwark of republicanism. Feminist efforts before the war had not been directed at eliminating conscription but, on the contrary, at developing a way of extending it to women as well. Thus the French military did not expect women to oppose mobilization,[29] nor did they need women's help to obtain men's enlistment.

American propaganda focused upon what Zeiger calls the mother–son "enlistment drama," contrasting the bad mother who feminized her son by trying to prevent his enlistment to the patriotic mother who resigned herself to letting her son do his manly duty. A few French propagandists toyed with variations on this narrative. Noëlle Roger's novel, *Feu sur la montagne: journal d'une mère 1914–1915* (1915), for example, depicted the shame of the patriotic mother of a shirker son. The mother berated herself for not having done her duty by teaching her son his. As she watched the troops march off she exclaimed: "Then, in this splendor of unanimous sacrifice, I thought of my son. Among all those mothers, I was ashamed of my security. Their anguish seemed to me a magnificent role that had been refused me."[30]

As this story suggests, the thrust of French propaganda was to convince French women that they were doing more than obeying the law in acquiescing to conscription; by countenancing the mobilization of their sons, they themselves were doing a signal patriotic service. In the rhetoric of commentators like Barthou and Roger, but also in the memoirs of women like the Baronne de la Grange and Mme Edouard Drumont, it was women, individually, who "gave" their sons to the war rather than the laws of conscription that took them.[31] The bulk of speeches, essays and stories, rather than depicting mobilization as a struggle between mothers and sons, feminine and masculine, showed French women voluntarily doing their duty by giving their sons, husbands and brothers to the nation, and praised them for it.[32]

Although the initial call to women was to "give" their men, it was soon evident that this was not to be a single sacrifice, completed when the men marched away. Women were going to have to give over and over again, not one son, but all, not once but several times, as the scene was to be restaged at the end of every leave. Finally women were to give up not just the presence of their men but their very lives. While the earliest propaganda tried to reconcile women to mobilization as a necessary but temporary absence, the focus quickly shifted to encompass and even to glorify male death as female sacrifice. Some commentators referred explicitly to the Spartan mother who, when told of the death of her five sons in victorious battle, rushed to the temple to give thanks.[33]

Accounts of mothers, already having lost several sons, joyfully offering up their last were staples of nineteenth-century war rhetoric[34] and readily appeared in France in the first years of the First World War. In his morale-boosting essay, *Voix de femmes* (1916), Ernest Gaubert evoked the ideal of Spartan motherhood in a peasant woman, a widow with two sons already killed on the battlefield, who presented her third and last son to the recruiting station: "If they have to kill you, she said, don't be too far away and at least make sure you kill some of the Boches first!"[35] Some propaganda extended the ideal to wives, fiancées and sisters, whose duty it also was to "give" the lives of their men to France.[36] In fact, the most famous "Spartan Mother" in French propaganda was a sister, Berthe Hasse. On 4 September 1914, Maurice Barrès printed in his weekly column Hasse's letter, the spiritual sister to the "Little Mother" letter that so outraged Robert Graves.[37] Like the "Little Mother" letter, the Hasse letter was probably not authentic, even though it was reported as such by Barrès and repeated by other reputable commentators such as Louis Barthou. The letter's author claimed to be a young woman from Lorraine writing to her brother Edward to inform him that four of his brothers were dead, the fifth badly wounded, and to exhort him: "Leave, my dear brother, sacrifice your life; . . . It's for us and for France. Think of your brothers and of your grandfather in 1870."[38]

Although it is unlikely that a real Berthe Hasse wrote this amazing letter to a real brother, there were certainly some French women who adopted such rhetoric in the early days of the war. The Prefect of the Aube reported that the wife of an important local industrialist had publicly stated: "I have only two sons, both soldiers at this moment. Even if I must weep for the rest of my life, I would sacrifice one of them if we are to be victorious." Newspapers published and praised letters from grieving wives and mothers who consoled themselves with the thought that they had "given to [their] country that which [they] held most dear in the world."[39] Such responses became so expected that when she met one mother who refused to play the role, Louise Delétang was surprised and confused. Her fruit and vegetable vendor had already lost three children to tuberculosis, and in December 1914 openly cursed the government for conscripting the two that remained. When Delétang's uplifting discourse on Fatherland, Duty and Virtue only infuriated the woman more, Delétang turned away in distress. What would be the fate of France, she later mused in her diary, if mothers refused "to inculcate in their children the religion of sacrifice and the acceptance of heroic and fertile death?"[40]

During the first months of the war, there was little criticism of the Spartan-Mother version of feminine patriotism, although a few commentators quickly identified some of the problems it posed and tried to resolve them. First of all, it omitted women who had neither sons nor husbands nor brothers to sacrifice. Sending off a distant cousin or a school friend did not quite qualify as patriotic service fulfilled. Paul Deleutre, in his compendium of patriotic anecdotes, opened the possibility that a woman without a man to "give" should give herself. Two "elegant young persons" on the Champs Elysées discussed their anxiety over brothers at the front. A third approached: "'Here's Laure. Laure, you have no one at the front, cheer us up a little bit.' The other looked at them. She gave a melancholy smile, then said very simply: 'That was unfair so I am going there myself, at least, as close as possible.' 'Yourself?' 'Yes, my guardian, Major L . . . has had me assigned to the temporary hospital in . . . (the name of a town in l'Aisne). I leave tomorrow.'"[41] He also told another supposedly true story of a sister who took her brother's place on the battlefield after he was killed.

A second way for women without men to contribute was to make themselves into prizes, or, as some articles suggested, sacrifices for the nation's heroes by marrying them. Newspaper articles, fiction and propaganda exhorted women to marry only a war veteran, preferably a wounded one, and praised them when they did so. "By generously and proudly consenting to marry these poor invalids or cripples of the war," a young French woman would "accept the sacrifice that she owed to her country," thought Maurice Barrès.[42] Marriage to a disabled veteran formed the plot of several wartime novels, such as René Boylesue's *Tu n'es plus rien* (1918), and Colette Yver's *Mirabelle de Pampelune* (1917), while the press lauded real-life examples in articles titled "A Hero's Marriage" and "A Glorious

Disabled Veteran Marries His Nurse" and condemned a woman who tried to divorce her amputee husband with a lecture on "The Duty of the Women of France."[43]

A second problem with the Spartan-Mother ideal was that with the death of the man, a woman's contribution ended. Few French women had, like Berthe Hasse, an apparently inexhaustible supply of men to sacrifice. Moreover, many commentators felt that the death of a loved man in the war, far from freeing French women from further war service, bound them to a continued effort not encompassed in the story of the Spartan Mother. Ernest Gaubert claimed to know a woman, who, after her husband was killed, took up work in a munitions factory; and Raoul Narsy, editor of the *Journal des debats,* printed a letter from a war widow who pledged to join "a regiment of women" if one was ever organized.[44] The most common solution, however, was to prescribe even more patriotic motherhood. Pauline Valmy told war widows that their job was to hide their tears and bravely raise their children to be true Frenchmen. They were to rebuild the home, even remarry, if possible, in order to have "battalions of cherubim."[45]

Finally, as the war continued and its appalling mortality became evident, the notion that men's death was their women's patriotic sacrifice became more grim than glorious. Michel Corday, who in his diary frequently skewered false sentimentality, particularly when displayed by women, ridiculed women who presented their men's deaths as their own sacrifices.[46] Critics began to find women who denounced "shirkers" morally repugnant.[47] Léon Abensour criticized the fashion for "héroïnes cornéliennes" but understood that women who declared themselves "happy" to have sacrificed their men had been taught this was how they were supposed to react "to leave to posterity the memory of a *beau geste*." But, he insisted, these were false models: "any mother worthy of the name will consider them with horror."[48]

Several women writers agreed with him. In her 1915 novel, *La veillée des armes*, Marcelle Tinayre presented the feminine ideal in the shape of a humble concierge, not as a Spartan Mother but as "the symbolic figure of the Mater Dolorosa" and speculated: "If there were women in the governments, there would be no more wars!"[49] Even Julie Daudet, widow and mother of hyper-nationalists, expressed doubts in her diary that motherhood could be appropriate war service. Contemplating her daughter's pregnancy in October 1914, Mme Daudet mused: "Isn't it a pity this year to be giving life *more than just motherhood*

when we see the void, the torture of human affections, when so many mothers cry for their twenty-year old sons?"[50]

Before the war, bearing and raising sons for France had assured some women that by performing this valuable national service, they were part of the Nation. In the first weeks of the war, the idea that mobilization was women's gift of men to France helped to reconcile women to the war. But in the long run, which the First World War turned out to be, the story of women's war service as first giving men life and then giving them up to death for the Nation was unsatisfactory for many French women. It seemed an inappropriate conception of feminine war service, even perverse, and certainly incomplete. Having sent their men to war, surely women should do something more to help them in this enterprise than to mourn and glorify their deaths.

Patriotic Femininity: Domesticity and Fashion

Commentators and women themselves, as revealed in their memoirs, struggled with the question of how to be feminine and warlike. Unfortunately for French women bedeviled by the question "What to do?" the answer that emerged in the public discourse was ambiguous, to say the least. The debate moved between two essentially opposite positions, although they were only occasionally acknowledged as such. One position argued that women would best serve the nation by remaining exactly as they were; the other argued that women could not remain as they were, but must live a different, better femininity during the war and in the future. Both views cast French women as the embodiment of the France for which their men were fighting. In the first story, France was gallant and gay, loving and caring, and innocent of any responsibility for the war. In the second, France's frivolity, light-mindedness and light morals had invited the current crisis, and only fundamental reform would see her through to victory. Maurice Donnay claimed: "Whatever the reason, it is the case that too many Parisiennes in recent years have been carried away in this sumptuary movement that itself carried us toward we didn't know what, but toward something, a revolution or a war . . . It was a war."[51]

In the first years of the war, headmistresses of girls' schools, politicians and journalists as well as a few memoirists – Maiten d'Arguibert for example – but especially novelists like Shéridan and Françoise Vitry advised or depicted the preservation of peacetime femininity as the essence of women's war service. By embodying and living the feminine, French women affirmed and kept alive French civilization. In 1915, the headmistress of the girls' *lycée* in Rouen exhorted the graduating class: "Let all those who will return to us find faithfully preserved the whole tradition of the France of our old epics: heroic France and GENTLE FRANCE." Julie Siegfried, head of the National Council of French Women, sounded the same message: "When those who have left return, what a delight for them if we stay that which we are in this moment."[52] This meant that women must live for others, especially for their children and their absent men. For many commentators, the wartime duty of mothers was to raise their children to be worthy of their hero fathers.[53] Yet patriotic femininity was to go beyond motherhood to infuse feminine existence. Esther Villeminot-Lapoulot claimed that the typical housewife was more than Coventry Patmore's "angel in the house," she was the angel in the Nation. "The warmth of a feminine heart" was not just to comfort her own family, but to warm France. "It is for the Women of France to pour out upon the Country the heroic breath that gives life and permits us to issue victorious from this crisis."[54]

Novelists depicted what this might mean in individual women's lives. Shéridan in *La grande blessée* (1917), Françoise Vitry in *Journal d'une veuve de guerre* (1919) and Charles-Henry Hirsch in *Mariée en 1914* (1916) told the same story. Their heroines were completely immobilized by the mobilization of the men in their lives. They thought constantly of the *cher absent*, reread his letters, "learned to wait" and, in the case of Hirsch's heroine, became pregnant. Their only war work was keeping the house and themselves as they were when their men left. Vitry's heroine rejoiced in her housework. "I prepared the house, I made it all fresh, all smart for when he would return. I made curtains of white lace for the windows and a pink spread for the bed."[55] Shéridan depicted his heroine's temporary defeatism as ceasing to care about her clothes and her looks, and her restoration to a proper, fighting spirit as a call to her seamstress. This duty did not end with the death of their men. At the conclusion of her novel, Vitry depicted femininity as both a personal and patriotic victory.

> But if I am the same as before, it's so he can recognize me, leaning from above . . . It's so he can say: "Of course, that's really her; she is what I made of her. If she laughs, it is because I loved her laugh." . . . No, I'm

not ashamed of my strength, my health, my bloom because I want to stay the same as His Dream, to the enchantment of our years of Happiness.[56]

The women's columnist Nadine and the memoirist Maïten d'Arguibert attempted to write this story for real, rather than fictional, heroines. In a series of articles in the spring of 1915, Nadine argued that various ordinary feminine tasks such as knitting, teaching children, doing housework and visiting family graves were patriotic service. Arguibert justified similar choices in her memoirs. After rejecting nursing as a possible response to the war, she decided that "the mission of the rear, . . . as long as the War lasts – and after" was to re-establish and strengthen the home because "[s]ince the war began, the French public makes up just one big family."[57] Thus both keeping and publishing this family journal amounted to war work, as did the various household tasks she recorded in it – fixing a crack in the plaster, moving furniture, helping with the house-cleaning.

In many of the commentaries, the femininity that equaled patriotism went beyond everyday peacetime requirements, since it was composed, at the core, of suffering. The smile, the freshly laundered curtains and plump babies only added up to feminine heroism if they were achieved as a triumph over tears. There could be no heroism without sacrifice and no sacrifice without suffering. Women's tears both honored and recompensed male bravery; they were its necessary counterpart. Dorgelès in *Les croix de bois* described a squad returning from the front, met by crowds of women, applauding and crying. "One woman wept, then others, then all of them . . . [in text] It was a homage of tears, past all the houses, and it was only in seeing them cry that we understood how much we had suffered . . . We advanced, ardor in our loins, opposing these tears with our pride as male conquerors."[58]

The favorite image of female suffering at home to balance male suffering on the battlefield was the war widow. Barrès hailed the spectacle of three or four hundred widows, "an immobile sea of black veils and white headbands," kneeling at a mass for the war dead. "What a magnificent tableau" he enthused, a delicious picture of "harmony, beauty, grief and austerity."[59] They could cry, "but they didn't cry out; they submitted to the sacrifice." They could cry but out of "the patriotism with which they cooperate in the national defense . . . they hide their tears and stifle their sobs, so as not to weaken the courage of their sons, their fathers, their husbands who struggle, suffer and die for France."[60]

The press printed supposedly true stories to teach the lesson that French women were to suffer in silence and that their silence was a sign of the strength of their patriotism. "The Dictation" in *Le Petit parisien* recounted the touching story of a schoolmistress who taught her young students the glory of patriotic sacrifice. Then one morning she received the notice of her beloved brother's death and a box containing his Croix de guerre. "She staggered, closed her eyes. Her clenched fingers squeezed the box. For an instant she thought she would die too. She stiffened herself to withstand the atrocious suffering and again started the dictation: 'My children, write: Love of country is one of the sentiments that most honors men's hearts.'"[61] Not only must she "stiffen herself," she must even manage to smile because her smile was proof of France's ultimate triumph. A correspondent in *Le Gaulois* told war widows: "Blessed be all of you for what you do, because it is thanks to you that victory returns wrapped in the folds of our flags, attracted by *your proud and sorrowful smile.*"[62]

While praising the exemplary patriotic behavior of French women, some commentators made pointed contrasts to pre-war behavior and also argued that not all French women had understood or accepted their wartime role. For these commentators, generally conservatives and Catholic moralists, the feminine demeanor of war service was not the preservation of pre-war femininity unchanged but a fundamental reform of it. Catholic propagandists like Abbés Coubé and Renoult recast their pre-war exhortations to women to be the saviors of France by returning her to the bosom of the Church into an even more heroic wartime mold. In a speech to the Patriotic League of Frenchwomen – preaching to the choir, this – Renoult invoked Joan of Arc and called French Catholic women "an invincible army" that could "remake France by the home" if they would only give up frivolity and materialism and dedicate themselves to child-bearing, housekeeping and prayer.[63]

In the favorite cliché, the war must turn egotistical dolls into self-sacrificing heroines. Almost all the stories of Michel Provins's collection *Ceux d'hier, Ceux d'aujourd'hui* (1916) develop this theme. In "Le Creusot," the war transformed a bored, neurasthenic *mondaine* into an energetic hospital administrator who forgot herself in the care of wounded soldiers. In "Le Mutilé," a cold, frivolous wife discovered sacrifice and devotion when her husband was wounded. "Loulou," an overprotective mother, became a Spartan Mother once she recognized her debt to *la patrie*.[64] The most insistent and widely-read advocate of this view was Académicien Maurice Donnay, who, in *La Parisienne et la guerre* (1916) and *Lettres à une dame blanche* (1917) described French women's wartime conversion to domestic duty in order to condemn their pre-war abandonment to luxury, materialism and immorality.

> It was war. So suddenly, from one day to the next, from the top to the bottom of the worldly or social ladder, the Parisienne will be transformed, or, rather, she is going to find herself, and, with courage and tenderness, she will do her duty, all her duty. The disorder, the independence, the egoism, the blindness, all that becomes order, discipline, altruism and lucidity.[65]

Donnay's moral did not go unchallenged. Louis Barthou and Léon Abensour, among others, argued that the war had not redeemed French femininity, since it had never needed reformation. Instead, the war showed the Frenchwoman as she always had been, despite the calumnies of salacious literature.[66] In his preface to Mme Paul Alexander Mellor's coffee-table book, *Pages inédits sur la femme et la guerre* (1916), Donnay trimmed his remarks in response to these critics. The image of the Frenchwoman as light-minded and loose-moraled, he argued, was a misapprehension based upon a view of the Parisienne purveyed in novels and plays. This was not the true Frenchwoman, whose worth had been revealed by her war service.[67] However, he did not argue that such Parisiennes had not existed, and he and other commentators continued to criticize French women, not only for their behavior prior to the war, but also for their wartime behavior. For the war might have chastened, but had not eradicated the "doll," and, during the war, when France's very survival was threatened, egotistical, frivolous femininity was more dangerous than ever.

Femininity could always be read in opposite ways. For Barrès, a conservative Catholic nationalist, a church full of silently praying war widows was an uplifting spectacle of feminine sacrifice and devotion; for an anticlerical republican nationalist, however, it could appear as a reproach, a defeatist demonstration, even an anti-war statement. A widow's mourning should be discreet lest it damage morale. But different readings did not depend entirely upon political outlook. For the republican politician Louis Barthou, a smiling countenance was the essence of feminine war service; but Michel Corday, another republican politician, attributed feminine gaiety to indifference, not to patriotism. Paul Geraldy's novel, *La Guerre, Madame* . . . made the same argument, but in the authoritative voice of the trench-fighter.[68] Published anonymously in 1916, the book claimed to be the journal of a soldier in Paris on leave (although Geraldy was a civilian). It recounted his revulsion upon encountering civilian life, always depicted as feminine. Women went to the theater, ate in restaurants and wore coquettish fashions in complete indifference to the war. "Two young women in deep mourning cross my path; they are talking very loudly, and from all that dull black emerge two faces of milk and enamel. I see beneath their veils the powdered cheeks, the thickened eye lashes, the too-vivid red of their lips."[69] Fabienne, the hero's former mistress, completed his disillusionment. She greeted him: "'You've put on weight' she said. 'And you have the Croix-de guerre. That's very good. Very smart, dearest!'"[70] For her, the war meant that it took more ingenuity to guarantee her own comforts. The only woman who appreciated the reality of the war was the mother of a friend, recently killed in action; and she had withdrawn into solitude (and darkness) because her suffering was so out of place in the feminine gaiety that ruled Paris. The narrator fled back to his unit at the front, revolted at the enormity of the betrayal he had witnessed. Of course he was soon killed, the Germans merely finishing off the victim of feminine treachery.

La Guerre, Madame . . . was the sensation of the spring of 1916, and set off a press campaign against Parisian frivolity and fashion.[71] The issue of fashion brought the question of the meaning of wartime femininity into the sharpest focus. In fashion, French civilization and French femininity came together. That Paris was the world center of high fashion was a sign of France's superior civilization. Mimi Pinson, the emblematic *midinette*, was both the embodiment of what was uniquely French about French civilization – its gaiety, insouciance, sophistication, style and wit – and the exemplar of French femininity. Like most other aspects of civilian life, the fashion industry ceased at the outbreak of the war. By the following spring, fashion (as well as theaters and restaurants) made a comeback. The question was, how to interpret this: as a sign of the strength of French civilization or as an affront to masculine sacrifice at the front? As fashion's main consumers, women, rather than the businessmen who ran fashion houses and published newspapers, were the center of this debate.

On the one side were the conservatives and moral reformers, often the same ones arguing that the war must reform French femininity, who demanded that women sacrifice fashion to the needs of the war and of the new France that would arise in the future. Barrès told French women of "all classes of society" that they were to cut consumption to create "new habits of simplicity and frugality." This was partly to conserve resources; but mostly it was to show solidarity of sacrifice with the soldiers. Corday condemned the spring fashions of 1916, "the short flared skirts, high heels, neat little hats with a peak, and low-cut blouses . . . [that] merely prove that frivolity and display have resumed their rights and made people forget the war." But it was not only social conservatives and misogynists who argued in this vein: the feminist Julie Siegfried insisted that among the sacrifices that the French woman must make for the war effort was "to simplify her ordinary life and her house-keeping, to alter her wardrobe without renewing it."[72]

This reaction, universal in the first months of the war and returning to prominence in the spring of 1916, did not remain unchallenged. In *La Grande revue* in November 1915, Aurel dismissed the criticism of feminine frivolity as frustrated puritanism using the war as an excuse to harangue against innocent fun. "Solidarity with our beloved soldiers does not require civilians to bury themselves."[73] Women's magazines and women's columns in the press, generally suspended in August 1914, began to reappear by the end of 1914 and in the spring of 1915. *Le Petit parisien* heralded the return of its fashion column, "The Feminine Week," as a sign of general confidence in the French army and "decidedly a happy presage of victory." It described fashion as the "mirror of the soul of the moment" and thus with a patriotic role to play, to represent France to France as "becoming once more frankly French with a little touch of the warrior, of the martial."[74] Moreover, fashion was a truly French industry that gave honest work to many women, war widows and orphans, so it behooved more fortunate French women to support it.[75]

Maurice Donnay was enough taken by these arguments that he was of two minds when the editor of a fashion magazine consulted him in February 1916 about resuming publication. On the one hand, Donnay thought fashion might improve morale; but nonetheless he advised the editor to wait. In *Lettres à une dame blanche*, he identified the core of the dilemma of attempting to read into femininity either patriotism or its reverse. Was the young woman in her flared skirt, high-heeled boots and tilted military-style cap saying "Me, I'm always there, indifferent to all the sorrow, all the ruins, so long as my hair curls"? Or was her message that of the indomitable vitality of French courage, style and civilization: "I am the Parisienne, grace, elegance, and this does not exclude either charity or bravery."[76] The same possibility of double meaning and misinterpretation clung to every formulation of femininity as women's essential wartime service.

Many French women experienced this paradox in their own lives. It made them restless and uncomfortable. Mme Drumont found that "the tranquillity and forced vulgarity of everyday occupations . . . [is an] impossible state that horribly irritates our nerves and when the evening comes, we are bruised, prostrate, submerged." For Nadine, it was more than irritation, it was guilt at continuing to live in comfort while men slept, ate and died in the mud.[77] Like Donnay, women often reacted with ambivalence to signs of the return of normal life, especially in its more frivolous aspects. Jane Michaux wondered how the reopening of cafés and theaters in January and February 1915 could be hailed as signs of high national morale when in August she had applauded their closing as a sign of national solidarity and seriousness of purpose. Which was the truth; or had six months of war so transformed reality? Mme Andrieu was slightly ashamed by her own delight in the spring fashions of 1915. Was this a sign of "strength of spirit," as her friends proclaimed, or was it deplorable feminine – national? – weakness?[78]

Motherhood was not enough; keeping the home fires burning and incarnating femininity were fraught with ambiguities. Maïten d'Arguibert's question continued to reverberate. "What to do? – What one did before. But everything is changed! – and everything is the same too, however! . . . What to do?"[79]

Women's Helping Hands: Charity and *Marraines de guerre*

Prepared mentally and emotionally, if not practically, by the prewar discussion of feminine patriotism, many comfortably-off women believed that their own mobilization was essential to the national defense. Since they envisioned a gender system based upon complementarity, it was inconceivable that men could fight the war successfully alone. In the first days of August 1914, the most striking demonstration of this belief was the rush to volunteer for the Red

71

Cross and to organize hospitals and ambulances. Of the many suggestions raised in the discussion of women's potential wartime service, only nursing had received official recognition and only the Red Cross had provided a concrete plan and the organizations to carry it out. The memoirs and journals of well-to-do women and girls express an almost universal desire to found hospitals or to nurse war wounded, and chronicle their efforts to serve the nation in this way. As we shall see in Chapter 5, for some women, nursing and hospital administration became their essential contribution to the war. However, for many others, the initial impulse ended in frustration due to lack of resources and connections but also due to lack of training, ability and finally, interest. Two examples were Mme Edouard Drumont, wife of the famous anti-Semite, and Lucie Delarue-Mardrus, a well-known poet and journalist. These two women both caught hospital fever in August 1914 and rushed to found hospitals and take nursing classes. Both soon gave up their hospital work, although only Delarue-Mardrus was self-aware enough to recognize why. "By curiosity, by contagious excitement, I came to serve at the hospital but I could only be a nurse without serious commitment and staying power."[80]

Commentators were quick to point to these failures to warn women that their urge to nurse wounded soldiers, although perhaps laudable, was usually inappropriate. Printing an article on 3 August 1914 that praised the Red Cross volunteers, *Le Petit parisien* changed its tune only three days later. "To Nurse the Wounded Soldiers: An Appeal to Women" requested inexperienced and unqualified women not to volunteer, suggesting they would do better to take care of children, work in the fields or roll bandages.[81] As feminine war service, nursing could never be the equivalent of male mobilization for combat because, the press claimed, the nation did not need all these nurses and because most women were not capable of the task. While virile masculinity was apparently the only requirement of soldiering, femininity was not a sufficient qualification for nursing. The feminine had to find a more universal application to war.

Women's first spontaneous efforts were to encourage the soldiers on their way to the front. The Marquise de Foucault's daughters, Mme Drumont, and many other women and girls gathered at the train stations and along the roadsides to cheer the passing troops and to hand out fruit, coffee, sandwiches, chocolate and cigarettes.[82] This led some women to organize canteens at the major train stations to provide more regular services for soldiers going to the front and later for the wounded on their way to hospitals in the rear. Some were run by the Red Cross, some by a new organization, the Green Cross, founded by Mme Bayard and Mme Monmory. Volunteering in a canteen appeared more appropriate to well-brought-up girls than nursing; it required no special training or scientific knowledge, it was less dangerous to morals since it did not involve touching male bodies, and girls often worked with their mothers. The Duchesse de Gramont provided a reassuring depiction of a train-station canteen in her memoirs: "[I]n all the train stations, canteens are springing up; girls spend the night in the station, the mothers knit and oversee the stove while their daughters supply the convoys of wounded or go from car to car on civilian trains, shaking their little metal bowls: 'For our wounded, please.'"[83]

The war quickly produced wounded soldiers but also prisoners of war, refugees, war widows and orphans as objects of patriotic, charitable concern. The sudden change from peace to war also created massive unemployment, especially among women in the textile and clothing trades. Later, the war created other "victims" in need of aid, disabled veterans, women, children and old people repatriated from the occupied territory, and the children of mothers employed in war industries. French women created a multitude of charitable organizations, both local and national, to meet these changing needs. *Paris charitable pendant la guerre*, published by the Central Office of Charities, listed hundreds for Paris alone,[84] while there were many similar organizations in every city and town in France, even in the areas occupied by the German army. The largest number served the soldiers. The Soldier's Package sent them writing paper, soap, flea powder, cigarettes, canned meat and chocolate; Soldier's Towel sent them towels, which, according to Abensour, "inculcated the habit of hygiene in almost all;"[85] Soldier's Warm Clothes sent long underwear, scarves, hats and mittens. The Green Cross provided food and drink at train stations; the Soldier's Home ran reading rooms and clubs for soldiers on leave. Many tried to help the wounded or the disabled. Some became large, well-publicized organizations. Mme Wallerstein's Clothing for the Prisoner of War by 1917 enrolled some three hundred women in making up packages to send to prisoner-of-war camps. *La Revue de Paris* and other papers publicized its work and wartime books that praised French women's war efforts like Léon Abensour's *Les vaillantes* (1917) and Jules Combarieu's *Les jeunes filles françaises et la guerre* (1916) devoted long laudatory descriptions to it.

In Germany and Great Britain, middle-class and elite women also rushed to volunteer their services in August 1914 as "fighters on the homefront," as German women proclaimed themselves. By the spring of 1915, despite some initial trepidation, the governments legitimated women's volunteer efforts. In Germany, the National Women's Service, formed as an umbrella organization to enroll women's charitable and patriotic organizations and coordinate their work, received government sanction and worked closely with the War Office as well as with local authorities. The British government, too, quickly recognized and supported some aspects of women's volunteerism.[86] By contrast, the French government moved more cautiously. Caught by surprise by women's volunteer mobilization, the first official reaction was to tell women to go home. Officials who had to deal with the flood of requests for authorization saw women's mobilization as distracting, if not positively destructive to the war effort. The Prefect of the Hautes-Pyrénées, for example, accused the ladies of the Red Cross of "zeal that is a bit theatrical . . . pushed to indiscretion" and recommended that a strict control be kept over their fund-raising so that it did not interfere with the government's needs.[87] Others, like M Dausset, an official in the Paris municipal government and Commandant G . . . of the army, both quoted in *Le Temps*, chastised women for wasting their efforts on ill-conceived endeavors.[88]

By the spring of 1915, officials in the French government and the military became more willing to concede that women's active support was sometimes necessary. However, they never moved to embrace women's volunteer efforts or to include prominent women in governmental commissions to the extent that occurred in Germany and in Great Britain. Besides an apparently stronger commitment to keeping the war an exclusively masculine enterprise that we will investigate in Chapter 7, there were several other stumbling blocks. One was doubt of women's administrative and financial abilities. Press stories accused "simple" women of being taken in by phoney claims or accused women themselves of engaging in fraud. The "fake Red Cross lady" was almost as common a home-front legend as the "fake nurse" was in war-zone lore.[89] More significant in the government's eyes was financial bungling in the administration of charities and also the proliferation of charities, each under its own "Lady Patroness," in rivalry with one another. To address these perceived flaws in women's volunteer organiz-ations, the government passed the law of 30 May 1916, which required charities to seek authorization from a regulatory commission and to submit their books to frequent audit.[90]

A second stumbling-block, unique to France, was religion. Although the *Union sacrée* had temporarily healed the breach – or at least called a truce in the struggle – between the Red and the Black, the Republic and the Catholic Church, the government and the military remained staunch defenders of rigid secularism. Given the history of women's mobilization for the Church, in the Patriotic League of Frenchwomen, for example, and the antecedents of women's wartime voluntarism in Catholic Social Action, the government suspected women were using war charities as a cover for Catholic proselytizing. The Right believed that the law of 30 May was an attack upon Catholic charities;[91] and indeed this was one of its intentions. Although the government usually kept its language carefully neutral, emphasizing only that charity organizers must be "suitable," when the Ministry of War authorized the Soldier's Home it explicitly banned all political and religious propaganda and ordered "a permanent surveillance" over the clubs to ensure compliance.[92]

Despite the government's distrust of their efforts, women and girls flocked to raise money for national "Days" that the government declared in support of various wartime charities (see Figure 3.1). Girls holding out bowls and shaking canisters, selling cockades, pins and miniature flags became a part of the everyday scene in urban France. According to *Le Petit parisien,* these young women were heroines, not only because of their patriotism but because they suffered. "Despite the frightful weather, icy mud and bitter wind, these sales-girls held out . . . Thus, on this morose day, didn't they also joyfully accomplish their duty as good French women?"[93] Maïten d'Arguibert reflected that for some girls, collecting money was indeed a trial of courage and endurance. "Begging . . . accosting passers-by, known, unknown, talkative, surly; . . . for the first time or the tenth, to repeat the same request, which you vary with two or three versions; to offer, to be refused, to offer again, to thank, it is like that from morning to night."[94] Over the course of the war, there were about twenty nation-wide collections, each raising several million francs for charities.[95]

In their memoirs, French women recalled their efforts to find satisfying war service. They often moved from one volunteer effort to another as needs, or their assessments of those needs, changed. For example, after troops stopped passing by, the Marquise de Foucault's daughters sought other ways to contribute. They

Figure 3.1 Poster proclaiming 14 July 1915 a collection day in Paris for war charities benefiting the combatants, the wounded, the convalescent, the crippled, refugees and prisoners by G. Picard. Courtesy of Dartmouth College Hood Museum of Art, Hanover, New Hampshire: gift of Edward Tuck, Class of 1882.

considered looking after village children so that their mothers could work; they also made pillows and foot-warmers for the soldiers at the front. Actress Lola Noyr, frustrated in her desire to become a nurse, turned to knitting mufflers and sending care packages. Maïten d'Arguibert's mother, appalled by the state of the refugees she saw passing through their town, joined a refugee aid group.[96]

A few women like Louise Weiss admitted that one criterion for volunteering was their own interest in the work. Weiss began her volunteer war work by setting up a hospice for refugees. Initially buoyed up by the generous response of her neighbors and the harrowing tales of the refugees, she shortly became disillusioned as the refugees complained and bickered. Then the local mayor asked her to set up a hospital for wounded soldiers. Warned by her first venture into humanitarianism, she was reluctant to take on this new assignment; but again, her sense of the importance of the work carried her for a while, even though she quickly became bored with the housekeeping involved and was repulsed by nursing. When her father insisted that she accompany him to Bordeaux, where the French government had taken refuge, she gave up her hospital work with relief. Returning later to Paris, she found her mother deeply committed to nursing; but Louise refused to join her. Instead, she volunteered to her aunt Sophie Wallerstein's charity, Clothing for the Prisoner of War, but this time kept her patriotic sensibilities firmly in check by her critical spirit. The result, in her memoirs, is a humorous, somewhat cynical depiction of this much-lauded charity.[97]

The war also impelled many civilian men into volunteer work. Some, like François Mauriac, who became an ambulance driver, devoted themselves entirely to their volunteer efforts. But more often, prominent men served as administrators or figure-heads for charities that were staffed and run by women. An example is the hospital that the Institut de France set up. The Institut provided the funds, Emile Picard of the Académie des Sciences was its financial officer, Frédéric Masson of the Académie des Sciences Morales et Politiques ran the daily operations; but the ADF supplied the staff.[98] In fact, Masson lent his authority to the mast heads of so many charities that he was called "our Joffre of charity."[99] Men might provide most of the money, the financial expertise and the *cachet* of their names, but women did the work, or so claimed the propagandists who promoted voluntarism as suitable feminine war service.[100]

Well-to-do French women claimed charity work as their own, uniquely feminine, contribution to the war. Their model, consciously for Catholic groups like the Noellists, was Catholic Women's Social Action, which before the war had identified the salvation of French society as women's mission. The crisis of the war abruptly broadened and secularized this task. If France's soul was at stake, so was French civilization. While French civilization and German *Kultur* slugged it out on the battlefield, elite French women claimed the survival of civilization on the home front as their special task. As Séverine announced to the staff of her magazine: "Men defend the soil; it is for us, women, to defend civilization!" before she assigned each of them to a charity.[101]

Charity was not only women's duty by virtue of a gender division of labor; women were deemed uniquely suited to its tasks. Their natural "maternal solicitude" made the care of the wounded, displaced and grieving their particular province. The desire to comfort, feed, clothe, even spoil the soldiers with canteens and care packages came from the same natural instinct. Even the charities' "obscure office work" was suited to the feminine capacity for attention to detail, devotion to duty and desire for anonymity.[102] Léon Abensour praised the charity work of well-known feminists and feminist organizations like the French Union for Women's Suffrage as proof that feminists were real women and that feminism and feminine devotion were compatible.[103]

In particular, certain services to the soldiers seemed to be only a modest extension of the care women provided to sons and husbands within the household. Women were also told, and believed, that it was their duty, rather than that of the Army supply department, to keep their men at the front as comfortable as possible.[104] Moralizing fiction and propaganda encouraged women and children to skimp on their own food to send treats to their men at the front, a form of support that became a real sacrifice by 1917 as the cost of living rose, shortages became endemic and rationing was introduced. Women's magazines encouraged the belief that women should provide for their men by instructing their readers what to send, giving recipes for "dainties" that soldiers were supposed to particularly relish and patterns for sewing and knitting soldiers' accoutrements.[105] Advertisers targeted this new market, touting toothpaste, tobacco, military accessories like belts and compasses, canned food and patent medicines as just what the soldier ordered. Screamed an advertisement in the *Petit parisien* in November 1914:

WOMEN OF FRANCE, KNIT! we can say today to mothers, wives, daughters, sisters, fiancées of our heroic soldiers. Send them very quickly everything they need to keep them from the terrible cold of nights in the trenches. But despite all the admirable efforts you make to relieve the suffering of our heros, how many of them, in the cold winter nights, will catch colds or bronchitis, grippe or pleurisy, or even, alas, consumption? Therefore, we cannot advise too often that the families who care for convalescent soldiers give them this excellent remedy for all bronchial and pulmonary afflictions, Goudron-Guyot.[106]

As this advertisement makes clear, another quintessentially feminine contribution was knitting for the first, and then the second, third and fourth winters of the war – socks, scarfs, helmets, mufflers, vests, sweaters, underwear. Women and girls who had never knitted before took up needles as an act of patriotic sacrifice (see Figure 3.2). Nadine, in her column of 20 March 1915, imagined an idle, luxury-loving girl saved from damnation when St Peter came upon her knitting needles and learned she had spent the winter knitting for soldiers. In Paris, according to numerous commentators, the *thé-tricot* [knitting-tea] had replaced the *thé-tango* [tango-tea] in fashionable circles.[107]

Even more essential than knitting was letter-writing, another task that propaganda hailed as particularly feminine. Descaves claimed that for men "the pen is heavier than the rifle," so it would be up to women to keep the lines of communication and affection open between front and *arrière*.[108] Besides, women would naturally be the best stokers of men's morale. Mothers would remind the soldiers of the homes for which they were fighting, while a sister, according to René Bazin, could chide her brother when he complained too much and inspire him to heroism with her admiration.[109]

In the spring of 1915, the creation and promotion of *marraines de guerre* [war god-mothers] transformed letter-writing from personal support of loved ones into an act of patriotism. The scheme originated in the press and was carried on in its pages. Barrès in *L'Echo de Paris* touted the Soldier's Family, a charity founded by Mlle de Lens; *L'Homme enchainé* publicized a similar effort organized by Clemenceau's daughter, Mme Jaquemaire. *Le Journal* then started its own organization for the "adoption" of prisoners of war, while other papers and magazines opened their classified columns to ads from soldiers seeking *marraines*.[110]

The *marraines de guerre* were a peculiarly French creation without close parallels in Britain or Germany. The scheme drew from

Figure 3.2 Drawing by L. Sabatier in the 1915 Christmas issue of *L'Illustration* depicting "The Son of the Maid." The caption reads: "A child of the class of 1915, moreover, and still so naive with his childish smile, telling about life at the front, about his first exploits as a soldier-boy perhaps! In his absence, Madame has knitted for him with fingers unused to such rough work a beautiful, warm sweater . . . And this son of the servant is welcomed into the home, itself missing someone in uniform, like a child of the family – this is the welcome that all our *filleuls* receive when they arrive at any home."

antecedents in Catholic women's charities that had "adopted" prison inmates and conscripts in order to convert them via correspondence.[111] However, it was the German occupation of northern France that inspired and justified this wartime pen-pal scheme. The name of Mme Jacquemaire's organization, the Charity of Combatants Without Family, revealed the thinking behind the plan. Women's main wartime mission was to support their men in combat, and to provide them with comforts and services, but especially to remind them of, and personify for them, the France that they were defending (see Figure 3.3). Commentators depicted such support as crucial

Figure 3.3 Postcard depicting one relationship between the "war godmother" and her soldier "godson." The *marraine* says: "My dear godson, I hope my little package will bring you pleasure" while the *filleul* replies: "Oh, my dear godmother, how you spoil me!" © Musée d'histoire contemporaine – BDIC, reproduction by Archipel.

to a soldier's morale, and particularly to his willingness to lay down his life. What, then, of the soldiers who had no women to sustain them in this way, soldiers without families, or soldiers whose families were sealed behind the battle lines in Occupied France? The themes of Catholic proselytizing and the German Occupation came together most explicitly in Barrès's promotion of *marraines de guerre*: letter-writing was to be the Christian mission of French women to France's sons temporarily orphaned by German barbarism.

As the scheme left the hands of its originators and entered popular culture, its Catholic coloration faded; but the imagery of war orphans remained strong. Although in fact many soldiers who had families acquired *marraines de guerre*, the discourse of the scheme's promoters and apologists always depicted the soldier "godsons" as cut off from the home front and bereft of all ties to *la patrie* except through the devoted attention of their "godmothers." Without their support, according to Henriette de Vismes, the main eulogist of *marraines* during the war, soldiers without families could easily lose their courage and their will, with "fatal results."[112] The *marraine's* letters were to ward off depression, *le cafard,* inspire her "godson" with patriotism and courage, applaud his victories, and especially, reconcile him to the patriotic sacrifice of his life. Vismes cited the letter of a nineteen-year-old soldier from the occupied north of France to explain this aspect of the *marraine's* role:

> How I love my country . . . I seek to make myself useful as best I can and I constantly ask to be sent to the most dangerous spots, but I find I am often discouraged because if I am brave, no one will congratulate me and if I die, no one will be informed and once my home is liberated, my mother won't even know where I fell or if I did well.[113]

In both fictional and supposedly real letters, soldiers claimed that having a *marraine de guerre* gave them the courage to die bravely and the consolation that they would be mourned. In one of Duplessis de Pouzilhac's tales, correspondence with a gentle, patriotic *marraine* turned a former Montmartre *apache* into a decorated war hero. Before entering his last battle he wrote to her: "Death will be sweet since I have found a little sister whose heart gave me a little affection."[114]

Susan Grayzel points out that some of the commentary and fiction imagined the relationship between *marraine* and *filleul* as an important transformatory experience for women as well. This was the case in Jeanne Landre's novel, *L'Ecole des marraines* (1917) in which a bored society woman was restored to a proper feminine role by becoming a *marraine* to a heroic but doomed lieutenant. When he died in battle, her own patriotic sacrifice was accomplished; she became part of the heroic France by having "given" her man, thus experiencing the suffering necessary for France's triumph.[115]

Marraines de guerre were not always female, as Visme reminded her readers. Civilian men, even convalescing soldiers, filled the role too; but in this one instance, contrary to all tradition, "the feminine outweighs the masculine."[116] By imagining letter-writing as feminine support for isolated soldiers, the *marraine* scheme helped reinforce wartime gender ideology. It drew upon the message of mobilization that had defined the battle front as masculine and physically separated from the feminine *arrière.* And it emphasized the important connection between them; the masculine combatant defended a feminine family, and that feminine family supported the war by supporting him. The *marraine* scheme was premised upon and helped elaborate the story of a feminine France for whom her sons fought and died. In Colette Yver's tale "La Marraine" (1915), a hospitalized soldier awaited a visit from his *marraine de guerre* who, though he had never seen her, had became "the image of France herself, the face of *la Patrie* . . . it was for her that he had fought and because of her support that he had been a hero."[117]

But if the feminine gendering of soldiers' pen-pals could create a version of women's war service that was both familial and national, it also opened the imagination to romance and eroticism. *Marraines de guerre* were, after all, only pseudo-mothers and sisters; in actuality they were women writing to unknown men. Fiction writers leapt upon this new plot device, and through it claimed the war as a terrain of romance. As Daniel Riche wrote in the introduction to his collection of short stories, *L'Amour pendant la guerre* (1917): "To support the sentimental preoccupations of men and women, God made *marraines de guerre*, war marriages, war flirtations."[118] The *marraine* scheme created the paradoxical possibility of an intimate relationship between complete strangers. According to a story in the magazine *Lectures pour tous*, "[t]o all its merits, [the *marraine de guerre* scheme] adds this attraction; a certain romantic air, something unexpected and a little mysterious."[119] Most of the fiction, plays and films about *marraines de guerre* played with the potential for mystery and deception – *marraines* who turned out to be long-lost mothers or estranged wives, or *midinettes* pretending to be *mondaines*, young women pretending to be elderly, elderly women pretending to be young, even men taking on female identities.[120]

The salacious humor magazine, *La Vie parisienne,* printed hundreds of requests from soldiers seeking *marraines de guerre.* Many of the 216 ads published in the 6 January 1917 issue indeed evoked the themes developed by the promoters of the *marraine* scheme. The soldiers were "very bored," "melancholy," "neurasthenic;" some were wounded. (One specified "one wound, two citations.") They were also "very alone," "isolated from all civilized life," "without family," and some "from the invaded territory." They were seeking affection, tenderness and gaiety, but also "moral comfort," "spiritual support," someone to be their "ray of sunshine." However, most combined such pathetic touches with requests similar to modern "personal" ads – "serious young man seeks gay, affectionate correspondent." As today, the ads described the men in terms calculated to appeal to feminine preferences for youth, good looks and high status. In this case, the status was provided by rank – most described themselves as officers – by branch of military service – aviation was a distinct plus – and by their decorations. Citations and Croix de guerre littered the page. Many of the ads hinted at romantic and sexual adventure with references to "sensitive" hearts and promises of "unforgettable pleasures" and the utmost discretion. The magazine promoted the erotic connection between *marraines* and their pen-pals in its cartoons, jokes and short stories. In one such, Loulette was amazed when her visiting *filleul* addressed her as "madame." How could he be so cold after the intimacy of their letters? "Oh, those letters . . . and those I received, that I opened slowly, so slowly to make the pleasure last!" Of course he quickly lost his formality (and his trousers) and the story ended in sighs, exclamation points and ellipses on Loulette's "delicious" divan.[121]

Promoters of the *marraine* scheme denied this narrative by insisting that the love that sustained the relationship was not romantic but familial or comradely. For example, in the 1917 play, "Marraines de Paris," a girl explained to her grandmother who objected to her writing to a strange man: "We don't love our 'god-sons' like future husbands, first of all because many of them are married; they are our sons, our little brothers. We write to them a little like they were childhood friends who are in trouble. No harm in that."[122] Vismes warded off the threat of sexuality with a series of portraits of typical *marraines de guerre* – a bereaved mother, a schoolgirl writing to a pretend big brother, a childless widow whose "poor little soldier" was the son she never had. There was not a lonely war widow or a romantic mademoiselle among them. Such narratives she consigned to "the cartoons, the theater and the cinema."[123]

The possibility of women corresponding with unknown men opened up two more potentially explosive themes, class and race. In many accounts, the *marraines de guerre* were educated, well-to-do Parisiennes, while their "godsons" were gawky country bumpkins making the "the first serious use of what they had studied in school so long ago."[124] The central scene was the arrival of the soldier on leave at his *marraine's* drawing-room, where he sat dumbstruck at the elegance of his surroundings and the graciousness of his hostess (see Figure 3.2). In this scene, the erotic potential was swamped by the class gulf. The *marraine's* mission was to introduce her simple hero to the civilization he was fighting to protect. Off they went on a whirlwind tour of Notre Dame, Napoleon's tomb and the Louvre, as she showed him "the beauty and grandeur of his country, of its History and of the Cause he defends."[125] But the abiding lesson was class conciliation. The lady recognized the simple courage and good heart of the typical *poilu*, while the soldier learned to appreciate *noblesse oblige*: "This sweet and devoted woman who spoke to them in the name of the friendship she had for them" taught the soldiers "wisdom, reason, moderation" and docility.[126] Post-war social harmony was assured.

Less central to the *marraine* plot, but still in evidence, was the issue of race. About 200,000 troops from France's colonies in West Africa served in France during the First World War, and some people worried about the disruptive potential of relations between them and French women. While soldiers worried about "their" women with black men, military authorities were more concerned that feminine contact would weaken what they idealized as the natural warrior spirit of African soldiers.[127] The popular press flirted with the image of the *midinette* and her *tirailleur africain* boy friend;[128] but the *marraine* story largely ducked the potential for interracial romance. In a play by Hary Mitchell, a black *poilu* arrived at his *marraine's* house complete with a bouquet of flowers for the sprightly young lady who had been writing to him, only to find out that his *marraine* was actually a middle-aged man. All is well that ends well; the masquerading *marraine* treated his *filleul* to a patriotic speech and a meeting with the Prime Minister, and became his *parraine* [godfather] instead.[129] Marcel Boulenger, in his acid satire on Parisian society women at war, used the possibility of a black *filleul* to explode elitist pretensions. His fashionable *marraine* copied Mme de Sévigné in order to give style to her little notes to her soldier, and relegated the job of finding appropriate treats to send him to her long-suffering servants. She imagined him as "one of the most distinguished young men;" he turned out to be black.[130] Boulenger presented race as a much more unbridgeable gulf than class, at least when gender was involved. Unlike the *parraine* in Mitchell's play, this *marraine* could have no civilizing mission toward the black soldier. His racial difference made him an illegitimate interloper in the great French family over which French womanhood presided.

The press and commentators like Abensour and Bontoux praised French women for their philanthropic war service. By knitting hats, writing letters, collecting money, sending treats and aiding war victims, French women were making an important contribution to the war effort. According to the many eulogists of women's patriotism, such charities softened the war's inevitable destruction while supporting its glory. And they demonstrated to the world that French civilization, whether defined as nurturing self-sacrifice or gay sophistication, not only survived but flourished under the test of battle. Yet almost every commentator also criticized French women's charitable efforts as well. Some attacked a particular kind of charity as being frivolous and unnecessary. "Lady hospital visitors" were a favorite target of satire, because it was claimed that in return for a few oranges and chocolate bars they wanted effusive gratitude and stories of heroism. If this charity gave too little and expected too much, Jeanne Landre criticized the *marraine* scheme for the opposite reason. It gave too much, and indiscriminately. Soldiers collected *marraines de guerre* in order to accumulate goodies, and wrote their own fake death announcements when they became bored. Landre also mocked what she considered the multiplication of trivial charities by creating fictional examples such as the BPSLF, the Bouton Pression Sur le Front, a charitable society formed to replace uniform buttons with metal snaps.[131] These were venial faults, however. Some critics claimed that ill-considered charity was actually harmful. Frédéric Masson fulminated against canteens that handed out food and drink to wounded soldiers without regard for their medical conditions.[132] Léon Abensour even argued that, given the unemployment of garment workers, well-to-do women should not knit for their soldier sons, but should buy knitted goods instead.[133]

The most common accusation was that, although perhaps laudable in their aims, women took up war charity in the wrong spirit. Critics like Donnay and Boulenger claimed that too often women volunteered out of boredom or to be fashionable rather than as an act of patriotic self-abnegation. Mme Daudet dismissed war charities as motivated by "desire for the top spot, for status that you defend inch by inch like a little fortress marked with a Red Cross."[134] Such women had no real devotion to the cause, and no staying power when rival attractions appeared. According to their critics, the most telling evidence of this feminine *légerté* was that some of the notable woman who had founded important charities in Paris in August abandoned them to go to Bordeaux in September. According to Jane Michaux: "[N]ot that they have given up on their devotion, nor on precedence, no! But due to one of those sudden shifts of the winds of fashion, from one day to the next there are no interesting wounded, workshops or charity canteens except in Bordeaux."[135] But of course this was no "sudden shift of the winds of fashion," it was a response to the government's panicky flight to Bordeaux in the face of the German invasion. And, as the wives and daughters of cabinet members and prominent politicians, many important patronesses went too.

On the one hand, the criticism represented a deflection upon these society women, always fair game, of anger and disappointment at the government for its cowardly behavior, criticism that neither the crisis of the moment, nor censorship, for that matter, permitted to be directed at its true object. Georges Lechartier pontificated: "Duty, for governments, is sometimes subtle. We cannot, we must not immediately judge them. But for ourselves in our own consciences, duty is always clear, precise, irrefutable."[136] But in fact, for the wives of government officials whom he was chastising, such duty was far from clear. Another reading of their behavior might have praised these women for dutifully accompanying their husbands to Bordeaux. The Weiss family exemplified the contradictory pulls upon feminine duty. Louise's father, Paul Weiss, was an official who moved to Bordeaux with the government. His wife, involved in hospital work in Paris, refused to go with him, so he ordered Louise to come to Bordeaux to be his housekeeper and hostess. Louise, who was also running a hospital at this point, closed her charity in order to obey. Which woman did her duty? The discourse of femininity as war service had no answer. What both praise and criticism refused to acknowledge was that the attempt to rework feminine domestic roles as war service was shot through with paradoxes. How could women truly devote themselves to the war when their first priorities always remained those of domesticity, of femininity? The spleen that women's war charities seemed to produce in their critics was an expression of vast unease with whole project of feminine war service. Instead of supporting the masculine war effort, the critics suspected women's activities as competing with it or even undermining it.

Commentators saved their most sarcastic judgements for the *marraine* scheme, whose sentimental purpose, whether maternal or romantic, struck critics as particularly damaging. They claimed that it led to confidence tricks and even outright fraud, that the high-flown hogwash typical of *marraines'* letters disgusted soldiers rather than inspiring them, and even weakened their fighting spirit. But the most prevalent charge was that rather than trying to support masculine resolve in the war, *marraines*, like Michaux' charity ladies, were furthering their own, feminine interests. Women became *marraines de guerre* to relieve boredom by initiating a flirtation or to seek a husband. For society ladies, writing to "godsons" and displaying their letters was just another kind of social snobbery; among young women, it led to a weakening of morals to which post-war commentators would point to explain French decline. By opening the war to romance, the *marraine* scheme undermined its true purpose.[137]

The most complete rejection of charity as women's war service came from the humorist Marcel Boulenger. His heroine, Charlotte, was a feather-headed society girl who pretended to be passionately involved in the war effort but in fact did all she could to maintain her *vie mondaine*. She dabbled at nursing, carried a bag of knitting around and collected "godsons." She "devoted" herself to charity by meeting several like-minded ladies every afternoon at a tea salon on the Champs Elysées. Every new version of women's war service was for Charlotte an opportunity to buy a new outfit. Her true devotions were fashion, flirtation and self-indulgence, and charitable war work gave her ample opportunity for all three, decked in patriotic bunting. For Boulenger, there was absolutely nothing women could do to support the war. Femininity and war were mutually exclusive, even hostile, terms, and to pretend otherwise was to countenance hypocrisy as comprehensive as Charlotte's.[138]

Charity of all sorts was undoubtedly well-to-do French women's major contribution to the war effort. If we include within this category writing letters and sending parcels to individual soldiers, then charity was the most common response of French women of all classes. Yet it was no less problematic than motherhood or the Eternal Feminine as a way of reconciling women and war. By their volunteer efforts, French women sought actively to support the war, and for this they received recognition and praise, but also criticism.

By stepping out of the immobility that mobilization had imposed upon them as the feminine role in war, by doing rather than simply being, women who organized and staffed charities disrupted the gender system upon which victory – and the fate of post-war France – seemed to rest.

Notes

1. For example, Jeanne Bouvier, *Mes mémoires ou 59 années d'activité industrielle, sociale et intellectuelle d'une ouvrière 1876–1935*, ed. Daniel Armogathe (Paris: Découverte/Maspero, 1983), p. 122.

2. Léonie Godfroy, *Souvenirs d'ambulance et de captivité (Noyon à Holzminden)* (Paris: Librairie de "L'Eclair," [1917]), 5: 149.

3. Colette, *Les heures longues* (Paris: Fayard, 1917), p. 326 (ellipses in text).

4. Emilie Carles, *A Life of Her Own: A Countrywoman in Twentieth-Century France*, trans. Avriel H. Goldberger (New Brunswick, NJ: Rutgers University Press, 1991), pp. 41–2; also, Pierre-Jakez Hélias, *The Horse of Pride: Life in a Breton Village*, trans. June Guicharnaud (New Haven, CT: Yale University Press, 1978), pp. 29–31 and Serge Grafteaux, *Mémé Santerre, A French Woman of the People*, trans. Louise A. Tilly and Kathryn L. Tilly, ed. Louise A. Tilly (New York: Schocken Books, 1985), p. 75.

5. Elisabeth de Gramont, *Mémoires: Clair de lune et taxi-auto* (Paris: Grasset, 1932), p. 36.

6. J. Delteil, *Les poilus* (Paris: Grasset, 1926), p. 28; Felix Klein, *Diary of a French Army Chaplain* (1915), excerpted in *World War I & European Society: A Source Book,* ed. Marilyn Shevin-Coetzee and Frans Coetzee (Lexington, MA: D. C. Heath and Company, 1995), p. 13.

7. Berthe M. Bontoux [Berthem-Bontoux pseud.], *Les françaises et la grande guerre* (Paris: Bloud et Gay, 1917), p. 9, and Jack de Bussy [Jacqueline Liscoät], *Refugiée et infirmière de guerre* (Paris: Eugène Figuière, 1915), pp. 5–7. For an analysis of public opinion at the outbreak of the war, see Jean-Jacques Becker, *The Great War and the French People*, trans. Arnold Pomerans (New York: St Martin's Press, 1986).

8. Baronne Jane Michaux, *En marge du drame: Journal d'une parisienne pendant la guerre, 1914–1915* (Paris: Perrin et cie., 1916), p. 16; Perreux, *La vie quotidienne des civils*, pp. 11–15.

9. Fernand Gregh, *L'age d'airain (Souvenirs 1905–1925)* (Paris: Editions Bernard Grasset, 1951), p. 165; Antoine Delécraz, *1914, Paris pendant le*

mobilisation: Notes d'un immobilisé (Geneva: Edition du journal *La Suisse, c.* 1915).

10. Louise Weiss, *Mémoires d'une européenne* Vol. 1: 1893–1919 (Paris: Payot, 1968), p. 177; also Delécraz, *1914, Paris*, p. 77; Donnay, *Lettres à une dame blanche*, pp. 165–72.

11. P. J. Flood, *France 1914–18: Public Opinion and the War Effort* (New York: St Martin's, 1990), pp. 24–33; Weiss, *Mémoires*, I: pp. 179–80; Yves Pourcher, *Les jours de guerre: La vie des français au jour le jour entre 1914 et 1918* (Paris: Plon, 1994), p. 71.

12. Michaux, *En marge du drame*, p. 41; Mme Andrieu in Camille Clermont, *Souvenirs de parisiennes en temps de guerre* (Paris: Berger-Levrault, 1918), p. 8.

13. Michel Corday, *The Paris Front: An Unpublished Diary: 1914–1918* (New York: E. P. Dutton & Co., 1934), p. 809; Archives Nationales (hereafter AN) F7 12937-8 shows many Prefects were astounded by this communiqué.

14. Weiss, *Mémoires*, I: p. 182.

15. Maïten d'Arguibert, *Journal d'une famille française pendant la guerre* (Paris: Perrin et cie., 1916), pp. ix–x.

16. Louise Delétang, *Journal d'une ouvrière parisienne pendant la guerre* (Paris: Eugène Figuière, 1935), p. 8; Marguerite Lesage, *Journal de guerre d'une française* (Paris: Editions de la diffusion du livre, 1938), p. 3.

17. Barthou, *L'effort de la femme française*; Masson, *Les femmes et la guerre de 1914;* Maurice Barrès, *Ce que peuvent et doivent faire les femmes* (Paris: Bloud et Gay, [1918]); Maurice Donnay, *La parisienne et la guerre* (Paris: Georges Crès et cie., 1916). For a feminist entry, see Siegfried, *La guerre et le rôle de la femme*. See Rageot, *La française dans la guerre* for a pronatalist view and Abbé Stéphen Coubé, *Le patriotisme de la femme française* (Paris: P. Lethielleux, 1916) for a typical Catholic contribution.

18. La Hire, *La femme française*, p. 45.

19. For example, Coubé, *Le patriotisme de la femme française*, p. 8 and Louise Zeys, "Aux femmes de France," *L'Echo de Paris*, 11 August 1914.

20. Zeys, "Les femmes et la guerre," p. 186.

21. Dr François Helme, "Menus propos d'un médecin," *Le Temps,* 28 April 1915.

22. Huss, "Pronatalism and the Popular Ideology of the Child," in Wall and Winter (eds), *The Upheaval of War*, pp. 329–67.

23. *La Revue philanthropique* 20 no. 38 (1917) includes numerous articles on this topics such as Dr V. Wallich, "Ce que feront les femmes après la guerre," pp. 474–89 and Dr Lop, "A propos de la dépopulation," pp. 569–79.

24. For feminists' wartime pronatalism, see Françoise Thébaud, "Le féminisme à l'épreuve de la guerre," in Thalmann (ed.), *La tentation nationaliste*, p. 26 and Christine Bard, *Les filles de marianne: Histoire des féminismes 1914–1940* (Paris: Librairie Arthème Fayard, 1995), pp, 64–6.

The Mobilization of Femininity

25. Chanoine Bernard Gaudeau, "Deux paroles de femmes françaises," *L'Echo de Paris* 7 August 1914; even more so, Maurice Barrès, "Le coeur des femmes de France," *L'Echo de Paris* 19 November 1914.
26. Barthou, *L'effort de la femme française*, pp. 4-5.
27. Courson, *La femme française pendant la guerre*, pp. 9-10.
28. Susan Zeiger, "She Didn't Raise Her Boy to Be a Slacker: Motherhood, Conscription and the Culture of the First World War," *Feminist Studies* 22 no. 1 (Spring 1996): 7-40; Cate Haste, *Keep the Home Fires Burning: Propaganda in the First World War* (London: Allen Lane, 1977), pp. 52-8.
29. French authorities identified socialists and anarchists as potential threats to mobilization, enrolling their names and addresses in the famous Carnet B for quick arrest in the event of war. They did not include feminists in this category despite their avowed pacifism. See Jean-Jacques Becker, *Le carnet B* (Paris: Editions Klincksieck, 1973).
30. Noëlle Roger, *Le feu sur la montagne: journal d'une mère: 1914-1915* (Paris: Attinger *frères*, 1915), p. 115.
31. Clémentine de la Grange, *Open House in Flanders 1914-1918*, trans. Mélanie Lind (London: John Murray, 1929), p. 7; Mme Edouard Drumont, *Le journal d'une mère pendant la guerre* (Paris: Attinger *frères*, [1916]), p. 11.
32. For example, Paul Deleutre [Paul d'Ivoi], *1914-1915: Femmes et gosses héroïques* (Paris: Ernest Flammarion, 1915) and Klotz, "La femmes française pendant la guerre," pp. 2564-6. A sentimental sub-plot in this narrative told of the anquish of mothers who gave their sons unknowingly. Both Lucien Descaves, *La maison anxieuse* (Paris: Georges Crès et cie., 1916), pp. 69-70 and *Le Petit parisien*, 15 October 1918, called to mind the plight of mothers who years before had abandoned their infant sons to Public Assistance and were "haunted" by the belief that they must now be at the front.
33. For example, Cunisset-Carnot, "La vie à la campagne: le patriotisme de nos paysans," *Le Temps*, 29 September 1915.
34. Elshtain, *Women and War*, pp. 70, 99-100 discusses the appearance of the Spartan mother in American Civil War discourse, for example.
35. Ernest Gaubert, *Voix de femmes* (Paris: Georges Crès et cie., 1916), p. 48.
36. Yvonne Pitrois, *Les femmes de 1914-1915: Vol. I: Les héroïnes* (Geneva: J.-H. Jeheber, [1915]), pp. 20-1; M. Eydoux-Démians, *Notes d'une infirmière 1914* (Paris: Librairie Plon, 1915), p. 111.
37. Ouditt, *Fighting Forces, Writing Women*, pp. 134-5.
38. Maurice Barrès, *Le coeur des femmes de France: Extraits de la Chronique de la grande guerre (1914-1920)* (Paris: Librairie Plon, 1928), pp. 86-8. Barthou, *L'effort de la femme française*, pp. 6-7.
39. AN F7 12937 Préfet de l'Aube to Interior Minister, 6 August 1914; "Admirable lettre d'une femme française," *Le Petit parisien*, 19 March 1915; "Une mère admirable," *Le Petit parisien*, 13 November 1914.

40. Delétang, *Journal d'une ouvrière*, p. 100.
41. Deleutre, *1914–1915: Femmes et gosses*, p. 6 (ellipses in text).
42. Barrès, *Coeur des femmes*, pp. 20–1; also Marie Laparcerie, *Comment trouver un mari après la guerre* (Paris: Albert Mericant, 1916), p. 72 and Bontoux, *Les françaises et la grande guerre*, pp. 199–203.
43. "Mariage d'un héros," *Le Petit parisien*, 12 July 1915 with a picture of the groom on crutches. "Le mariage d'un poilu aveugle," *Le Petit parisien*, 19 August 1916; "Un glorieux mutilé épouse son infirmière," *Le Petit parisien*, 28 April 1916; "Le devoir des femmes de France," *Le Petit parisien*, 9 March 1916.
44. Gaubert, *Voix de femmes*, p. 59; Raoul Narsy, *La France au-dessous de tout: Lettres de combattants rassemblées* (Paris: Bloud et Gay, 1915), p. 68.
45. Pauline Valmy, "La guerre et l'âme des femmes," *La Grande revue* 19 no. 10 (December 1915): 308; also Eydoux-Démians, *Notes d'une infirmière*, pp. 100–10.
46. Corday, *The Paris Front*, p. 185
47. Catherine Slater, *Defeatists and Their Enemies: Political Invective in France 1914–1918* (Oxford: Oxford University Press, 1981), p. 20; Abel Hermant, *La vie à Paris (1916)* (Paris: E. Flammarion, [1917]), pp. 154–6 and Descaves, *La maison anxieuse*, pp. 42–7.
48. Léon Abensour, *Les vaillantes: Héroïnes, martyres et remplaçantes* (Paris: Librairie Chapelot, 1917), pp. 21–2.
49. Marcelle Tinayre, *La veillée des armes: – Le départ: août 1914* (Paris: Calmann-Lévy, 1915), p. 143. Julie Siegfried gave a similar speech at the Musée social on 13 January 1915, published as a pamphlet, *La guerre et le rôle de la femme*. As Sara Ruddick argues in "'Woman of Peace': A Feminist Construction" in Lonrentzen and Turpin (eds), *The Women and War Reader*, pp. 215–16, the Mater Dolorosa is not necessarily an anti-war image; she can call for revenge.
50. Julie Rosalie Céleste Daudet, *Journal de famille et de guerre 1914–1919* (Paris: Bibliothèque-Charpentier, 1920), p. 48.
51. Donnay, *La parisienne et la guerre*, pp. 24–5.
52. Siegfried, *La guerre et le role de la femme*, p. 9; Margadant, *Madame le Professeur*, p. 240.
53. For example, La Hire, *La femme française*, pp. 17–18; 45–6; Nadine, *Rêves*, pp. 96–8, 112–14 ; Valmy, "La guerre et l'âme des femmes."
54. Esther Villeminot-Lapoulot, *Aux femmes de France: De la lutte au triomphe* (Sens: Imprimerie J. Chapron, 1916), p. 11.
55. Françoise Vitry, *Journal d'une veuve de guerre* (Paris: Maison française d'art et d'édition, 1919), p. 34. Maurice Level, "Monique ou la guerre à Paris," *La Vie parisienne* 55 no. 7 (17 February 1917): 151–4 made fun of such stories. His heroine enthusiastically greeted her *permissionaire* husband with the assurance "je n'ai touché à rien," except, of course, his

razors had disappeared under her cosmetics, his suits into a wall-cupboard
in the hall and she had replaced his desk with a divan.

56. Vitry, *Journal d'une veuve de guerre*, pp. 92–3.

57. Arguibert, *Journal d'une famille*, pp. xiii, xv. Other examples are
Mme Andrieu in Clermont, *Souvenirs des parisiennes*, and Daudet, *Journal
de famille*.

58. Roland Dorgelès, *Les Croix de bois* (Paris: Albin Michel, 1919), pp.
237–8.

59. Barrès, *Coeur des femmes*, pp. 23–4.

60. Masson, *Les femmes et la guerre*, p. 7; "Le vice-président de la Douma
salue les femmes françaises," *Le Petit parisien*, 3 July 1916. Valmy, "La guerre
et l'âme des femmes," p. 305; Pierre Mille, "Les femmes," *Le Temps*, 22
September 1915; and Henri Robert, "La femme et la guerre," *La Revue
mondiale*, (May 1917): 244–5 also equated women's silence and hidden
tears with heroism.

61. "La dictée," *Le Petit parisien*, 13 January 1916.

62. Narsy, *La France au-dessous*, p. 17 (emphasis in text); similarly
Barthou, *L'effort de la femme française*, p. 11 and Siegfried, *La guerre et
le role de la femme*, pp. 12–15.

63. Abbé Joseph Renoult, *Le coeur de la française* (Evreux: Imprimerie
Ch. Hérissey, 1916); Coubé, *Le patriotisme de la femme française*.

64. Michel Provins, *Ceux d'hier, ceux d'aujourd'hui* (Paris: La Renaissance du livre, 1916).

65. Donnay, *La parisienne et la guerre*, p. 26.

66. Barthou, *L'effort de la femme française*, p. 3; Abensour, *Les vaillantes*, pp. 18–21; *Le Petit parisien*, 23 August 1915 claimed Deleutre's
propaganda collection, *1914–1915: Femmes et gosses héroiques* refuted
slander about French women's decadence.

67. Maurice Donnay, preface to Mme Paul Alexandre Mellor, *Pages
inédites sur la femme et la guerre: Livre d'or* (Paris: Devambez, 1916),
pp. 15–19.

68. First published in *La Grande revue* in March 1916, then in book
form by Georges Crès et cie. First published with the author's name in 1922.

69. Geraldy, *La Guerre, madame,* pp. 36–7. The 'false' widow was a
favorite target of criticism. See Hermant, *La vie à Paris (1916)*, pp. 113–
14 and Marcelle Capy, *Une voix de femme dans la mêlée* (Paris: Librairie
Paul Ollendorff, 1917), pp. 106–7.

70. Geraldy, *La Guerre, madame*, p. 25.

71. Pourcher, *Les jours de guerre*, pp. 170–4.

72. Barrès, *Ce que peuvent faire*, pp. 1–2; Corday, *The Paris Front*, p.
150; Siegfried, *La guerre et le rôle de la femme*, p. 8; also Delécraz, *1914
Paris*, p. 87.

73. Aurel [Mme Alfred Mortier], "Moeurs de guerre," *La Grande revue*
19 no. 9 (November 1915): 29.

74. "La mode féminine en temps de guerre," *Le Petit parisien*, 30 November 1914; also *L'Illustration* 72 no. 3747 (26 December 1914): 501 for praise of the new military fashion touches.

75. *Le Petit parisien*, 5 April 1915 and 25 May 1915.

76. Donnay, *Lettres à une dame blanche*, pp. 124-5.

77. Drumont, *Journal d'une mère*, p. 20; Nadine, *Rêves*, p. 28.

78. Michaux, *En marge du drame*, pp. 152-3; 185-6; Andrieu in Clermont, *Souvenirs des parisiennes*, pp. 65-6.

79. Arguibert, *Journal d'une famille*, p. 2.

80. Lucie Delarue-Mardrus, *Mes mémoires* (Paris: Gallimard, 1938), p. 190; Drumont, *Journal d'une mère*.

81. "La Croix-rouge est prête," *Le Petit parisien*, 3 August 1914; "Pour soigner les blessés militaires: Appel aux femmes," *Le Petit parisien*, 6 August 1914 ; "Avis aux femmes qui veulent contribuer à la défense de la patrie en danger," *La France de Bordeaux et du Sud-Ouest*, 2 August 1914; Delécraz, *1914 Paris*, p. 66.

82. Marquise de Foucault, *A Château at the Front*, trans. George B. Ives (Boston: Houghton Mifflin Company, 1931), pp. 31-2; Drumont, *Journal d'une mère*, p. 27.

83. Gramont, *Mémoires*, pp. 84-5. *La Vie parisienne* 53 no. 2 (9 January, 1915) mocked the popularity of colored-cross charities by announcing "La Croix-rose," a new charity that would find "gallants" for wives whose husbands were at the front.

84. Office central des oeuvres de bienfaisance, Paris,*Paris charitable pendant la guerre* (Paris: Plon, 1915); also Mme Emile Borel, *La mobilisation féminine en France (1914-1919)* (Paris: Imprimerie <<Union>>, 1919) and Georges Lechartier, *La charité et la guerre* (Paris: Bloud et Gay, 1915).

85. Abensour, *Les vaillantes*, p. 109.

86. Ute Frevert, *Women in German History from Bourgeois Emancipation to Sexual Liberation*, trans. Stuart McKinnon-Evans (New York: Berg, 1989), pp. 160-1; Arthur Marwick, *Women at War 1914-1918* (London: Croom Helm, 1977), pp. 27-47.

87. AN F[7] 12938, report of the Prefect of Hautes-Pyrénées, 16 August 1914.

88. "Assistance et chômage" *Le Temps*, 22 August 1913; "Idées de derrière le front", *Le Temps*, 10 July 1915.

89. See "La fausse dame de la Croix-rouge," *Le Petit parisien*, 6 May 1917; Delétang,*Journal d'une ouvrière*, p. 72 and Charles Foley's novel, *La guerre vécue* (Paris: Librairie Jules Tallandier, 1915), pp. 89-106.

90. Thébaud, *La femme au temps de la guerre de 14*, p. 113.

91. James McMillan, "French Catholics: *Rumeurs Infâmes* and the Union sacrée 1914-1918," in Shevin-Coetzee and Coetzee (eds), *Authority, Identity and Social History of the Great War*, pp. 122-4; Louis Rivière, "Le contrôle des oeuvres de guerre," *Le Correspondant* 226 (10 March 1916): 856-86.

92. SHAT 7N 175 EMA-Oeuvres.

93. "La Journée Albert Ier," *Le Petit parisien*, 16 November 1914.

94. Arguibert, *Journal d'une famille*, p. 116.

95. Thébaud, *La femme au temps de la guerre de 14*, pp. 113-14.

96. Arguibert, *Journal d'une famille*, p. 114; Lola Noyr in Clermont, *Souvenirs des parisiennes*, pp. 191-201; Foucault, *A Château at the Front*, pp. 13-19.

97. Weiss, *Mémoires*, I: pp. 182-220. Weiss also wrote publicity for another charity, Le Secours aux dépôts d'Eclopés. This brought her to the attention of Senator Justin Perchot, who hired her as his secretary, thus ending her benevolent career.

98. Martha Hanna, *The Mobilization of Intellect: French Scholars and Writers During the Great War* (Cambridge, MA: Harvard University Press, 1996), p. 53.

99. Lechartier, *La charité et la guerre*, p. 51. Lechartier tells of a woman who when talking to Masson about a particular charity, was startled when he asked who had founded it and what its object was. Embarrassed, she revealed that he himself was the founder.

100. Zeys, "Les femmes et la guerre," p. 179. Masson protested in "Et les vieux?" *L'Echo de Paris*, 2 August 1914 that charity was *not* the exclusive domain of women.

101. Account of one of the staff members, Marthe Pattez in Clermont, *Souvenirs des parisiennes*, p. 179.

102. Bontoux, *Les françaises et la grande guerre*, pp. 114-30; Mme René Accollas in Clermont, *Souvenirs des parisiennes*, pp. 106-16.

103. Abensour, *Les vaillantes*, p. 97.

104. For example, Frédéric Masson, "Tricotons!" *L'Echo de Paris*, 9 August 1915 called upon women to disregard government assurances that supplies for the soldiers were sufficient. Only French women could give to the soldiers the little personal touches so necessary to morale.

105. See, for example, *La Vie féminine*, when it reappeared in 1916, and the column, "La Semaine féminine" in *Le Petit parisien* in 1915.

106. *Le Petit parisien*, 3 November, 1914 .

107. Nadine, *Rêves*, pp. 76-8; Michaux, *En marge du drame*, pp. 123-5.

108. Descaves, *Maison anxieuse*, p. 37.

109. René Bazin, "Elles écrivent," *L'Echo de Paris*, 8 February 1916. By contrast, if women filled their letters with trivial troubles and selfish complaints, they would damage soldiers' morale, warned "Courier féminin" in *La Vie féminine* 2 (4 March 1916).

110. Susan Grayzel, "Mothers, *Marraines* and Prostitutes: Morale and Morality in First World War France," *The International History Review* 19 no. 1 (February 1997): 70-2; Thébaud, *La femme au temps de la guerre de 14*, pp. 141-2; Henriette de Vismes, *Histoire authentique et touchante des marraines et des filleuls de guerre* (Paris: Perrin et cie., 1918), pp. 24-35 and appendices, pp. 261-96.

111. Alix, *Croix-rouge*, pp. 104-5; Thébaud, *La femme au temps de la guerre de 14*, p. 107.

112. Vismes, *Histoire authentique*, pp. 71-3, also "Marraines de guerre," *Lectures pour tous* 18 no. 8 (15 January 1916): 616.

113. Vismes, *Histoire authentique*, p. 21; also, Victor Jacquet, *Lettres à une marraine: Notes d'un fantassin* (Paris: La Maison française d'art et d'édition, 1920), p. 85. According to the military postal censor, SHAT 7N 955 EMA contrôle 15 August-15 September 1918, soldiers' letters to their *marraines* were more imbued with patriotic enthusiasm than their letters to their families.

114. Paul Duplessis de Pouzilhac, *Les mouettes aux croix-rouges: contes médicaux de guerre* (Paris: A. Maloine *et fils*, 1917), p. 142. Vismes quotes several similar letters in *Histoire authentique*, pp. 100-10.

115. Grayzel, "Mothers, *Marraines* and Prostitutes," pp. 72-5; Jeanne Landre, *L'école des marraines* (Paris: Albin Michel, 1917).

116. Vismes, *Histoire authentique*, p. 10.

117. Colette Yver, "La marraine," *Lectures pour tous* 18 no. 1 (1 October 1915): 55.

118. Daniel Riche, *L'amour pendant la guerre* (Paris: Editions J. Ferenczi, 1917), p. iv.

119. Jacques Freneuse, "La marraine," *Lectures pour tous*, 26 no. 1 (1 October 1916): 66.

120. Besides the stories already cited, see Henry d'Yvignac, *J'avais une marraine* (Paris: Editions des Gémeaux, 1918); Jean Louis Vaudoyer, *Les permissions de Clément Bellin* (Paris: Calmann-Lévy, 1918); Mary Florian [Marie Leclerq], *On demande une marraine ...* (Paris: Calmann-Lévy, 1919); André Warnod, "Le filleul de Lily," *Le Petit journal*, 16 December 1915; Didier de Roulx [André Janssen] *Petite marraine* (Paris: Jouve et cie, 1916); *Marraines de Paris: scènes de guerre par un zouave* (Paris: Jouve, 1917). Thébaud, *La femme au temps de la guerre de 14*, p. 145 cites two wartime films, "Marraines de guerre" by Léonce Perret and "Madame et son filleul," by Maurice Hennequin, Pierre Veber and Henry de Gorsse. The latter was a film version of a very popular play by the same title that ran in Paris from September 1916 until the end of the war.

121. Tank, "Simple erreur," *La Vie parisienne* 55 no. 1 (6 January 1917): 17.

122. *Marraines de Paris*, p. 11.

123. Vismes, *Histoire authentique*, p. 9.

124. Ibid., p. 86.

125. Ibid., p. 175.

126. Ibid., p. 256.

127. Marc Michel, "Soldats et travailleurs d'outre-mer dans la guerre française," in *Les sociétés européennes et la guerre de 1914-1918*, ed. Jean-Jacques Becker and Stéphane Audoin-Rouzeau (Paris: Publications de l'Université de Paris X-Nanterre, 1990), p. 405.

128. Jennifer Keene, "'Another than an American type of white man,' African-American and West African Soldiers in France during World War One," unpublished paper, 1997.

129. Hary Mitchell, *La marraine: comédie en un acte* (Paris: Librairie Théâtrale, artistique et littéraire, 1916).

130. Marcel Boulenger, *Charlotte en guerre ou le Front de Paris* (Paris: La Renaissance du livre, 1917), pp. 38–40.

131. Arguibert, *Journal d'une famille*, pp. 128–34; Louise Ibels, *Une journée à l'hôpital: 20 lithographies en couleur* (1916), p. xi; Landre, *L'école des marraines* , pp. 84–5, 123–6, 218, 317–19.

132. Masson, *Les femmes et la guerre*, pp. 26–30; also Francis Marre, "Conseils d'hygiène pratique à ceux qui sont restés," *Le Correspondant* 200 no. 4 (25 August 1914): 719–24.

133. Léon Abensour, "Les femmes et l'action nationale," *La Grande revue* 19 no. 10 (December 1915): 48–9.

134. Daudet, *Journal de famille*, p. 41; Donnay, *Lettres à une dame blanche*, pp. 7–8; Boulenger, *Charlotte*.

135. Michaux, *En marge du drame*, p. 47.

136. Lechartier, *La charité et la guerre*, p. 15.

137. Vismes, *Histoire authentique,* pp. 1–6 lays out the criticism she intended to refute; see also Louis Narquet," La française de demain d'après sa psychologie de guerre," *La Revue bleue* 56 no. 18 (21–28 September 1918): 600; Bontoux, *Les françaises et la grande guerre*, p. 187; and Perreux, *La vie quotidienne des civils*, pp. 34–6.

138. Boulenger, *Charlotte*. It is perhaps no surprise that after the war, Boulenger migrated from conservatism to fascism and became a propagandist for Mussolini in France.

4

War Heroines/War Victims

In the story of August 1914, told and retold in propaganda, memoirs and diaries, French men marched resolutely away to war while French women stayed behind to cheer and to cry. One of the few dissenting voices to this story belonged to Madeleine Pelletier, feminist and socialist, psychiatrist and political activist. In her unpublished diary, she contemplated a different picture of war's meaning for gender. As the soldiers marched out of Paris, they shouted cat-calls and sexual insults at the female spectators. Some women responded with obscenities of their own, but others acquiesced. "A young woman in front of me allowed herself to be kissed by at least a hundred men. She was a woman of easy virtue, that was clear, but even so, her kisses were not salacious. She thought she was performing a good action; giving men about to risk their lives some courage."[1] Kisses for courage, but also, perhaps, kisses for protection. Felix Klein, an army chaplain, commented that all the women's tears were not necessarily for the men who marched away but also for what might happen to themselves if these men were not victorious.[2] The kisses were prophylactics, sexual access traded for protection against sexual abuse. In their ribald march, the soldiers reminded Pelletier of what unbridled masculinity might do. The feminine left behind, suppressed and silenced, might also become women abused.

The mobilization scene depicted war as separating the genders – men to the front, women to the rear – but war, even in theory, did not solely involve men. As we have seen, it required women to wait, to weep and to be worthy. But it also positioned women as potentially the prey. If one objective of war was to kill men, another was to possess women. As Pelletier feared, the First World War was to be no exception. Soldiers themselves experienced conquest less as the capture of enemy soldiers or territory than as the conquest of women. Jean Giraudoux, one of the few Frenchmen to taste conquest in this war, wrote in his war diary for 20 August 1914 that it was only when he was being served breakfast by two very nervous German girls in a captured Alsatian village that "at last we have the impression of being conquerors."[3] And it was not soldiers alone who understood conquest in these terms. According to Michel Corday, "A cocotte, as she kissed her bully, who was joining his unit, remarked: 'Go and rape lots and lots of them!'"[4] Conquest, rape, this was what was supposed to happen to enemy women; but certainly some French women remembered 1870: they knew they were not immune to this fate if the French armies were not victorious. Nadine called upon her readers to remember and pray for those who were protecting them, "those who died to defend your white bedrooms ... and without hesitation, on your knees, with a sigh or a sob, thank those who permit you to remain virgins and Frenchwomen."[5]

By the middle of August, only two weeks after war began, it became clear that the French armies were not going to be victorious, at least not immediately. The German armies overwhelmed Belgian resistance, halted the French advance in Alsace and Lorraine and bore down upon France. As we have seen, most French civilians were unaware of this until the shocking communiqué of 29 August; but by then it was hardly news to the residents of northern France. Mme Dromart recalled in her memoir that within a week of the declaration of war, Belgian refugees began streaming through her village near the Franco-Belgian border, spreading panic with their tales of German atrocities.[6] Before it was halted in the Battle of the Marne, in early September and pushed back, the German army had penetrated over one hundred miles into France; cavalry patrols roamed within eight miles of Paris. The French drove the Germans back at the Marne, and the battle then extended westward in the "race to the sea." By early January 1915, the opposing lines stabilized into what would become the front until the spring of 1918. In the intervening three years, offensives and retreats on both sides had only local consequences, leading to the capture of a bit more territory or the liberation of territory captured in 1914. In March 1918, the war went on the move again with a massive German offensive that reached further into France than any attack since the fall of 1914, but halted without a decisive breakthrough by early June. In mid-July came the Allied counter-offensive, which, by October, liberated French towns like Cambrai and Lille, long in German hands. For four years, the German army enveloped ten departments,[7] comprising about 6 per cent of French territory and 12 per cent of French population. On the Allied side of the front, thousands more French lived within the war zone amidst the maneuvering of the French and British and later American armies, and under the constant threat of German attack.

Civilians on both sides of the line came under military authority, which accorded scant respect to their rights or needs. In his indictment of the German occupation, Georges Gromaire recognized the similarity between the German occupation of northern France and the French military occupation of the war zone, but nonetheless concluded that the German occupation was fundamentally different. The French army, in the war zone, imposed only indispensable constraints and "left commerce and industry the greatest possible liberty compatible with the conduct of the war." The German army, he argued, completely suppressed all civilian liberty.[8] This authority was undoubtedly harsher upon those under German control because, while French commanders assumed the willing cooperation of the French population, German commanders assumed that there would be both active and passive resistance. As a result, the Germans often used the threat of imprisonment and even death to insure obedience to their regulations. But in fact, on the French side, "the greatest possible liberty compatible with the war" did not add up to much liberty at all. Leaving punishments aside, we find that war zone regulations controlled and disrupted civilian life in very similar ways on both sides of the line. Both armies strictly rationed civilian food, censored mail, restricted travel even for short distances, imposed curfews, billeted soldiers in civilian homes, requisitioned civilians' property, goods and services, banished civilians judged to be in the way and ordered evacuations.[9] For commanding officers, whether French or German, the overwhelming priority was the needs of their armies.

The war created enormous suffering for all the inhabitants of the war zone. For women it posed particular problems, but also particular opportunities. As the potential booty of conquest, women figured as real and symbolic victims of the war and the German occupation of French territory; what happened to them, and what was imagined as happening to them, represented the suffering of the nation as a whole, invaded, pillaged and raped. On the other hand, the invasion and Occupation created a terrain for feminine heroism. By the dignity of her suffering, French womanhood could represent civilization's moral victory over barbarism. As Maurice

Barrès wrote: "This suffering is all necessary to national salvation; as for victory, it is simply the sum of all this suffering."[10] By suffering courageously, women held out the promise of the ultimate victory to be awarded to the braver and more righteous, if physically weaker, combatant.

With the opportunity for suffering and heroism came considerable risk. As symbols of France martyred but France triumphant, women in the war zone stood upon a national pedestal. Intimations that their behavior might be more self-interested than self-sacrificing, more materialistic than noble, could send them crashing down. Stories of the *petit poilus* in their trenches cannily operating by the "system D" to provide for their own comfort appealed by showing the human side of France's defenders. However similar behavior by women in the war zone made them suspect – that they betrayed their femininity, or worse, that their femininity betrayed the war. With the war on their doorsteps and in their homes, French women in the war zone still found the task of reconciling "woman" and "war" an impossible one.

French Women in the War Zone: Servants or Spies?

Before they could be victims or heroines, French women had to negotiate existence in the war zone. In contemporary conceptions the war should have occurred in an exclusively masculine space. Femininity as a set of values and practices, and women as its chief carriers, were not supposed to intrude; they were dangerous to war's successful enactment. And yet women were there, in the war zone, not through any misguided effort to contribute to the war by masculinizing themselves, like, for example, women who wanted to be militarized (see Chapter 7), nor through any equally misguided effort to feminize the war, like volunteer nurses (see Chapter 5), but because the war had engulfed them. These women could not be held at fault for being in the war zone; they had not left their proper sphere to seek out the war. As Princesse Marie de Croÿ replied to the German doctor who told her she should have stayed home and had nothing to do with the war, "But I was at home. I was taking care of my own. It is you people who came and tore me away."[11] Thus, in conceptual as well as practical terms, women's existence in the war zone was problematic.

In August 1914, like women throughout France, women in what quickly became the war zone suffered from anxiety for their husbands, sons and brothers in the army and from the lack of official news that caused rumors to run wild. But here, the rumors found substantiation in the sight and stories of refugees fleeing before the German invasion.[12] In the fall of 1914 and again in the spring of 1918, but in fact throughout the whole war, women had to decide whether to stay put or to join the exodus. Duty to family could mandate staying put. There was family property to protect; as the Marquise de Foucault wrote in the spring of 1918, "in the event of a German advance, it is impossible to leave Pronleroy [her château] in the hands of the servants."[13] A sense of loyalty to husbands and sons in the army also led women to reject evacuation. Clémentine de la Grange felt that to abandon her home would betray her soldier son. After he departed to join his regiment, she wrote in her diary: "To leave the place where he has bidden me goodbye will be impossible. I shall look for some duty to fulfil, if dangerous so much the better. I shall feel nearer to him."[14] Similarly, Marguerite Lesage accepted her husband's charge to keep the family sugar refinery in operation as a sacred trust that she could not abandon without somehow tarnishing his "patriotic self-sacrifice."[15]

But, on the other hand, duties to children seemed to require that they and their mothers be removed from harm's way. Isabelle Rimbaud's niece Nelly was torn between her father-in-law's insistence that she and her young child stay on the family farm to keep it safe for his son, and her own belief that motherhood required her to seek a safer refuge for her child.[16] Such dilemmas did not concern Clémentine de la Grange, whose children were grown; but they bedeviled Marguerite Lesage and other mothers. When Lesage finally decided to flee to protect her little girls, she nonetheless agonized over the decision. Had it been a betrayal of her husband? "However, did my four young girls and I need to stay imprisoned – for how long? – walled off from all news, good or bad, from our loved ones? I don't think that my husband would had asked that of me. I think that he would have ordered just the opposite for me, and himself as well."[17]

Neither civilian nor military authorities provided much help to women who faced this decision. They themselves had little reliable news, and often received and issued contradictory and impractical orders.[18] However, correspondence to and from the Prefects and Sub-Prefects of the invaded regions reveals that the government and the army had very mixed feelings about the civilian population caught in the war zone, and did not always put civilian interests

gov't responsible

first when they gave out or withheld information, counseled calm or ordered evacuation. Sometimes they discussed civilians as "hearths," the essence of France that the French army must protect. But often in the same communications, another concept took precedence; civilians in the war zone were "useless mouths" and impediments to military activity, clogging roads and trains.[19] In this view, women and children ceased to represent the France that French men were dying to defend and became expendable in order to protect the army. As a result, government and military officials often gave women false or incomplete information about the dangers they faced and mixed messages about whether they should go or stay. The government was not above using the presence of women to forestall a civilian evacuation that would hinder the military from retreating in an orderly fashion. The Prefect of the Meurthe-et-Moselle boasted that he had stopped a panic in Nancy, set off by a (true) rumor that the railroad station and post offices were being evacuated, by walking around town with his wife on his arm.[20] Often, by the time authorities advised evacuation, women and their families could not escape because, as was the case in Nancy, rail service had already stopped and roads were under bombardment.

The military and the government shared the fantasy of war splitting society into gendered zones. Women and children were to be sheltered in a separate space, the *arrière*: thus women who found themselves in the war zone were out of place. They lost their symbolic significance as embodiments of France and became hindrances, perhaps even dangerous. As the front stabilized after the Battle of the Marne, the military's policy toward women in the war zone became clearer, combining exploitation with suspicion. Women's sole purpose in the war zone was to serve the troops; but even the important services they rendered did not make their presence desirable.

Military authorities depended upon women in the army's rest areas to house and feed soldiers and, by their mere presence, to create an atmosphere of "normal life," of the France that disappeared in the trench world. The novelist André Foucault depicted a general who described rest areas in these terms:

> The rest area begins, you see, Madame, where there are four stones cemented around a window, where a fountain spills into its basin, where there are civilians. And the incontestable quality of a true civilian is to wear a skirt. A skirt that goes by in the street, that is rest; whether it's ugly, whether it's graceful, that is relaxation.[21]

103

The most famous woman in the French war zone was Madelon, the heroine of a pre-war song that became popular with soldiers and civilians alike during the war.[22] A barmaid with a heart of gold, Madelon gave each soldier the illusion that she was his sister or his sweetheart while remaining true to her own man. Propaganda insisted she existed in real life too; *Le Petit Parisien* published a sketch in 1915 of Marie, "the little maid of the front," whose life story seems directly cribbed from the song.[23]

During the first months of the war, soldiers recalled with appreciation the services that the women provided in the villages through which they passed. Once the trench war set in, however, soldiers began to depict the war-zone women who sold them drinks or eggs or the use of a kitchen in quite different terms. Their hearts were not gold with loving kindness but with greed. To Henri Barbusse, the women in the rest area assigned to the troops in his novel were crones who squeezed the soldiers for every *sou*. Their slogan, he claims, was *Pourvu que la guerre continue!* so that the money would keep rolling in.[24] The memoirs of Elisa Rossignol provide an interesting contrast. As a young girl in Alsace during the war, she watched her mother scheme to have soldiers billeted in their house because this was the only way to get food for herself and her two children.[25] In the war zone, the army was often the only source of income, since either the war itself or the army's regulations destroyed virtually all other economic activity. However, in the soldier's mind, his sacrifice and hardship was more than the equivalent of anything that the civilian population had endured and entitled him to whatever he could take.[26] Women who lived in areas that changed hands during the war found that French soldiers looted as easily as German soldiers did, and acted as if they were in conquered territory. In André Foucault's novel about life in the war zone, the heroine complained that while some of her soldier lodgers were polite and considerate, others "cross my threshold as if they were in conquered territory, ready to *me tutoyer*."[27]

For this novelist, lapses in linguistic respect were the worst form of abuse; he refuted those who imagined the billets as one big brothel. The soldiers, his heroine stated, were far too exhausted to take advantage of the war-zone women.[28] However, this was not always the case. Besides food and shelter, soldiers hoped and expected that women in the war zone would provide them with sex. As with eggs and wine, soldiers expected women to sell sex at reasonable prices and complained and became hostile and sometimes violent if the women they approached were not interested.[29] Because military authorities made it clear that they tolerated civilians in the war zone only to serve the army, it is not surprising that relatively few women officially complained of rape. Nonetheless the military police did investigate a few charges, mostly concerning the rape of young girls.[30] To address this problem, the army eventually authorized war-zone brothels.[31]

A soldiers' newspaper, *Face aux boches*, proposed a much more radical idea: that wives be allowed to visit their husbands in the rest areas.[32] This was directly contrary to army regulations, which prohibited visits by wives even to soldiers posted in the *arrière*. For nearly a year, until the army established a leave policy, the train stations of the war zone saw skirmishes in a sex war. The military police had instructions to check the travel permits and hold for questioning any suspicious persons, specified as journalists, photographers and women. "Ladies are prohibited from visiting their husbands, whether in the regular army or mobilized reserves who are part . . . of the troops stationed in the area. Therefore, interrogate all women who arrive by train as to the purpose of their trip and their husband's situation, or that of their lover. Ask to see their family passbook."[33]

Women with money, automobiles and well-placed connections could make an end run around the train-station gauntlet and could usually depend upon the civilian population of the war zone, their loved one's friends and even sometimes his commanding officers to help defeat the vigilance of the military police. Every account written by a woman living in the war zone, from the Marquise de Foucault to Elisa Rossignol, the *cheminot's* daughter, recounted clandestine visits from soldiers' wives that they abetted.[34] Meanwhile, the military police expended a considerable amount of time and personnel chasing around after "suspicious" women.[35]

What was the army's rationale in this effort? According to Michel Corday, it was to "keep the army in complete isolation, thus protecting it against sentimental weakness."[36] Elisabeth de Gramont, like many women, found the exclusion of wives ridiculous when prostitutes were admitted to the war zone with special passes, no less. She tackled military officials about what she considered an insulting regulation. "The whore, a general explained, is a necessary distraction, while the wife, who represents the home, weakens the soldier's heart."[37] To keep the soldiers in fighting trim, they had to be kept away from feminine influences. The feminine, the realm of affection and sentiment, was the danger, not the healthy masculine pursuit of sex. The war zone was to be kept exclusively masculine.

But there were more serious suspicions against women in the war zone than that they were stealing from soldiers' pockets or weakening their hearts. Obviously out of place, women were easily suspected of being spies. This suspicion rained down upon refugee women and local girls going on errands, upon Marguerite Lesage traveling for her business, upon women drivers employed by the French army and upon Clémentine de la Grange, even though she was accompanied by a British general![38] Nor was it necessary that women move around; Dorgelès suspected that the daughter of his landlady in Monpoix was a spy because she was pale, intent, and followed the soldiers' conversation without saying anything.[39] Rumors flew about women in the border region who signaled to the enemy by hanging out laundry in certain patterns.[40] Suspicion even dogged the footsteps of war-zone nurses. The British General Walter Kirk complained: "Now the whole country is full of secretive females with fancy Red Cross outfits, subject to no form of control. Many undesirables must be included among their activities and it is an obvious means of access for hostile agents."[41] The message of all this was that women in the war zone were out of place and therefore dangerous. By breaching the masculine world of war, they threatened to betray it.

Heroines of the Invasion: Emilienne, Marcelle, Julie and the Others

If women could be the villains of the war zone, they could also be its heroines. The image of male heroism was forged in the trench war, where the *petit poilu*, dirty but cheerful, displayed French resourcefulness in the face of superior German force.[42] In the *poilu*, French humanity shamed German dehumanization. The typical French heroine was also usually *petite* and *simple*, but she was dignified and her courage was moral rather than physical. She embodied French *civilisation* triumphing over German *Kultur*. The story of the 1914 invasion belonged to her.

There were a few popular heroines of the home front – Denise Cartier, the young Parisian victim of a German bomb, for example, or Madeleine Daniau, the baker's daughter.[43] However, most of the women celebrated in the press and propaganda as French heroines derived from the invaded territory in the fall of 1914. The many speeches, articles and books that lauded French heroines often cited particular stories to celebrate larger groups of anonymous women:[44] heroic PTT employees who reported German positions to the French headquarters even as the invasion raced down upon them;[45] nurses who remained beside the wounded when shells began to fall; teachers and postmistresses who provided leadership in their villages after male officialdom had fled. The most renowned of these heroines, who stood in the public mind as representing many others, were Marcelle Semmer of L'Eclusier, Emilienne Moreau of Loos, Sister Julie of Gerbéviller, and Mme Macherez of Soissons; all four won the Legion of Honor or the Croix de guerre for their actions.

Emilienne Moreau was a seventeen-year-old schoolteacher in Loos (Pas de Calais) (see Figure 4.1). According to her own account, as well as the numerous press reports, she courageously suffered

Figure 4.1 Invasion heroine Emilienne Moreau receiving the Croix de guerre from General de Sailly on 27 November 1915. De Sailly told her "I congratulate you and I admire you . . . You honor the women of France. For them you are a beautiful and comforting example." © Bibliothèque Nationale de France, Paris.

through the German occupation of her town: saw her father die of privations, her young sister wounded by a German shell, her brother killed in battle. When the British counterattacked, she nursed their wounded under shellfire, singing the Marseillaise the while. After German soldiers ambushed her nursing station, she picked up a gun and shot back.

Marcelle Semmer of L'Eclusier (Somme) was also young, only twenty, also an orphan, and lived near a lock on a canal in Picardy. After the French army was forced to retreat across the canal, Semmer opened the swing bridge and threw the key to the mechanism into the canal to prevent the Germans from crossing in pursuit. She then helped French soldiers escape across the lines. Arrested by the Germans, she declared: "I am an orphan. I have only one mother, France, and it does not bother me to die."[46]

Mme Macherez of Soissons was a different sort of woman; sixty-four years old, the influential widow of a senator, she was the president of the local chapter of the ADF. When Soissons was evacuated, Mme Macherez remained behind to run the nursing station she had set up. She presented herself to the German commander as the representative of the mayor and negotiated for the care of her patients and the safety of the town. According to the story, she successfully prevented the Germans from burning Soissons by declaring: "You must shoot me first."[47]

The story of Sister Julie is very similar to Mme Macherez's. A sixty-one-year-old nun of the Sisters of St Charles who headed a hospital in Gerbéviller (Meurthe-et-Moselle), she refused to leave her post when the town's evacuation was ordered and the bombardment began. After the Germans arrived, she stoutly defended the wounded under her care, refusing to cede them as prisoners of war. "An officer entered with his soldiers. He came up to my wounded. The poor little ones trembled. And me, well I put myself between them and him and I said: 'Don't you touch them, they are wounded.'"[48] Her negotiation with the German commander was also credited with saving the town from "fire and massacre;"[49] Poincaré himself awarded her the Legion of Honor.

Taken together, these accounts and others like them were intended to present a unified story of female heroism. No official effort at propaganda produced this narrative; it developed spontaneously and rapidly in the press from bits of information culled from military bulletins, soldiers' accounts and interviews in response to readers' interest. Those who had been unfortunate enough to have experienced German conquest first hand found themselves forced into the role of *raconteur*. The Marquise de Foucault commented on a visit to relatives in Angers in January 1915: "All are very curious to meet a person 'who has seen the Boches pass.' I am beginning to learn how to deal with the story of the invasion – the details that make an impression. My audience is interested . . . wants an encore."[50] They wanted to understand the invasion in a way that could not be obtained from the military communiqués, which, after 29 August, had lost some credibility anyway. These heroines' stories depicted the invasion's impact upon ordinary civilians; they gave an intimate view of its horrors. But they also offered an antidote; they turned the inexplicable French defeat into a moral victory.

The heroine was to be an example to women on the home front, to demonstrate the qualities expected of all French women during the war. As General de Sailly told Emilienne Moreau when he awarded her the Croix de guerre: "You honor the women of France. For them you are a beautiful and comforting example."[51] In a speech at the Sorbonne in 1917 honoring Marcelle Semmer, Deputy Klotz from the invaded department of the Somme defined what it was that their stories taught: "This admirable little daughter of Picardy so represents the qualities of the French woman, from her simple origins and her exemplary dignity, her grave character and her gentle manners to her magnificent will."[52] Even though in this case, the core of the story was quick thinking and decisive action, the heroine's example was one of moral character and demeanor rather than of intellect or action, moral character that would sustain the France of the *arrière* as it had sustained French women in the war zone. Nonetheless, to turn these accounts into moral fables suitable to French womanhood as a whole required some careful pruning.

First of all, the ideal heroine was small, young, pretty, and, if possible, orphaned like Marcelle Semmer, "all blonde, all fresh,"[53] or Emilienne Moreau, "thin, small, modest under her orphan's veil, such a fragile young girl."[54] In many other cases, such as Germaine Sellier, aged 23, who helped Mme Macherez nurse the wounded in Soissons, Louise Simon, aged 17, who took a horse and cart on to the battlefield to bring wounded to a nursing station, and especially Clotilde Boucry, aged 16, who decoyed a German patrol into a French ambush, storytellers made much of the youth, beauty and small size of their heroines.

Not all heroines were young and little, yet in these stories they often became so regardless of reality. *Le Petit Parisien* described Sister Julie as "this black and white flower" and a series of postcards celebrating her exploits depicted her as young and beautiful. A magazine cover from 1916 shows this delicate flower to be a stout and rather grim elderly woman.[55] But if the heroine could not be young and little, she could be simple and above all, feminine. Sister Julie, "robust and simple," was a "mother hen, running here and there to care for her chicks."[56] Mme Macherez presented the most problems to this stereotype: not only was she elderly, she was a powerful personality in the town of Soissons even before the war. Accounts of her exploits, like that published by Louis Barthou in 1917, could not avoid her competence and sang-froid, but they softened the image with feminizing vignettes, such as that she braved bombardment to find a blanket for an abandoned child,[57] or by assimilating her actions to the duties of the typical housewife. Léon Abensour wrote: "All this Mme Macherez did simply, without posturing, without speech-making. She protected her city and her fellow townspeople in the same way she would have protected herself or her property, like a shrewd and prudent housewife, like a woman with a head and a heart."[58]

Three words most often qualified the heroine's action: calm, devotion and self-sacrifice. Commentators erased any sign of bravado from their accounts. Emilienne Moreau reputedly conducted herself before the enemy with "calm dignity." "Under Prussian insolence, she kept the calm of a pride that will not bend."[59] Mme Macherez and Mlle Sellier walked amid the bombardment of Soissons "tranquilly, with an even step."[60] Sister Julie, at her post in Gerbéviller was "the example of courage and abnegation."[61]

The central moment in most of the stories was the confrontation of the frail French woman and the brutal German officer. In tale after tale, French civilization, embodied in French femininity, cowed and conquered German brutality by its nobility, courage and moral rectitude. *Tel qu'ils sont* (1915) by Hélène Leune is a compendium of such stories in which anonymous heroines faced down and showed up German *Kultur*.[62] Marcelle Semmer's lines: "I am an orphan. I have only one mother, France. And it does not bother me to die," were the most famous, but we hear them echoed in many other stories. Emilienne Moreau claimed that when a soldier treatened to shoot her if she didn't hand over her bicycle, "I cried, so shoot then! . . . A crime more or less, what does it matter to you!"[63]

Mme Macherez dared the officer who wanted to burn Soissons, "You must shoot me first." A first-person story printed in the *Petit Parisian* supposedly by Sister Gabrielle, a nun who headed a hospital in Clermont-en-Argonne, claimed for her repeated confrontations, with suitably heroic lines, of course. When German officers broke into her hospital, "I said to them simply: 'You are here in a house devoted to suffering. You may not go any further,'" and the Germans desisted, promising to protect the hospital. When the occupying commander threatened to burn the town, the nurse berated him: "Your officers gave me their word that the hospital would be spared. They have broken it. Never would a French officer behave like this," and again, triumphed. But her last encounter was the most dramatic. A German sentinel had been wounded by a sniper and the commander threatened to have all the inhabitants shot in retaliation. Once again, our heroine confronted him: "If you think that you must have a life to compensate for your soldier's wound, take mine; I am ready, but do not massacre a crowd of innocents!" And once again, her intervention saved the town.[64]

The heroine's bravery came from moral rectitude; her exploits were always to save others. This was quite different from the aggressive bravery of soldiers. Although sometimes praised as "like" a soldier, it was not a heroine's role to play the soldier's part. Military-type actions causing death and destruction crossed the gender divide; belying the feminine, they were inappropriate for heroines. So what did the French public make of Emilienne Moreau, undoubtedly the most celebrated of all invasion heroines? Although her story included caring for an invalid father and nursing wounded soldiers, at its center Moreau picked up a gun and shot it, killing German soldiers. This scene obviously fascinated and repelled French readers. The rest of her story varied little from account to account, but the dramatic climax was veiled in mystery and confusion. In some accounts she shot two Germans, in some three and in others, five. Abensour asserted she threw a hand grenade as well.[65] What was billed as her own memoirs, published serially in *Le Petit Parisien*, is even less definitive.[66] Up until the fatal episode, the story appeared with little censorship. However, from the moment Moreau picked up the pistol, the censor's scissors hacked it into meaningless fragments. What she did with the pistol disappeared in supposedly censored passages.[67] The account published in the family reading magazine, *Lectures pour tous*, omitted any mention of the gun at all by concluding with her nursing soldiers.[68]

In all the accounts, what legitimated Moreau's action, whatever that action was, was her overriding impulse to save an innocent French life. As in Sister Julie and Sister Gabrielle's stories, soldiers' wounds infantilized them, making them the proper care of women. In her memoirs, Moreau led up to the drama by emphasizing the childlike helplessness of her charge, "reduced to immobility, able to do nothing to save himself . . . What seemed to me so abominable was this ambush upon a poor boy, incapable of the least movement!" This was the moment she picked up the gun and the text plunged into the void. When coherence returned, it began: "My conscience told me, nevertheless, you have saved a wounded soldier!"[69]

The second lesson of Moreau's story was its denouement, when she returned to her feminine self. Abensour concluded his account of her bravery with this caution.

> However, don't let's see her as a fanatic, a virago drunk with carnage. To save her own life or that of a wounded soldier, to chase the enemy out of her town, she donned for several moments a personality that is strange to her nature and she was astonished to recognize herself when the danger passed. "I quickly recovered my young woman's weakness" she says after recounting one of her exploits." . . . I was seized by an immense disgust."[70]

These lessons were not lost on contemporaries. Marcelle Tinayre, a well-known novelist, compared Moreau with Flora Sanders, the British woman who fought with the Serbian army, eventually being awarded the rank of sergeant. According to Tinayre, the French public saluted Sanders "but in its admiration there is a little bit of . . . Our old Latin instinct protests when a woman is no longer content to admire a doublet and breeches but wants to wear those breeches!" By contrast, "little Emilienne Moreau of Lens (*sic*) is also a heroine who has valiantly won the Croix de guerre. Only, if she acted like a soldier, she did not turn herself into a soldier. The heroine has remained a young woman."[71]

Although the heroines were acclaimed for having done extraordinary things, their admirers depicted them as ordinary French women. Sister Julie was "like all of the nuns and most of the matrons of our small towns."[72] Emilienne Moreau was just an ordinary young schoolteacher; the PTT heroines were like the young women you might see in any post office. Thus, the heroine was potentially Every Woman; she was one's neighbor, she could be oneself. As Emilienne Moreau claimed: "I did nothing more than any French woman would have done in my place."[73]

The presence of Sister Julie – or Sister Gabrielle or Sister Rose or Sister Louise – in the firmament of French war heroines underlined the inclusiveness of patriotism. The heroine as nun was the perfect symbol of the *Union sacrée*, "French and Christian," as *Lectures pour tous* reminded its readers of Sister Julie.[74] The cover of *J'ai vu* of 20 May 1916 showed side-by-side photos of Emile Combes, the anti-cleric, and Sister Julie, over the title *L'Union sacrée*. While one could interpret the award of the Legion of Honor and the Croix de guerre to nuns as a return of the Republic to the embrace of the Church, the nuns' actions carried the opposite message. In redirecting their devotion and self-sacrifice away from God and toward France in the form of the wounded soldier and in courting martyrdom for the Nation – "If you think you need a human life . . . take mine" said Sister Gabrielle – these nuns' stories rallied the Church to the Republic.

The heroine of the invasion story was the replica of the Joan of Arc popularized before the war by both Catholic and Republican nationalists – young, innocent, physically weak but morally unconquerable in her innocence, faith and rectitude. Even when she died a martyr – rare in these stories – her heart, like Joan's, untouched by the enemy's crime, still beat out the patriotic drum roll. According to the propagandist Berthe Bontoux, retreating German soldiers discovered Marie Messin nursing two wounded French soldiers. As "a cowardly means to avenge themselves for their defeat," they shot her. She died in the arms of the advancing French army, murmuring "I am happy to have served France. I die content."[75]

In these stories, it was not women's service to France that made them heroines; it was that they *were* France, France invaded but France triumphant. The message of the heroine was that moral strength is superior to physical strength and right gains the victory over might. "Thus, in the towns of invaded France, the women, for their part, vanquished the German by immaterial weapons and, in the midst of bloody war, revived the spirit of justice and humanity."[76] Sometimes, as with Mme Messin, this was in apotheosis; but more commonly in these stories, the victory occurred on the battlefield, when the French army retook Soissons or Loos. The stories of these frail French women confronting and cowing hulking Prussians proclaimed in the dark years of trench war what must be the ultimate outcome of the confrontation of France and Germany.

Victims of the Occupation: Rape, Abduction and Seduction

The heroine of the invasion story came from territory reconquered by the Allies early in the war. However, ten departments and more than two million French civilians remained under German control until the fall of 1918. One reason for the lack of heroines from the occupied territory was, of course, that communications were cut between these areas and France. A few potential heroines were repatriated and enjoyed a brief moment of publicity when they published their stories upon returning home. The wife of the Belgian Minister of Justice, Mme Carton de Wiart, who was taken to Germany as a hostage, is an example.[77] However, stories of repatriated women lacked a satisfying denouement compared to stories of invasion heroines. Despite the dignity, calm and devotion of someone like Mme Carton de Wiart, Belgium and the north of France remained in German hands. Boorish German *Kultur* remained in possession regardless of the civilized behavior of the French women.

Instead of heroines, what the Occupation had was victims. In his speech celebrating the heroism of Marcelle Semmer, Deputy Klotz called to mind the women of the occupied territory: "What pity grasps our hearts when we call up the most sorrowful image of all, that of French women who, for more than two years, must submit to the yoke of the invader. O women of our invaded departments, I am wrong to speak of our pity. I should say our admiration for you, the victims."[78] The Occupation story was part of a larger narrative of victimization in which France herself was pillaged, wounded and raped. Commentators commonly referred to cities in the occupied territory as "martyred" or "wounded."[79] Atrocity stories abounded, especially in 1914 and 1915 and again in 1918, of German soldiers who raped French women and chopped off French children's hands.[80] But the term "atrocity" encompassed a much larger terrain in French writing about the occupied territory: "it is the fact of being occupied that is the atrocity."[81] And the thought of French women under German domination raised more complicated emotions than horror and outrage. As the historian Ruth Harris argues, in the public discourse about rape and its projected outcome, i.e. children conceived of German seed, what was at stake was less the suffering of French women than the potency of French men.[82] French masculinity was under attack, and upon French masculinity rode victory or defeat, the fate of the Nation.

For every story of a female French martyr, mutilated, killed, raped or "Forced into Slavery,"[83] there was also a story of accommodation and complicity between French women and German soldiers. The central issue was, of course, sexual contact, which the victim story defined as rape but which skeptics implied was what would be called during the Second World War "horizontal collaboration." If women in occupied France could be martyrs, they also might be traitors, and the longer the Occupation lasted, the more suspicions grew.

The most vivid image of France, innocent victim of German aggression, was that of the raped woman. Harris points out that it was only by brandishing this image that France, one of Europe's great powers, could be paired with inoffensive little Belgium. The atrocity stories published in government reports, pamphlets and newspapers and illustrated in posters and cartoons portrayed German soldiers as brutes and sadists preying upon French women and girls, "defiled innocents" whom they not only raped but also often mutilated. According to Harris, this story expressed "the traumatized sentiments of an invaded nation" – impotence, violation, dismemberment.[84]

The rape story, and the other popular atrocity story, that of severed hands, date from the period of the invasion in the first months of the war. They began to recede in public discourse by the summer of 1915 as France adjusted to trench war as a fact of daily life. Already early in 1915, the story of the rape of France via the rape of French women began to be transformed into a story of France's triumph over suffering through feminine power. The story became a debate over its projected consequence, the children, always imagined as sons, conceived of the rape.

The discussion of the children conceived in the rape of French women by German soldiers began with an article in *Le Matin* on 7 January 1915. It continued in the daily papers like *Le Temps* and *Le Petit Parisien* and also in Catholic, medical and feminist journals and even in Cabinet meetings throughout the spring of 1915.[85] While ladies excitedly discussed the subject in charity meetings, pundits as far removed from one another as Maurice Barrès and Jane Misme agonized in print over it.[86] The issue inspired novels like Charles-Henri Hirsch's *La Chair innocente* (1915) and plays like Maurice Soulié's *1914 à 1937* (1916).[87]

The question was, as Misme phrased it in the title of her article, "What is to be done with the Unwanted Little Ones?" Some advocated – even demanded – abortion as the only way to cleanse France of the German taint; others subscribed to the doctrine that French women's mother-love would conquer all.[88] In practice, French policy was similarly divided. The government refused to permit abortion; instead it established procedures by which women could bear such children anonymously and abandon them to Public Assistance. By searching Public Assistance files, the historian Judith Wishnia has been able to identify 123 cases that followed these procedures and several hundred more that may be hidden in the records.[89] Only one woman, Joséphine Barthélemy, was tried for killing a child conceived in rape by German soldiers, and she was acquitted.

In the realm of public discourse, however, "redemptive motherhood," in Anne Cova's phrase, won out over vengeance and racial purification.[90] Not only would French women rise above their pain to save these unfortunate children from abortion and infanticide, they would redeem them from the brutality of their fathers for humanity and civilization and, in the crowning victory of maternity over biology, make good French patriots of them. This was one more way for French women to vanquish German barbarism. When Dr Adolphe Pinard argued against abortion as a solution for the rape victims, he asserted that to bear and raise the infants thus conceived was "the only humane conduct, which has the greater merit of showing the world the depth of the gulf that separates our civilization from what they call their '*Kultur*'!"[91] This was the plot of both Hirsch's novel, *La Chair innocente* and of Soulié's play. While Hirsch made the case for redeeming motherhood, Soulié turned the son into his mother's avenger. Conceived in the rape of a French woman by a German soldier, the hero of the play grew up to seek out his father and kill him. Thus France would not only endure; through her sons she would ultimately triumph.

The stories of rape and the discussion of the "Unwanted Little Ones," like the heroine stories that flourished in this same period, expressed anxiety, fear and outrage, but then mastered these disturbing emotions by a transcendent moral that proclaimed France as the true victor after all. And the agent of this transformation was French womanhood, in Abensour's words, "by the sovereign magic of her grace united with her clear reason, the image of the spirit of France."[92] However, no such magic transformed the Occupation. For four long years, French civilians lived "in agony" "under the boot," "under the iron fist."[93] The victim as victor did not explain this situation. As the war and the Occupation dragged on, stories of heroines and victims faded from the popular press, replaced by tales of endurance in which the ordinary events of daily life and even survival itself became proofs of moral ascendency. While those on the home front were encouraged to believe that "holding on" – "Pourvu qu'ils tiennent" – guaranteed French victory, those in occupied France were depicted as living a Calvary for which the outcome could only be salvation.

For the population of the occupied territory, their contemporaries in France and also for many historians, the most significant trial in the long martyrdom of the Occupation was the deportation and forced labor of young women. The postal censor reported in 1918 that, as long-occupied cities were liberated, the story their inhabitants most frequently told was about "l'odieux enlèvement des jeunes filles"[94] [the odious abduction of young women]. In her survey of the First World War memorials, Annette Becker discovered that this was one of the few events of the Occupation commemorated in public monuments.[95]

This episode in Easter week 1916 occupies the central place in most of the writing about the Occupation as well. For example, during the war the French government published a series of reports on German atrocities. The first volumes presented rape as the most characteristic and heinous crime, but the last three volumes, published in 1916 and 1917, replaced rape with the *enlèvement*, qualifying it as "the most brutal and most revolting" of German atrocities. In 1916, the Ministry of Foreign Affairs even published a separate booklet in English about the affair as an appeal to American public opinion.[96] For Pierre Bosc and Georges Lyon, both writing about occupied Lille in 1919, it was "the unqualifiable crime," outstripping pillage, bombardment, arson and even rape.[97] And so it remained. Even in recent studies by the historians Annette Becker and Françoise Thébaud, the *enlèvement* retains its status as the most shocking episode of the Occupation.[98]

The story, shorn of its sensationalism, is a relatively simple one. By 1916, there was an acute food shortage in the occupied territories, less for the civilian population, by then largely fed by international relief organizations, than for the German army. A labor shortage in the countryside exacerbated the problem; meanwhile, severe unemployment reigned in the cities. The obvious solution to the shortage of farm labor occurred to the Germans as it occurred to the British government about a year later; just as the British authorities would recruit young women into the Women's Land Army to work in agriculture, the German authorities tried to recruit the unemployed of Roubaix and other cities into field labor. Very few people responded to the German appeals for workers, so the Germans resorted to conscription. Under the conventions signed in the Hague in 1907, conquered people could not be forced to work for the war effort against their own side, so the order informing the population of the call-up promised that the work would not be war-related. Beginning on Good Friday in April 1916, German military police moved from house to house in most of the districts of Lille, Roubaix and Tourcoing, selecting about 25,000 persons for forced labor. Smaller round-ups followed in August 1916 and in January 1918. After packing a small bag, conscripts were marched to the train station and shipped off to destinations in the countryside, where they worked under guard in the fields and on the roads. Some of the Easter-week conscripts returned home at the end of August; the rest returned by November.[99]

Most contemporary accounts of the *enlèvement* and the histories based upon them, including Annette Becker's recent book, *Oubliés de la Grande Guerre*, claimed that the vast majority of the deportees were teenage girls and women. In fact, this was not the case. After extensive work in the archives of the Nord, the historian Judith Wishnia has concluded that fewer than one-third were female.[100] Yet it was the minority of young women among them who gave the name and the meaning to this event.

Compared with stories of rape and severed hands, the *enlèvement des jeunes filles* seems benign. In fact, it is not clear that it was legally an atrocity at all; unlike that of the male forced laborers who dug trenches and transported war material,[101] these women's work did not manifestly contravene the contemporary rules of war. For the modern reader, knowing the horrors that awaited deportees in the Second World War as well as the fact that Britain conscripted its female population during that war, the story of the forced labor of some eight thousand women in occupied France hardly seems like a good candidate to stand as the exemplar of French victimization and German barbarism.

This is the story stripped of its sensationalism, however; it was in the accretion of details that the horror resided. The stories told by contemporary propaganda and repeated by historians moved through a number of interrelated scenes, each one focusing upon a different crime, specific to gender, age and class. By defining the victims as young ladies, these scenes raised a banal story of wartime oppression into a multivalent atrocity that represented the martyrdom of the entire Occupation.

The first moral of the *enlèvement* story was that the Germans had no respect for the most basic values of any society, let alone civilized society, i.e. family, especially motherhood. As Bishop Charost of Lille admonished General von Graevenitz, "This, to dismember the family, by tearing youths and girls from their homes, is not war; it is for us torture and the worst of tortures – unlimited moral torture."[102] The whole story was an example of German barbarism; but it was the opening scene that most specifically delivered this message, when indifferent or brutal soldiers dragged young girls from their mothers' arms.[103] Georges Lyon in his 1919 *Revue des deux mondes* article declared that soldiers "literally ripped young women from maternal arms," including one girl from her mother's deathbed: "At the deathbed, where the priest has come to administer extreme unction, are poised two young and tender hands, which, in a few minutes, should close the beloved eyes. But nothing stops the tyrant, who has already marked his victim: the pious consoler is pitilessly dragged away."[104] A protest issued by a number of major French women's organizations used identical words but switched the roles in the scene; in their account it was mothers "cruelly ripped from their husbands, from their children."[105] Pierre Bosc's account turned the scene again by focusing upon the suffering of the mothers left behind. Several, he claimed, "rolled on the floor in the grip of terrible nervous spasms," and at least one died as her daughter was dragged down the street. Lest the reader miss the point, he drove it home.

> In the name of the dignity of woman, in the name of respect for childhood, in the name of the rights of fathers and mothers, in the name of the inviolable character of the family, all these insolently trampled underfoot during the events of April 1916, the population of the occupied North of France demand from the civilized world exemplary punishment of the guilty for these sacrileges.[106]

The second moral was that the Germans had no respect for the values of higher civilization, such as the delicacy of femininity and the refinement of class. Although most of the women conscripted were domestic servants, textile and garment workers,[107] in all the stories they appeared as gently-reared young ladies. A succession of scenes showed the Germans imposing conditions that were degrading to their status. Georges Lyon whipped himself into a froth of indignation on this subject:

But the young girl, this select, delicate creature, preserved by the most vigilant solicitude from every strong wind! The young girl, brutally carried off from her home, forced to leave her mother or grandmother whom she had piously assisted in all the cares of the home, she is going to be first taken to some waiting pen, then to the train station, then in a cattle car that carries a multitude of these exiles at a snail's pace, to arrive, finally, at some stable or improvised shed into which the deportees are piled by the hundred – mixed with *filles tout court* (women of the street), forced to endure their vulgar insults, their trashy talk, their obscene gestures. The heart rebels at such ignominy.[108]

They were transported in cattle cars and housed in insalubrious hovels with dirt floors and no plumbing; they were then forced to do dirty, exhausting work like digging cabbages, hoeing fields and chopping wood. Of course, France transported conscripted soldiers in cattle cars, and most peasant women lived in similar houses and did similar work. But that was the essence of the Germans' crime in these scenes, their violation of gender and class status, as Lyon's fantasy of fragile young girls piously keeping house suggests. Both Gromaire and Celarié illustrated this in vignettes in which "little, delicate, refined, blonde young women" just out of boarding school were forced to dig potatoes, hoe beets or make charcoal.[109] Other accounts focused upon the breach of gender norms. Jeanne Régamey pointed out that the women were made to do "not only the soldiers' 'housekeeping' in the barracks and depots, but also the hard work of day laborers." Gromaire ironically referred to the Germans as "perfect feminists" in their failure to observe a proper gender division of labor.[110]

The most heinous of the German crimes encapsulated in the story of the *enlèvement des jeunes filles* was its assault upon purity, the mixing of young ladies with *filles tout court* as Lyon expressed it. Celarié claimed in the conclusion of one of her pamphlets: "Of everything that the Boches have done, the offense to young French womanhood is the most unpardonable."[111] In almost every account, the central scene was the medical examination, which apparently most of the conscripted women had to undergo. This included a humiliating vaginal examination, which the authors described in euphemism, for example as a medical examination "that is imposed upon certain persons of dubious morality."[112] Carried out without privacy by military doctors, the examinations were degrading; but the atrocity consisted in being examined at all: as Yvonne X lamented "'They' treat us like streetwalkers!"[113] Surrounding this scene clustered others, varied in their details, but all depicting assaults upon modesty – lodging the women in a house next to a brothel, guards propositioning them, "honest" women housed with prostitutes and forced or lured into prostitution themselves.[114] In all, rape hovered just beyond the text.

These scenes focused the erotic promise of the *enlèvement* story that permeated the entire narrative, beginning with its title. *Enlèvement* means "carrying off," but it also means "abduction" and "rape." Thus, by calling the conscription of women the *enlèvement des jeunes filles*, even the driest commentator, such as Boulin, opened the door to sexual fantasy. Most commentators, however, made no effort at objectivity, but played the story for all it was worth. On the first page of her propaganda pamphlet, *Emmenées en esclavage*, Henriette Celarié established the key element of the atrocity by calling the conscripted women "French virgins."

This outrage drew far more upon the fears raised in the invasion and rumors that surrounded the conscription than upon the testimony of the women who actually experienced it. The first posted notice that women were to be conscripted immediately provoked fears of sexual servitude. Despite the statement that the conscripts were to work in agriculture, the residents of Lille, Tourcoing and Roubaix assumed that the Germans were taking "their" women to be "femmes à Boches" – to clean house, cook and provide sexual services for the German soldiers. What other reason could there be for conscripting women than to use them as – women? The news of the conscription that reached unoccupied France and other countries also assumed this. In Italy, the *Popolo d'Italia* reported that the women were transported to provide for the sexual needs of German soldiers. In France, newspapers reported similarly, though in more veiled terms (see Figure 4.2). By contrast, the stories conscripted women themselves told to Bishop Charost after their return to Lille had a different slant. Although many remembered with outrage the medical examination, and some had other stories of sexual harassment to tell, for all of them the core of the story was physical privation, their treatment as prisoners, and the back-breaking work.[115]

Why did a story of privation, imprisonment and forced labor of both men and women turn into a story of the sexual exploitation of women? This returns us to the gendered terms in which war was imagined. As mobilization was polarized by gender – the men marching away, the women staying behind – so too was victory

Figure 4.2 Cartoon in the *Echo de Paris*, 1 August 1916 commenting upon the deportation of young women from Lille the previous April. Identified as "At Lille," the German officer says: "So you don't like Germany? Germany will love you!"

and defeat. In victory, the men were to march home and the women were to cheer. In defeat, the men were killed and the women were raped. Since France was traditionally represented as a woman, what happened in the Occupation could only be rape, but not rape transcended in the triumph of a maternal France, as happened in the invasion story of the "Unwanted Little Ones." This was rape that had to be endured, "jusqu'au but," the chalice drained to the last drop.[116] Celarié's informant Yvonne Y declared " despite all the suffering, all the sorrow, we remained steadfast . . . We knew that, finally, we would be victorious, we couldn't not be."[117] Imagined in this way, the *enlèvement des jeunes filles* became the perfect metaphor for the Calvary of the Occupation as a whole.

And yet, doubts crept into the story. Was what happened rape, or was it more nearly seduction or prostitution? Several of the vignettes of the *enlèvement* story, while implying rape, suggested other possible interpretations. For example, Boulin told of a German administrator who rode about the countryside propositioning conscripts who caught his eye with promises of pretty clothes and lighter work. Celarié also alluded to German guards who made "shameful propositions" – which, of course, the French women "indignantly repulsed."[118] But what if women in the occupied territory did not repulse German advances, but gave in to them, or even welcomed them? This possibility haunted the accounts that cast women as the symbol of Martyred France. If women actually acquiesced, then the whole story of France's Calvary was belied. If Occupied France were not a martyr but a harlot, where was the French moral superiority upon which victory depended?

The relations between the civilian population in the occupied territory, always imagined as female, and the German occupiers have inspired flights of historical imagination but little credible research. In all probability, there can be no general assessment of the relationship, which inevitably changed over time and place,[119] besides more incalculable variables such as the outlook of a particular commanding officer or the behavior of individual soldiers and civilians. Nonetheless, the historians who have studied the Occupation have tried to summarize the relationship between French and Germans, and almost always have done so by qualifying the extent and emotional content of sexual relationships.

British historian Richard Cobb in *French and Germans, Germans and French* (1983) imagined that a cozy domesticity developed between French women and their German occupiers based upon propinquity and their similar positions of powerlessness.[120] Georges Gromaire, Françoise Thébaud and Marc Blancpain regard this scene with considerable skepticism, arguing that sexual relationships resulted mostly from German domination and perhaps from mercenary motives, rather than from the affectionate companionship that Cobb imagined.[121] While in Cobb's story the couple of French woman and German soldier was a triumph of humanity, for the others it was victimization.

Deborah Buffton's assessment is the most reserved, perhaps because it is the only one based upon archival research. As a whole, her thesis counters the view that the population experienced the Occupation as one long atrocity. She argues that "many things in the Nord continued as before, some completely unaffected by the wars and occupations" and that the population adapted rapidly to the changes they did experience. The majority of the population, she claims, continued their lives as best they could, keeping to themselves as much as possible. Few welcomed the Germans, even though some came to accept and enjoy the company of the soldiers billeted upon them.[122]

The ambivalence of these assessments mirrors the suspicions, anxieties and fantasies of the time. Both during and after the war, trench-fighters' letters, newspapers and fiction were permeated with the fear of personal betrayal by "their" women behind their backs.[123] For example, in Roland Dorgelès's novel, *Les Croix de bois*, which in 1919 won the Prix Fémina, every mention of a wife or girlfriend immediately or eventually turns into a vignette of infidelity and betrayal. Since the trench-fighter was sacrificing his life for France, the France that "she" represented, her sexual infidelity became treason. In these stories, the villain was a shirker on the home front; but Henri Barbusse, in *Le Feu*, upped the ante by locating the scene of sexual betrayal behind the German lines in occupied France. In Barbusse's story, Poterloo disguised himself as a German soldier to sneak across the lines into Lens in order to visit his wife. As he recounted later to his buddies, before knocking on her door, he reconnoitered, peering through a window:

> There were heads of men and women with a rosy light on them, round the round table and the lamp. My eyes fell on *her*, on Clotilde. I saw her plainly. She was sitting between two chaps, non-coms., I believe, and they were talking to her. And what was she doing? Nothing; she was smiling . . . She was smiling. She was contented. She had a look of being well off, by the side of the Boche non-com . . . Not a forced smile, not a debtor's smile, *non*, a real smile that came from *her*, that she gave.[124]

The woman's smile that propagandists like Louis Barthou and Raoul Narsy hailed as France's secret weapon that cemented the front and the *arrière* and guaranteed French victory,[125] this she bestowed on the enemy! The trench-fighter replaced occupied France as the martyr in this version of wartime Calvary, and occupied France played Judas. The denouement was inevitable; as in Geraldy's novel, *La Guerre, Madame . . .,* the woman's treachery led directly to the soldier's death.[126]

Suspicions of French women's behavior in the occupied territory took less apocalyptic forms as well. Although banned from the press to avoid damaging morale, rumors and salacious stories made the rounds. That inveterate gossip, Michel Corday, remarked in his diary on 29 March 1917 that rumors were flying about the civilians evacuated with the Germans in their withdrawal: "It is fairly generally stated that some of the women taken away by the Germans in their retreat went of their own free will, since they had had relations with the Germans and did not dare to face their families again."[127]

In almost all wartime writing and imagery, French women in invaded and occupied France remained on their pedestal as simultaneously heroines and victims, who triumphed and endured as France must triumph and endure. Nonetheless, the *guerre d'usure*, as the French labeled the trench war, also wore down the promise of this image. The slogan of the famous cartoon – "Pourvu qu'ils tiennent!" – when applied to occupied France expressed the anxiety that even if France eventually won, the cause might already have been lost. France might already have given in, have betrayed herself. Focusing upon French women's bodies, violated, impregnated, abducted, seduced by Germany, wartime fears about the effects of the invasion and occupation foreshadowed what was to be the post-war assessment of the consequences of the First World War for France. Although France would win the war, she would lose herself in the process.

Notes

1. Cited in Felicia Gordon, *The Integral Feminist*, p. 146.

2. Klein, *Diary of a French Army Chaplain*, excerpted in Shevin-Coetzee and Coetzee (eds), *World War I & European Society*, p. 4.

3. Jean Giraudoux, *Campaigns and Intervals*, trans. Elizabeth S. Sergeant (Boston: Houghton Mifflin Co, 1918), pp. 27–8.

4. Corday, *The Paris Front*, p. 46. Such fantasies returned in 1918, when the French army was once more on the offensive. The postal censor reported as an example of good morale a soldier who wrote to his girlfriend that when he invaded Germany, he would rape "ces superbes gretchens" (cited in Stéphane Audoin-Rouzeau, *La guerre des enfants 1914–1918: essai d'histoire culturelle* (Paris: Armand Colin, 1993), p. 82).

5. Nadine, *Rêves de guerre*, pp. 18–19. For memories of 1870 see Lesage, *Journal de guerre*, p. 18; Isabelle Rimbaud, *Dans les remous de la bataille*

– *Charleroi et la Marne* – *Reims* (Paris: Librairie Chapelot, 1917), pp. 40-2; La Grange, *Open House in Flanders*, p. 34.

6. Marie-Louise Dromart, *Sur le chemin du calvaire* (Paris: La Maison Française, 1920), p. 3.

7. Aisne, Ardennes, Marne, Meurthe-et-Moselle, Meuse, Nord, Oise, Pas-de-Calais, Somme, Vosges.

8. Georges Gromaire, *L'occupation allemande en France (1914-1918)* (Paris: Payot, 1925), p. 65.

9. For historians' accounts of the Occupation, see Gromaire, *L'occupation*; Deborah Buffton, "The Ritual of Surrender: Northern France Under Two Occupations, 1914-1918, 1940-1944," Ph.D. dissertation, University of Wisconsin, 1987; and Annette Becker, *Oubliés de la grande guerre: Humanitaire et culture de guerre 1914-1918: populations occupées, déportés civils, prisonniers de guerre* (Paris: Editions Noêsis, 1998), pp. 27-53. Madeleine Havard de la Montagne, *La vie agonisante des pays occupés: Lille et la Belgique: Notes d'un témoin octobre 1914-juillet 1916* (Paris: Perrin et cie., 1918) is a good eyewitness account. Historians have not studied civilian life on the French side of the war zone. See Jacques Meyer, *La vie quotidienne des soldats pendant la grande guerre* (Paris: Hachette, 1966), pp. 335-48 for the soldiers' perspective. Marguerite Lesage's *Journal de guerre* is an excellent memoir of life in the war zone.

10. Maurice Barrès, preface to Havard de la Montagne, *La vie agonisante*, p. iii.

11. Marie de Croÿ, *Souvenirs de la princesse Marie de Croÿ* (Paris: Librairie Plon, 1933), p. 134.

12. See for example, Foucault, *A Château at the Front,* pp. 6-47; Rimbaud, *Dans les remous*, pp. 28-34; Mme Emmanuel Colombel, *Journal d'une infirmière d'Arras: août-septembre-octobre 1914* (Paris: Bloud et Gay, 1916), pp. 23-33.

13. Foucault, *A Château at the Front*, p. 222.

14. La Grange, *Open House*, p. 6.

15. Lesage, *Journal de guerre*, p. 9.

16. Rimbaud, *Dans les remous*, p. 64.

17. Lesage, *Journal de guerre*, pp. 3-6; also Colombel, *Journal d'infirmière d'Arras*, pp. 32-3.

18. Clermont, *Souvenirs de parisiennes*, pp. 8-16; Colombel, *Journal d'infirmière d'Arras*, pp. 23-33; Marguerite Daugan, *Mon séjour à Péronne pendant l'invasion (25 août 1914-25 avril 1915)* (Nancy: Berger-Levrault, 1926).

19. AN F[7] 12937-8 guerre de 1914, rapports des préfets; Pourcher, *Les jours de guerre*, pp. 76-7.

20. AN F[7] 12938 guerre de 1914, rapports des préfets.

21. André Foucault, *Cahiers d'une femme de la zone* (Paris: Ernest Flammarion, 1918), p. 94; also see Dorgelès, *Les Croix de bois*, p. 233; Meyer, *La vie quotidienne des soldats,* pp. 335-6.

22. Charles Rearick, "Madelon and the Men - in War and Memory," *French Historical Studies* 17 no. 4 (Fall 1992): 1001-34.

23. Henry de Forge, "La petite bonne du front," *Le Petit parisien,* 18 November 1915; also a similar sketch by the same author, "La vieille fille du front," *Le Petit parisien,* 30 December 1915.

24. Henri Barbusse, *Under Fire,* trans. W. Fitzwater Wray (London: Dent, 1926), pp. 73-81. Dorgelès, *Les Croix de bois,* pp. 106-14, described women in the war zone in similar, although less vicious, terms.

25. Elisa Rossignol, *Une enfance en Alsace, 1907-1918* (Paris: Editions Sand, 1990), pp. 181-2.

26. Meyer, *La vie quotidienne des soldats,* p. 336.

27. A. Foucault, *Cahiers d'une femme de la zone,* p. 13; also Foucault, *A Château at the Front,* pp. 50-3, 65; Lesage, *Journal de guerre,* pp. 210-12; and Pourcher, *Les jours de guerre,* pp. 250-2.

28. A. Foucault, *Cahiers d'une femme de la zone,* pp. 91-9.

29. Meyer, *La vie quotidienne des soldats,* pp. 336-49.

30. SHAT 16 N 2405 permissionnaires.

31. According to Dr Léon Bizard, *Les maisons de prostitution de Paris pendant la guerre* (Poitiers: Société Française d'Imprimerie, 1922), p. 3, in them women worked 18 hours a day, serving 50 to 60 men and earning from 400 to 500 francs a day.

32. Stéphane Audoin-Rouzeau, *Men at War 1914-1918: National Sentiment and Trench Journalism in France During the First World War,* trans. Helen McPhail (Providence, RI: Berg, 1992), pp. 129-31.

33. SHAT 16 N 2541 GQG divers. Odette Busand, "Cohabitation prohibé," *La Française,* 16 October 1915. *La Vie parisienne* published a series of salacious stories about the issue from December 1914 until the summer of 1915, when the leave policy was instituted.

34. Foucault, *A Château at the Front,* pp. 112, 189-91; La Grange, *Open House,* pp. 110-11, 116; Lesage, *Journal de guerre,* pp. 77-8; Rossignol, *Une enfance en Alsace,* pp. 200-3.

35. SHAT 16 N 2541 GQG divers.

36. Corday, *The Paris Front,* p. 60, also Perreux, *La vie quotidienne des civils,* pp. 28-9.

37. Gramont, *Mémoires,* p. 101.

38. Julie Wheelwright, *The Fatal Lover: Mata Hari and the Myth of Women in Espionage* (London: Collins & Brown, Ltd, 1992), pp. 103-4; Giraudoux, *Campaigns,* p. 31; Lesage, *Journal de guerre,* p. 49; La Grange, *Open House,* p. 113. On military drivers, see Chapter 7.

39. Dorgelès, *Les Croix de bois,* pp. 127-9.

40. Wheelwright, *The Fatal Lover,* p. 104.

41. Cited in Wheelwright, *The Fatal Lover,* p. 125.

42. Charles Rearick, *The French in Love and War: Popular Culture in the Era of the World Wars* (New Haven, CT: Yale University Press, 1997), pp. 6-10.

43. Both Cartier and Daniau were child heroines. See Audoin-Rouzeau, *La guerre des enfants,* pp. 135–6 and Thébaud, *La femme au temps de la guerre de 14,* p. 78.

44. Pitrois, *Les femmes de 1914–1915;* Abensour, *Les vaillantes;* "Le livre d'or de la bravoure féminine," *Lectures pour tous* 18 no. 8 (15 January 1916): 598–603; Léa Béraud-Camourtères, *Au service de la France: Les décorées de la grande guerre* (Gravure et Impression SADAG, s.l., s.d).

45. Alfred Capus, *Le personnel féminin des PTT pendant la guerre* (Paris: Imprimerie nationale, 1915); "Une téléphoniste décorée de la croix de guerre," *L'Illustration* 76 no. 3937 (17 August 1918): 158.

46. Klotz, "La femme française pendant la guerre," pp. 2564–6.

47. "Deux vaillantes femmes," *Le Petit parisien,* 6 June 1916.

48. "La cornette protectrice des blessés: Soeur Julie à Gerbéville," *Lectures pour tous* 18 no. 8 (15 January 1916): 579.

49. BMD dos 940.3 Héroïnes de la Guerre 1914–18, clipping 29 September 1914. There were other nuns who were praised for virtually the same actions, for example, Sister Louise of Nancy, Sister Gabrielle of Verdun, Sister Rose of Saint-Die, and Sister Gabrielle of Clermont-en-Argonne.

50. Foucault, *A Château at the Front,* p. 127.

51. "L'Héroïne de Loos reçoit la Croix de guerre," *Le Petit parisien,* 28 November 1915.

52. Klotz, "La femme française pendant la guerre," p. 2566; "Une jeune fille française," *L'Illustration* 75 no. 3856 (27 January 1917): 66.

53. BMD dos 940.3 Guerre 1914–1918 press clipping, "Les femmes <<Croix de guerre>>" journal title missing, 2 February 1916.

54. "L'héroïne de Loos," *Le Petit parisien,* 4 December 1915.

55. Thébaud, *La femme au temps de la guerre,* p. 77; *J'ai vu,* 20 May 1916.

56. "La cornette protectrice," p. 579.

57. Barthou, *L'effort de la femme française,* pp. 8–11.

58. Abensour, *Les vaillantes,* p. 174.

59. "L'Héroïne de Loos."

60. "Deux vaillantes femmes."

61. BMD dos 940.3 Héroïnes de la guerre 1914–18 press clipping 29 September 1914.

62. Hélène Leune, *Tel qu'ils sont: Notes d'une infirmière de la Croix-rouge* (Paris: Librairie Larousse, 1915).

63. Emilienne Moreau, "Mes mémoires," *Le Petit parisien,* 2 January 1916. (Ellipsis in text.)

64. R. M., "Dans l'Est: A Clermont-en-Argonne. Le dévouement d'une femme sauva la population," *Le Petit parisien,* 11 November 1914. Anonymous in this article, the nun's name was Marie Kosnet, in religion Sister Gabrielle, according to Abensour, *Les vaillantes,* pp. 161–6.

65. Abensour, *Les vaillantes,* pp. 215–6.

66. Moreau, "Mes mémoires," *Le Petit parisien*, 2–16 January 1916. As Françoise Thébaud comments: "On ne sait pas si la réalité est digne du feuilleton ou si le feuilleton impose ses lois à la réalité" (*La femme au temps de la guerre de 14*, p. 79).

67. Moreau, "Mes mémoires" *Le Petit parisien*, 8–9 January 1916.

68. "Le livre d'or," pp. 593–4.

69. Moreau, "Mes mémoires" *Le Petit parisien*, 9 January 1916.

70. Abensour, *Les vaillantes*, p. 216 (ellipsis in text).

71. Marcelle Tinayre, "Un été à Salonique," *Revue des deux mondes* (1 June 1917): 616–7 (ellipsis in text).

72. Maurice Barrès, "L'âme des reines," *L' Echo de Paris*, 4 November 1914.

73. "Lettre d'Emilienne Moreau," *Le Petit parisien*, 3 December 1915.

74. "La cornette protectrice;" Thébaud, *La femme au temps de la guerre de 14*, p. 77.

75. Bontoux, *La grande guerre*, p. 66.

76. Abensour, *Les vaillantes*, p. 175.

77. Georges Brouilly, "Prisonnière des allemands; notre interview de Mme Carton de Wiart," *Lecture pour tous* 18 no. 8 (15 January 1916): 568–77; "Mme Carton de Wiart raconte sa captivité," *L'Echo de Paris*, 11 September 1915.

78. Klotz, "La femme française pendant la guerre."

79. For example, Marie de Croÿ, *Le martyre des pays envahis* (Paris, 1933); Henriette Celarié, *Le martyre de Lille* (1919); Emile Basly, *Le martyre de Lens, Trois années de captivité* (1918); Léon Bocquet, *Villes meurtries de la France. Villes du Nord* (1918). This language continues, as in Dominique Gallez, "Lens, cité martyre 1914–1918," *Revue du Nord* 65 no. 259 (1983): 691–705.

80. Stéphane Audoin-Rouzeau, "Bourrage de crâne et information en France en 1914–1918," in Becket and Audoin-Rouzeau (eds), *Les sociétés européennes*, pp. 167–9; Ruth Harris, "The 'Child of the Barbarian': Rape, Race and Nationalism in France During the First World War," *Past & Present* no. 141 (November 1993): 170–206; Stéphane Audoin-Rouzeau, *L'enfant de l'ennemi 1914–1918* (Paris: Aubier, 1995), pp. 33–98; John Horne, "Les mains coupées: <<atrocités allemandes>> et opinion française en 1914," *Guerres mondiales et conflits contemporains* 43 no. 171 (July 1993): 29–45.

81. Annette Becker, "D'une guerre à l'autre: mémoire de l'occupation et de la résistance: 1914–1940," *Revue du Nord* 76 no. 306 (July–September 1994): 454.

82. Harris, "The 'Child of the Barbarian.'" There was nothing subconscious about this message: Dr Paul Rabier elaborated it great detail in *La loi du mâle: à propos de l'enfant du barbare* (Paris: Vigot frères, 1915).

83. Title of a propaganda pamphlet by Henriette Celarié, *Emmenées en esclavage* (Paris: Bloud et Gay, 1918).

84. Harris, "The 'Child of the Barbarian,'" pp. 172, 190.

85. Ibid.; Audoin-Rouzeau, *L'enfant de l'ennemi*; and Thébaud, *La femme au temps de la guerre de 14*, pp. 58–9.

86. Daudet, *Journal de famille*, p. 88; Maurice Barrès, "Une loi nécessaire," *L'Echo de Paris*, 10 February 1915; Jane Misme, "Que fera-t-on des petits indesirés?", *La Française*, 6 February 1915.

87. Audoin-Rouzeau, *L'enfant de l'ennemi*, pp. 78–9 lists seven novels and short stories on the subject published between 1915 and 1918 and even a film, Abel Gance's *J'accuse*, begun in 1917 although it did not open until 1919.

88. Audoin-Rouzeau, *L'enfant de l'ennemi*, pp. 106–64 traces this debate in detail.

89. Judith Wishnia, "Natalisme et nationalisme pendant la première guerre mondiale," *Vingtième siècle*, no. 45 (January–March, 1995): 37–8.

90. Cova, *Maternité et droits des femmes*, p. 199.

91. Cited in Audoin-Rouzeau, *L'enfant de l'ennemi*, p. 129.

92. Abensour, *Les vaillantes*, p. 140.

93. Havard de la Montagne, *La vie agonisante des pays occupés (1918)*; Ernest Colin, *Saint-Die sous la botte* (1919); Albert Droulers, *Sous le poing de fer: Quatre ans dans un faubourg de Lille* (1918).

94. SHAT 7 N 955 EMA contrôle. Etat de l'opinion en France d'après le contrôle de la correspondance, 15 October–15 November 1918.

95. Becker, "D'une guerre à l'autre," pp. 456–9.

96. *The Deportation of Women and Girls from Lille* (New York: George H. Doran Company, 1916); Audoin-Rouzeau, *L'enfant de l'ennemi*, pp. 83–4.

97. Georges Lyon, "Dans Lille occupé," *Revue des deux mondes* 49 (1 February 1919): 537–66; Pierre Bosc, *Les allemands à Lille* (Paris: Editions de Foi et Vie, 1919), p. 164; also Gromaire, *L'occupation allemande*, pp. 463–5; Pierre Boulin, *L'organisation du travail dans la région envahie de la France pendant l'occupation* (Paris: Presses universitaires de France, 1927), p. 80.

98. Thébaud, *La femme au temps de la guerre de 14*, p. 57; Becker, *Oubliés de la grande guerre*, pp. 68–77.

99. Boulin, *L'organisation du travail*, pp. 77–87, 92–5; Gromaire, *L'occupation allemande*, pp. 277–93; Buffton, "Ritual of Surrender," pp. 103–4; Thébaud, *La femme au temps de la guerre de 14*, pp. 55–8; Becker, *Oubliés de la grande guerre*, pp. 68–77.

100. Judith Wishnia, "Forced Labor of Women in World War I: The 'Raffles' of 1916," unpublished paper delivered at the Western Society for French History, November 1998. The one contemporary account that reported the actual percentage of male to female deportees, although in fragmentary fashion, was the Ministry of Foreign Affairs propaganda booklet, *The Deportation of Women and Girls from Lille*.

101. The deportation and forced labor of French and Belgian men and boys was much more extensive, much more long-term, and in many cases in direct violation of the Hague agreement: see Boulin, *L'organisation du travail.*

102. *The Deportation of Women and Girls*, p. 16.

103. BMD dos 940.3 Guerre 1914–18, press clippings, Jeanne Régamey, "Les femmes d'Alsace-Lorraine astreintes aux travaux forcés," 17 April 1918; Henriette Celarié, *Les jeunes filles déportées par les allemands* (Paris: Bloud et Gay, 1918) and *Emmenées en esclavage.*

104. Lyon, "Dans Lille occupé," pp. 556–7.

105. BMD dos 940.3 Guerre 1914–918. The protest came from the Conseil national des femmes françaises, the Union française pour le suffrage des femmes, the Société pour l'amélioration du sort de la femme, the Union fraternelle des femmes, the Société du suffrage des femmes, and the Croisade des femmes françaises. Cécile Brunschvicg read it at a public meeting at Trocadero organized by La Ligue des droits de l'homme in December 1916 and published it in *La Renaissance* in February 1917. See Thébaud, *La femme au temps de la guerre de 14*, pp. 57–8 and Bard, *Les filles de marianne*, pp. 50–1.

106. Bosc, *Les allemands à Lille*, pp. 170, 172–3.

107. Wishnia, "Forced Labor of Women," determined that nine-tenths of the deportees from Roubaix were working-class. Several letters in *The Deportation of Women and Girls from Lille* reported that most young people of good family initially rounded up were quickly released.

108. Lyon, "Dans Lille occupé," pp. 556–7.

109. Gromaire, *L'occupation allemande*, pp. 250–2, 267–9; Celarié, *Les jeunes filles déportées par les allemands.*

110. Régamey, "Les femmes d'Alsace-Lorraine;" Gromaire, *L'occupation allemande*, pp. 247, 440.

111. Celarié, *Emmenées en esclavage*, p. 16.

112. Boulin, *L'organisation du travail*, p. 81; Bosc, *Les allemands à Lille*, p. 172; Lyon, "Dans Lille occupé," p. 561.

113. Celarié, *Emmenées en esclavage*, p. 8.

114. Gromaire, *L'occupation allemande*, p. 271; Lyon, "Dans Lille occupé," p. 561. Celarié, *Les jeunes filles déportées par les allemands* includes a story of girls forced into prostitution by their guards who sold them to soldiers for bars of chocolate.

115. Boulin, *L'organisation du travail*, pp. 92–5. Celarié drew both of her pamphlets from testimony collected by Charost, shaping it to her own purposes.

116. Lyon, "Dans Lille occupé," p. 561.

117. Celarié, *Emmenées en esclavage*, p. 11.

118. Boulin, *L'organisation du travail*, p. 95; Celarié, *Emmenées en esclavage*, p. 10.

119. The relationship would have differed in the trigger-happy days of the invasion from the psuedo-normalcy of the period of trench war, and differed again during the savagery of the retreat in 1918. The same relations probably did not obtain in rural communities and in cities, in areas close to the front and in communities well to the rear.

120. This topic takes up a third of Cobb's 30-page essay upon the 1914–1918 Occupation in *French and Germans, Germans and French: A Personal Interpretation of France Under Two Occupations 1914–1918/ 1940–1944* (Hanover, NH: University Press of New England, 1983), pp. 11–19.

121. Gromaire, *L'occupation allemande*, p. 442; Thébaud, *La femme au temps de la guerre de 14*, p. 60; Marc Blancpain, *La vie quotidienne dans la France du Nord sous les occupations (1814–1944)* (Paris: Hachette, 1983), pp. 306-7.

122. Buffton, "Ritual of Surrender," pp. 61; 136-7.

123. Annick Cochet, "L'opinion et le moral des soldats en 1916 d'après les archives du contrôle postal," 2 vols. Thèse pour le doctorat, Paris X-Nanterre, 1986: II: 323-6, 347; Audoin-Rouzeau, *Men at War*, pp. 131-3; Roberts, *Civilization Without Sexes*, pp. 32-41; Rearick, *The French in Love and War*, pp. 13, 20.

124. Barbusse, *Under Fire*, pp. 156-7 (emphasis in text).

125. Barthou, *L'effort de la femme française*, pp. 11-12; Narsy, *La France au-dessous de tout*, pp. 16-17.

126. See Smith, "Masculinity, Memory," in Shevin-Coetzee and Coetzee (eds), *Authority, Identity and the Social History of the Great War*, pp. 251-73 for an interesting analysis of the themes of French masculinity lost and redeemed in Dorgelès's *Les Croix de bois* and Barbusse's *Le Feu*.

127. Corday, *The Paris Front*, p. 240. Thébaud, *La femme au temps de la guerre de 14*, p. 49, whose grandmother was one of the women deported, has a different view of this retreat.

5

White Angels of the Battlefield

In June 1914, Marie Rabut attended a fair in Dijon. Wandering among the various booths, she poked her head into the Red Cross tent set up as a model ambulance. Staring at the stretcher and sterilizer she thought: "Oh my God, would war be possible?" In that moment, five years of nationalism rose within her and "a more vibrant gust of patriotism" swept her to the registration table, where she signed up to take a first aid course.[1]

Six weeks later, the same gust reached gale force. Rabut spent the last days of July alternately at Dijon's Red Cross depot, helping to inventory donations, and searching the town for news. When mobilization was announced, her Red Cross group held a meeting to launch their first aid station. The doctor who had trained them gave a solemn speech: "The hour has come to put into practice the lessons your intelligence and docility have received; show yourselves worthy of your title as *ambulancières* of the Association of French Ladies!"[2] Less than a month after completing her certificate, Marie Rabut was going to war, and thousands of French women were going with her.

In Paris and in every provincial city and town, women, and men, too, rushed to join one of the three branches of the French Red Cross and petitioned local officials, the Service de Santé Militaire [Military Medical Service] and the Ministry of War to offer their services. Aristocrats like the Marquise de Foucault demanded authorization to turn their châteaux into hospitals, while members of the political elite like Mme Tailliandier, wife of a deputy in Arras, worked with local officials to transform schools, convents and even casinos into nursing facilities. Village mayors approached educated young women like Louise Weiss to organize hospices in country houses and train stations. In some instances, as in Arras, the cooperation between churches and local governments in these hasty preparations was a dramatic enactment of the *Union sacrée*. Prefects reported: "The evident results are worthy of praise."[3]

An unprecedented demonstration of national solidarity across gender and between Church and State, "this hospital passion," as Dr Lejars called it,[4] was less successful at bridging the gulf of class. While elite women founded hospitals and middle-class women volunteered to staff them, working-class women were excluded. Although many were swept up by the same patriotic fervor, they could not afford to work without pay. The *Petit Parisien* reported on 3 August 1914 that a group of dressmakers had joined the UFF, proudly declaring "We have come to do our duty." However, Maria Léra discovered that although these young working women knew that they would not earn wages, they assumed that at least the Red Cross would provide their meals. When they learned that this was not the case, they left in disappointment. The seamstress Louise Delétang also wished she could volunteer: "If only I were rich . . . if only I had the time!"[5]

Nevertheless, the largest number of French women's personal accounts of the war are nursing memoirs, while most of the memoirists who did not nurse, like Delétang, wished they could. Even Mme Daudet, who depicted her own devotion to family, in the form of the great Léon, as a superior version of feminine war service, did not escape nursing envy. Waiting for her son's arrival at a train station, she reported: "From time to time a nurse crosses the tracks, dressed all in white with a certain coquetry, Red Cross on her bonnet and on the obligatory arm band, the other cross, that of prayers, on a chain at her chest. Secular nuns, if I may call them so: I envy them and if I had not been absorbed this year by all my family cares, I would have joined them."[6]

Volunteer nursing was the only female war service the French government recognized before the war, and from the first days of August 1914, when Parisians cheered Red Cross volunteers in the street,[7] to the end of the war it remained the most popular representation of French women's patriotism. In the iconography of posters and postcards, the begrimed, bloody, unshaven *poilu* paired with the clean, solicitous nurse, white-robed with a red cross on her veil; this was the image of the masculine and the feminine in wartime guise. The French government rewarded nurses' valor with decorations; nurses were even sanctified by death in the line of duty. Thus, of all the French women involved in the First World War, nurses would seem to have been the most worthy, if not to stand level with the soldier in the national pantheon, at least to be included in the tableau in a supporting role.

But the inclusion of the nurse in the war story barely survived the war. While the stone and bronze of war memorials and the pages of fiction and popular memoirs commemorate the trench-fighter, nurses have disappeared.[8] During the war, innumerable propagandists praised France's "white angels of the battlefield," and personal accounts of war nursing found a wide and appreciative audience. After the war, however, the memoirs of France's volunteer nurses soon went out of print, and today are difficult to find. There is no nurse's story to complement Henri Barbusse's *Under Fire* or Marc Bloch's *Memoirs of War*. A couple of reactions to "hospital passion" offer clues to the failure of nurses' stories to implant themselves in popular memory.

José Roussel-Lépine wrote a comical chronicle in the *Revue des deux mondes* of a nursing station deep in provincial France. He skewered the self-importance of its organizers, who exhorted the volunteers to remain at their posts even under enemy fire – in a town four hundred kilometers from the frontier! He mocked the staffers' preoccupation with their uniforms, their devotion to elaborate techniques of bandaging, and their consternation when their first patient arrived, dirty, smelly but "not a trace of blood. He has all his limbs! The three nurses are disappointed!" Toward the end of the article, however, the joke slipped away. As the trains of wounded began to arrive, the comic characters turned into caring nurses. The reader might conclude that all those bandaging drills had paid off; but this was not Roussel-Lépine's point. Instead he drew the lesson that women's nursing was simply instinctive, a mother's care for her son. There was no need for preparation or even patriotism; in reality women did not act for the Patrie but for "Pitié," he claimed.[9]

While to Roussel-Lépine women's efforts to do something official for the war effort were laughable, to Dr Félix Lejars they were deplorable. He was the head doctor at the military hospital of Villemin in Paris and responsible for inspecting and authorizing local auxiliary hospitals. Undoubtedly he had to deal with many pushy people in the early days of August 1914, but despite a few perfunctory acknowledgments of the Red Cross's good intentions, his account is a thorough indictment of "hospital passion." According to Lejars, those who wanted to open hospitals were motivated solely by ambition. Every woman of the *beau-monde* wanted to head her own hospital, regardless of unsuitable premises and her lack of nursing credentials. When Lejars refused his approval, such women went over his head, using political connections to get authorization for their pet facilities. And when the government fled Paris, they went too, to swank around Bordeaux in their Red Cross uniforms and talk about "my hospital." Lejars's rancor is palpable. These were powerful women who did not recognize his authority; they knew how to get what they wanted, how to get things done; they were accustomed to being in charge. Good officer material, one might say; but to Lejars, they were the antithesis of women. Unlike Roussel-Lépine, he did not grant them the saving grace of maternal instinct. Instead, he portrayed them as having abandoned femininity in pursuit of social status and political power. By doing so, they betrayed womanhood, the war and France.[10]

Together, Roussel-Lépine and Lejars suggested what happened to the story of French women's wartime service as volunteer nurses. If women tried to insert themselves into the drama of the war, to create a patriotic role for themselves in the hospitals and ambulances, they were ridiculous or even dangerous. Not only did they undermine gender, their selfish pursuits were detrimental to the war effort. However, if women remained appropriately feminine, domestic, submissive and maternal, then there was no war story, in fact there was no story at all, just women being women, the Eternal Feminine.

Of course, Lejar's criticisms were extreme; but in most prop-aganda and personal accounts of wartime nursing, we find similar, although more muted assessments. The true nurse – *la vraie* – the angel of mercy and devoted surrogate mother to the *petit poilu*, whose feminine nature supported the war effort, was usually shadowed by the false nurse, suspected of putting her own, i.e. feminine, interests ahead of the national, i.e. masculine, ones. Instead of supporting the war, the false nurse tried to hijack it, to undermine the virile national regeneration that was its justification and its ultimate purpose.

When the true nurse won out, as she usually did in nurses' personal accounts, she relegated the false nurse to the category of the exception that proved the rule. But then she faced an even more potent rival for the Nation's attention, the object of her devotion, the wounded soldier. All agreed that volunteer nursing was maternal and personal rather than abstract, national service; that while the soldier served France, the nurse served the soldier. She was never a heroine in her own right. Her patriotism was worked on his body, her commitment to the national cause was expressed in her devotion to him. Nurses' memoirs became eulogies to the suffering and martyrdom of French masculinity.

The Service de Santé and the Red Cross

When French women volunteered to nurse, they responded to a desire to demonstrate their patriotism and to contribute to France's defense. But they also filled a real need. The French government had begun to train military nurses in 1909, but in 1914 there were less than one hundred of them.[11] For its nursing staff, the Service de Santé depended upon conscripts, nuns and Red Cross volunteers, who, in 1908, were admitted to military hospitals, including Val-de-Grace and Villemin in Paris. In 1913, the Ministry of War and the high council of the Red Cross exchanged representatives to ensure that the volunteer organization understood and prepared for its role in the army's plans. As a result, mobilization orders went out to nearly 23,000 Red Cross nurses in August 1914.[12] Besides this, the Service de Santé counted upon local Red Cross organizations to set up, fund and staff auxiliary hospitals as needed. But the first weeks and months of the First World War proved murderous beyond anyone's plans. Although trench warfare would acquire an evil reputation, in fact the war of movement in the first months, the retreat and the Battle of the Marne, produced the highest French casualty rates. Medical officers like Alfred Mignon in Verdun later admitted that the Service de Santé's plans were seriously flawed. For example, they envisioned only the briefest of medical attention at the front; all wounded were to be evacuated immediately by train to hospitals well to the rear. However, there were no provisions for getting wounded from the battlefields to the train stations or, at the other end of the trip, from the train stations to the hospitals.[13] Nor had the Service de Santé correctly predicted the kinds of wounds it would face. In 1907 the army doctor César Legrand wrote that modern warfare mostly produced "humanitarian" gunshot wounds that were small, clean and rarely fatal.[14]

Mme Colombel's account of an auxiliary hospital in Arras run by her mother, Mme Tailliandier, is one example among many of the way the war quickly overwhelmed the Service de Santé's plans. As the wife of a deputy, and head of the local chapter of the Patriotic League of Frenchwomen as well as of the elite Red Cross branch, the SSBM, Mme Tailliandier was a civic leader with considerable organizational experience and political and social clout. When war was declared, the Prefect of the Pas-de-Calais asked her to join the efforts of the SSBM with those of its rival organization, the UFF, to organize an auxiliary hospital in Arras. Her religious connections secured the use of an old convent and her social status gathered around her "numerous local ladies" to raise money and collect linens. Within a week, Tailliandier had set up a 180-bed "dream hospital." Then the volunteers waited in increasing nervousness, counting sheets, practicing their bandaging techniques and getting on one another's nerves. Suddenly, in the last week of August, the first wounded arrived; but these were not men with nice, clean, bullet wounds, but men with gaping holes in their sides, crushed legs, shattered jaws, dirty, bloody, disoriented, moaning, screaming. Mme Colombel described the scene on 28 August, her first day nursing. Before noon all the beds were filled, and horribly wounded men sprawled in the corridors and on the floors of the wards. The shelves of bandages, the boxes of morphine ampoules were empty. At 7.00 p.m., suddenly fifty more wounded poured in; Mme Colombel recalled she was so tired and panicked she burst into tears. The "dream hospital" had turned into a nightmare.[15]

The Red Cross organizations desperately tried to meet the double challenge of the rush of volunteers and the flood of wounded. Prior to the war, the training to become a Red Cross nurse had not been particularly difficult, but it had been fairly lengthy and expensive. The UFF, for example, had given classes lasting a few weeks, followed by a brief period of hospital work and capped with an exam for certification in first aid to become an *ambulancière*. However, a volunteer nursing diploma required a year of further course work, a year of hospital work and a second exam, in all costing about one thousand francs. At the beginning of the war, the UFF claimed to have fully trained 8,500 nurses and the SSBM claimed over ten thousand; but both figures were probably over-estimates.[16] Once the war began, training became much speedier, and focused upon dressing wounds. Thousands of women crowded into class-rooms hastily improvised in town halls and hotels to learn the rudiments and acquire the certificate that could admit them to an auxiliary hospital or the diploma that might be a passport to an ambulance at the front. The actress Lola Noyr recalled: "I never studied a role with as much fervor as I studied the essentials of bandaging the wounded."[17]

The Service de Santé's arrangement with the Red Cross required the Red Cross not only to administer and staff its auxiliary hospitals but also to supply and fund them. However, despite much generosity, especially at the beginning of the war – Mme Tailliandier was able to raise 18,000 francs for her hospital in Arras in one day in the first week of the war[18] – the flood of wounded quickly swamped the Red Cross's financial resources. By the spring of 1915, most auxiliary hospitals had come to rely upon state subsidies, paid per soldier treated. In return, the Service de Santé came to rely much more heavily upon the Red Cross for nurses than it had ever intended.

The army's plans called for volunteer nurses to work in the *arrière* only; Article 133 of Service de Santé regulations, to which Red Cross officials had agreed, barred them from the war zone. Marie Rabut recalled that at her ambulance's organizing meeting, the head doctor had warned her not to imagine herself "Miss Florence Nightingal [*sic*] . . . to take aid and comfort to the wounded on the battlefield."[19] But even before the war, some Red Cross officials, like the volunteer nurses themselves, chafed at this restriction and hoped that it might collapse during a real war. In his 1907 sketch of women's wartime nursing, Dr Legrand advised Red Cross groups not to spend their entire budget setting up auxiliary hospitals, but to set funds aside for a possible "new mission." If a war occurred on French soil, Legrand believed it would be impossible to exclude women from the battle zone.[20] And this is what happened. At first, the French retreat turned several Red Cross auxiliary hospitals, like those of Mme Tailliandier in Arras and Mme Macherez in Soissons, into *ad hoc* front-line nursing stations. Owing to what Dr Mignon termed "administrative gerrymandering" [*chinoiserie administrative*],[21] some obviously front-line sectors, such as Verdun where he served, retained their designation as in the *arrière*, and thus continued to employ volunteer nurses in great numbers; but the exclusion of the Red Cross from the battle zone still applied *en principe*.

In the spring of 1917 the Ministry of War ordered the admission of Red Cross volunteers to the war zone, and in July they became the standard staff in the *auto-chirs*, the mobile surgical units. In February 1918, they were admitted to front-line dressing stations. Concerted pressure from various constituencies caused these breaches in the wall between front and rear, military and civilian, masculine and feminine. One was elite women with impressive nursing diplomas and even more impressive political connections who lobbied the Service de Santé for front-line assignments. A second was the public acclaim of nursing "heroines" during the invasion.

The exploits of Sister Julie and Mme Macherez proved women's usefulness even in the most dangerous locales, which publicly refuted the army's claim that women could not nurse in combat zones.[22] Doctors were a third source of pressure. Many, like Mignon, had become familiar with Red Cross nurses in auxiliary hospitals and wanted to take their teams with them when they were assigned to front-line duties. For example, when setting up a surgical unit attached to the Fourth Army, Major Guyot wrote to the Service de Santé requesting permission to enroll Mme Boisboissel as his head nurse. His experience working with her at a hospital in the rear had led him to appreciate her "high professional quality and the authority she exercises over her collaborators."[23]

The most important pressure upon the Service de Santé regulations, however, was the war's relentless drain upon manpower. By the spring of 1917, the Ministry of War had already begun to "weed out" conscripts who had been sent to work in vital industries to return them to combat units (see Chapter 6) and to employ women for non-combat jobs (see Chapter 7). In this circumstance, it was unconscionable to assign soldiers to nursing duties when women had proved capable in the job. Nonetheless, the army did not welcome more volunteer nurses; it first turned to paid workers, whom military administrators expected to be more docile and more amenable to dirty work than Red Cross ladies.

In 1916 the army created the status of Temporary Military Nurse, a paid position for the duration of the war, opening war nursing to working-class women for the first time. Louise Delétang noted in her diary on 15 August 1916 that a friend had been hired in this new status at Val-de-Grace: "Forty francs a month, three meals a day, working hours from 7.00 a.m. to 7.00 p.m. including meal times. Sweep, clean the wards, make the beds, empty the pails and bedpans or then in the kitchens, peel the vegetables, wash the dishes, etc."[24] Delétang's friend was delighted, but Delétang less so; the program was too late, she thought, to attract the many working women who had wanted to nurse at the beginning of the war. By the summer of 1916 they had found factory jobs, also essential to the war effort, that paid a good deal more than the Service de Santé offered.

Although the army eventually hired about 30,000 women as military nurses, they did not solve the nursing shortage. The pay was too low, the work too demanding and the job status at once too restrictive and too insecure. The women had to sign contracts that bound them to the Service de Santé until six months after the end of the war, although, of course, the army could fire them at any time. The Service de Santé did finally increase the wages, but only in October 1918, too late to improve recruiting efforts.[25] And, although these nurses could supplement volunteers in housekeeping chores and routine care, few had the education to replace the diploma-endowed Red Cross nurses in operating rooms and hospital administration. However, some military doctors saw the arrival of paid nurses as a chance to dispense with volunteers altogether, much to the dismay of Justin Godart, the Undersecretary of State in charge of the Service de Santé.[26] In order to avoid losing valuable volunteers, he issued new regulations for Red Cross nurses in military hospitals, granting them the same benefits in terms of working hours, vacations, sick leave, meals, lodging and transportation provided to the paid nursing staff.[27] Finally, because of the continued shortage of trained nurses, the Service de Santé approved "in principle the employment of Nurses in front-line medical units, but only when an insufficient number of male nurses proves detrimental to the wounded." Since the nursing shortage continued – in August 1917, for example, the officer in charge of medical staffing in Creil, north of Paris, informed his superiors that he could not operate his first aid stations owing to a shortfall of 216 nurses – Red Cross volunteers were welcomed, sometimes enthusiastically, sometimes grudgingly, into the war zone.[28]

At the height of their activity, the three branches of the French Red Cross fielded some 63,000 nurses who staffed 1,480 auxiliary hospitals and provided hundreds of nurses to the military hospitals, hospital ships, dressing stations and mobile surgical units.[29] Dr Mignon summarized the extent of volunteer nurses' duties as they expanded during the war.

> According to regulations, the nurses were charged with maintaining the wards and giving the sick and wounded the care that the doctors judge appropriate. They were to prepare and maintain the necessary equipment for operations and the dressings, and also to monitor closely the seriously sick and wounded. They were to participate in administering drugs, distributing food and maintaining the bodily cleanliness of the hospitalized; and be on duty day and night. They could be used to direct the kitchen, the linen and the clothing departments. Implicitly, the instructions admitted that nurses could administer anesthetic and serve as operating assistants.[30]

Although Mignon suggested that nurses' participation in these last procedures was unusual, already in 1915 one nurse wrote from her auxiliary hospital on the Côte d'Azur:

> I do all the anesthesia whether chloroform or ether. We have had up to twenty-one operations in a day; this was the record but fifteen to seventeen is very common. We do all the sterilizations in our laboratory, also how many times I am still on my feet at one in the morning . . . Never did I work like this before the war.[31]

The French Red Cross is justly proud of its record in the First World War. More than twenty volunteer nurses were killed at the front – the SSBM claimed thirteen such martyrs – while many others died of communicable diseases, particularly typhoid fever, contracted in their war service. Nearly one thousand received the Croix de guerre.[32] Each of the societies publicized its own particular heroines, such as the UFF's Mme Quiquet in Rheims and the ADF's Mme Macherez and also Mme Charlotte Maître, decorated four times for bravery under fire.[33] Praise poured in from all sides; the Republican politician Louis Barthou, Abbé Stéphen Coubé and Dr Mignon all delivered similar eulogies. As Mignon wrote, "No Red Cross volunteer failed to heed the call."[34] But with the praise came criticism. From the first days of August, the Red Cross female volunteers provoked uneasiness; was it really possible for so many women to go to war? How would it affect them? How did it affect the war and the Nation?

The White Angel and the *Mondaine*

Compared with the meager pre-war discussion of women's role in war, wartime literature on this subject was voluminous; and, in virtually all of it, whether documentary, laudatory or critical, nursing took pride of place. As Léon Abensour wrote in 1917: "Whoever thinks of French women in 1914 sees a young nurse draped in a white or blue veil, very gay despite her monastic headdress displaying the blood-red cross. The Red Cross is, of all the immense activities of French women, the best-known and the most popular, in truth we could say the only one known and the only popular one."[35] Nonetheless, wartime literature failed to resolve the contradictions of pre-war discourse. For most commentators, volunteer nursing was the ultimate feminine war service; yet whether it was *military* service, whether the nurse was truly engaged in the masculine war, remained in dispute. Catholic commentators tried to deal seriously, if a trifle nervously, with the precedent set by their recently beatified heroine, Joan of Arc; although she had been called to fight, modern women were called to nurse, they maintained.[36] Feminists more bluntly equated soldiering and nursing. For example, Louise Zeys called attention to the parallel mobilization of soldiers and Red Cross volunteers: "During the night of 1 August, all the nurses on *active duty* received their mobilization orders . . . they joined the military trains that carried our troops toward the East and in compartments reserved for nurses in *uniform* they were acclaimed by all as new comrades. Weren't they going to campaign together?"[37] Mobilized together, performing a common duty, nurses and soldiers would share the same risks, the same war (see Figure 5.1). "Many comport themselves as true soldiers and have already been cited as such in dispatches," confirmed Mme Pérouse, head of the UFF. Dr Anna Hamilton thought it appropriate for soldiers to salute nurses.[38]

Figure 5.1 *Le Miroir*, 10 August 1914 reported: "Red Cross ladies depart for Belgium. . . . Mothers, wives, sisters of the combatants also depart for the battlefields to lavish their cares, their encouragement, their consolations on the unfortunate wounded. In Paris and in most of the provincial towns, ambulances are hastily, but perfectly, organized." © Bibliothèque Nationale de France, Paris.

But such an easy assimilation of the feminine to the masculine military project struck many observers as silly, or worse, as demeaning to the real war heroes, the soldiers. Antoine Delécraz snickered at an acquaintance who ceremoniously doffed his hat to any woman wearing Red Cross insignia, even a maternity home attendant![39] Military officials and satirists alike condemned women's apparent lust for uniforms of their own,[40] while the conservative columnist Lucien Descaves chastised nurses for "playing" at nursing while the men they were pretending to emulate certainly were not playing at soldiering. In particular, he condemned women's desire for recognition for their war service; if heroes could die in obscurity, he sanctimoniously intoned, then nurses should not seek publicity.[41]

Much less controversial, although difficult to integrate into the masculine experience of war, was the depiction of the nurse as simultaneously mother and nun and definitely all woman, repeating and expanding the themes that had emerged before the war. The most popular image was the nurse as mother and the *petit poilu* as her infant. A song of the period, "Adieux à l'Hôpital," is an example: "There we found rest/ and to bandage our booboos/ women's hands . . . Sweet nurse/ now when everything is black/soften the despair/ like a mother!"[42] However, religious imagery also arose easily from the history of nursing. Red Cross uniforms copied nuns' habits, with their long sleeves and impractical coifs, in a conscious effort to appropriate to their wearers not only the qualities of nuns but also the respect and privileges society accorded to them, for example, the ability to travel alone and to associate closely, even intimately, with men not of their immediate family, without jeopardizing their reputations or their caste.

Virtually all the eulogists of volunteer nursing stressed the nurse's vocation and her devotion, often alluding to nurses as "secular nuns."[43] Jack de Bussy in her novel *Refugiée et infirmière de guerre* made the parallel with religious service explicit: "I am very highly impressed by the monastic aspect of all these women, the volunteer nurses who have broken with civilian life, that is to say, home, family, friends, habits, to consecrate themselves to the War Wounded."[44] But it was not only the monastic costume, the renunciation of the world and the devotion to a Cause that publicists emphasized, it was also the ideal of absolute self-abnegation and obedience. According to the Catholic writer Georges Docquois, the nurse was an anonymous acolyte in a secular religion in which the doctor stood in for Christ: "For their pure devotion, their wordless pity, they desire no other recompense than these five words from the head doctor: I am satisfied with you."[45] Marcelle Capy dispensed with the doctor/priest and depicted the nurse as a guardian angel, wrestling directly with the devil for the soul of her patient. "For these wounded creatures, the nurse must dispute with death . . . She is the savior, the good in battle against the forces of darkness."[46]

From mother to nun, the image of the volunteer nurse rested on essential womanhood. In wartime novels it was not training that made a nurse, it was femininity. Charles Foley's *Sylvette et son blessé*, for example, contrasted the failure of Mme Heltoux, a scientifically *diplomée* but unfemininely ambitious nurse, with the success of Sylvette, devoid of training but brimming with a tender heart, feminine devotion and "grandmother's recipes and old wives' remedies."[47] Even for Drs Lejars and Mignon, who demanded thoroughly professional staffs, a nurse's womanly qualities were as important as her technical training. It was women's voices, their way of moving, bending over, or sitting at the bedside and especially, "the infinitely consoling balm of the womanly hearts" that reassured the wounded in ways male attendants could not.[48] For others, like the song quoted above, it was a woman's hands or her smile.[49] This was the image of nursing that captured the public imagination – and the female imagination in particular. As Jules Combarieu noted in his wartime study of girls' education:

> To be a nurse! To have a right to this title of humility that the most beautiful ideas have made a title of nobility! To wear – with coquetry, of course, like the brave, young officers wear theirs – this blue and white uniform to which its insignia of devotion add the mysticism of a religious robe and which constitutes, in time of war, the supreme elegance of womanhood! Since the beginning of the war, this was the dream of many young girls.[50]

The hands, the smile, the heart, the womanly elegance – they were to achieve a larger victory than to ease the pain of wounded soldiers; they were to heal France! Many writers claimed that the masculine camaraderie of the trenches was solving "The Social Question;" several eulogists of the Red Cross made similar claims for volunteer nursing. The Red Cross promoted its volunteers as "ladies." In fact, their unpaid status, that to Red Cross publicists guaranteed their selfless devotion to the Nation, really did guarantee their social class; few working-class or even middle-class women could afford to pay their own way. The feminist Marguerite Durand and the socialists Capy and Pelletier criticized the Red Cross for shutting out the vocation and nursing talent of less well-to-do women;[51] but for many commentators, the Red Cross's elitism promoted national reconciliation. Devoid of the autonomy, sexuality and material self-interest that coarsened the femininity of lower-class women, Red Cross nurses exuded a "moral force," according to Dr Lejars.[52] Through the experience of nursing poor (but heroic) peasants and workers, elite French women would learn to esteem "the popular soul," while their patients would learn the error of their revolutionary doctrines.

> Later, after the war, when life returns to normal, there is bound to be a reciprocal and more penetrating understanding between [the nurse] and the men of the people . . . Because of her, yesterday's wounded who is tomorrow's electorate, will, after the war, mistrust revolutionary doctrines and be saner and clearer-thinking. The Red Cross, healer of the body, will have contributed to making a new soul in generations of Frenchmen.[53]

It will not escape the reader that it was the lower class that was supposed to modify its politics and that future electors were envisioned as male; this was a vision of national reconciliation based upon an acceptance of the status quo in terms of both class and gender subordination. The nurse, far from being an adventurous or emancipating figure, was presented as powerfully conservative.

But although devotion and motherhood were values beyond criticism, other aspects of femininity as embodied in volunteer nursing drew attacks. If, to the Red Cross's supporters, femininity translated into self-sacrifice and conservation of the social order, to its critics femininity spelled frivolity, fashion, sexuality, romantic adventure and social chaos. The Red Cross, the critics claimed, licensed women to pursue selfish desires, obviously at odds with France's wartime interests, under a hypocrite's veil of patriotic devotion.

The nun, secularized and trained, was the model of the "true" nurse; her opposite, the *mondaine*, was the favorite example of the rival image, the false nurse. Pre-war novels about "emancipated women" had already identified educated women and career women with *la vie mondaine*; all had abandoned their natural feminine devotion to home and family for lives of pure selfishness.[54] Translated to the wartime scene, the *mondaine* embraced, rather than abandoned, the world, the flesh and the devil and volunteered to nurse to increase her social capital, to fill her empty hours and to pursue sexual pleasure. While the true nurse inhabited a cell with the nursing manual at her bedside like a breviary,[55] the "fashion-plate nurse" arrived in a limousine, dripping with jewelry and self-importance. "With sounding horn and sparkling brass, the limousine advances ceremoniously down the teeming street. Inside, bosom high, all in white, pearls at her ears, a Red Cross nurse . . . Grave gentlemen gallantly salute the *grande dame* who is playing angel."[56] Commentary and fiction, both during and after the war, imagined plots of conversion made conventional by the pre-war pseudo-moralistic *romans de moeurs* and antifeminist novels; again and again, nursing war victims converted *mondaines* to true femininity. After depicting the frivolous behavior of Society Ladies who volunteered to nurse at his hospital, Dr Lejars intoned: "A few among them understood; they renounced their habits and their worldly illusions, and made themselves humble and silent."[57]

The image of the nurse-as-*mondaine* informed almost all the criticism of Red Cross nurses, from socialist pacifists like Capy, quoted above, to Catholic moralists and nationalists. A typical claim was that women volunteered only in order to be able to wear the Red Cross uniform, thus perpetuating the pre-war "doll" who would go to any length to be in fashion. For such women, war service was just another aspect of their social lives, "a sport, a new game, a more enthralling variation of flirtation and the tango."[58] What mattered to them was to be admitted to a "chic" hospital; the new social delineator, smirked Marcel Boulenger, was the answer to the question: "In which hospital does she work?"[59] Rather than promoting a social *Union sacrée*, volunteer nursing had created a new arena of social competition. According to the conservative columnist Lucien Descaves, Red Cross volunteers "cared for the poor wounded as if they were their brothers, it is true; but they only have brothers, no sisters."[60]

More serious charges followed. If the ideal volunteer was trained as a nurse and obedient as a nun, *les élégantes de la première heure* were both ignorant and independent. Used to getting their own way, they refused to subordinate themselves to a doctor's authority. For Dr Lejars, the perfect nurse was silent and anonymous – and Society Ladies were neither.[61] Their conception of nursing, it was claimed, was to give out smiles and treats to handsome young officers –

nothing dirty, coarse or painful. Docquois imagined the reactions of one such: "And then, and then, when I heard that we're only going to get common soldiers, well, my dear, really! It's no longer the least bit interesting . . . What! Having had all these lovely coifs made to turn the heads of some vulgar, penniless foot-soldier?"[62] But the portrait was even more damning; Docquois suggested that this woman then quitted her hospital to flee the threatened invasion. And he was not alone in branding the nurse-*mondaine* as a coward; nurses' uniforms, we learn from Dr Lejars and several other commentators, were especially popular in Bordeaux in the fall of 1914, linking nurses with the "cowardly" behavior of the government that had abandoned Paris to take refuge there. Masson went further, claiming a disproportionate number of nurses in Biarritz![63] Although none of the serious commentators accused "false" nurses of treason, such stories appeared so frequently in newspapers and novels early in the war that one Prefect became worried about security at hospitals: "There are too many women in hospitals and ambulances," he warned.[64]

The key failing of the nurse-*mondaine* was her sexuality.[65] When represented as a nun or a mother, the nurse was asexual – and so was her patient; the soldier became a soul to be saved or a child to be nurtured. The *mondaine*, by contrast, brought sexuality with her; her patients were, first and foremost, men. Thus she exploded the neat gender sequestration that the war rhetoric had ordained, that masculinity was locked in combat on the battlefield while femininity waited in abeyance at home.

Almost all the contemporary light fiction that dealt with wartime nursing featured as the main plot device the romantic connection between a volunteer nurse and her soldier (usually officer) patient. Sometimes it was the nurse's maternal care that sheltered romance, as in Foley's *Sylvette*; sometimes, more shockingly, it was the nurse's nun-like posture. In Maxime Formont's novel *La dame blanche*, the wounded soldiers followed the heroine with their eyes. "When they saw her pass by, in her immaculate robe of a seraphim, she gave the impression of a young girl by the transparency of her face, the freshness of her eyes. But her charm was that of a woman."[66] Who and what was she, they speculated: a *mondaine*? a *femme libre*? an actress? And they were, of course, right; her virgin's veil did indeed cover a dark past of sexual experience.

This was the plot convention already laid down in Lechartier's pre-war novel – volunteer nursing as redemption for fallen women;

but here it expanded to imbue nursing itself with erotic implications. For the hero of Henry d'Yvignac's novel *J'avais une marraine* (1918), the romance with his nurse began the moment she first helped him to his bed. "I had to accept help to get to my bed – from her! What humiliation! I slid my arm around her delicate neck, but when I removed it, I profited . . . by caressing her where her veil let escape a few fine curls of gold."[67] The relationship between nurse and wounded became one of mutual seduction.

As in fiction about *marraines*, all the popular genres in which nursing figured during the war, whether *romans de moeurs*, novels of moral uplift, satiric sketches, comedy and even the soldiers' trench newspapers,[68] portrayed nursing as essentially a means of intimate, romantic contact between upper-class young women and strange men (see Figure 5.2). And it was a romantic connection with a purpose: love of country came a distant second to love of a good man. A girl's true aim in volunteering to nurse war wounded was not to serve her country; it was to further her own feminine interests. Such was the equivocal result of conceptualizing women's war service as personal devotion; in these stories, instead of seeing the Nation in the body of her wounded patient, the nurse saw the man.

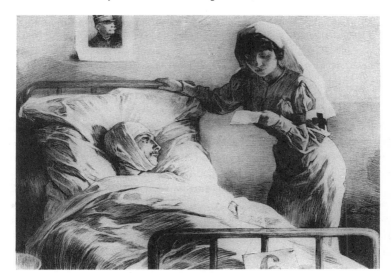

Figure 5.2 "Les Sublimes." A magazine illustration of the romantic relationship between nurse and wounded. © Bibliothèque Nationale de France, Paris.

This view was not confined to the pages of fiction; critics accused women of volunteering to nurse either from a frivolous addiction to flirtation, otherwise frustrated by the absence of young men in wartime society, or from the single-minded pursuit of matrimony.[69] The popular psychologist Dr Toulouse linked the rush of young women to volunteer to the great losses of young men in the first months of the war, not because of women's patriotic recognition that their services were desperately needed, but rather because of their suddenly reduced chances on the marriage market: "The husband hunt has become a big deal for the young woman and remarkably assists her duty to aid the wounded," he dryly remarked.[70]

Behind these criticisms lurked the fear that nursing spelled the end of sexual innocence for young women. In turn-of-the-century novels and moralistic tracts, the scene of the young woman clandestinely reading a medical book had come to represent the corruption of feminine innocence by modern life.[71] Now, the literary trope had become reality. As Dr Toulouse sermonized:

> The war came and the most sheltered young woman enrolled in the nursing corps. The mystery of the other sex, which had been strictly kept from her, was brusquely revealed in the beds of pain of wounded soldiers . . . The young woman now knows. She is aware, she no longer lowers her eyes as before, and she sees clearly ahead of her, in the world and in life.[72]

Toulouse did not entirely condemn this eventuality, even though he regretted it. But for others, it was the final plunge down the slope of female emancipation into the pit of gender chaos from which France was finally arising owing to French soldiers' demonstrations of manliness in the trenches. What was the point of the war at all, if women's war experience negated men's? Formont drove the point home in *La dame blanche*: nursing was not suppose to emancipate women, it was suppose to make evident and acceptable their necessary subordination to men. As a result of her nursing, his heroine rejected her pre-war feminism: "'Now,' she went on, 'man is our champion, our hero, even our god. A poor god who dies for us, to save us from the Beast's fury! Woman realizes what she owes him.'"[73] But the specter of nursing as an open road to sexual emancipation, cultivated in this novel as in so many others, was too strong to be dissipated by such a last-minute conversion.

Critical evaluations of nurses were not confined to a few misogynists and conservatives; they pervaded the wartime literature that
explored women's relationship to the war. Commentator after
commentator, republicans, socialists and feminists, as well as clerics
and conservatives, in chapters usually titled "White Angels," followed
their eulogies to nurses' devotion and feminine healing powers with
doses of criticism. Lechartier, who had done so much to popularize
the Red Cross before the war, protested: "Everyone has a lot of bad
things to say about the Red Cross. Each has his own dart to throw,
usually a scandalous one, an amusing anecdote or a worrying or
terrible story to tell on the subject. And each waits while his
neighbor tells his story in order quickly to tell a worse one." He
dismissed "abuses" as insignificant beside the invaluable services
that the Red Cross provided,[74] but in other commentary, the
depiction of the "false nurse" – ambitious, frivolous, wanton –
claimed as much space – or more – as did that of *la vraie*.[75] Without
doubt, the volunteer nurse, although held up as the best way for
women to support the war, was an ambivalent figure.

Volunteer Nurses and Trench-fighters

Those who experienced the First World War found it notoriously
difficult to write about. In 1914 Europeans were heirs to a coherent
set of concepts and images and a glamorous rhetoric that purported
to convey the true meaning of war, full of courage, heroism, self-
sacrifice and manly honor.[76] During the war, official language in
France perpetuated this view, in which, for example, soldiers always
"fell on the field of honor." Although Paul Fussell argues that the
"eyewash" churned out by the press repulsed British trench-fighters,
French historians have found that, in their own writings, soldiers
sustained some of the same myths.[77] Especially early in the war, there
was no other vocabulary available. Gradually realist, pessimist, and
even absurdist and pacifist modes began to challenge the traditional
heroic formula, beginning with Henri Barbusse's *Under Fire* (1916).
In the 1930s, a new wave of war literature appeared that deepened
the bitter, ironic current, for example Céline's *Voyage au bout de
la nuit* (1932) and Jean Renoir's film *La Grande Illusion* (1937).[78]
However, although these works have entered the canon, at the time
they represented a small ripple in a tidal wave of the Myth of War
Experience from which, George Mosse argues, not even such anti-
war novels as Remarque's *All Quiet on the Western Front* were totally
exempt.[79]

Women's wartime experience was even more constrained by myth than men's. Men, writing from their authenticating experience as soldiers, could place themselves within the rhetoric of heroism or on its margins, the better to engage it in a kind of guerrilla war, exploding its concepts to reveal the grim and absurd realities beneath. But one way or the other, they conceived of war as an appropriate male domain; the writers did not have to explain or justify men's relationship to the war – war was a given of masculinity. And their memoirs helped to commemorate the First World War as exclusively, obsessively masculine.[80]

By contrast, commentators on women's wartime experience, whether critics, apologists or memoirists, had to justify women's excursion into war literature and into the experience of war that it claimed to represent. Léonie Godfroy, a Red Cross volunteer nurse who was captured when Noyon fell to the German army, tried to explain in the introduction to her brief memoirs how it was she was writing a war memoir and why it differed so much from other such literature.

> But when, giving in to the affectionate curiosity of my friends, I decided to write up part of my memories, I realized that the tableaux I was going to evoke differed in fundamental ways from most of those you see in the newspapers every day. This is caused by a difference in point of view ... War appears to be something abominable or something sublime, depending upon the side one experiences. *I must declare that I saw only the somber side. This is women's share.* Those of us whom chance or vocation draw into the vast drama must resign ourselves to seeing only the saddest of realities. To men in the first rank of danger go the superb spirits, the epic spectacles of the battlefield. To us, the other side of the picture ... We don't meddle with the heroes in the apotheosis of combat. They come to us *afterwards*, bloody, exhausted, mute. It is not surprising that our memoirs often seem like nightmares, while there is joy in theirs – a sort of superhuman joy.[81]

Before the war, Georges Goyau had depicted nursing as a women's war, fought "a fold of the landscape" away from the masculine battlefield. Similarly, Godfroy constructed a masculine and a feminine war operating next to each other, not in space, like Goyau's alternative army, but in time; for Godfroy, the woman's war was the war that happened after the masculine war. Godfroy feared that this grim feminine war might be interpreted as an anti-war.

The simplest way for women to stake a claim upon a war experience was not to define a rival feminine war but to embrace the masculine war myth of self-sacrifice for one's country and to claim it for women. The volunteer nurse was well positioned to make this claim, but it excluded her from the critical position on the margin. Even a pacifist like Vera Brittain was unable to escape the rhetoric of military heroism,[82] and none of her French counterparts was able to sustain even Brittain's level of analysis. An incident, an episode might elicit a critical response; but this could not encompass the whole experience. To reject the mythic war instantaneously removed the female author from war's universe and left her no ground from which to launch her re-evaluation. To be in the war at all, women had to accept, at least partially, the heroic myth. As a result, it is not surprising that the memoirs of wartime nurses are unconvincing either as literature or as historical records. Few memoirs resolved the tension between the rhetoric of heroic sacrifice and the reality of dirt, pain, fear and fatigue, with most memoirs swinging from one mode to the other without any attempt at reconciliation. For example, Noëlle Roger began her description of a ward of seriously wounded soldiers with the claim that "each of these men had had his glorious adventure." She then depicted a man brought from the operating table shrieking in pain, a rigid, terrified victim of tetanus and a shell-shock case engulfed in hallucinations. However, her intent was not irony; she did not seem to notice – or could not express – that none of these were glorious adventures.[83]

The memoirs of French women who volunteered to nurse during the First World War are a mixed genre, including obvious propaganda literature written in the obligatory language of chivalry as well as documentary chronicles of women's war experience. The first predominated in the early years of the war: Hélène Leune's *Tel qu'ils sont: Notes d'une infirmière de la Croix rouge*, published in 1915, is an example.[84] By 1916, the cast of "little heroes" and "white angels" that people the earlier memoirs began to give way to more realistic descriptions of nursing routine. Rather than the relationship of one ideal nurse to "her" wounded, these memoirs usually depicted the institutional shape of nursing; sometimes the life of the hospital or ambulance itself became the subject of the memoir, as in La Boulaye's *Croix et cocarde* (1919).[85]

Not surprisingly, the accounts that broke most consistently with the high diction of the War Myth were published after the war was over. Clemenceau's daughter, Madeleine Jacquemaire, wrote the most hard-hitting of French nursing accounts, *Les hommes de bonne volonté* (1919). It interspersed accounts of soldiers' suffering with vivid depictions of the back-breaking, soul-destroying work of nursing at the front. As the title suggests, Jacquemaire wrote this fictionalized memoir to eulogize the honor, courage and sacrifice of the French Common Man; but in place of the standard "high diction" is an unremittingly downbeat tone: these men often suffered unnecessarily. Like the trench-fighter of so many memoirs, Jacquemaire depicted a combat in which the main enemy was not the Germans, but the living and working conditions of the war, the bureaucratic procedure of the army, and even her own supervisors. And, like Barbusse's famous novel published three years earlier, Jacquemaire questioned the validity of war and her role in it. In a monologue by her alter-ego, Mme Berton, Jacquemaire imagined the nurse's role as the attendant at the *corrida* who patches up the wounded horses and whips them back to their feet, once more to face the bull's horns. Yet in the end, Jacquemaire backed away from Barbusse's concluding call to pacifism: Must we do this? she asked, and replied immediately, "Yes, for it is the price of victory."[86]

Despite the differences in experience and in the discourse that described them, most nursing accounts shared many themes with each other and with the commentary on nurses' war service. Nursing as the feminine equivalent of military service, the nurse as nun and as mother were images that the nurses themselves found persuasive. The main differences between their views and those of the commentators were ones of emphasis. None broke entirely with the dominant discourse.

Most of the accounts presented volunteer nursing as similar to, or even the equivalent of, men's military service. For example, La Boulaye claimed veteran status for herself and her fellow nurses. After a particularly harrowing operation, she wrote: "French women soon will have two years of campaigning: we are no longer cadets [*des bleues*]."[87] Some memoirs substantiated the critics' fears that wartime nursing would emancipate women. French nurses did not produce the adventure stories so common to British, American and even German volunteers; the war was too close to home to qualify as exotic travel.[88] Nonetheless, nursing brought increased independence and public worth. Léonie Godfroy explained that the need for her nursing skills transformed her in her own eyes and those of her society. "A young girl, in ordinary life, is nothing or next to nothing. For the first time I was going to be someone, I would have a personal role to play, I would count in the world."[89]

The nurses almost invariably used a rhetoric of service, sacrifice and devotion to describe their own motivations in volunteering and to depict the "true" nurse. Sometimes the ideal nurse was literally a nun (see Figure 5.3);[90] for others, the she was merely nun-like.

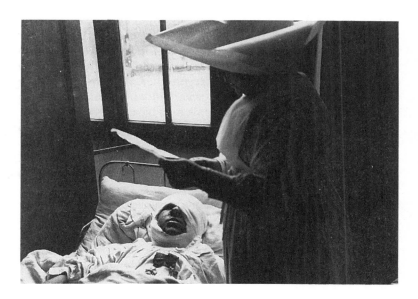

Figure 5.3 Sister Gabrielle of Clermont-en-Argonne. "The devotion of this woman saved the population," reported the *Petit Parisien*, 11 November 1914, crediting her with cowing the German invaders who threatened to massacre the whole town in retaliation for a sniper. Courtesy of ECPA Ivry-sur-Seine, France.

> Suddenly, personality fades under the uniform. You only feel an immense desire to do good, the absolute consent of your whole self to discipline. You become that anonymous being who obeys the sound of a bell, the doctor's gesture, the patient's call, who stands respectfully at the head of the bed and who takes on every chore, even the most repulsive: these humble chores, how sweet they seem to me![91]

Maternal imagery was less pervasive, appearing mostly in accounts from nurses in convalescent hospitals. In these stories, the wounded were always *petits* and the nurse's job was to wait on them, scold them and "spoil" them with treats and attention.[92] Perhaps maternal rhetoric rang less true for some volunteers because they experienced conflict, rather than continuity, between hospital and family roles. While commentators condemned nurses who "deserted" their posts, the nurses themselves discovered that the job of "mothering" wounded soldiers did not exempt them from their own family obligations. Mme Colombel recalled dutifully visiting her husband at his request, although to do so required her to leave her hospital post in Arras at the height of the German advance in September 1914. And just as dutifully, Juliette Martineau cut short her visit to her family despite her mother's protests to return to her hospital when it was suddenly inundated with wounded.[93] In neither case did the woman have a moral imperative to guide her choice. The analogy of nurse to mother did nothing to clarify the situation.

But if motherhood was attenuated as a motif in nurses' accounts, the romantic/erotic theme that ran through so much of nursing fiction and commentary was almost entirely absent. In a public letter, one nurse complained about the nursing romances so popular with serial writers.

> Please don't believe those cute stories that come out several times a week on the fourth page of the newspaper: the model hospital installed in an old château; the wounded officer always decorated with the Croix de Guerre, whose wound is always serious but aesthetic; the young nurse, white and blonde under her veil who, this year, has abandoned the tango for the Red Cross . . . Invariably they fall in love, will fall in love, or already have been in love.[94]

The only account that gave any credence at all to the romance plot was a letter from a nursing friend that Juliette Martineau published in 1916; but for her, the war, not romance, was the serious business of life. That she spent her time flirting with officers proved her hospital was part of the feminine *arrière* where "the timorous, the old maids and the flabby bourgeoises" held sway, and thus not real war service at all. She explained: "I keep my flirts like I used to keep my dolls. The day a new distraction appears, I'll shove them in the cupboard; so recommend me to the General . . . I'm a warrior pigeon. What a humiliation for us in these times not to be able to carry a gun!"[95] Most nurses rejected even this scenario by portraying themselves either as "white angels," all asexual devotion, or as hardworking, exhausted professionals. Both images banished romance from the scene.

By contrast, the accounts did admit criticisms of snobbery, feminine ambition and competition in volunteer nursing. Most concurred that some women were drawn to nursing because it had become fashionable, and the "false" nurse, when she appeared in their pages, was usually portrayed as a *mondaine*, like Mlle Fachemine, whom La Boulaye used as the foil to her ideal nurse, Sister Rosalie. She reminds one very strongly of Mme Heltoux in Foley's novel, *Sylvette et son blessé,* technically well-trained but eaten up with social ambition and without the requisite feminine heart. So pervasive was the cliché of the nurse-*mondaine* in her diamonds that Jacquemaire, by way of pointed contrast, insisted that her heroine's leather wrist-watch was her only jewelry.[96]

But in many accounts, it was not individual nurses who were bad, but a system of nursing that pitted women against one another. Both Jacquemaire and La Boulaye claimed that nuns resented Red Cross volunteers and hindered their work when they could.[97] And in 1916, when the army medical service created the paid position of Temporary Military Nurse, it also created a new rivalry, suggested in the title of La Boulaye's memoir, *Croix et cocarde,* the cross being the Red Cross badge and the cockade, the insignia of the military nurse (see Figure 5.4).[98] But the most disruptive conflict was the rivalry of the three separate Red Cross organizations. The Society to Aid Wounded Soldiers (SSBM), founded in 1864, saw the Association of French Ladies (ADF, 1879) and the Union of Women of France (UFF, 1881) as interlopers; the more recent foundations accused the SSBM of snobbish exclusivity.

In the street [white] vestals come across other vestals dressed in blue. These women who wear on their foreheads the sign of redemption, of mercy and peace – the cross of the Savior Jesus – exchange no greetings. They cough insolently. "That's the enemy society that competes with us and steals our patients, a worthless society, Johnny-come-latelies . . . civil servants' wives and shop girls."[99]

Wartime volunteer nursing, as nurses themselves depicted it in their memoirs and published diaries, was quite similar to the way it was viewed by contemporary commentators. It was the feminine version of national patriotic service, similar, if not equivalent, to military service for men. True nurses were nun-like and maternal;

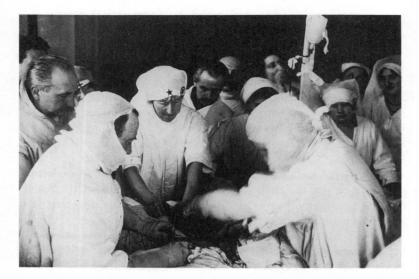

Figure 5.4 Red Cross and army nurses work together at a field hospital. Notice the cockade on the headdress of the nurse in the center, the cross on the nurse behind the orderly at the left. © Musée d'histoire contemporaine – BDIC, reproduction by Archipel.

they were also feminine and professionally competent. False nurses, to the extent that nurses admitted they existed, also exhibited many of the qualities of which commentators complained; they were socially ambitious, self-interested and lacked true devotion to the vocation of nursing France's wounded heroes.

However, nurses did modify the portrait of wartime nursing in interesting ways. In their depiction of the false nurse, for example, they never suggested that romantic or prurient interest was the basis of her failings. Typically they viewed the inevitable physical intimacy with strange men that was inherent in the job either neutrally or as a drawback that experience eventually overcame. Several of the nurses recalled their first exposure to the naked male body – and their reaction was either revulsion or aesthetic distancing. Louise Weiss and Lola Noyr recalled that on their first day of nursing they were almost paralyzed by contact with male bodies. When the local *curé* fulminated against a young woman's doing such work, Weiss was flabbergasted: "Where I felt nothing but disgust, he imagined voluptuousness!"[100] By contrast, Roger and La Boulaye compared their first sights of naked men to Renaissance paintings, and Jacquemaire, to a Greek vase.[101]

The nurses also had a somewhat different view of the organizations in which they served, the Red Cross, the hospital and the military, than what the commentators represented. Although commentators accused women of being snobbishly competitive as individuals, the nurses themselves blamed the way wartime nursing was organized for creating and exacerbating competition between nurses and institutions. And in later memoirs in particular, they often blamed the military authorities that oversaw the administration of their hospitals for many of the problems that they faced as nurses. According to Jacquemaire, "The doctors and officials of the Medical Corps, from the orderlies up to the Inspector-General, do not suffer nurses gladly. 'Women have no place in the army so they should stay home,' they claim."[102] One woman doctor protested in the pages of the *Revue philanthropique* that the creation of the Temporary Military Nurse proved the Service de Santé believed Red Cross nurses to be "blue-stockings of medecine" and preferred "the rough servant, devoted but uneducated, who blindly obeys their prescriptions." By driving out trained nurses, she argued, the military was jeopardizing the care for the wounded.[103] La Boulaye was the most detailed and direct in her criticism of how the military ran its medical auxiliaries. Her auxiliary hospital was alternately flooded with wounded and then, just as suddenly, depleted and threatened with closure. Nowhere in her account did she editorialize to criticize the military, nor did she need to; the disorganization, inefficiency and waste she described is sufficient indictment.[104]

In La Boulaye's account and those of several others – Colombel, Jacquemaire, Julie Crémieux – a view of the volunteer nurse tentatively emerged that was not encompassed by the commentary literature and not comprehensible in the terms of its discourse of heroes, nuns and mothers. It was the image of the nurse as the feminine equivalent of the trench-fighter. These accounts showed war nursing to be a kind of physical and emotional assault, a relentless succession of horrors and exhaustion that would stand – almost – comparison to the conditions described in Barbusse's *Under Fire*. They depicted the wounded not as noble heroes, but as only too frail mortals, torn apart in a brutal war. They certainly provided many examples of great courage in the face of suffering and of human dignity under appalling conditions, but neither did they flinch from showing fear, pain, panic or venial sins like disobedience, drunkenness and abysmal morale. And although they all surrounded their own work with a frame of feminine devotion and compassion, the picture itself was grim. Colombel described being overwhelmed with horrendously wounded men in a non-stop triage, an exhausting sequence of dressings, operations and death. Crémieux, working in field hospitals, added round-the-clock bombardment and lack of sleep. To this Jacquemaire added mud, bone-chilling cold, rats, rotten food, lack of letters and lack of clean underwear. Jeanne Antelme, serving on the Turkish front, included brutal heat, polluted water, insects and a typhoid epidemic, and La Boulaye, a pneumonia epidemic. Almost all recalled breaking down, emotionally, or physically, at some point, as well as bouts of *le cafard* – depression. Both La Boulaye and Antelme stopped keeping their diaries, upon which their memoirs are based, due to emotional and mental exhaustion.[105] Many of the nurses even claimed to share danger and risk death with the soldiers. Léonie Godfroy was captured and spent some months in a prison camp. And Roger went one better; her *Carnets*, she claimed, was the diary of a war martyr, a nurse who had died when a flu epidemic swept the hospital in which she worked.[106]

If, for these nurses, the major enemy was the war itself, the military was not exempt from blame. Like the trench-fighter memoirists, a few of the nurses depicted military authority as an obstacle, if not an outright enemy. Just as junior officers complained of futile paperwork, Jacquemaire railed against the all-important Form 46 that had to be filled out for each wounded man before medical treatment could begin. The military personnel and the staff doctors, in her account, had rule-books in place of hearts and put their own comfort and routines ahead of the welfare of the wounded. At one point, Colombel did the unthinkable from the perspective of the nurse-as-nun; she disobeyed the surgeon under whom she found herself working, giving chloroform to a howling soldier when the surgeon had refused to sedate him.[107]

But in one important way, these nursing memoirs differentiated themselves from the accounts of front fighters. In almost all the writings of trench soldiers, the hero was less an individual than a group of buddies, a brotherhood, in Mosse's term, like Barbusse's *Under Fire*, subtitled *History of a Squad*. Dr Mignon witnessed similar solidarity in front-line nursing, where women were welded into an enduring team by mutual dependence, urgency and suffering. "To my knowledge, no such team broke up and none merited the cliché that women cannot get along."[108] French nursing memoirs, however, did not focus on such teams of nurses. Their authors rarely drew portraits of their colleagues except as ideal types – *la vraie* or *la mondaine*. From a few references,[109] we can speculate that friendships between nurses in hospitals, as between soldiers in the trenches, were often important to making their lives and work bearable; but such glimpses are rare.

Volunteer nurses could easily have portrayed themselves as a feminine collectivity; they had an obvious model before their eyes in the Catholic nursing orders, which had endowed French nursing with both the form and language of sisterhood. However, the nurse-memoirists chose not to do so, and for good reason. By constructing the war as a combat to remasculinize the French nation, the war myth had not only excluded French women from the war story, it had positioned femininity as hostile to the war. Anything women did to contribute to the war, even nursing its wounded heroes, was suspect. Women, by their collective efforts, however well intentioned, risked losing the real war, the war to restore French masculine supremacy. Inevitably, to represent nursing as a collective female war experience would raise the specter of an alternative feminine war, undermining or even opposing the national war effort.

Volunteer nurses suppressed the sisterhood of nursing in their memoirs in order to insist that they were fighting the same war as the soldiers, the masculine war, the trench-fighters' war. Their accounts focused almost all their attention upon the relationship between the nurse and the wounded soldier, not as a romantic or erotic tie, but as one between comrades in arms and accomplices in suffering, in league against the brutal enemy and the callous authorities. But even then, nurses could not risk claiming an equal experience to the soldiers', an equal sacrifice to the national cause; since masculinity had to triumph, it was not a camaraderie of equals but of the nurse as acolyte to the soldier's heroism. Exhausted or frightened or sick as she was, it was his suffering that caused hers. Antelme wrote: "You know, those agonies, they tear the soul, and to know your impotence to stop that suffering, that is the worst of all."[110] As her emotional anguish reflected his physical pain, so too did her war experience reflect his. Rather than commemorating a unique feminine experience, in account after account memoirists subordinated the nurse's story to the soldiers'.

In the end, the nurses' memoirs, like the commentaries, left intact the incongruity, even the opposition, of women and war. As targets of as much criticism as praise, nurses in their memoirs absolved themselves of the charge of pursuing feminine emancipation, solidarity and values at the expense of masculine suffering by subordinating their wartime experience to the soldier's story. Rather than script a role for the volunteer nurse to stand alongside the soldier in the war story, even the grimmest and most "realist" of the nurses' memoirs placed the wounded soldier on a pedestal and the nurse, head bowed, at his feet, her emotional suffering a tribute to his sacrifice. In their personal accounts, France's nurse memoirists helped erase their own experiences from the war story. Their works did not reshape the war myth to include women; instead they commemorated the First World War as the trench-fighters' war and confirmed the essence of the war experience as masculine.

Notes

1. Rabut, *Les étincelles*, p. 6.
2. Ibid., p. 11.
3. Borel, *La mobilisation féminine,* pp. 16–17; Foucault, *A Château at the Front,* pp. 85–7; Colombel, *Journal d'une infirmière d'Arras,* pp. 20–4; Weiss, *Mémoires,* I: 187–91; AN F⁷ 12937–12939 reports from Prefects to the Minister of the Interior (cited, the Prefect of Calvados), also Delarue-Mardrus, *Mes mémoires,* pp. 190–1 and Mme Henry Taudière, *En pensant aux absents: Histoire de l'ambulance de Absie (de septembre 1914 à mai 1915)* (Paris: Plon-Nourrit et cie., 1915), pp. 9–17.
4. Félix Lejars, *Un hôpital militaire à Paris pendant la guerre: Villemin, 1914–1919* (Paris: Masson et cie., 1923), p. 98.
5. "La Croix-rouge est prête," *Le Petit parisien,* 3 August 1914; Maria Léra [Marc Hélys, pseud.], *Cantinière de la Croix-rouge 1914–1916* (Paris: Perrin et cie., 1917), p. 7; Delétang, *Journal d'une ouvrière,* p. 213.
6. Daudet, *Journal de famille,* p. 61; also Andrieu in Clermont, *Souvenirs de parisiennes,* pp. 37–8.
7. "La Croix-rouge française," *Le Temps,* 3 August 1914.
8. Becker, *Les monuments aux morts* found only one war memorial that included the figure of a nurse, in the chapel of Douaumont. Even the memory of the renowned Scottish Women's Hospital has almost vanished from the Abbey of Royaumont, according to Crofton, *Women of Royaumont,* p. xi.
9. José Roussel-Lépine, "Une ambulance de gare," *Revue des deux mondes* (1 and 15 June 1916): 665–84; 910–34.

10. Lejars, *Villemin*, pp. 97–127.

11. Leroux-Hugon, "Les dames blanches," in Kniebiehler *et al.* (eds), *Cornettes et blouses blanches*, p. 96.

12. Ruault, *Cent ans de Croix rouge*, p. 37; Jean-Pierre Fournier, "Evolution du Service de santé militaire française pendant la guerre de 1914–1918" (Thèse, Montpellier III, 1996), p. 99.

13. Fournier, "Evolution du Service de santé," pp. 467, 618; Dr Alfred Mignon, *Le Service de santé pendant la guerre 1914–1918* (Paris: Masson & cie., 1926–7), IV, pp. 196–7.

14. Fournier, "Evolution du Service de santé," pp. 617–18; Legrand, *L'assistance féminine en temps de guerre*, p. 75; also Lespine, *Les hôpitaux de la Croix-rouge*. The hygienist Francis Marre was still writing about "humanitarian bullets" in *Le Correspondant* 200 no. 5 (5 September 1914): 880–5.

15. Colombel, *Journal d'une infirmière d'Arras*, pp. 13–40.

16. Ruault, *Cent ans de Croix rouge*, p. 144; B. Cohen, "Visites de la Société Internationale," *Revue philanthropique* (1916): 139–43; Leroux-Hugon, "Emergence de la profession," in Kniebiehler *et al.* (eds), *Cornettes et blouses blanches*, p. 51–4; Fournier, "Evolution du Service de santé," p. 98.

17. Noyr in Clermont, *Souvenirs de parisiennes*, p. 191; Léra, *Cantinière*, p. 7.

18. Colombel, *Journal d'une infirmière d'Arras*, p. 13

19. Rabut, *Les étincelles*, pp. 11–12.

20. Legrand, *L'assistance féminine en temps de guerre*. pp. 197–8, 239–41.

21. Mignon, *Le Service de santé*, VI: p. 200.

22. BMD dos 331 Ambulancière, "Faut-il féminiser intégralement les ambulances?" [*Le Journal*, 1916?].

23. SHAT 16 N 2682 and 2683; GQG, Direction de l'arrière, Service de santé personnel.

24. Delétang, *Journal d'une ouvrière*, p. 296.

25. "Doctoresses et infirmières," *Le Petit parisien*, 8 October 1918; Thébaud, *La femme au temps de la guerre de 14*, p. 85.

26. SHAT 7N 159 main d'oeuvre féminine circular 1 August 1916 and 7N 170 Etat majeur de l'armée, Service de santé instructions 8 March 1916, 11 April 1916 and circular 20 June 1916.

27. Lejars, *Villemin*, pp. 150–2.

28. SHAT 16N 2682 GQG DA Service de santé personnel.

29. The SSBM provided approximately 35,000 nurses, the UFF some 20,000 and the ADF about 8,000, according to Ruault, *Cent ans de Croix rouge*, p. 44. These figures refer only to the fully qualified nurses; Leroux-Hugon, "Les dames blanches," p. 96, estimates that 500,000 French women in all volunteered in hospital work during the war.

30. Mignon, *Le Service de santé,* IV: p. 206.
31. Dr Anna Hamilton, "Service des gardes-malades de la Maison de santé protestante de Bordeaux pendant la première année de la guerre," *Revue philanthropique* (1916): 370–1.
32. The SSBM earned more than 500 croix de guerre, the UFF, 300 and the ADF, 133; Ruault, *Cent ans de Croix-rouge,* p. 51.
33. "Les femmes de France," *Le Petit journal,* 14 December 1915 and "Les <<Dames Françaises>> pendant la guerre," *Le Petit journal,* 31 December 1915; Bérard-Camourtères, ed., *Au service de la France,* pp. 6–7; "Une héroïque française reçoit la Légion d'honneur," *Le Petit parisien,* 13 August 1917; Paul Fuchs, "Après la thèse, l'exemple: Madame Maître, femme soldat," *Je sais tout* 13 no. 143 (15 October 1917): 393–4.
34. Barthou, *L'effort de la femme française;* Coubé, *Le patriotisme de la femme française;* Mignon, *Le Service de santé,* I: p. 124.
35. Abensour, *Les vaillantes,* p. 85.
36. Coubé, *La patriotisme de la femme française,* pp. xii–xiii; Maurice Barrès, *Autour de Jeanne d'Arc* (Paris: Librairie Ancienne Edouard Champion, 1916), pp. 73–4.
37. Zeys, "Les femmes et la guerre," p. 177 (emphasis in text).
38. "Les Femmes de France," *Le Petit journal,* 14 December 1915; Dr Anna Hamilton, "Service des gardes malades," *Revue philanthropique* (1916): 373.
39. Delécraz, *1914, Paris,* p. 58; also Aurel, "Moeurs de guerre," p. 34.
40. Lejars, *Villemin,* p. 145; Roussel-Lépine, "Une ambulance de gare," p. 12.
41. Descaves, *La maison anxieuse* , pp. 81–3; also Masson, *Les femmes et la guerre,* pp. 19–20.
42. Léon Schneider, *Au bruit du canon: poésies et souvenirs de guerre* (Paris: Editions littéraires et musicales du Reveil Chansonnier, s. d.).
43. For example, Delétang, *Journal d'une ouvrière,* p. 429 and Daudet, *Journal de famille,* p. 61.
44. Jack de Bussy, *Refugiée et infirmière de guerre* (Paris: Eugène Figuière, 1915), p. 154.
45. Docquois, preface to Geneviève Duhamelet, *Ces dames de l'hôpital 336* (Paris: Albin Michel, 1917), p. 7. The preface claims that Duhamelet, a prolific novelist, was also a Red Cross nurse.
46. Capy, *Une voix de femme,* p. 135.
47. Charles Foley, *Sylvette et son blessé* (Paris: E. Flammarion, 1917), p. 46. Roussel-Lépine, "Une ambulance de gare," p. 682 also contrasted the "diplômée, oh! très diplômée, très suffisante, très digne" with the true nurse "bonne, simple, et vraie. Votre soeur plutôt que votre maître. Une femme avec toute la douceur, toute l'intelligence, toute la vivacité, tout le dévouement."
48. Mignon, *Le Service de santé* , IV: pp. 207–8, 299 and Lejars, *Villemin,* pp. 143–8.

49. Eydoux-Démians, *Notes d'une infirmière*, p. 19; Barthou, *L'effort de la femme française*, p. 17.

50. Jules Combarieu, *Les jeunes filles françaises et la guerre* (Paris: Librairie Armand Colin, 1916), p. 136.

51. Bard, *Les filles de marianne*, p. 56; Capy, *Une voix de femme*, pp. 81–2; Gordon, *The Integral Feminist*, p. 142.

52. Lejars, *Villemin*, pp. 161–3.

53. Courson, *La femme française pendant la guerre*, pp. 41–2; also Renée d'Ulmes, *Auprès des blessés* (Paris: Librairie Alphonse Lemerre, 1916), pp. 29–30.

54. Maugue, *L'identité masculine*, pp. 54–64.

55. Roussell-Lépine, "Une ambulance de gare," p. 669.

56. Capy, *Une voix de femme*, pp. 84–5; also Deleutre, *1914–1915; femmes et gosses*, pp. 2–4 .

57. Lejars, *Villemin*, p. 145. Many novels used this plot, for example Bussy, *Refugiée*; Pierre de Valrose, *Une âme d'amante pendant la guerre 1914* (Paris: Perrin et cie., 1916) and Provins, *Ceux d'hier*.

58. Abensour, *Les vaillantes*, p. 92; also Foley, *Sylvette*, p. 7; Lejars, *Villemin*, p. 145; and Narquet, "La française de demain," p. 566.

59. Boulenger, *Charlotte*, pp. 124–5; Michaux, *En marge du drame*, p. 135.

60. Descaves, *La maison anxieuse*, pp. 80–1.

61. Lejars, *Villemin*, p. 145. Lejars carried out this injunction in his own work. In his chapter on hospital personnel, he named all the male staff – colleagues, medical assistants, pharmacists, even orderlies – but not a single nurse. Mignon, *Le Service de santé*, I: pp. 39–40 also insisted upon self-effacement and deplored independence, but he did not refuse to celebrate his nurses' achievements. He recorded the citations of nurses in his sector, I: pp. 300–1.

62. Docquois, preface to Duhamelet, *Ces dames de l'hôpital*, p. 10; also la Grange, *Open House in Flanders*, pp. 194–5.

63. Lejars, *Villemin*, p. 102; Corday, *The Paris Front*, p. 12; Michaux, *En marge*, p. 47; Masson, *Les femmes et la guerre*, p. 13.

64. AN F⁷ 12939, Haute-Vienne. See *Le Petit parisien*, 15 October and 11 December 1914 for stories about "false" nurses and Pierre Decourcelle, *Les marchands de Patrie*, a serial novel published in *Le Journal* in 1916 for a typical nursing espionage story.

65. Theweleit, *Male Fantasies*, I: pp. 79–100 identifies in post-war German *Freikorps* novels the contrast of the true "White Nurse," maternal, protective and conservative, with the false "Red Nurse" who is a working-class whore. Red Cross propaganda had insured that no "Red Nurses" appeared in French wartime writing; but the nurse-*mondaine* admitted some of the sexuality of the "Red Nurse" that had been erased from the "White Nurse" in both cultures.

66. Maxime Formont, *La dame blanche* (Paris: A. Lemerre, 1917), p. 15.

67. Yvignac, *J'avais une marraine*, pp. 58–9.

68. Audoin-Rouzeau, *Men at War 1914–1918*, p. 131.

69. Masson, *Les femmes et la guerre*, pp. 19–20; Bontoux, *Les françaises et la grande guerre*, p. 148; Combarieu, *Les jeunes filles*, pp. 139 and Louise Bodin, "Voyons, mesdames," *Voix de femmes* no. 8 (19 December 1917).

70. Dr Edouard Toulouse, *La réforme sociale: Question sexuelle de la femme* (Paris: Bibliothèque Charpentier, 1918), pp. 71–2.

71. Dottin-Orsini, *Cette femme qu'ils disent fatale*, p. 246.

72. Toulouse, *La réforme sociale*, p. 12. Not all commentators saw this revelation as inevitable. Masson, *Les femmes et la guerre*, p. 24, suggested that if unmarried women were allowed to nurse at all, they must be confined to dressing "le doigt, la main tout just, et peut-être le bras."

73. Formont, *La dame blanche*, p. 25.

74. Lechartier, *La charité et la guerre*, p. 27.

75. For example, Masson, *Les femmes et la guerre*; Abensour, *Les vaillantes*; Lejars, *Villemin*; Bontoux, *Les françaises et la grande guerre*.

76. Paul Fussell, *The Great War and Modern Memory* (New York: Oxford University Press, 1975); Cruickshank, *Variations on Catastrophe;* Samuel Hynes, *A War Imagined: The First World War and English Culture* (London: The Bodley Head, 1990).

77. Cochet, *L'opinion et le moral des soldats* ; Audoin-Rouzeau, "Bourage de crâne," in Becker and Audoin-Rouzeau (eds), *Les sociétés européennes*, pp. 171–2.

78. Mary Jean Green, "1914–1918: La grande guerre," in Denis Hollier, ed., *De la littérature française* (Paris: Bordas, 1993), pp. 795–801.

79. Mosse, *Fallen Soldiers*, pp. 198–9; also Rose Maria Bracco, *Merchants of Hope: British Middlebrow Writers and the First World War, 1919–1939* (Providence, RI: Berg, 1993).

80. Until very recently, the literary criticism of First World War writings excluded women's writing from war literature. See, for example, Maurice Rieuneau, *Guerre et revolution dans le roman français de 1919 à 1939* (Paris: Klincksieck, 1974). As Hynes, *A War Imagined*, pp. 158–9, points out, combatants alone were presumed to know the truth of the war.

81. Godfroy, *Souvenirs*, p. 5 (emphasis in text).

82. Claire Tylee, *The Great War and Women's Consciousness; Images of Militarism and Womanhood in Women's Writings, 1914–1964* (Iowa City, IA: University of Iowa Press, 1990), pp. 47–74.

83. Noëlle Roger, *Les carnets d'une infirmière* (Paris: Attinger frères, 1915), 1: pp. 22–9. Roger, a pseudonym for Hélène Pittard, was a prolific novelist. It is not clear if this work is indeed the diary of an anonymous nurse, as she claims, or the product of her own observation and imagination.

84. Hélène Leune, *Tel qu'ils sont: Notes d'une infirmière de la Croix-rouge* (Paris: Librairie Larousse, 1915) and a similar piece, Eydoux-Démians,

Notes d'une infirmière (1915) appear to be pseudo-memoirs. They report, as if personally experienced, atrocity and nobility stories that show up in other propaganda of the period.

85. M. de La Boulaye, *Croix et cocarde* (Paris: Librairie Plon, 1919). Others include Colombel, *Journal d'une infirmière d'Arras*; Jeanne Antelme, *Avec l'armée d'orient: Notes d'une infirmière à Moudros* (Paris: Emile-Paul frères, 1916) and Julie Crémieux, *Croquis d'heures vécues, 1914–1919* (Fourmies: Imp. Bachy, 1934).

86. Madeleine Clemenceau Jacquemaire, *Les hommes de bonne volonté* (Paris: Calmann et Levy, 1919), pp. 265–6.

87. La Boulaye, *Croix et cocarde*, p. 223; also Crémieux, *Heures vécues*, p. 39.

88. For example, Grace McDougall, *A Nurse at War: Nursing adventures in Belgium and France* (London, 1917). The only similar French title is Antelme, *Avec l'armée d'orient*. See Henriette Donner, "Under the Cross – Why V. A. D.s Performed the Filthiest Task in the Dirtiest War: Red Cross Women Volunteers, 1914–1918," *Journal of Social History* 30 no. 3 (Spring 1997): 687–704 and Regina Schulte, "The Sick Warrior's Sister: Nursing During the First World War," trans. Pamela Selwyn, in *Gender Relations in German History: Power, Agency and Experience from the Sixteenth to the Twentieth Century*, ed. Lynn Abrams and Elizabeth Harvey, (Durham, NC: Duke University Press, 1997), pp. 121–41.

89. Godfroy, *Souvenirs*, p. 6.

90. Eydoux-Démians, *Notes d'une infirmière,* depicted Sister Gabrielle as the perfect nurse; for La Boulaye, *Croix et cocarde*, it was Sister Rosalie.

91. Roger, *Carnets*, 1: p. 11.

92. For example, Roger, *Carnets*, 2: p. 4 and Taudière, *En pensant aux absents, passim.*

93. Colombel, *Journal d'une infirmière d'Arras*, pp. 83–4; Juliette Martineau, *Journal d'une infirmière* (Angers: Imprimerie G. Grassin, 1916), pp. 28–9. Mignon, *Le Service de santé*, IV: p. 297 recognized this dilemma.

94. Docquois, preface to Duhamelet, *Ces dames de l'hôpital*, pp. 16–17 (ellipses in text).

95. Juliette Martineau, "Les infirmières au front," *La Renaissance* 4 no. 4 (22 January 1916): 23–4.

96. La Boulaye, *Croix et cocarde*; Jacquemaire, *Bonne volonté*, p. 37.

97. La Boulaye, *Croix et cocarde*, pp. 137–8; Jacquemaire, *Bonne volonté*, pp. 10; 21–2.

98. Numerous circulars from the Service de santé bear witness to this rivalry, exacerbated in some cases by vindictive behavior toward the Red Cross volunteers by some doctors and hospital administrators. See SHAT 7N 170 circular 20 June 1916 and SHAT 7N 159 circular 1 August 1916, from the Sous-secrétaire d'Etat du Service de santé militaire. By contrast Dr Lejars, *Villemin*, pp. 161–67, clearly preferred his Red Cross nurses and heaped scorn upon the paid nursing staff.

99. Martineau, *Journal d'une infirmière*, pp. 2–3. Lejars, *Villemin*, p. 156 recommended that Red Cross nurses from different organizations should not be assigned to work together.

100. Weiss, *Mémoires*, I: p. 192; also Noyr in Clermont, *Souvenirs de parisiennes*, p. 202.

101. Roger, *Carnets*, 1: p. 24; La Boulaye, *Croix et cocarde*, p. 89; Jacquemaire, *Bonne volonté*, p. 151.

102. Jacquemaire, *Bonne volonté*, p. 91, confirmed by SHAT 16N 2682 GQG DA Service de santé personnel.

103. Une doctoresse, "La profession d'infirmière en France," *Revue philanthropique* (1916): 238–40.

104. La Boulaye, *Croix et cocarde*.

105. In her novel, *Ces dames de l'hôpital*, pp. 156–7, Duhamelet set her characters a game of defining *le cafard*; but the nursing accounts make it clear that it was no game but seriously debilitating. See, for example Colombel, *Journal d'une infirmière d'Arras*, pp. 37–40, and Jacquemaire, *Bonne volonté*, pp. 234–6 as well as La Boulaye, *Croix et cocarde*, and Antelme, *Avec l'armée d'orient*.

106. Godfroy, *Souvenirs d'ambulance*; Roger, *Carnets*, 1: pp. 5–9.

107. Jacquemaire, *Bonne volonté*, especially the vignettes "Septs cents pieds gelés" and "Les Rentrants;" Colombel, *Journal d'une infirmière d'Arras*, pp. 100–1.

108. Mignon, *Le Service de santé*, IV: p. 298. For a British example, see Crofton, *Women of Royaumont*.

109. For example, Jacquemaire's gratitude toward her assistant, *Bonne volonté*, pp. 83–4 and Crémieux's description of falling asleep on a friend's shoulder in a dug-out, *Heures vécues*, p. 46.

110. Antelme, *Avec l'armée d'orient*, p. 36.

6

French Women in the War Economy

When interviewed about her recollections of the First World War, Mme Norman fondly recalled her fifteen-year-old self and the thrilling days of the fall of 1914: "The work of the harvest fulfilled my aspirations: the outdoors, physical exercise suited my temperament and my excellent health. Sixty-five years later I still wonder by what miracle we succeeded with that first harvest."[1] But Madame X of the Limousin had different memories. A young woman in 1914, she was left by her husband's mobilization with a three-year-old child and all the work of their farm. The war was no time for exciting adventure, but for unremitting labor, made more difficult by her fears for her husband and her worry that she was neglecting her son's upbringing. It is little wonder that she greeted the armistice and her husband's return with relief. "We returned to our own work," she recalled with satisfaction.[2]

Two different women, two different memories of work during the war: but their experience may not have been so different. During the war, the same woman might feel all of these things: pride in accomplishment, fatigue and resentment, longing for pre-war routines. Their experience was often an ambiguous one, and official policy and contemporary discourse underlined and exaggerated its ambiguities. What the public, including women themselves, wanted from women's work changed abruptly and frequently during the war. Sympathy and praise were shadowed by suspicion and blame. Women workers were victims, left in the lurch by mobilization; they were heroines, cheerfully shouldering patriotic tasks; they were profiteers, making money from male sacrifice; they were victims again, forced by the war and enticed by their own weaknesses to neglect their true duties to their children upon whom rode the future of France. It is not surprising that both at the time and in their memories decades later, the women who replaced men in the French workforce during the war had difficulty interpreting their own experience.

169

Initially the government did not intend to mobilize women, or indeed, any civilians, into a war economy. Like civilian life in general, the economy was to vanish for the duration; and in fact, mobilization virtually shut it down, particularly women's jobs in textiles, the garment industry and domestic service. Once the economy began to revive, these sectors remained in deep recession.[3] In July 1915, although male wages had returned to, or even exceeded, pre-war levels, most women were making, at best, only three-quarters of what they had earned a year earlier. It took Parisian garment workers until the fall of 1918 to achieve wages comparable to what they had been making before the war.[4]

At the Bordeaux Conference of 20 September 1914, the Ministry of War realized that the government must revitalize the economy in order to fight the war, particularly to produce munitions. In the spring of 1915, the newly created Undersecretary of Artillery, Albert Thomas, began to recommend that munitions factories hire women; but the big push to replace a male industrial labor force with a female one did not begin until the summer of 1916, when all available men were needed for the battle at Verdun. By the end of the war, there were about 430,000 women employed in the defense industries, about one-quarter of this labor force.[5] Although these women continued to earn less than men by as much as 40 per cent, nonetheless they earned considerably more than in "women's work," and this was as true in the provinces as it was in Paris. In the Dauphinais, for example, although a woman working in a munitions plant earned only about two-thirds of what a man earned, this was still one or two francs more a day than she could earn as a textile worker or shop girl.[6]

In his wartime study of the French economy, Charles Picquenard identified a number of attitudes that defined women's place in the workforce. He concluded that although supply and demand had much to do with women's limited employment options and low wages, it failed to explain everything. Also at work was "the very lively prejudice of both employers and workers that insists that a woman must not earn as much as a man."[7] In many people's minds, women's role in the wartime labor market was not primarily an economic issue, but a moral one. As the economic historian Laura Lee Downs has argued, while employers claimed to pay men by the value of their work, they claimed to pay women according to their needs – as women.[8] Earning money meant spending money, and spending money spelled emancipation. The desire to curb feminine independence lurked within government policy and private charity toward women in the first years of the war, burst forth in the criticism of replacement workers in 1916 and 1917, and saturated the debate over maternity that dominated discussion and policy regarding working women in the last year of the war.

Such attitudes betrayed considerable ambivalence about mobilizing women to the war effort, especially when this involved women doing work traditionally done by men. In anecdotes that accused working women of indulging themselves in fine clothes, fancy food and alcohol while their men died in the trenches, commentators expressed their disapproval that women should benefit from war work. This attitude developed into an extended discussion of working women's (un)fitness as mothers. The presumed conflict between work and maternity had been a theme in the discussion of mobilizing women into the labor force since the effort began; but it assumed steadily larger proportions from 1917 to the end of the war and beyond. The discussion of workers' maternity explained why, although the French economy might continue to need women workers to replace the men who had died in the war, and although many French women, bereft by these same deaths of male support, might need to work, it would be best for all – men, women and especially for France – if women retreated from the workforce, or at least from masculine jobs. Women like Mme Norman who had been hailed as patriots, doing valiant service in the national defense in 1914, by 1917 were the cause of pursed lips and shaking heads; their efforts had endangered the race.

The Sacred Debt to National Solidarity

Convinced that any war would be short, and mesmerized by the immediate needs of the military, the government had made no plans to mobilize the economy nor had it considered how civilians would support themselves in their immobility. Conscription law, dating from 1905 and revised as recently as August 1913, included the principle of compensation to support the conscript's family in time of war; but no law had turned this principle into policy. As soon as mobilization was announced, however, mayors and Prefects warned the Minister of the Interior that some kind of aid from the State had to be forthcoming immediately. Local funds for public assistance would be woefully inadequate to provide for the many women and children suddenly left destitute.[9] On 5 August, the legislature created

military allowances [*allocations militaires*] to support the dependants of mobilized soldiers left in financial need. The law authorized
the payment of 1.25F per day to needy adult dependants – essentially
wives and elderly parents – with a supplement of 0.50F for each
dependent child under the age of 16.

What was the government's purpose in creating this allowance?
The socialist feminist Marcelle Capy saw in the military allowances
society's recognition of its collective responsibility toward "whoever
finds himself deprived of work or support." She proclaimed: "One
granted allowances. It was no longer a matter of a favor, an 'assistance,' but of a right."[10] If it was such a right, however, it was not
one granted to women, but to men. Georges Rendel, writing in 1915
on "The Theory and Practice of Military Allowances in France,"
called the allowances "the discharge of a national moral debt" owed
to the soldier, and Senator Paul Strauss stated: "It gives the combatants complete confidence and security about the fate of their loved
ones."[11]

Despite its apparent simplicity, the program of military allowances proved very difficult for local officials to administer. In keeping
with the practice of public assistance, many officials thought their
duty was to deny as many applications as possible to save public
funds.[12] Initially they often denied the applications of women who
had any property, who worked or whose children worked, who they
thought could work, or whose benefits, when the children's supple-
ments were added, seemed too high. They also treated the mandated
payment as a maximum and granted lower amounts, especially
to peasant women, claiming that the full benefit would be an
incitement to idleness.[13] Maurice Barrès believed that some officials
played political favorites as well, refusing allowances to the families
of soldiers who had voted for the opposition or who were practicing
Catholics.[14]

Historians generally agree with contemporary criticism; the
program started badly – so badly, in fact, that in the fall of 1914,
some soldiers deserted after their wives had been denied allowances.[15] However, the distribution of benefits gradually liberalized
until it reached almost all servicemen's wives and families. Besieged
with complaints, the Ministry of the Interior issued circular after
circular, instructing commissions to interpret the law "in the wide
spirit of justice and humanity." The most controversial expansion,
advocated by socialists and syndicalists, extended benefits to non-
marital "companions" and illegitimate children.[16]

Two weeks after establishing the military allowances, the government also created national unemployment benefits at the same basic rate. However, the Ministry of Labor viewed most women's occupations as "ancillary" and thus ineligible for benefits.[17] Also, women could not receive both unemployment benefits and a military allowance, since the first required them to have been self-supporting while the second required them to have been dependent. The government ignored the situation of many working-class women who had depended upon their husbands' or sons' wages as well as upon their own to support their families. In the government's eyes, a woman could be a dependant or a worker but not both, and in either case, her daily allowance would equal only a fraction of the family's former income.

The military allowance was intended to solidify morale by assuring the soldiers that the gender system would be maintained in their absence, that their dependants would remain dependent and protected. But the payment was so low, lower even than typical women's wages, that it drove many women on to the job market, where they joined the legion of women whom the war had thrown out of work. Although policy-makers were immediately aware of this problem, the government did little to address it. New proposals came from private organizations like the Women Students Association, who called for a register of all unemployed women with professional qualifications to be used to recruit replacements for men in laboratories, schools, the civil service and industry.[18] They envisioned an economy functioning during the war; but in August 1914 the only sector of the economy that the government deemed necessary to the war effort was agriculture. The government's only specific effort to fight female unemployment was to "repatriate" unemployed Parisian women to their rural places of origin.

Promoted by the Comte de Las Cases, Senator from the Lozère, endorsed by the Minister of Labor and recommended by the Prime Minister, repatriation would kill two birds with one stone; it would relieve unemployment in Paris and provide labor needed for the harvest. The Central Syndicate of Farmers of France organized the effort, subsidized by the railroads and the government, who jointly picked up most of the cost of train fares to the countryside.[19] However, Couyba in the Ministry of Labor reported that the program was not popular with its intended beneficiaries. "I have encountered certain difficulties. Poverty brings with it a sort of prostration and moral decadence. Many women said 'What would we do there?'"

They also worried that by leaving Paris, they would jeopardize their rights to unemployment benefits or military allowances. Coubya dismissed these questions, asserting "the women and children that we send back will find something to do there" and promising that the Ministry was taking all the measures possible to ensure the continued payment of military allowances. Meanwhile, Las Cases blithely assumed that, in the countryside, thousands of women and their children could "easily be housed and fed cheaply and could even be of some help."[20] Probably wisely, few women entrusted their survival to such cavalier planners.

For the vast majority of unemployed women without resources, the only recourse was to charity. Fortunately, in the panoply of war charities that elite women organized in August 1914 to aid the soldiers, refugees, the wounded and prisoners of war, they did not ignore destitute women and their families. One such charity was the Association for the Protection of Widows and Orphans of the 1914 War, headed by the Duchesse d'Uzès. Frédéric Masson lent his name and considerable publicity skills to another, "For the Women," founded in late August 1914 to help unemployed women in the spirit of feminine nurturing: "Oh, French sisters, be sweet to one another, be tender, be generous, be humane! Bend over these sad lives and listen to the songs that arise, the songs and the sobs. Be fraternal to the forsaken, the abandoned, the isolated! Oh French sisters! Let's be regenerated by love while we wait to be regenerated by victory!"[21]

This was a far cry from Capy's idea of social rights. Such charities usually doled out only a small amount of financial assistance with a large amount of advice. "Being humane" often meant inspecting housekeeping, overseeing childrearing and scrutinizing morals. The Association for the Protection of Widows and Orphans of the 1914 War used the opportunity of handing out ten francs a month to visit the beneficiaries in their homes, bringing them, in the words of one admirer, "the even more indispensable, moral support that cares for children with a mother's heart." Aided by the Dames du Calvaire, these benevolent ladies were particularly interested in sending children to religious schools.[22]

The most common form of charity designed to aid unemployed women was the *ouvroir*, or charity workroom. In August and September 1914, elite women opened hundreds of sewing work-rooms, supported by their own money and by private donations. Organizers saw them primarily as charities, to provide emergency subsistence and moral protection to needy women. Many paid

Charity workrooms

derisory wages – the journalist Maria Léra praised one that paid only 25 sous a day[23] – or provided a midday meal in lieu of wages. The most publicized and highly praised were the workrooms run by the Red Cross, such as the one housed and funded by the Institute de France. Intended to supplement the military allowance, the Red Cross's *ouvroir* paid women one franc to work four hours a day. They were forbidden to work longer "for fear that without them, their homes would be abandoned."[24]

These charity workrooms were intended to be short-lived, until the war ended, or, as victory receded into the future, until the economy recovered. But month followed month without the needle trades rebounding. The continuing depression was due in part to a decrease in the demand for clothing and to the large number of women seeking work, but also to the proliferation of workrooms that operated as charities rather than as employment. Socialists and labor leaders pointed that by paying less than the market value for labor, charity workrooms were actually hurting the unemployed by depressing wages. As both the war and unemployment dragged on into the winter, some of the *ouvroirs'* supporters began to agree. In December 1914, the Women Students Association condemned *ouvroirs* that undercut wages as unproductive and unpatriotic.[25]

The solution was for workrooms to become businesses by making uniforms, blankets and other material for the army. Some well-connected women, like Valentine Thomson, editor of *La Vie féminine* and daughter of the Minister of the Navy, secured government contracts for their workrooms, as did women's trade unions; but in general, military procurement officers preferred to contract with established entrepreneurs.[26] The only recourse for most workrooms was to become sub-contractors, or sub-sub-contractors, a move that left them back where they started, paying starvation wages.

Edouard Herriot, the leftist mayor of Lyons, publicized the scandal of the sub-contracting system that exploited the charity workshops. He spoke to the legislature of his own efforts to help the war effort and give work to unemployed women by running an *ouvroir*. When he obtained a sub-contract to finish two hundred pairs of army pants, he thought the effort was on a firm footing. However, after completing and dispatching the work, he received the contractor's bill for damaged work, thread and other materials, which came to more than the contract itself – Herriot ended up paying out of his own pocket.[27] Politicians on the Left, like Herriot, and feminists like

Gabrielle Duchêne, had been trying for several years to regulate home work, and in December 1913 had finally pushed a bill through the Chamber of Deputies; but it had languished in the Senate ever since. The war, however, shone a different light on the garment industry. Its workers were now war victims, thrown out of work or deprived of their natural support by mobilization. What is more, they were making uniforms for their husbands and sons; it was scandalous that they should be exploited by war profiteers. Herriot's revelations and emotional speeches by other leftist politicians led to the passage of labor regulations for home work in the garment industry in July 1915.[28]

Louise Delétang, a Parisian seamstress and labor activist, kept a diary during the war.[29] Familiar with the bureaucracy in her neighborhood as well as with the garment industry, Delétang was involved in all aspects of the unemployment crisis in the first months of the war. Her local government, that of the 5th *arrondissement* in Paris, delegated the task of investigating applicants for military allowances to schoolmistresses. Delétang's former schoolteacher asked her to help, since she knew many women of the neighborhood. Delétang took on the job with enthusiasm, pleased to assist women in emergencies. She reported that the women she interviewed were "calm and resigned," but very anxious about their husbands' safety and their families' survival (pp. 13–15). However, as the workload increased, her sympathy for the applicants waned; insistent upon their rights, they insulted the staff and sat chatting while the administrators "worked day and night" (p. 24). She had more sympathy for working women like herself.

The unemployment crisis hit women like her immediately. On 8 August, she reported in her diary, "Everywhere it is a ceaseless chase for work. Worry about tomorrow deadens the anguish over separation. So many women say to me: 'If I had work, I wouldn't ask for anything more'" (p. 16). Active in the Working Women's Association (*Association Ouvrière*), she helped the group set up an *ouvroir*, but was shocked to discover that it could not even pay as much as the unemployment benefits (p. 27). Even so, it was better than another workroom she discovered. Housed in a former automobile showroom on the Champs Elysées, the organizers used the big windows to display the working women "like strange beasts," in an effort to encourage sympathy and raise money. Meanwhile, the women worked six and a half hours a day in return for a meal (pp. 61–3). In December, her workroom joined several others to create the Federation of Organizations of Female Work ("what a long name," she commented) in order to obtain military contracts that would permit them to pay a living wage. They found, however that the military preferred to get the work done below cost by charity workrooms (pp. 101–2). Later Delétang concluded that charitable *ouvroirs* were "maladroit, sterile and even demoralizing . . . they sacrifice charity's resources by favoring the exploiter without much improving the lot of the exploited" (pp. 187–8).

Many of her diary entries in this first year of the war recounted her own efforts to find work that would keep her alive. In January 1915, in the absence of better alternatives, she agreed to sew pillowcases for a big department store's white sale. With complicated pleating, hemstitching and buttonholes, each case took an hour and a half to complete. When she, her sister and mother all worked on the job, they could only make 2.40F a day, less than a third of their pre-war wages. However, all other piecework was nearly as badly paid, be it gloves, pajamas, men's trousers, military coats, or shirts, each of which they tried in the weeks to come. In February, Delétang sighed: "I've changed jobs again . . . Twelve jobs, thirteen miseries" (p. 133). Only in the spring did the garment industry begin to pick up – fueled in part by orders for mourning clothes; but wages and hours still were short. Several of Delétang's friends, skilled dressmakers, worked for a fashion house in the morning and still sewed at a workroom in the afternoon (p. 175). In the summer the workrooms began to close as work became more generally available, though still at below-normal wages.

The French government hesitated even to recognize the problem of female unemployment in the first months of the war. Owing to its belief in a short war, it regarded the economic mobilization of women as unnecessary. Women's role was to wait passively for their men, their natural protectors and supporters, to return. To help them do this, the government quickly authorized military allowances, while private individuals, mostly elite women, organized charities. Meanwhile, as Herriot claimed to the Senate and as Delétang's diary substantiates, the government was willing to exploit women's unemployment to obtain goods at cut-rate prices, all the while denying that women's work was necessary to the war effort. There was one important exception, however: French peasant women. Because the war began in August, agriculture could not close down like the rest of the economy. The crops could not wait the two or three months that French men would need to beat Germany and return to the fields. If France was to eat, if her defenders on the frontiers were to eat, at least this group of French women had to be mobilized.

The Heroines of the Harvest

Peasants were the one group of women upon whom the French government counted for immediate action. The war had broken out in the midst of the harvest; elderly men, young boys and especially women would have to complete it. On 6 August, Prime Minister René Viviani issued "An Appeal to French Women:"

> Rise up, then, French women, young children, daughters and sons of the fatherland! Replace in the work of the fields those who are on the fields of battle. Prepare to show them, tomorrow, the soil cultivated, the crops harvested, the fields sown! In these grave times, there is no lowly labor. Everything is great that serves the country. Rise up! To action! To work! Tomorrow there will be glory for everyone.
> Long live the Republic! Long live France!

Prefects and journalist who saw women take over the harvest credited it to this stirring appeal;[30] but feminists like Léon Abensour and Jane Misme thought it superfluous. Peasant women, they pointed out, were accustomed to helping the men in the fields at harvest time.[31] But officials and feminists did agree that the 1914 harvest was a success due to women's work.

The Republic had called, peasant women had responded; and France had its first war heroines, the strong, "simple," dignified *paysannes*. In the *Echo de Paris*, Catholic novelist René Bazin celebrated one of them. "No one can say that Aimée Cotereau wept in public. Small in stature she was, indeed, but brave, too, able to keep her heart in silence, accustomed for centuries to being put to the test . . . She didn't sing like a true drover but she kept the team going straight, saying the needed words in her little voice."[32] Charming, even when dressed in trousers, blushing when praised, so gay at her work that cleaning hops became "an improvised dance," the peasant woman rose to the challenge with feminine grace.[33] The most marvelous of all were the women behind the plow, celebrated by feminists, socialists and conservatives alike as the perfect symbol of feminine patriotism in action.[34] The only appropriate monument to their efforts was their own figures standing tall in the fields, "silhouettes that appear as clear-cut as bronze statues on the national horizon."[35]

Michel Augé-Laribé, the Secretary General of the National Confederation of Agricultural Associations and the leading analyst of wartime agriculture, suspected that the sudden spate of newspaper articles lauding peasant women did not result from simple admiration; it was a calculated effort to raise morale by convincing the French population that their food supply was secure.[36] Touched off by the fact that the war had interrupted the harvest, fears of food shortage were magnified by memories of the Franco-Prussian war. By 6 August, Parisians were already stockpiling food, and items such as salt, macaroni and bottled gas disappeared from store shelves.[37] The monumental image of the peasant woman in her field had a calming influence.

But the story of the peasant heroine struck deeper chords as well. Propagandists created for peasant women a role not unlike that of the invasion heroines, symbolizing in their feminine fragility ("small of stature"), their endurance and their miraculous achievements, the inevitable triumph of France over Germany. While the invasion heroine demonstrated the superiority of French civilization over German *Kultur*, the French peasant woman embodied the endurance and strength of nature and tradition compared to the bumptious technology and modernism of Germany.[38] As the war dragged on, peasant women's willingness to endure and to produce came to mean more than a necessary food supply; paired with the endurance of the men in the trenches, it signified the deep-rooted strength of France. In 1916 René Bazin placed the two figures side by side in the patriotic pantheon. Peasant women, he wrote,

> brought in the harvest of 1914, then sowed and brought in the harvest of 1915, then again sowed and brought in the harvest of 1916; many are discouraged; others have been vanquished by the extent of the effort; but most have held out, like the men in the trenches. The war supported as much by the daughters of France as by her sons! What a magnificent gift offered to the absent ones and to the country![39]

Extravagant praise of peasant women's accomplishments had a less noble political purpose; it excused the government from addressing the problems that the war had created for peasant agriculture. The battle of the 1914 harvest was won, certainly; but, as even Bazin admitted in 1916, those that followed were not so successful. If he had waited a year to write his praise, he would have had to explain the food shortages in 1917 and 1918. There was a serious labor shortage in the countryside, and all the panegyrics to the heroism of the French peasant woman could not fill it.

France had a finite labor force that was required to fight the war, produce armaments and produce food, all at the same time. In this three-way tug-of-war, despite the military's occasional lip-service to agriculture's importance, agriculture always placed a distant third. However, the victory of the 1914 harvest appeared to justify this ranking. If French women could win this battle unaided in 1914, then they could do it again and again and again. In the spring of 1917, the government published another appeal "To All the French Men and Women of Our Countryside" to repeat the miracle of 1914: "You are working for French Victory and Peace. The Country has confidence in you. The Country counts on you."[40] And, if the harvests came up short, as they increasingly did, then the culprit was close at hand. The peasant woman was a convenient scapegoat for the shortcomings of a wartime agricultural policy that, according to Augé-Laribé, was much better at "imposing sacrifices and regulations on the peasants, much less able to find the means to aid them to accomplish their work."[41]

Even before the war, social conservatives had blamed peasant women for the depopulation of the countryside and the decline of rural life, the backbone of French civilization. Tempted by the luxuries of the city, girls refused to marry peasants, giving them the choice of celibacy or renouncing their vocation – for, in this literature, farming was not merely a job, it was a spiritual calling.[42] During the war, when food production became peasants' patriotic duty, the "abandonment of the soil" became tantamount to desertion in the discourse of the left as well as the right. Jeannine, writing in the syndicalist paper, *La Bataille*, admonished peasant women in language similar to that of René Bazin in the *Echo de Paris* and Emmanuel Labat in the *Revue des deux mondes*. Her duty, above all, was to "Hold Out in the Fields," as one of Bazin's articles proclaimed. She must shun the bright lights and easy money of the city, and listen to "the commandment of the instinct of life, the call of the land and of her ancestors, the commandment and call of the Fatherland itself."[43]

In 1914, the French peasant woman was a war heroine; by 1917 she was a potential deserter. Interviews with peasant women conducted by historians in the 1970s suggest that they saw themselves in relationship to these images. They claimed credit for having accomplished "miracles," and they were proud that they had stayed on the land. But their stories departed in major ways from the myths. Mostly they recalled their wartime experience as back-breaking work: "It was hard . . . It wasn't fun." "In the fields morning 'til night."[44] Success depended less upon their own strength, will-power or patriotism than on the size of the farm and, especially, the composition of the labor force.

First of all, the story of peasant women's triumph in the harvest of 1914 was something of a fiction. Some young men remained at home until the end of August, while some older men, initially called up for guard duty during mobilization, were sent home in September. This was the case with Mme B's father in Gençay. Despite the mobilization of her husband and the farm servants, with her father and two teenage brothers at home, the gender division of labor hardly changed: "For them, it was the field work, for us it was the house-work," she recalled.[45] In 1914, there was a labor shortage, but not yet an absolute dearth. If some farms were suddenly deprived of key workers, others still had labor to lend or to sell. In the moment of crisis, the impulse was to pull together.[46]

But this was a strategy that could not continue for long. The demands of the military dug deeper and deeper into the supply of men working in agriculture, so that farms not only had less labor power for themselves, they also had less to lend. About 30 per cent of the active male labor force had been mobilized in 1914; by 1918 this had risen to 63 per cent, and even higher for peasants who did not enjoy the exemptions that benefited workers in transportation, mining and heavy industry.[47]

How successfully women could replace men on the farm depended to a large degree upon its size. Large farms that depended upon teams of hired hands, like Marguerite Lesage's sugar beet operation or the Breton farm where Pierre-Jakez Hélias's parents worked, suffered from the mobilization of their laborers, but could often fill their places by mechanization, hiring women or, later in the war, imported labor gangs or prisoners of war.[48] This type of operation also benefited most from the agricultural leaves instituted in 1915. Small marginal operations also survived, and even sometimes prospered, because much of the work had been done by women and children anyway, while the adult men had hired themselves out. During the war, it was the products of the farmyard – eggs, milk, poultry, vegetables – that profited most, rather than grain, which was requisitioned and price-controlled.[49] Mme X from the Limousin, interviewed in the 1970s, recalled that when the war broke out her husband was renting land on a share-cropping contract. On their own small plot of less than an acre they raised vegetables and fattened a few cows and pigs for market. After the 1914 harvest, she gave up the share-cropping contract, supporting herself and her small child on the produce of her garden and animals. She believed herself to have been better off than women left in charge of bigger farms because, although her work was hard, it was familiar.[50] Françoise H from the Beauce, also interviewed in the 1970s, recalled that, on the small farm her parents owned, she and her mother were able to keep the farm going with only occasional hired help to plow, plant and maintain their tools. "My mother had three little fields. I recall that I went to cut the hay and the wheat. It was hard. We didn't have any cows yet. In [19]18 we started by buying a cow and a horse. My mother had the fields plowed and sowed and I was the one to cut them. That wasn't easy."[51] Nevertheless, they prospered, as the cow and the horse attest.

By contrast, it was often difficult to keep medium-sized farms going. Abruptly or gradually stripped of manpower, draft animals and fertilizer, the woman left in charge often had no option but to cut back or cease production altogether. The journalist Maria Léra, traveling in the Poitou in 1917, reported that peasant women were working themselves to death, but were still unable to make ends meet. One war widow wrote to René Bazin to defend peasant women whom he charged with "abandoning the soil." She explained

> Although I myself drive our horses, who are too strong to be entrusted to the old men or the boys, and I load the wagons, I'm not making the value of the rental contract owing to the poor harvest and the increases in wages . . . At present, I can only sow wheat in two-thirds of the land that should be planted in grain. Thus, certain deficit for next year. If I stay on, the little that my husband left to his children will be swallowed up.[52]

The most important factors in the family farm's survival were the size, gender and age of the labor force. Families in which the men were not conscripted because of age, health or an exemption, worked through the war years with the least disruption to gender roles and the most opportunity for profit. In Mme B's family, in which her father and teenage brothers continued to work the fields, the mobilization of her husband and two farm servants meant that occasionally she had to do unaccustomed tasks, such as driving the oxen. But otherwise her work remained the same. By contrast, on Mme T's family's farm, her father struggled through the harvest in 1914 with the help of his daughters, but the mobilization of his son and his son-in-law meant the farm was no longer viable. He gave it up in 1915.[53]

Some women later expressed pride in having learned masculine skills. Mme Norman reported that her older sister Suzanne became a "true miller knowing her trade" during the war, while another sister won admiration for her talent in stacking hay.[54] Despite her father's failure to keep the farm in operation, Mme T's memories of her 20-year-old wartime self sound like the peasant heroine of propaganda: "I myself plowed, an opportunity that I took. I did the *piare* – they said that of women who replaced the men."[55]

But for many, pride in accomplishment was swallowed in pain, frustration and exhaustion. While to the peasant woman of propaganda, plowing was the ultimate triumph, to Emilie Carles it was a source of bitter pain:

> Before he left, Joseph [her brother] taught me to plow. The hardest part wasn't so much dealing with a mule or a yoke of cows as holding on to the handle. I was not tall. I remember we had an ordinary plow, the swing type, with a handle designed for a man. It was far too high for me. When I cut furrows with that contrivance, I got the handle in the chest or face every time I hit a stone. For me plowing was the road to Calvary.[56]

For the sixteen-year old who would become Mme G, the situation was more desperate. With two older brothers in the army, two younger ones in school, an invalid father and a mother tied to his bedside, all the farm work fell upon her and her fourteen-year-old brother. Despite their relentless work, the farm's output fell, and her desperation is evident in her memories, recorded by Martine Benoit sixty years later.

> It was two children who had to maintain and exploit the farm, as best as we could. We worked hard but we lacked management . . . production fell off and the amount of sowed land diminished . . . We were often overwhelmed with fatigue and discouragement. In our conversations, in our ideas, we took voyages to free us from our misery.[57]

The future Mme G and her brother earned no recognition or compensation for the four years' toil that kept their family's farm solvent. When their elder brother returned from the army, he took over the farm as his father's heir, and the two younger children were demoted to the rank of farm servants.

The success of French agriculture during the war depended mostly upon the resources available to peasant producers, and these progressively dwindled, while the government's efforts to fill the gaps were, in Augé-Laribé's words, "fatally incoherent and provisional."[58] In particular, the government's policies to provide agricultural workers in the form of immigrants or prisoners of war, or the much-publicized programs to use schoolchildren during their summer vacation as field hands[59] were woefully inadequate and unadapted to peasant agriculture. The program that peasant women demanded and eagerly awaited, agricultural leaves for peasant soldiers, was also the biggest disappointment. Begun in the spring of 1915 and used intermittently thereafter, the policy deployed soldiers to help in the seasons of heaviest farm work. However, as one local official reported, peasant women had definite expectations of the policy, which the government had no intention of fulfilling.

> When a woman comes to consult me on this subject, saying that she wants her husband, son or brother to receive a two-week leave to help with the hay-making or similarly urgent work, I tell her that it is possible to let her have a man, but that I can't promise that this man will necessarily be her husband, son or brother, since they may not be available. So she refuses . . . These women don't want to understand that one man might get a leave while another would not. This is a distinction that escapes them. They want their husband, brother, cousin, son or nephew; they don't want anyone else. So they prefer to predict failure – and spread recriminations about the military and civil authorities.[60]

The misunderstanding here was on both sides. If the peasant woman refused to understand the army's priorities, the creators and administrators of this policy refused to understand the realities of small family farms. Although peasant women were obviously very anxious to secure leave for their own relatives, they also wanted farm workers who would fit into the division of labor that obtained on their own particular farms. One man was not as good as another; a worker who had to be instructed and supervised as well as housed, fed and paid was not worth the trouble. The program worked best on large commercial farms, where farm laborers truly were interchangeable; but even there it did not solve the labor problem. Military priorities came first, and if the military's need for manpower coincided with peak agricultural seasons, as was the case in the spring and early summer of 1916, 1917 and 1918, all agricultural leaves would be abruptly canceled, and farmers who had contracted for their help would be out of luck. The Marquise de Foucault wrote in her diary on 28 June 1916: "There is no way of obtaining manual labor, either civil or military . . . all agricultural permits are withdrawn as a result of a movement taking shape toward the north . . . My head keeper Voisennet begins, with very ill grace, to turn the hay with feminine help."[61]

The increasing shortage of resources was not the only factor that sapped peasant women's ability to reproduce the triumph of the 1914 harvest. The whole rural community, women included, had been driven by the crisis of the outbreak of the war; but as the war continued, morale sagged. The Comtesse de Courson evaluated peasant women's morale in the winter of 1915 like this:

> The task of the peasant woman is heavy, and for the past eighteen months they have accomplished it admirably, although perhaps today with a little more lassitude. In 1914, some of the field work was completed by the men before they left for war, by the little soldiers of the class of [19]15 and by a large number of Territorials who were still there to do their share of the work. The summer of 1915 was more difficult to get through; the mourning, the deep anxiety pressed on these peasant women, many of them knowing today that the empty places at the hearth will stay that way for ever. Despite the crushing weight of physical and emotional fatigue, they continued, with few exceptions, to face up to the necessities of the war.[62]

These "exceptions" would become less exceptional. In the spring, the military censor reported increasing complaints from peasant women: "Moving letters written from the countryside show us women killing themselves with work without being able to replace the men who fight or who are dead."[63] This was a year before the crisis in national morale that affected the whole French population, civilian and military. By 1917 Labat feared out-and-out defeatism, not due to German or Bolshevik propaganda but to the "nightmare" of the war that engulfed peasant women. "Sometimes a woman, overcome with fatigue, sat at the side of the road, calling to her neighbor who was passing by, bent under the same burden, saying: ' We are worse than beasts of burden. Why are we working like this? Let's stop working. Famine will come, and at once the war will be over.'"[64] In fact peasant women did "hold out," as Jean Jacques Becker concluded in his study of wartime morale – most of them had no other choice, after all; but they were no longer the national heroines they had been four years earlier.

Doing Men's Work: *Remplaçantes* and *Munitionettes*

As a feminist Marcelle Capy was delighted that women were tackling "masculine" jobs and earning high wages in the French war industries. But as a socialist she worried about conditions in the factories, and as a pacifist she was repulsed by the work's militarist implications. After her first visit to a munitions plant, she pondered how "maternal arms that cradle life at its beginning, now day and night make murderous machines."[65] Was such work really in women's best interests? To find out, Capy took a job at a Parisian factory, and then published a long article in *La Voix des femmes*, a socialist women's magazine, describing her work as a *munitionette*, as the press dubbed the women munitions workers.[66]

Capy admired her co-workers, whose courage and competence proved the anti-feminists wrong about women's abilities. Women *were* up to the task, and they certainly deserved every *sou* they earned at this work. However, this was not work that any feminist, certainly not a pacifist socialist like Capy, would wish upon women. Capy vividly evoked the brutal nature of the factory work – noisy, dirty, exhausting and dangerous – and especially the long, long working days that left women with no time for themselves or their families. Was this an opportunity for women, or was it the worst sort of exploitation? Louise Delétang, herself a garment worker and no stranger to long hours, thought that the opportunities of munitions work were largely illusions. Yes, the armaments plants paid much better than sewing shirts; but they taught no skills. When the war was over and men returned, the women would be out on the street with nothing to show for their years of labor.[67] And both Capy, the socialist, and Delétang, the conservative, worried that in the meantime women workers would have lost their essential identities as mothers and centers of the family. Besides being factory workers, Capy reminded her readers that her co-workers were "mothers, wives, fiancées." What was this work doing to them? She worried that such factory work made women "silence their wounded tenderness."[68]

Ambivalence clung to the women workers who replaced men in the economy. Often they were blamed for exactly the same things for which they were praised. By working hard in "masculine" jobs, they supported the nation; yet they undermined it by jeopardizing the gender order. If they contributed indispensably to victory on the battlefield, they also threatened the nation's future by putting its children at risk. Women workers and their supporters could argue that future risks were justified by current need, that the risks were much less than the critics supposed, and that women gained – strength, self-confidence, respect – by the experience; but the only sure way out of the dilemma was to insist that the harm would be transitory because the work was only temporary. After the war, when the men returned, the gender order would snap back into place. Women would willingly exit jobs that belonged by right of suffering, sacrifice and victory as well as by gender to France's men, and they would return to their primordial tasks of bearing and raising the next generation.[69]

This dilemma was certainly not something official policy had intended. Although, by the end of September 1914, the government had revised its assumption that the French economy could shut down for the duration of the war, it did not soon envision a female labor force. At first, the government helped revive selected industries – munitions, mining, the railroads – by releasing mobilized workers to them. It was late in 1915 before Albert Thomas, the Under-secretary of Artillery in the Ministry of War, advised industrialists to consider women as a potential labor pool. Only in the summer of 1916 did this recommendation become an order.[70]

In April of 1916, Thomas created the Committee on Female Labor [*Comité du travail féminin*] to study the potential use of women in industry and to make recommendations. Headed by Senator Paul Strauss, the committee included economists, doctors, politicians, officials, and representatives of the women's movement and women's trade unions. The labor economist Charles Picquenard was a member, and Marcelle Capy later served as a consultant to the committee.[71] In May, Thomas issued a directive to the heads of all industries working for government contracts, ordering them to replace male workers with female and "to develop new technical processes to increase production and help the women in their work."[72] As the battle of Verdun drained the supply of combatants, the "weeding-out" process intensified, replacing mobilized or mobilizable men with women and sending the men to the front.

187

This would continue until the final months of the war, when businesses of all kinds began to envision a reconversion to peacetime conditions and the return of a male labor force.

The increase in the number of women employed in previously male occupations varied from industry to industry. In many sectors of the economy, the increase was gradual but steady, as businesses began to pick up in 1915 at the same time as more and more male employees were mobilized. In others, such as munitions and transportation, openings for women closely followed the ups and downs of government policy. It was not until 1916 that the government created public employment offices and began to publicize and coordinate hiring women workers.[73] The Ministry of War also supported volunteer organizations, such as the National Agreement of Female Recruitment Charities, run by national women's organizations, to recruit qualified women. However, job placement still remained very decentralized, with each government department and each enterprise responsible for finding its own labor force.[74]

The French government could not control the female labor force, because it never officially mobilized women. One writer in *La France militaire* in January 1916 called for women's conscription: "Individual liberty has its limits set by the national interest, especially when the defense of the country is at stake. Men are required to carry arms; leisured women must be able to be mobilized – if need be – for work in offices or workshops, to provide care in hospitals, etc."[75] A year later, the government began to entertain this idea. In December 1916, Senator Henry Bérenger introduced a bill to register "all French persons of either sex" from the age of 17 to 60 for conscription to the labor force.[76] A month later, the government presented its own version of civil conscription, which modified Bérenger's proposal by including the requisition of goods as well as labor and by excluding women from compulsory mobilization. Instead, women could enroll voluntarily as "a sort of transition" between "liberty and constraint."[77]

The *Grande review* published a series of articles that not only supported the conscription of women but also made clear what motivated the project. Besides evoking the Revolutionary *levée en masse* and heaping disdain upon "idle women," the authors pointed to the recent German law of civilian mobilization. They implied that France must follow suit to prevent Germany from winning the war of attrition.[78] However, the legislature proved hostile to the idea of forced labor, and even to the voluntary conscription of women. Nor did French women support it. Louise Delétang reported that as early as November 1916, rumors of "civil requisition, the mobilization of all women" upset women who were waiting to collect their military allowances. "One of them cried: 'Oh no! I won't work in their factories and get my hand cut off! No, no, I won't go.'"[79] Although this proposal would have fulfilled feminist demands for a national service for women equivalent to military service, feminists did not rally to it. Instead, Jane Misme argued that it was silly to think that conscripting women would solve the labor shortage. All the women who were capable of useful employment were already working; the women who were left had no useful skills. What they needed was not conscription, but job training and apprenticeship programs. In some trades, she pointed out, employers were more willing to train foreigners than women.[80] In the end, the Senate passed the part of the bill that authorized requisitioning goods, but sent the section that concerned the conscription of labor back to committee, where it quietly expired.

Despite the lack of result, the proposal to conscript women led politicians to praise French women for their voluntary mobilization and to acknowledge their many crucial roles in the war economy. A Senate sub-committee extolled the women

> who, ever since 1914, have saved our agriculture, our commerce, even certain of our industries, in our countryside, our cities and our suburbs and who have taken over the plow, the shop, the bookkeeping in place of the husband, father or brother mobilized in the trenches or the factory.
>
> And especially, how can we not celebrate the voluntary enrollment of more than five hundred thousand French women and girls in our gunpowder factories, in our pyrotechnic plants, in our munitions workshops, in our marine arsenals, even in our steelworks?[81]

By early 1917, the mantle of feminine patriotism slid from the shoulders of the peasant women and was draped around the *remplaçantes*, i. e. women who replaced men in the economy. The new favorite was the *munitionette.*

The image of these new war heroines developed gradually during the first two years of the war. Public attention first fell upon the most visible of the replacement workers, such as the women fare collectors on Paris tramways. As the government began the campaign to recruit women into armaments factories, the *munitionettes* moved to the head of the parade of images of French women at war. Like the invasion heroine, the nurse and the peasant woman, the *munitionette* was even occasionally paired with the trench-fighter to represent the masculine and the feminine of France at war. According to Gaston Rageot, the woman munitions worker deserved a prominent place in war memorials, which should depict "a big French soldier wearing his greatcoat and helmet and, next to him, leaning toward him and trembling, offering him, not a laurel wreath, nor flowers, but a fruit of the war, a grenade – a little woman in a factory bonnet."[82]

Beginning in the fall of 1915, the popular press ran regular features depicting replacement workers. *Lectures pour tous* imagined a man who had fallen asleep in September 1914 and had just awakened in January 1916. The article followed its Rip Van Winkle on the tram and the metro, to the post office, the bank and City Hall; in each venue he was astonished at the "curious spectacle" of women at work, charming, gay and competent. *Je sais tout* went this device one better by arranging for a reporter, Jane Simone, to work as a *remplaçante* – making munitions, punching tickets on the tram, waiting table in a café – with a photographer in tow.[83] These articles and others like them combined the picturesque with some factual information about qualifications, wages and hours. Their main purpose was to celebrate the ubiquity and the versatility of French women in the wartime economy.

Altogether, the press created a striking image of the *remplaçante* – young, pretty, cheerful and fashionably dressed (see Figure 6.1). This working woman was already familiar to readers of the Parisian popular press; she was the *midinette*, the stereotyped seamstress, whose youth, style and insouciance cloaked the poverty and drudgery of garment work. The war added a new requirement to this stock image: a sentimental patriotism in which love of country was embodied in love of a man. Paul Strauss, head of the Committee on Female Labor, acknowledged that, of course, women worked to earn money, but

> they have another purpose: it is to come to the aid of their dear husbands, to send them every week, most of them, the packages that are so anticipated and welcomed with infinite gratitude. By a touching reversal of roles and responsibilities, the wife is, in this moment, the protectress of her husband.
>
> In working in these establishments where she can risk her health or even her life, in the ultimate act of tenderness, she also puts her heart on the line by cooperating to safeguard the being who is as dear to her as her country's safety.[84]

Figure 6.1 The *munitionette*, competent but feminine; a shell-case cutter in a munitions works at St Etienne. © Musée d'histoire contemporaine – BDIC, reproduction by Archipel.

Although the image of the woman war worker was clear, her identity was vague. Who were these women and girls? Employers claimed that most were the female dependants of their mobilized male workers. Le Creusot classified women job applicants by a priority system based upon their male relative's war record and service to the factory, with war widows and orphans of former employees topping the list.[85] Labor statistics show that most of the women had worked before the war, mostly as domestic servants, garment workers, or textile workers or in other kinds of factory work.[86] Most contemporaries believed, however, that patriotism had drawn flocks of homemakers and leisured girls from their kitchens, salons and boudoirs into the labor force. In a letter to the Committee on Female Labor, Albert Thomas described the munitions workers as women "torn from the hearth." Angèle Bory d'Arnex believed *munitionettes*, like trench fighters, were drawn from all classes of society – "more than one bourgeoise slipped in among the working women;" both were united in camaraderie and devotion to the patriotic cause.[87]

In the publicity about the woman war worker that flourished in the middle years of the war, two related but contradictory themes emerged. One was that the war worker was a novelty, an exotic curiosity; the other was that she was Every Woman, feminine, domestic and classless. In this way, propagandists publicized women's presence on formerly masculine terrain while soothing the anxiety caused by such obvious changes in the gender division of labor. Although depicting women in strange new environments, the articles reassured their readers that the women themselves were unchanged. By hiding the fact that most were women who had worked before the war and would need to continue to work once the war was over, this discourse allowed the French public to sustain its belief in an ideal society of female homemakers and male breadwinners that would be reconstituted after the war.

These themes merged in an almost obsessive interest in the workers' clothing that juxtaposed oddity and femininity. Often journalists spent more lines describing what women workers wore than what work they did. That many of the new women workers who were most in the public eye – tram workers, mail carriers, Métro workers – wore uniforms fascinated reporters. For example, the uniform of the tramway ticket-seller was "a black smock, a kind of little fatigue cap coquettishly tilted over her hair, a number badge in silver thread pinned to her shoulder, satchel slung like a bandolier"[88] (see Figure 6.2). The masculine aspects of the uniform – fatigue cap, number badge, bandolier – were feminized; the cap was small and coquettish, the numbered badge embroidered in silver thread and pinned on like a piece of jewelry. Louise Delétang absorbed the message of such descriptions; she found the new women tram conductors "serious, alert, not masculine." "This was not the virago who, to prove her equality with men, rigged herself out in men's clothes; no, she had feminized the cap by framing it with waves of chestnut hair."[89]

Munitions workers presented no such reassuringly feminine image. *Lectures pour tous*, after minutely detailing the work clothes of tram conductresses and Métro ticket-takers, noted merely that munitions workers wore smocks.[90] In fact, many wore trousers. A *Petit Parisien* article on "Workers' Fashions in the Munitions Factory" explained that ordinary women's clothes were dangerous around quickly-moving, powerful machinery. The fact that many women adopted male attire was not a sign of their masculinization, but a simple safety precaution.[91] Instead, propagandists feminized the

Figure 6.2 A woman driver and fare collector on the Paris tramway, July 1917. © Musée d'histoire contemporaine – BDIC, reproduction by Archipel.

factory workers with the feminine diminutive nickname, *munition-ette*, and focused on their after-work dress and activities or their exceptionally womanly bodies to prove they remained normal girls. In a series of vignettes, Bory d'Arnex showed them applying make-up, chatting about fashion, the cinema and children, and affirming their femininity as well as their Frenchness by their love of the countryside. The *Petit Parisien* turned trouser-wearing women baggage-handlers into charming, opulent young amazons, who "call to mind the firm, vigorous flesh of a Rubens. Sometimes their hair is magnificent."[92]

Propagandists insisted that women inevitably brought womanliness to whatever they did. A favorite motif was to contrast the inferno of the factory hall with the feminine grace of the workers; munitions workers were like dancers, "a symphony of movements."[93] As Laura Lee Downs has argued, employers played this game too, implicitly justifying the presence of women in war industries by describing their jobs as analogous to housework. When women finished airplane parts or shells, they were polishing jewelry; when they measured explosives, they were dipping sugar; when they shaped shells, they were knitting; while assembling fuses was a kind of embroidery.[94] Employers and propagandists claimed, as the *Petit Parisien* did for tramway workers, that women shouldered these new tasks "as if this work was completely natural, as if she had never dreamed of another destiny."[95]

In 1917, the rising cost of living and the wave of strikes in which women workers played prominent roles clouded the image of the charming, patriotic girls who assembled shells or sold tickets on the tram to support themselves, their men and their country. The strikes began in the fall of 1916 and multiplied in January 1917; but the one that captured Parisian attention was the "smiling strike," the seamstresses' walk-out in May.[96] From there, the strikes spread into textiles, food processing, retail sales and, most controversially, into the munitions industry. At its height in Paris in the spring and summer of 1917, the strikes involved about 100,000 workers and nation-wide, perhaps 300,000, most of them women.[97]

At least some of the women strikers had an agenda that included socialism and an end to the war. In June, striking women from a gunpowder factory in Toulouse sang the *Internationale*; elsewhere women chanted: "Give us back our *poilus.*" As the strike waves continued into 1918 and became more aligned to syndicalist programs, and also more male-dominated, explicit demands for peace became more common. However, specific issues varied from plant to plant; some women struck to protest against abusive foremen and demanded to be treated with respect. Women workers at a gunpowder factory in Toulouse protested against wage reductions as punishment for absences – unfair, they claimed, to women, who had to cope with family and government bureaucracy – for example, the need to collect military allowances and ration cards – as well as work.[98] Other strikes protested over cuts in piece rates or other speed-up tactics or demanded the "English week." This paid Saturday afternoon holiday, a priority of the labor movement, was popular with women workers, who, struggling with the claims of the workplace and the home, found time off without loss of pay particularly attractive. The key demands in every strike, however, were pay hikes to compensate for the increased cost of living.

The cost of living had been rising since the beginning of the war; but in 1917 it shot up precipitously. The winter was unusually cold, and since France's coal-producing Nord was occupied by German armies, coal was in short supply. Bread and potato supplies were controlled, but the price of meat soared and milk and butter were hard to come by at any price. Sugar was so scarce – also as a result of the German occupation – that on 1 January 1917 the government ordered pastry shops to close two days a week, and in March issued sugar ration cards. In May it began the same pattern with meat by ordering two meatless days a week, during which butchers and restaurants were forbidden to sell meat, with the prospect of meat rationing in the future. Lack of coal forced laundries to close, newspapers raised their prices for the first time in living memory and clothing and shoe prices rocketed.[99] Also legislation that had limited the work day, mandated Sunday off and imposed safety measures had been abrogated or was not being enforced, and manufacturers were lowering piece rates to cut costs and increase production. It is no wonder that workers struck.

Although the most studied aspect of the French home front, the strikes were rarely mentioned by the commentators who eulogized women's war work, except of course, those writing in the socialist papers like *L'Humanité* and *La Bataille*. This was partly due to timing – many of the books and articles, like Abensour's *Les Vaillantes*, were already published or in press by the summer of 1917. It was also due to censorship, which restricted the publication of information about strikes in the war industries to prevent their spread and to protect morale. But it was mostly because the image of a striker was difficult to reconcile with the image of the *munition-ette* that the popular press had constructed. Only those who sympathized with feminism and socialism saw the connection. Marie de La Hire was one of the few propagandists outside the socialist press who commented on women strikers. She argued that, by taking part in the war effort, they had come to recognize their own worth

Figure 6.3 The "smiling strike;" *Midinettes* on parade in Paris, May 1917. © Bibliothèque Nationale de France, Paris.

and were now joining male workers to stand up for themselves and for the advancement of their class.[100]

The popular press reported the strike of the *midinettes* largely favorably.[101] The strikers made good use of their press image, parading in their best clothes and singing to create a festive impression (see Figure 6.3). Alice Brisset, who had been one of the strikers, recalled:

> It was my first strike, that was in the midst of war, the capital in anger. We went to turn out the sewing industry by going into the workshops. It was like a ground-swell; everything that had accumulated at the bottom rose to the surface. Plus the sidewalk has always been a little bit the *midinettes*' domain. In happier days, we paraded there, singing, to celebrate St Catherine's day.
>
> But now, the street belonged to us: "Our 20 *sous*! The English week! Give us back our *poilus*!"[102]

The public generally found them attractive and amusing. Michel Corday recorded in his diary on 22 May, "The strikes of 'midinettes' are spreading. The appearance of their processions is quite novel. They are young women, mostly in navy blue costumes. They laugh. They sing. An enormous number of policemen keep them in order."[103] Since their targets were the big fashion houses and wealthy women, they were not perceived to be a threat to the daily lives of ordinary folks nor, of course, to the war effort.

But striking shell-fitters and gunpowder-makers were a different story. The labor activist Gabrielle Duchêne recalled that "the public became bad humored when the less decorative, but so much more moving, masses of factory women paraded, demanding 'their poilu!'" Public authorities rebuked these women for endangering the country. Albert Thomas, himself a socialist, asked strikers at the Schneider factories in Harfleur, "Have you thought of the seriousness of the mistake you are making? Have you thought of the enemy, who isn't going to interrupt his work? Of your brothers, your husbands who are impatiently waiting for the means of defense that you provide them?"[104]

But criticism went beyond such chiding. Enthralled and frightened by the Revolution in Russia, which had begun, after all, as a women's strike, some people quickly concluded that the women strikers were a similar advanced guard of the social revolution in France. The postal censor recorded this evaluation from a Parisian's letter: "Hordes of these bareheaded women with their hooligan brats are spreading revolution. We are heading straight for a patched-up peace, or worse. It's all very depressing." Surrounded by strikers on a café terrace, Michel Corday thought helplessly of the French Revolution. In a final escalation of fear, the strikers became wild women, "the crazy women in the powder factory," as one Toulouse resident described them. After the war, Louis de Launay pointed to the strikes as proof that women were unfit to work outside the home. In his mind, a combination of irrational passion and defeatist propaganda drove the women strikers into a frenzy.[105] When on strike, women were no longer spunky *munitionettes*; they became that nightmare, the furies who destroy all order and civilization.

Press censorship kept this image from wide dissemination during the war; but it did nothing to constrain another negative assessment, that of the woman worker as war profiteer. This view encompassed the strikers, asserting that they were unjustly exploiting the crisis of the war for their own benefit. William Oualid and Charles

Picquenard concluded that while the *midinettes* had had cause for complaint, the *munitionettes* had none. They struck merely to profit from the moment to acquire some "false luxuries."[106] Inevitably, critics contrasted the women on strike with the men in the trenches. Louise Delétang, who must have been one of the most conservative garment workers ever to have lived, wrote in her diary on 20 May 1917: "To profit from the war to demand the English week, it's a bit like blackmail. Have they the [English] week, the ones who are getting killed to protect all the *munitionettes* and *midinettes*, some of whom were not afraid to kill those whose job it is to maintain order?"[107] – a reference to stories of striking "furies" attacking policemen.

The public perception of women workers as war profiteers went far beyond the strikers, however. It arose from a number of indisputable facts. First, women were working in jobs that had been vacated by men who were now at the front. This particularly disturbed some soldiers. The censor of military mail reported in 1916 that men who were being "weeded out" of the factories to be sent back to the army "have it in for Parisiennes and all women who go to work in the factory."[108] The second fact was that women were earning higher wages than was their customary lot. Munitions workers, it was widely believed, were earning "fantastic salaries," and to these they added military allowances.[109] Maria Léra reported her conversation with a lady in Nantes, well known locally for her charitable works: "Workers' families, she told me, even those where the father is in the army, have never been more comfortable, thanks to the allowances and the work of women and young boys." Did this please the charitable lady? Not at all, because instead of using their money wisely, women workers squandered it, to the detriment of all. "Workers' families don't deprive themselves of anything, and, to a certain degree, they are responsible for the high price of certain goods for which they don't even try to bargain."[110] And here entered the third fact, the sharp increase in the cost of living, explained as working women's fault.

Official reports and government policy reinforced the belief that inflation and shortages were due, not to wartime conditions or to economic mismanagement, but to the selfishness of individuals, women in particular. In the Dauphinais, for example, a report in early 1916 by a departmental committee investigating the causes of inflation placed a large part of the blame on the high wages paid to munitions workers and the military allowances.[111] Meanwhile, government policies pointed to another female culprit, the peasant woman. Since she had supposedly saved the 1914 harvest without help, the government ignored production problems in agriculture or blamed them upon the selfishness of the peasants. It requisitioned grain, wool and cattle at prices below the cost of production and then penalized farmers who shifted to crops that were not requisitioned. It prosecuted peasant women who sold butter and milk at what public opinion claimed were scandalous prices without considering the shortage of cows and the much increased costs of keeping them.[112] In the increasingly common scuffles in markets between peasants selling produce and urban women consumers, the police sided with the consumers, and were more likely to arrest the peasants for price-gouging or even to blame them for causing the disturbance than to arrest the shoppers who destroyed or looted their goods.[113] Public opinion indicted peasant women for withholding goods from market and for charging "fabulous prices" in order to salt away nest-eggs.[114] If peasant women willingly took over their men's work in the fields, it was less for patriotism than for profit; while their husbands and sons "were dying gloriously" to defend the country, they were socking away the spoils.[115] Heroine in the fall of 1914, by 1917 the peasant woman was a war profiteer as well as a deserter.

The problem was not only that women were making money; they were also spending it in ways disruptive to society and to the war effort, or so claimed their many critics. The most common criticism of women workers during the war, and especially of munitions workers, was that they spent their money recklessly on what Oualid and Picquenard called "false luxuries:" clothes, hats, the new high-heeled boots, lingerie, perfume, jewelry – Marie Diemer claimed that women wore "diamond combs" into the factory – and, most distressing of all, "they all wear, not the muslin stockings that before were worn by even the most elegant of them, but *silk stockings!*"[116] The fashion, make-up and hair-dos that propagandists argued proved working women's essentially femininity, in the eyes of their critics became evidence of deplorable frivolity. Nor were peasant women immune to this criticism: "Just as in town, one can see shortened skirts, knee-boots, hats copied from the latest fashion magazine. The traditional headdress is no longer worn except by very old women. Every young girl has a bicycle. In the countryside, money abounds and young countrywomen make sure that everyone knows it."[117]

And then, there was food. The middle class explained the increase in the price of fruit, meat and milk products and sugar by claiming that munitions workers were gorging themselves on *charcuterie*, cream, fruit and pastries, paying whatever price was asked. A typical munitions worker, Bory d'Arnex reported, bought oranges by the dozen.[118] The gastronomic equivalent of silk stockings, however, was chickens, which, critics claimed, women workers devoured at a great rate and without regard to price. Léra recorded what supposedly was a typical exchange between a maid and her mistress when the former returned from the market: "'Did you get a chicken? – A chicken? Mademoiselle will have to go to buy one herself. You can't find anything for less than 6 or 7 francs. Mme X bargained one down to 5.50F. She would have gotten it, but a munitions worker came in, threw down 6 francs and took the chicken without even looking at it."[119] In a remarkably hostile article, Magd-Abril depicted the life of working women; work takes up two lines and hedonism the rest.

> Let's depict the life of the woman war worker in a glance as rapid as the hours of this same life, devoured by the double fever of work and pleasure. She rises before dawn. Does she work all day? From dawn to dusk she is in movement, using up her feeble strength in the Dantesque setting of the munitions plant. At nightfall she leaves the workshop, no longer feeling any fatigue because she rushes to take her hair to the hairdresser, her fingers to the manicurist. She goes home, pretty as a *femme du monde*, kisses her children and takes them to dinner at a neighboring dairy bar. Afterwards, everyone goes to the cinema and gives up sleep to follow in the imagination some hero of popular romance . . . The *midinette* whose fiancé was killed by the enemy consoles herself this Saint Catherine's day, not with a paper bonnet like last year, but with one in fine lace. And the widow dries her tears by giving her little girl a beautiful doll that says "papa."[120]

Nor were such views confined to the Right; CGT leader Raymond Péricat raged: "Go to the industrial suburbs and see them coveting furs and wearing boots that go up to their knees! At the cinema, the theater, they all laugh, they all enjoy themselves . . . Their sons, their husbands, their fiancés fall, cut down by machine-guns and they all accept the fact without flinching."[121]
Péricat felt working women's consumption habits betrayed their men. What concerned other critics was the disruption of class hierarchy. Dressed like *femmes du mondes*, buying food, clothing and entertainment previously reserved for the middle and upper

classes, working women were the *nouveaux riches*, while the bourgeoisie were the *nouveaux pauvres*, or so the critics feared. Léra concluded her dialogue of mistress and maid with the mistress's lament: "It's dreadful, murmured the old lady, choked with indignation. Where are we going?"[122]

But class disruption was not the worst of it; there was also gender disruption. For if working women were dressing and eating like ladies, they were drinking, smoking, swearing and fornicating like men, or so said the critics. "Like overwork, debauchery awaits the working woman, debauchery and alcoholism. Because in taking on men's work, woman has taken on his vices as well . . . And those who have remained pure boast to imitate the allure and language of the others." Even socialists concurred: "It is shocking to see and hear the factory girl or woman talk in a vulgar and excessively coarse fashion." Working women must remain feminine.[123] But conservatives believed this was impossible, because, they asked: "What remains of the woman, the mother, in this *munitionette* in blue overalls and trousers, with the hair shoved under a protective cap, with the sharp look and the brisk and precise movements that contact with machines brings?"[124]

Not only were working women responsible for the breakdown of class and gender, they were also responsible for prolonging the war. This was the repeated message of the revolutionary, pacifist wing of the labor movement. Péricat exploded at a union meeting in December 1916: "If the feminine element wasn't so egotistical, the war would have ended long ago, but the women only think of earning money to treat themselves to jewels and clothes."[125] The postal censors reported that some soldiers expressed similar sentiments, accusing both women factory workers and peasant women of prolonging the war for their own profit.[126] These were opinions that people expressed privately in letters or in closed meetings; but the cartoonist Henriot made them public in a famous cartoon published in 1917. It showed a woman, holding a child by each hand, standing in the street of a factory town, explaining to a gentleman: "Yes of course, besides the allowance, I earn 8 to 9 francs a day making shells . . . unfortunately the war won't last for ever."[127]

In the wartime discourse about working women, the spunky patriot working for her man and her country metamorphosed into the vain profiteer who risked all social order in pursuit of her selfish interests. Republicans and feminists like Abensour, Misme, and the

Petit Parisien applauded the one, while conservatives like Léra, Magd-Abril, and the *Correspondant* and revolutionary socialists like Péricat and *La Bataille* deplored the other. Rarely did commentators try to reconcile the two sides of the portrait. Occasionally a writer would point out that *munitionettes'* wages and peasant women's earnings were not so high as opinion imagined, or that they were justified by inflation. A few more straightforwardly defended women's right to earn whatever they could and to spend it as they liked. "This money that they spend, it is the price of their work. They have earned it, painfully, courageously, honestly," wrote Louise Bodin in the socialist magazine, *Voix des femmes*.[128] If, by their war work, they were able to raise their standard of living, surely this was all to the good. Ernest Gaubert defended peasant women's nest-eggs by pointing out they proved peasant women's optimism, their care of their families and their commitment to the soil: "She has thought of her husband. She has dreamed of future harvests. She has faith in them."[129]

Women replacement workers did not respond in print to the propaganda that romanticized them or to the barrage of criticism that vilified them. Unfortunately, we have no memoirs comparable to those of the peasant Emile Carles nor a diary of a munitions worker like that of the garment worker Louise Delétang. No oral history project has recorded the memories of *munitionettes* or tram drivers sixty years later as the Sound Record Department of the Imperial War Museum in London has done for British munitions workers or as some French historians and ethnographers have recorded the memories of elderly peasants. Our best views inside the lives of munitions workers come, not from workers themselves, but from journalists. Marcelle Capy and an anonymous "neutral journalist" from the *Petit Parisien* each worked incognito in munitions factories for several weeks and published accounts of their experiences.[130] Their reports detailed the long hours, petty rules, stress, fatigue and risk of accidents that were the universal components of wartime factory work, components that figure hardly at all in either the praise or the criticism. They deplored the absence of training that excluded women from technical knowledge and skills, delighted in the camaraderie of the women with whom they worked, and watched closely the mixed reactions of the men who worked with them and supervised them. They described the inadequate safety precautions and washing, eating and toilet facilities and the overcrowded public transportation that made a long, exhausting workday even longer and more stressful. The *Petit Parisien* journalist wondered how her co-workers coped:

> We work for ten hours. With meals included, this makes a workday of eleven and a half hours. At 6:15 [in the morning] I have to be in the Métro. Seven in the evening has rung before I get home. Long day, very long. In anguish I ask myself: "What does this feel like to those who still have to do the housework, make the dinner, get provisions to take to the factory the next day? When will they read a newspaper? When will they write to him who is out there? [i. e. in the trenches].[131]

But although she stated that the primary goal of her adventure was to "make the woman worker's voice heard," this she could not do. What did working women think about their new jobs and about their role in the war? How did they interpret their circumstances?

The only extended personal accounts that we have of replacement work come, not from the factory floor, but from behind desks: Jeanne Baraduc who taught in a boys' secondary school, and Marguerite Lesage, who ran a sugar factory, both kept diaries of their experiences and later published accounts based upon them.[132] Like all replacement workers, they were doing unfamiliar jobs to which they had acceded by wartime necessity. They were nervous about their abilities to perform adequately, seeing their jobs more as a duty than an opportunity. Each imagined herself as mobilized and compared her work to that of the soldiers. But at the same time, they saw where this analogy broke down. Lesage wrote on 17 March 1916:

> There are times when I wonder if I'm going to give in to *le cafard*, as the *poilus* call it [i. e. depression]. I doubtless have many good reasons to do so, and especially overwork: the factory, the fields, inventory (right now I have only bad seeds), the cares and worries of dealing with the personnel, the loss of animals, work, correspondence; it is a lot for one lone woman. The future and education of my daughters, which should be my top priority, preoccupies me also and all this in complete insecurity, without any assurance of tomorrow, at the mercy of a German success, even if only momentary and local!
>
> Yes . . . but having mentally run through this list for the thousandth time, it is enough to think of our soldiers – and in what conditions! – to think, once again, that as long as I can, I must be worthy of them and stay here (pp. 96–7; ellipses in text).

Whatever they did, they did not do as much or sacrifice as greatly as the men they replaced. Although both came to feel competent at their new jobs, they did not feel that they deserved them. Imagining the men marching home victorious, they both hoped that they would be pleased to give up their wartime responsibilities and return to familiar, feminine occupations.

Both Baraduc and Lesage faced disapproval for trying to do a "man's job" and had to withstand efforts to undermine their positions. Baraduc had difficulty with the oldest students, who constantly defied her authority and challenged her expertise; but worse were those who treated her with exaggerated gallantry: "Of all my students, these I like the least. They harass me by incessantly reminding me that I am out of place" (p. 101). Lesage had similar problems with her husband's friends. When she turned to one for advice about the factory, "he went on about the question of the difficulties of the situation. He judged them insurmountable by a woman (he didn't say, such as me). But he had an idea (oh, yes!). I had only to write to the administrative council that after reflection, I was afraid I could not direct the business well and propose as director . . . the visitor's own nephew!" (p. 25; ellipses in text).

By the time Jeanne Baraduc wrote her account in 1919, she had come to believe that her problems had not arisen from a lack of knowledge or teaching skill or the weakness of her brain or her character, as critics had implied. At fault were gender relations; and in her memoir she struggled to articulate this perception. She was willing to attribute some of her difficulties in teaching boys to "atavistic" gender differences; but she felt the older boys had learned their anti-feminist attitudes and behaviors. These boys imitated the attitudes of the wider society, which belittled women and regarded them with contempt. This was not, in her mind, an issue of her lack of "natural" authority, but of her students' learned disrespect (pp. 61–2).

In Marguerite Lesage's account, an edited diary, we can follow her as she wrestled with this issue. Initially, she did not think of herself as actually replacing her husband at the head of the business; he would remain the *patron*; she was merely his handmaiden (p. 9). However, the business could not function in this way. Like everyone else, Lesage expected a short war; she had also believed that her husband would direct her via his letters. Neither expectation was fulfilled. Her husband was taken prisoner and her communication with him was severely restricted. Furthermore, the war radically altered manufacturing, so that her husband's advice was often not helpful even when he could give it. The war had created a shortage of labor and coal, but a luxuriant growth of regulations. In addition to these problems, her factory was in the war zone, briefly occupied by the Germans. But the German depredation was nothing compared to that of the French army, which requisitioned buildings for a munitions dump, camped in sown fields, set up checkpoints that prevented workers from reaching the factory, disregarded Lesage's official authorizations and in general impeded her efforts to maintain production. As the war progressed, her diary became a record of her personal war with the army, a war in which she saw herself as a *poilu* (p. 136).

Problems like these faced every farmer, merchant or manufacturer during the war; but Lesage also faced the disbelief and self-doubt that she, as a woman, could and should run a business. At first she justified her perseverance by her husband's absence. She told a meeting of local industrialists who questioned her decision to run the factory that "because all healthy men (I did not dare say 'brave men!') are at the front, their wives must safeguard their positions." But in her diary she admitted that this response was "too easy" (p. 28). She was beginning to feel that she was not just a stand-in for her husband, but a manufacturer who deserved to be taken seriously in her own right. In December 1916, on a trip to Paris to lobby the Ministry of Agriculture for help in her battle with military requisitioning, Lesage met the wife of manufacturer of agricultural machines who, like Lesage, was running a factory. "Well! I'm not alone to cry and live in worry and annoyance. Other women are as courageous as I am; that's an encouragement and an inspiration" (pp. 131–2).

Lesage was proud of her proven competence, but was also concerned about its implications for post-war gender relations. At first she was pleased that the resolution she thought she lacked developed quickly on the job. On 4 November 1914, after a staff meeting, she wrote: "As it turns out, I find I adapt myself rather well to my new life. I will not write that I have become 'brave' but I no longer have those feminine fears of the dark, of burglars, of . . . mice! My nervousness has given way to great calm" (pp. 26–7; ellipses in text). And with resolution came leadership. She had imagined that the factory would run itself; but a revolt of workers who feared a renewed German occupation forced her personally to take charge. After persuading the workforce to return, she reported happily: "The factory is doing well: I showed it to my girls this afternoon with some pride" (p. 30). Her battles with bureaucrats also made her assertive and self-confident, something which pleased but also worried her. A neighbor complimented her: "'You were so timid before,' Mme N. V. told me, 'your husband won't know you!' This remark made me wonder. Yes, I have acquired something of a 'personality.' But . . . will it please Maurice? Well, when he is here, I'll try to lose this 'personality:' Like some wartime constructions, it will be easier to demolish than to build!" (p. 139; ellipses in text).

Their experience as replacement workers challenged both Marguerite Lesage and Jeanne Baraduc to reconsider their assumptions about the naturalness of gender. Both women came to believe that it was not their female nature that impeded their wartime duties, but people's attitudes toward femininity. If the war had proved to both of these women that the traditional gender system was not "natural," like Mme X, one of the peasant women whose words opened this chapter, they believed that it was, nonetheless, desirable. Just as the propaganda maintained, they saw their excursion into "men's work" as a patriotic duty they would relinquish when the soldiers returned. Neither completely embraced the image of the plucky, charming *remplaçante*; but they certainly took in and repeated the message of that image, that whatever the war called upon them to do, it would not change French women. A friend rebuked Lesage for not being more pleased at receiving a commendation: "'What do you want, then, Madame? he asked, raising his arms toward heaven . . . What I want, is my husband and all of my men to return, to become a mother and housewife again. Am I not also a wife and a daughter and a sister?" (pp. 75–6; ellipses in text).

Workers, Mothers and the Future of France

"The Factory, Baby Killer!" – screamed the headline in *Le Matin* on 6 December 1916. In the article, Dr Adolphe Pinard demanded that pregnant women and nursing mothers be banned from employment in munitions factories. National production, he declared, was fatally interfering with "the production of the child," which must be woman's highest task. His opinions came as no surprise to his fellow doctors. A well-known professor of obstetrics at the Paris Faculty of Medicine and vice-president of the League Against Infant Mortality, Pinard had been airing his pronatalist and eugenicist opinions for the past twenty-five years. Three days before, he had urged the

Academy of Medicine, without success, to endorse the ban.[133] Then he took his cause to *Le Matin*, and set off a vociferous public debate. Paul Strauss, president of the League Against Infant Mortality, but also the head of Thomas's Committee on Female Labor, rebutted Pinard's position in the Academy and in the press. Stating the position of the Ministry of Armaments, he claimed that women's work was essential to the war effort, and that it could be, and was being, made safe and reconcilable with motherhood. Other doctors, women's rights advocates and socialists weighed into the argument on both sides, and the popular press reported the debate, blow by blow.[134] This argument involved little that was new. Before the war, doctors, clergymen, feminists – social critics and commentators of all stripes – had locked horns over how women's capacity to work outside the home could be reconciled with their reproductive capacities. Pronatalist campaigners had colored the discussion with cataclysmic prophesies.[135] When Albert Thomas decided that munitions factories needed to recruit women, he did not lose sight of this concern. He chose Strauss to head the committee because Strauss had authored the 1913 law that established maternity leave, and charged him "to arrange it so that the factory would not put a brake on the birthrate nor lead to increased infant mortality, either by a premature expulsion of the product of conception, or by obstacles to maternal nursing, or by favoring the abandonment of the child to a nurse."[136] As the historians Mathilde Dubesset, Françoise Thébaud and Catherine Vincent point out, the discussion in the Committee and the popular press throughout 1916 had emphasized accommodation. The Committee recommended not only what jobs women could safely take over from men, but also how the workplace could be adapted to women's total "well-being," particularly as mothers. It undertook numerous investigations of women workers' health and safety, lodging, the sanitary facilities of factories, etc.; but its main interest was in facilities that would enable mothers and expectant mothers to work. The Committee's recommendations led to the law of 5 August 1917, which required large factories to provide nurseries and permit women to nurse during working hours without loss of pay.[137] Some women's rights advocates like Léon Abensour hailed the Committee's work as "a complete success" and enthusiastically described the canteens, nurseries and workers' barracks as models of caring employment. Others thought more should be done. Marie de la Hire, for example, argued that the protections provided for women in the munitions industries should be applied universally and permanently.[138]

It was into this scene of reconciliation and reform that Pinard dropped his bombshell. His testimony to the Academy of Medicine reopened the issue of maternity and factory work that the Committee on Female Labor was supposed to have closed, at least for the duration of the war, and sent the Committee and its supporters scrambling. The war had raised the stakes in this debate for both sides. Supporters of women's work emphasized that the war effort depended upon women munitions workers. Dr Jacques Amédée Doléris, usually a strong pronatalist, concluded: "However painful it is to subordinate such a lofty cause as the future of France, it is nonetheless obligatory at present to assure industrial vitality by an intense effort until the victory."[139]

On the other side, the argument of the pronatalists was stronger than ever in face of the horrific mortality on the battlefield. Pinard and his supporters never ceased to point out that the future of the French "race" was in jeopardy. As Marie Diemer wrote in September 1917: "In our country especially, where the birthrate is so weak, what terrible repercussions if the factory tears woman from her first duties and suppresses the mother in her! . . . The factory destroys health and, like the war, it kills, but the youngest, the weak, it kills the future."[140]

"Scientific" evidence in this debate was sparse. The few studies of the impact of factory work on reproduction and child-rearing could be interpreted in different ways. Pinard based his proposal to ban pregnant and nursing women from factory work on figures showing a general decline in the birth rate and a rise in infant mortality. Strauss cited a study by Dr Bonnaire of four hundred pregnant factory workers to support his claim that factory work was reasonably safe and could be made safer.[141] Nonetheless, virtually all the voices in the debate assumed that factory work was indeed dangerous to women's health and to their reproductive capacities. Besides obvious dangers to any worker regardless of sex such as toxic chemicals and unguarded machinery, all agreed that a woman's reproductive capacities exposed her to unique risks from standing, vibration, lifting heavy objects and excessive fatigue. There were dangers of a moral and social origin as well. The piecework system, they claimed, led women – but not men – to overwork themselves in an effort to earn more. Those who sympathized with women workers attributed this to their desire to support their families, while their critics laid it to their greed for luxuries.[142]

The question that triggered the debate was how dangerous these factors were and to what extent they could be reduced or eliminated. In reply to Pinard's conclusion that only removing women from the factory would provide sufficient protection, Strauss and most of his colleagues on the Committee on Female Labor argued that regulations and benevolent intervention could make the risks of factory work acceptable. The Academy of Medicine agreed and, instead of endorsing Pinard's proposal, recommended a set of reforms, including placing women workers under a doctor's supervision.[143] The Academy of Medicine's concern over this question was not entirely disinterested. Doctors saw a new realm of work in industrial medicine, and here claimed for themselves the role of arbiters of the national interest, weighing in each case the interests of France, present and future.

But this did not satisfy Pinard and others who agreed with him. They doubted that such measures would be effective – and rightly so, since a survey by the Committee on Female Labor discovered that the law of 5 August mandating nurseries had had little effect.[144] But opponents raised other dangers of factory work to maternity that these reforms did not even attempt to address. Work and the money it brought led to female emancipation of the most noxious sort. Pinard declared: "Children, these bothersome hindrances, are seen by some women of little scruple as limiting their freedom to use their time as they wish and as an obstacle to earning maximum profits working at exceptionally well-paid jobs."[145] This argument, if taken to its logical conclusion, implicated all women, not just pregnant and nursing women, and would have excluded them, not just from munitions factories, but from all work outside the home.

Why did this issue, which had been percolating nicely on the back burner, heat carefully controlled by the Committee on Female Labor, suddenly explode in the government's face? The reason probably had less to do with what was going on, or not going on, inside munitions factories and working women's wombs than with what was happening in the trenches. It is no coincidence that this debate engaged the public at the same time as morale in the army and in the civilian population was plummeting. In *Civilization Without Sexes*, Mary Louise Roberts has argued that the discourse about women's behavior in post-war France expressed anxieties about the outcome of the war, a France victorious but a France weakened, perhaps fatally.[146] The year 1917 saw the development of several such arguments that identified women as the potential weak link whose selfish and unpatriotic behavior might undermine the war effort. From heroines of the harvest, peasant women in 1917 were suspected of deserting (the soil) and profiting from the food shortages. *Munitionettes*, once plucky and patriotic, were now also profiteers and dangerous revolutionaries. The debate over factory women's maternity was the most politically and emotionally charged of these discussions.

In 1917 and 1918, the survival of France troubled more than pronatalists like Pinard; but the real source of their concern was not women factory workers, but French soldiers. By 1917, everyone knew that the rhetoric of glorious battles and heroic deaths covered a reality of mud and terror and suffering, both physical and psychological. Would the soldiers hold out? From the winter of 1917 through the spring of 1918, the unvoiced and unvoiceable fear was that the soldiers would not be able to withstand the battering any longer, and that after all the sacrifices – the battle of the Marne, the bombs dropped on Paris, Lille's young women abducted, the heroic defense of Verdun – France would be defeated. Looking beyond victory or defeat, beyond Republic and even *patrie*, this debate focused upon the survival of French identity, French civilization, the French "race." It sidestepped contemplation of what would follow if French men failed in battle by arguing that France's annihilation – or salvation – actually rested in the wombs of French women. If French women would do their duty "to give birth and give birth and give birth once again," in the words of Dr Doléris,[147] then France was saved.

In this tense climate, we can understand why evidence made so little impact and why radical solutions struck chords even while practical solutions prevailed. We can also understand another peculiarity of the debate, that no one consulted working women. Although reports to Committee on Female Labor or to the Minister of Labor recorded the words of a few working women, these disappeared from the public discussion, which drew upon abstractions like Dr Bonnaire's four hundred pregnant workers or stereotypes like Magd-Abril's worker who ran from factory to manicurist to movie theater.

The debate constructed working women as incapable of identifying or defending their best interests. Of course, it drew upon a long history of women's legal irresponsibility that placed them under male protection and control. The context of the war heightened concern for women's dependence; bereft of their "natural" protectors, women were in greater need of State protection. As the government had stepped into the role of the male provider when it granted military allowances to soldiers' dependants, in regulating women's work the government also took on the role of husband and father to protect women not only from other men who would abuse them but also from their own irresponsible behavior. Baronne Brincard claimed:

> They rush upon the work with a kind of intoxication composed of their patriotic ardor and a horror of the strain that will soon grip them, and then also their inexperience of their own strength and ignorance of the most elementary laws of hygiene . . . Thus, at the moment they become "men" by their ant-like work (with a dexterity and speed superior to the masculine average), they show even more clearly that their weakness must be protected against themselves, against their own courage and want of foresight.[148]

The same qualities – assiduousness, speed, patriotism – that made it possible for women to replace men in the labor force also spelled their downfall if more responsible heads did not intervene.

Since the Committee on Female Labor, as well as all the other parties in this discussion, argued that women workers did not know what was good for them, there was no need to consult them. From this debate one would never know that thousands of women workers were on strike at this very time. Marcel Frois, a member of the Committee, even claimed that despite the munitions workers' long hours, "not a single complaint arose from the women workers."[149] In fact the demand of women strikers for the "English week" could have supported proposed reforms to prevent overwork; but of course their main demand, higher wages, had no place in the debate at all.

Women's rights also had very little place in the discussion. Only a few feminists objected to Pinard's proposed ban on the grounds that it abridged women's right to work.[150] Even for feminists, the main terrain of the debate was women's value to the Nation. This is not surprising, considering the context of the war. At a moment when France had ordered most young men to subordinate their individual rights to national duty to the point of sacrificing their lives, it was difficult to make an argument in favor of women's right to work when, where and how they chose.

However, the debate over factory women spilled over into a discussion of women's role in post-war France. Each side extended its arguments into the projected post-war period when, each predicted, the current crisis would continue and its wartime proposals would still be valid. Supporters of women's work pointed out that all economists agreed that the deficit in French manpower would continue after the war. As Auguste Pawlowski argued, France would need to turn once more to women. While conservatives bemoaned the sad necessity of women's work, feminists like Léon Abensour, Pawlowksi and Raymond Thamin hailed it as progress towards the equality of men and women that was their goal. The generalized incorporation of women into industrial personnel would be the prelude to their economic and social emancipation. The vote would surely follow.[151]

Pronatalists pointed to the battlefield deaths to argue that there would be an even more urgent need after the war to increase the French birth rate. The feminists, they claimed, had the priorities wrong. Although women who had lost their male providers in the war might need to work, feminists' delight in it was misplaced. Women's "true role" was "as reproducer of the species," and, according to Dr Wallich, "repeopling France" would be the crucial task for all lucky French women after the war.[152] In fact, some feminists agreed with him. In March 1916, Marguerite de Witt-Schlumberger, President of the French Union for Women's Suffrage, kicked off a new initiative, "Moral and Social Action in Favor of Maternity."[153] In an article ruminating on "The Duties of Tomorrow," the former Minister of War, Alexandre Millerand, summed up and dismissed the whole issue: "Although woman is a marvelous worker, she must above all be a mother; that is her first duty; there is no social interest above this."[154]

Although officially opposed to natalism, which they identified as right-wing and militarist, the male labor movement sided with the pronatalists in the discussion of women's role in the post-war economy. In 1917 a series of articles appeared in *La Bataille* that railed against capitalists who tore and feminists who enticed women from their homes to the detriment of the working-class family. For their author, Adolphe Hodée, the proposed nurseries and day-care centers were part of a plot to snatch workers' children away. The paper's women's columnist, Jeannine, disagreed with his vehemence but not with his conclusions; the woman must withdraw from the workforce in order to save the worker's home.[155]

When the chronological focal point shifted from the present to the future, from war to peace, the strength of the opposing positions shifted as well. In the present of 1917 and 1918, the overwhelming need for war *matériel* was self-evident, and even those, who generally opposed women's work on eugenic grounds accepted its wartime necessity. But when contemplating the future, maternity gained the upper hand. This is most evident in the case of Doléris, who in 1917 spoke in support of Strauss's position in the Academy of Medicine, but in 1918 co-authored a book that argued that in the future women's duty would be to give birth and that her essential national value was her womb.[156] In this imagined post-war world, social critics eased their discomfort at the sight of trouser-clad females running drill presses by consigning them to a future in the boudoir and nursery. Any commentator who wrote approvingly of women's future in the workforce could be dismissed with a pointed reference to repopulation and the duties of motherhood. Thus, the editor of the *Revue politique et parlementaire* appended a note to Pawlowski's article defending the place women had acquired in the labor force during the war: "We wish to remind our excellent collaborator that there is also in France a problem of the birthrate that dominates all others and particularly that of the labor force."[157]

When discussing the wartime situation, commentators gestured to the desirability of women's having babies and went on to elaborate schemes that would allow them to work nonetheless; when they imagined post-war society, the dynamic reversed. Now many critics acknowledged briefly that some women might need to work, but then devoted most of their energy to proposals designed to keep them at home. While Henri Joly thought that women could be encouraged to stay home by denying them apprenticeships and child-care facilities, others believed that schools must teach girls their duty to bear and raise children. Some proposed rewards for women who stayed home and had babies, "an elegant little cross of honor," for example, or even a vote.[158] Dr Toulouse resuscitated the pre-war feminist demand for compulsory national service for women, but, in this instance, less as a fulfillment of citizenship than as an incentive to motherhood. Women who had three children by the age of 30 would be exempted and the service would be designed to be "so disagreeable in practice" that women would prefer maternity.[159]

Commentators on rural France gave peasant women much the same advice; while it had been their wartime duty to cultivate the land, their post-war duty would be to repopulate it. As had been the case in the fall of 1914, commentators told peasant women that their task was larger than that of other French women; staying at home and bearing children would not be enough. After all, before the war the peasant woman had caused the countryside's problems with her desire "to be a lady."[160] After the war, she would have to continue to pull her weight in the garden, the poultry yard, the cow barn and even the fields. These social critics who feared urban women's emancipation saw the peasant woman as a valuable antidote. Emmanuel Labat suggested that her pride in her sacrifice and commitment to the soil represented a positive kind of "feminism," although she "knows neither its name nor what it's about," that might even merit the vote.[161]

In these commentators' minds, there was no contradiction in constraining urban women to give up their work while urging peasant women to keep at theirs. Critics did not envision for post-war women a life of idleness; they saw the home as the proper place for women to work. Their domestic work included, of course, frequent child-bearing, childrearing and housekeeping, but also work on the farm and sewing, preferably for their own families but, if need be, for the market as well. Erased from their vision of the future was any memory of the exposés of 1915 of exploitation in the garment industry. It was only unnatural work, masculine work, work that "tended to take women out of their natural role" that endangered them, their reproductive capacity and France's future. If the work was done in the home then it was appropriate to women's abilities and to their needs, and commentators smiled upon it. After the war, the dictates of science, the needs of the Nation, and the traditional gender division of labor would finally coincide. It was a comforting vision.

The discourse about women's work in post-war France that developed from 1917 to the end of the war prepared and justified the demobilization – i. e. firing – of the female labor force as soon as the armistice was declared. On 13 November, only two days after the armistice, Louis Loucheur, who had replaced Albert Thomas as Minister of Armaments, informed women working in the defense industry:

> In response to an appeal from the French Republic, you forsook your traditional pursuits in order to manufacture armaments for the war effort. The victory to which you have contributed so much is now assured; there is no more need to manufacture explosives . . . Now you can best serve

your country by returning to your former pursuits, busying yourselves with peacetime activities.[162]

Workers who left by 5 December would receive a month's wages as a bonus. Private employers simply began to fire women as they closed down, cut back or retooled their operations. Although André Citröen predicted a massive economic expansion that would continue to pull women into manufacturing – in fact, he even worried about a shortage of female labor – by February 1919, Citröen had cut the labor force at its Javel plant from approximately 11,700 workers, of whom about 6,000 were women, to 3,300 workers, all male.[163] Women in the tertiary sector, such as the mail carriers, tram drivers and schoolteachers, kept their jobs longer and were fired more selectively, as the men they had replaced – or who could replace them – were demobilized. Nonetheless, the result was the same; by the summer of 1919, most replacement workers had lost their jobs. While some did receive severance pay, most were dismissed without any resources but the meager unemployment benefits.

Women workers had no recourse against being fired. Throughout the war, both propaganda and policy had designated them as replacement workers; press depictions had nearly always declared that their motives were primarily patriotic and that they were eagerly awaiting the return of "their" men to whom they would relinquish the jobs that were not really theirs. How could women refuse to give way before the claims of these men, now returned victorious? Nonetheless, some did protest. *La Vague*, a small-circulation socialist paper edited by Marcelle Capy, printed several letters in the spring of 1919 from women distressed by their treatment. Wrote one woman: "My husband has been in the army for the last six years. I worked like a slave at Citröen during the war. I sweated blood there, losing my youth and my health. In January I was fired, and since then have been poverty-stricken."[164] What Louise Delétang had predicted when she advised girls not to get jobs in the munitions factories had come to pass. Once the war was over women workers were out on their ears, without having acquired any status or skills that would support them in the peacetime economy.

This is not, however, a full summary either of the discourse about women's role in the post-war economy or of its reality. Commentators had indeed predicted and demanded women's return to the home, and the labor policies that obtained in the days and months after the armistice ensured that most women were evicted from their wartime jobs. But many of them could not just "go home," since they were responsible for supporting themselves and often others as well, and many commentators recognized this. Except for the most dogmatic antifeminists,[165] all pronatalists realized that at least some women would need to work, both to support themselves and to help rebuild France. Jules Amar, for example, who thought it was enough if women were "pretty and socially pleasing and devoted," agreed that they should take on "besides their domestic tasks, those trades in which it is not preferable to hire men."[166] As Laura Lee Downs points out, what distinguished the discussion in France over women's work from a similar discussion taking place in England at the same time was the French call to rebuild France. While the British simply evoked a return to "normalcy," the French were imagining a New France.[167] And to rebuild France, a better France, French women would have to do more than return to their pre-war lives. They would, of course, need to produce many more babies than they had before the war; but they would also be needed in new sectors of the labor force now being defined as feminine. The discussion of women's work in post-war France narrowed the parameters of feminine work from the latitudinary era of the war, when handling baggage, driving trams and operating lathes were all exquisitely feminine, but expanded it in comparison to pre-war expectations. In a long article on the problem of female demobilization, Abensour solicited the opinions of officials, labor leaders and feminists. All agreed that women should work in "truly feminine industries," such as sewing, ribbon-making, textiles and jewelry-polishing, but they also mentioned the manufacture of chemicals, telephone equipment and parts for automobiles, bicycles and the railroad.[168] Even writers like Louis de Launay, who thought that women were inherently disruptive in the industrial labor force, argued that there would still be a place for them after the war – a limited place to be sure, but a place "of proportions unknown before."[169] Alongside the programs to entice women to stay home, commentators and policy-makers continued to discuss proposals to reconcile the workplace with women's maternal duties. These proposals did not evince the enthusiasm for the issue that Paul Strauss had demonstrated in 1917; but they recognized, reluctantly, that the Nation would continue to need women workers.[170]

This discourse drew a horizontal gender line through work. Work requiring skill, strength, knowledge, responsibility or authority –

and which was well paid – was masculine; work requiring manual dexterity – those "delicate fingers" – and a tolerance for monotony, as well as qualities more traditionally considered to be feminine, like delicacy, patience and nurturing, was women's work. Such arguments legitimated what Laura Lee Downs has described in the metalworking industry as the reclassification of labor that took place in France in the two years after the war. After a year of firing women workers, in the fall of 1919 manufacturers began to rehire them, for precisely those jobs that required manual dexterity, speed and tolerance for mindless repetitive motion, that is, jobs in the new mass production manufacture of products like telephone equipment, bicycles, and light bulbs.[171] And, predictably, such work was paid "women's wages:" the gap between male and female wages in metalworking, which had closed during the war to 18 per cent widened to 30 per cent or more.[172] Similarly, while women mail-carriers (strength) and tram drivers (strength, responsibility and authority) disappeared so completely that in the 1960s newspapers hailed the few newly-hired women bus drivers as pioneers, the women who opened and shut the gates at Métro stations remained on the job.[173]

As this discourse "reclassified" women's work, it also brought the image of French women in wartime full circle. Women had begun the war as dependent victims who needed support and protection. But then peasant women became war heroines, a status that, in 1916, passed to replacement workers, especially to *munitionettes*. These women, depicted as charming and plucky, embodied the nation "holding on" with the same cheerful determination imagined to prevail in the trenches. In 1917, however, under the pressure of food shortages and anxiety for the progress of the war, the image of the female war worker began to carry the nation's fears rather than its hopes; they, and not the soldiers, became potential deserters, profiteers and traitors. Throughout, whether patriotic heroines or selfish profiteers, women workers had figured as active participants in the war economy and agents of the war's outcome. Now, in the discourse about women's post-war roles, they had become the war's passive victims once more, and the projected losses of their wombs stood in for the real loss of hundreds of thousands of French men in the war.

Notes

1. Roger Laouénan, *La moisson rouge: Les bretons dans la grande guerre* (Paris: Editions France-Empire, 1987), p. 56.
2. Martine Benoit, "Les femmes et la guerre de 14-18; Témoignages," *Le Peuple français*, (July–September 1978): 30.
3. Charles Picquenard, "La guerre et la question des salaires," *La Revue bleue* 54 no. 3 (29 January–5 February 1916): 67–9.
4. Marcel Cachin, "L'ouvrière parisienne pendant la guerre," *Le Petit parisien*, 14 January 1915; Jonathan Manning, "Wages and Purchasing Power," in *Capital Cities at War: Paris, London and Berlin 1914–1918*, ed. Jay Winter and Jean-Louis Robert (Cambridge: Cambridge University Press, 1997) I: pp. 264–9.
5. Downs, *Manufacturing Inequality*, pp. 21–30, 39–41; Gerd Hardach, "Industrial Mobilisation in 1914–1918: Production, Planning, and Ideology," in *The French Home Front, 1914–1918*, ed. Patrick Fridenson (Providence, RI: Berg, 1992), pp. 61–2; Monique Bonneau, "Les femmes et la guerre de 1914–1918: Les ouvrières et l'industrie de guerre," *Le Peuple français* (July–September 1979): 17–18.
6. Flood, *France 1914–18*, p. 76.
7. Picquenard, "La guerre et la question des salaires," p. 74.
8. Downs, *Manufacturing Inequality*, pp. 106–7.
9. AN F⁷ 12937-8, reports of the Prefects, August 1914.
10. Capy, *Une voix de femme*, p. 53.
11. Georges Rendel, "Théorie et pratique des allocations militaires en France," *Revue philanthropique* 19 no. 36 (1915): 70; Paul Strauss, "La guerre et les lois sociales," *La Revue bleue* 53 no. 7 (27 March–3 April 1915): 100. See Thierry Bonzon, "Transfer Payments and Social Policy," in Winter and Roberts (eds), *Capital Cities*, pp. 288–9.
12. The Prefects' reports of August and September 1914 in AN F⁷ 12937-9 contain numerous suggestions for saving money, for example, scrutinizing applicants' savings account records.
13. "Rapport de M Capart sur les allocations militaires en France," *Revue philanthropique* 20 no. 38 (1917): 286–94; "La distribution des secours," *Le Temps*, 4 September 1914; Frédéric Masson, "Pour les femmes," *L'Echo de Paris*, 25 August 1914, and 30 August 1914; Thierry Bonzon, "The Labour Market and Industrial Mobilization, 1915–1917," in Winter and Roberts (eds), *Capital Cities*, p. 185.
14. Maurice Barrès, "Préfets et commissaires, ayez tous du coeur," *L'Echo de Paris*, 2 December 1914.
15. Becker, *The Great War and the French People*, p. 19.
16. Ministère de l'Intérieur, *Décrets, arrêtés et circulaires concernant l'application de la loi du 5 août 1914 sur les allocations aux familles des mobilisés* (Melun: Imprimerie administrative, 1917); Jean-Louis Robert, "La

CGT et la famille ouvrière 1914-1918: première approche," *Le Mouvement social* 116 (July-September 1981): 60.

17. Memo from the Minister of Labor in *Revue philanthropique* 19 no. 36 (1915): 16-19; Bonzon, "Transfer Payments," pp. 291-3.

18. Delécraz, *1914 Paris,* pp. 66-7.

19. Louise Zeys, "Aux femmes de France," *L'Echo de Paris,* 11 August 1914 ; Paul Delay, "Le rapatriement des provinciaux de Paris," *L'Echo de Paris,* 12 August 1914; Michel Augé-Laribé, *L'agriculture pendant la guerre* (Paris: Presses universitaires de France, [192?]), p. 68; Viviani's memos to the prefects printed in *Revue philanthropique* 19 no. 36 (1915): 14-16. According to André Créhange, *Chômage et placement* (Paris: Les presses universitaires de France, 1933), p. 9, the government spent more than 200,000FF on the program.

20. AN F²² 542 Lutte contre le chômage; Delay, "Le rapatriement des provinciaux de Paris."

21. Masson, "Pour les femmes," *L'Echo de Paris,* 18 August 1914. Masson continued to tout this charity in *L'Echo de Paris* throughout 1914 and 1915.

22. René Lavollée, "Pour les veuves et les orphelins de guerre," *Le Correspondant* 226 (10 February 1916): 533-4; "L'oeuvre des veuves et orphelins de la guerre," *Le Petit Parisien,* 21 February 1916.

23. Maria Léra [Marc Hélys], *Cantinière de la Croix-rouge 1914-1916* (Paris: Perrin et cie., 1917), pp. 19-27.

24. Lechartier, *La charité et la guerre,* pp. 10-13. Office central des oeuvres de bienfaisance, *Paris charitable,* pp. 66-82 reported 102 *ouvroirs* run by the various Red Cross societies. It also lists *ouvroirs* run by religious orders, the Protestant Church, women's organizations like the Ligue patriotique des françaises and the Ligue pour le droit des femmes, and even by women's magazines.

25. BMD dos 940.3 Guerre 1914-18; Clotilde Mulon, "Rapport sur l'Office d'utilisation des femmes pendant la guerre," 6 December 1914.

26. AN F²² 542 Lutte contre le chômage, Rapport sur les commandes de lingerie militaire, 21 August 1914; APP Db 352 Marchés - Rapport de la Commission chargée d'examiner les marchés conclus par l'Etat depuis le debut de la guerre, 5 April 1917.

27. Jean Morel, "La guerre et la question des salaries," *La revue bleue* 54 no. 3 (29 January-5 February 1916): 78-9.

28. Mary Lynn Stewart, *Women, Work and the French State: Labour Protection and Social Patriarchy 1879-1916* (Montreal: McGill-Queen's University Press, 1989), pp. 67-72; Bard, *Les filles de marianne,* p. 73; William Oualid and Charles Picquenard, *Salaires et tarifs: Conventions collectives et grèves* (Paris: Presses universitaires de France, 1928), pp. 282-92.

29. Delétang, *Journal d'une ouvrière.*

30. Rageot, *La française dans la guerre,* p. 12; Créhange, *Chômage,* p. 2; AN F⁷ 12937-8 Prefects' reports.

31. Abensour, *Les vaillantes,* p. 35; Misme, "La guerre et le rôle des femmes," pp. 205-6.

32. Réné Bazin, "Celle qui ne savait pas," *L'Echo de Paris,* 27 October 1914 .

33. Barthou, *L'effort de la femme française,* p. 18; "La terre qui vit," *Le Petit parisien,* 6 August 1916; Cunisset-Carnot, "La vie à la campagne: Le patriotisme de nos paysans," *Le Temps,* 29 September 1915; also "Vaillantes françaises," *Le Petit parisien,* 20 September 1914, one of the first encomia in the popular press to peasant women.

34. Courson, *La femme française pendant la guerre,* p. 14; Capy, *Une voix de femme,* p. 46; Bazin, "Celle qui ne savait pas."

35. Nadine, *Rêves de guerre,* p. 138; also La Hire, *La femme française,* p. 63 and Barthou, *L'effort de la femme française,* p. 18. One senator campaigned to have the work of peasant women recognized with a special medal: "On donnera le Mérit agricole à nos paysannes," *Le Petit parisien,* 21 July 1915.

36. Augé-Laribé, *L'agriculture pendant la guerre,* pp. 66-7.

37. Jean-Jacques Becker, *1914: Comment les français sont entrés dans la guerre* (Paris: Presses de la fondation nationale des sciences politiques, 1977), pp. 514-15; Tinayre, *La veillée des armes,* pp. 12, 45, 58; Léra, *Cantinière,* pp. 11-12; Michaux, *En marge du drame,* p. 16.

38. Bontoux, *Les françaises et la grande guerre,* p. 54.

39. Réné Bazin, *La campagne française et la guerre* (Paris: Ch. Eggimann, 1916), p. 6.

40. AN F^{12} 8018^1 Mobilisation civile, 21 February 1917.

41. Augé-Laribé, *L'agriculture pendant la guerre,* p. 173.

42. Michel Gervais, Marcel Jollivet and Yves Tavernier, *La fin de la France paysanne de 1914 à nos jours,* Vol. 4 of *Histoire de la France rurale,* ed. Georges Duby and Armand Wallon (Paris: Seuil, 1976), p. 168.

43. Emmanuel Labat, "La terre pendant l'épreuve. Le devoir paysan," *Revue des deux mondes,* 87 no. 41 (1 September 1917): 179; Bazin, "'Tenir' aux champs," *L'Echo de Paris,* 26 October 1915; Jeannine, "La femme aux champs," *La Bataille,* 24 October 1917. Even Augé-Laribé, *L'agriculture pendant la guerre,* pp. 91-2, felt it was immoral for peasant women to take city jobs. By contrast, Lucien Léauté, "Plaidoyer en faveur des cultivateurs," *La Bataille,* 3 April 1917, objected to the accusations that peasant women were deserters and recommended giving them help in the fields.

44. Christiane Germain and Christine de Panafieu, *La mémoire des femmes: Sept témoignages de femmes nées avec le siècle* (Paris: Editions Sylvie Messinger, 1982), pp. 125-6; Laouénan, *La moisson rouge,* p. 45.

45. Benoit, "Les femmes et la guerre," p 28.

46. Becker, *The Great War,* pp. 13-17.

47. Augé-Laribé, *L'agriculture pendant la guerre,* pp. 65-6.

48. Labat, "Le devoir payson," p. 156; Gervais *et al.,* *La fin de la France paysanne,* pp. 39-44; Lesage, *Journal de guerre;* Hélias, *The Horse of Pride.*

49. Augé-Laribé, *L'agriculture pendant la guerre*, pp. 177-9.

50. Benoit, "Les femmes et la guerre," p. 30.

51. Germain and de Pannafieu, *Mémoire des femmes*, pp. 125-6. Mme D of Aslonnes told a similar story to Benoit, "Les femmes et la guerre," p. 28.

52. Bazin, "'Tenir' aux champs." Also Maria Léra [Marc Hélys pseud.], *Les provinces françaises pendant la guerre* (Paris: Librairie Académique, Perrin et cie., 1918), pp. 202-3, 249-52.

53. Benoit, "Les femmes et la guerre," pp. 28-9.

54. Laouénan, *La moisson rouge*, p. 56.

55. Benoit, "Les femmes et la guerre," p. 29.

56. Carles, *A Life of Her Own*, p. 60.

57. Benoit, "Les femmes et la guerre," pp. 29-30.

58. Augé-Laribé, *L'agriculture pendant la guerre*, p. 69.

59. Perreux, *La vie quotidienne des civils*, pp. 79-80; Augé-Laribé, *L'agriculture pendant la guerre*, p. 83; Audoin-Rouzeau, *La guerre des enfants*, pp. 61, 165; Lavarenne, "Nos écoliers aux champs," *Je sais tout*, 12 no. 130 (15 September 1916): 257-65; Borel, *Mobilisation*, p. 45.

60. *Le Petit parisien*, 3 July 1915.

61. Foucault, *A Château at the Front*, p. 193.

62. Courson, *La femme française pendant la guerre*, pp. 12-13.

63. SHAT 7N 955 EMA 15 April-15 May 1916, also Colette, *Les heures longues* , pp. 374-5 and Becker, *The Great War*, pp. 227, 232.

64. Labat, "Le devoir paysan," pp. 162-3.

65. Marcelle Capy, "Femmes de peine," *La Vie feminine*, ns. no. 2 (4 March 1916).

66. Marcelle Capy, "La femme à l'usine," *La Voix des femmes*, 28 November, 5, 12, 19 December 1917 and 2 January 1918.

67. Delétang, *Journal d'une ouvrière*, pp. 220-1.

68. Capy, "La femme à l'usine" (19 December 1917); Delétang, *Journal d'une ouvrière*, pp. 313-14.

69. For example, "Dans les usines de guerre: Les femmes produisent des munitions et des armes dont se servent leurs maris, leurs frères, leurs pères," *Le Petit parisien*, 10 February 1916.

70. Hardach, "Industrial Mobilisation," pp. 61-2; Downs, *Manufacturing Inequality*, pp. 39-41; Thébaud, *Le femme au temps de la guerre de 14*, pp. 31-2.

71. Cova, *Maternité et droits des femmes*, p. 211 and La Hire, *La femme française*, pp. 112-13. Thomas became Minister of Armaments in December 1916. He resigned from the government along with his socialist colleagues in September 1917 when Clemenceau became Prime Minister.

72. Cited in Bonneau, "Les femmes et la guerre de 1914-1918," p. 18. See La Hire, *La femme française*, pp. 112-16 and Marcel Frois, *La santé et le travail des femmes pendant la guerre* (Paris: Presses universitaires de France, 1926), p. 14 and *passim* on the Comité du Travail féminin.

73. Downs, *Manufacturing Inequality*, p. 51; Créhange, *Chômage*, p. 44; Perreux, *La vie quotidienne des civils*, p. 57.

74. BMD dos 331 Office du travail féminin; Borel, *Mobilisation*; Arthur Fontaine, response to Paul Strauss, *La Revue bleue* 53 no. 7 (27 March–3 April 1915): 105; SHAT 7N 159 main d'oeuvre féminine, circular 14 October 1916. Oualid and Picquenard, *Salaires et tarifs*, pp. 63–4.

75. "Les moyens de <<tenir>>: Le devoir de production et d'action." *La France militaire*, 27 January 1916.

76. AN F^{12} 8018 Mobilisation civile, Sénat no. 480: Proposition de loi, instituant la mobilisation civile et organisant la main-d'oeuvre nationale en France et dans les colonies, Henry Bérenger, (29 December 1916).

77. Ibid., Projet de loi, no. 30; Senate report no. 77 (1917).

78. Paul Deprade, "Le service de guerre obligatoire," *La Grande revue* (December 1916): 193–200; Deprade, "L'organisation du service de guerre obligatoire," *La Grande revue* (January 1917): 461–71; Un sapeur, "Le préjugé des effectifs et la mobilisation civile," *La Grande revue* (February 1917): 584–611. In fact, the German Auxiliary Service Law did not conscript women; Daniel, *War From Within*, pp. 65–85.

79. Delétang, *Journal d'une ouvrière*, p. 307.

80. Jane Misme, "Il faut orienter et former l'activité féminine," *La Française*, 17 February 1917.

81. AN F^{12} 8018 Mobilisation civile, Senate report no. 77 (1917).

82. Rageot, *La française dans la guerre*, pp. 4–5; also La Hire, *La femme française*, p. 112; Baronne Brincard, "L'armée féminine de la défense nationale," *Revue hebdomadaire* (19 May 1917): 347. Women munitions workers were included in a parade on 20 October 1918 in Paris honoring the conscripts of the class of 1920, according to Delétang, *Journal d'une ouvrière*, p. 441.

83. "Les hommes combattent, les femmes travaillent," *Lectures pour tous* (15 January 1916): 604–12; Jane Simone, "Journal d'une 'remplaçante.'" *Je sais tout* 12 no. 130 (15 September 1916): 319–28; also Francis Miomandre, "Chez les amazones," *La Vie parisienne* 55 no. 7 (17 February 1917): 154–7; Jules Chancel, "Nos remplaçantes," *Le Petit journal*, 27 January 1916; "Quinze jours comme ouvrière de la défense nationale," *Le Petit parisien*, 19, 20, 21, 24, 27 July 1916; and a series of articles celebrating various *remplaçantes* in *Le Petit parisien*, from 15 August 1916 to 9 October 1916.

84. Paul Strauss, "Le travail féminin dans les usines de guerre," *Revue philanthropique* 19 (1917): 119; also Albert Thomas's speech to the munitions workers of Saint-Chamond, reported in *L'Illustration* 73 no. 3786 (25 September 1915): 338–9 and the propagandists Bontoux, *La grande guerre*, p. 50; La Hire, *La femme française*, p. 108; and Rageot, *La française dans la guerre*, p. 18.

85. Henri Joly, "De l'extension du travail des femmes après la guerre," *Le Correspondant* 266 (10 January 1917): 13. Perreux, *La vie quotidienne*

des civils, p. 57 claimed that some employers devised a point system for their priority lists, with war widows rating 20, sisters of those killed in action 10, wives of wounded soldiers 5 and of prisoners of war, 2.

86. Jean-Louis Robert, "Women and Work in France During the First World War," in Wall and Winter (eds), *The Upheaval of War*, p. 262; McMillan, *Housewife or Harlot*, pp. 132–3. Historians of British and German women war workers have reached similar conclusions: Braybon, *Women Workers in the First World War*, pp. 47–50; Woollacott, *On Her Their Lives Depend:*, pp. 17–22; Daniel, *The War From Within*, pp. 38–49.

87. Frois, *La santé et le travail des femmes*, p. 138; Angèle Bory d'Arnex [Jacques Vincent pseud.], *Parisiennes de guerre (1915–1917)* (Paris: Editions de la France, 1918), p. 248.

88. "Les hommes combattent, les femmes travaillent," p. 605; also Chancel, "Nos remplaçantes;" "Celles qui remplacent les mobilisés: Brosseuses et receveuses de tramway," *Le Petit parisien*, 5 September 1916.

89. Delétang, *Journal d'une ouvrière*, pp. 55, 148.

90. "Les hommes combattent, les femmes travaillent," p. 609.

91. "La tenue des ouvrières dans les fabriques de munitions," *Le Petit parisien*, 20 August 1916.

92. Bory d'Arnex, *Parisiennes*, pp. 249–51, 258–9; "Celles qui remplacent les mobilisés: Femmes débardeuses et femmes d'équipe," *Le Petit parisien*, 9 October 1916. Both L. Dorliat in Clermont, *Souvenirs de parisiennes*, pp. 218–19 and Yvonne Sarcey, "La visite des universitaires des annales aux usines Citroën," *Les annales conferencia; journal de l'Université des annales* (1918): 276 pointed to the workers' love of flowers as feminizing the factory.

93. "Une travailleuse de l'usine de guerre," *L'Illustration* 74 no. 3816 (22 April 1916): 380, also Borel, *Mobilisation*, pp. 48–9; Rageot, *La française dans la guerre*, p. 4; Abensour, *Les vaillantes*, p. 73.

94. Downs, "Les marraines élues de la paix sociale? Les surintendants d'usine et la rationalisation du travail en France 1917-1935," *Le Mouvement social* 164 (July–September 1993): 59 and *Manufacturing Inequality*, p. 83; also Rageot, *La française dans la guerre*, p. 4; "Les hommes combattent, les femmes travaillent," pp. 608, 610; La Hire, *La femme française*, p. 96.

95. "Brosseuses et receveuses de tramway;" "Les hommes combattent, les femmes travaillent," pp. 608–12; La Hire, *La femme française*, pp. 101–2.

96. Georges Yvetot, "Grève souriante," *La Bataille*, 24 May 1917. *Le Petit parisien* front-page coverage began on 17 May; also BMD dos 331 grèves 1914–1918, press clippings.

97. Becker, *The Great War*, pp. 205–16; Monique Bonneau, "Luttes ouvrières: Les grèves de 1917 et 1918," *Le Peuple français* (April–June 1979): 24–9; John N. Horne, *Labour at War: France and Britain 1914–*

1918 (Oxford: Clarendon Press, 1991), pp. 176–89; Mathilde Dubesset, Françoise Thébaud and Catherine Vincent, "Female Munitions Workers of the Seine," in Fridenson (ed.), *The French Home Front*, pp. 203–7; Thébaud, *La femme au temps de la guerre de 14*, pp. 258–64 ; Oualid and Picquenard, *Salaires et tarifs*, pp. 330–400.

98. AN F⁷ 12986 Guerre de 1914, Haute Garonne, report 9 June 1917.

99. Pourcher, *Les jours de guerre*, pp. 129–45; Horne, *Labour at War*, p. 395; Manning, "Wages and Purchasing Power," pp. 257–9.

100. La Hire, *La femme française*, pp. 134–5.

101. BMD dos 331 grèves 1914–1918, press clippings.

102. Cited in Madeleine Colin, *Ce n'est pas d'aujourd'hui . . . femmes, syndicats, luttes de classe* (Paris: Editions sociales, 1975), p. 75.

103. Corday, *The Paris Front*, p. 253. Une actrice de la Comédie française, *La vie frivole pendant la guerre* (Paris: Ernest Flammarion, 1931), pp. 129–30 remembered the *midinette* strike as "souriante . . . même fleurie." Delétang, herself a garment worker, was not so enchanted. She described them on May 26 as raucous and vulgar. But then, she frowned upon strikes: *Journal d'une ouvrière*, p. 338.

104. Duchêne cited in Bard, *Les filles de marianne*, p. 77; Thomas cited in Bonneau, "Les grèves de 1917 et 1918," p. 25.

105. Becker, *The Great War*, pp. 216, 221; Corday, *The Paris Front*, pp. 254–5; Louis de Launay, "Problèmes économiques d'après la guerre: la main-d'oeuvre," *Revue des deux mondes* 271 (January–February 1919): 168.

106. Oualid and Picquenard, *Salaires et tarifs*, pp. 359, 367.

107. Delétang, *Journal d'une ouvrière*, pp. 337–8.

108. Cited in Cochet, "L'opinion et le moral des soldats," II: p. 347.

109. Dubesset *et al.*, "Female Muntions Workers," p. 90 note that police spies in cafés found this belief was widespread. Commentators, like Narquet, "La française de demain," p. 602 repeated it in print.

110. Léra, *Les provinces françaises pendant la guerre*, p. 14.

111. Flood, *France 1914–1918*, pp. 124–5. C. Vallée, "La vie chère – ses causes," *La Nouvelle revue* (1 November 1918): 10–18 endorsed this view.

112. Augé-Laribé, *L'agriculture pendant la guerre*, pp. 153–6; Jean-Louis Robert, "The Image of the Profiteer," in Winter and Roberts (eds) *Capital Cities*, pp. 120–2.

113. Pourcher, *Les jours de guerre*, pp. 155–6; Laouénan, *La moisson rouge*, pp. 247–8

114. Comment from a postal censor, 10 October 1916, cited in Cochet, *L'opinion et le moral des soldats* II: p. 464; Becker, *The Great War*, p. 122; Augé-Laribé, *L'agriculture pendant la guerre*, p. 173; also Narquet, "La française de demain," p. 629 and SHAT 7N 955 EMA Section de contrôle, 15 February–15 March 1918.

115. André Ducasse *et al.*, *Vie et mort des français, 1914–1918.* (Paris: Hachette, 1959), p. 259; Narquet, "La française de demain," pp. 629–30; Becker, *The Great War*, pp. 119–20.

116. Magd-Abril, "La vie d'une famille ouvrière pendant la guerre," *La Renaissance* 6 no. 5 (2 March 1918): 1-3 (emphasis in text); Marie Diemer, "Les usines de guerre et la main-d'oeuvre féminine," *L'automobile aux armés* 13 (September 1917): 38; also Corday, *The Paris Front*, p. 148 and Delétang, *Journal d'une ouvrière*, pp. 221-2.

117. Cited in Becker, *The Great War*, p. 122.

118. Bory d'Arnex, *Parisiennes*, pp. 252-3; also Narquet, "La française de demain," p. 602.

119. Léra, *Les provinces françaises pendant la guerre*, pp. 7-8.

120. Magd-Abril, "La vie d'une famille ouvrière," p. 3.

121. Speech in a meeting of the Comité de défense syndicaliste, 16 December 1917, cited in Robert, "La CGT," p. 62.

122. Léra, *Les provinces françaises pendant la guerre*, p. 8.

123. Diemer, "Les usines de guerre," p. 38; Marianne, "Libre Propos," *Voix des femmes* 6 (5 December 1917); also Ducasse *et al.*, *Vie et mort*, pp. 263-4 and Delétang, *Journal d'une ouvrière*, p. 341.

124. Diemer, "Les usines de guerre," p. 38.

125. Robert, "La CGT," p. 62; also Georges Yvetot, "Travailleuse, viens à nous!" *Voix des femmes* 1 (31 October 1917).

126. Cochet, *L'opinion et le moral des soldats*, II: pp. 326, 464; SHAT 16 N 2405 Permissionnaires, Contrôle postal, 27 July 1917.

127. Henriot [Jean Henry Maigrot], *De l'arrière au front; Croquis de Henriot* (Paris: E. Fasquelle, 1917).

128. Louise Bodin, "Voyons Mesdames . . ." *Voix des femmes* 6 (5 December 1917).

129. Gaubert, *Voix de femmes*, p. 31.

130. Capy, "La femme à l'usine," and "Quinze jours comme ouvrière de la défense nationale," *Le Petit parisien*, 19-27 July 1916.

131. "Quinze jours comme ouvrière de la défense nationale," *Le Petit parisien*, 27 July 1916.

132. Jeanne Baraduc [Jeanne Galzy pseud.], *La femme chez les garçons* (Paris: Payot et cie., 1919) and Lesage, *Journal de guerre*.

133. Frois, *La santé et le travail des femmes*, pp. 119-37; Dubesset *et al.*, "Female Munitions Workers," pp. 194-200; and Stewart, *Women, Work and the French State*, pp. 189-90. See William H. Schneider, *Quality and Quantity: The Quest for Biological Regeneration in Twentieth-Century France* (Cambridge: Cambridge University Press, 1990) for an account of Pinard's career in these movements. In 1917 he was undoubtedly the best-known obstetrician in France.

134. For example *Le Petit parisien*, 14, 21, 23 February 1917 and the *Revue philanthropique* 19 (1916) and 20 (1917). For socialist opinion, see Jeanne Bouvier, "L'usine de guerre, tueuse d'enfants," *L'Action féminine* 47 (March 1917) and Adolphe Hodée, "La maternité: fonction sociale," *La Bataille*, 27 August 1917. For discussions of the debate, see Cova, *Maternité*

et droits des femmes, pp. 213-17 and Dubesset *et al.*, "Female Munitions Workers," pp. 194-7.

135. Besides the works on pronatalism already cited, see Alisa Kraus, "Depopulation and Race Suicide: Maternalism and Pronatalist Ideologies in France and the United States," in *Mothers of a New World: Maternalist Politics and the Origins of Welfare States*, ed. Seth Koven and Sonya Michel (New York: Routledge, 1993); Philip E. Ogden and Marie-Monique Huss, "Demography and Pronatalism in France in the Nineteenth and Twentieth Centuries," *Journal of Historical Geography* 8 no. 3 (1982): 283-98; Offen, "Depopulation, Nationalism, and Feminism," pp. 648-76.

136. AN F^{22} 538 Rapport de M le professeur Bué sur la protection de la maternité ouvrière pendant la guerre; also Frois, *La santé et le travail des femmes*, pp. 138-9.

137. On the work of the Committee see Dubesset *et al.*, "Female Munitions Workers, " pp. 194-200; AN F^{22} 534 crèches; 538 Rapports divers; 539 Hygiène; Frois, *La santé et le travail des femmes*, pp. 127-32.

138. Abensour, *Les vaillantes*, pp. 73-4; La Hire, *La femme française*, p. 118.

139. Dr Jacques Amédée Doléris and Jean Bouscatel, *Néo-malthusianisme: Maternité et féminisme: Education sexuelle* (Paris: Masson et cie., 1918), p. 254.

140. Diemer, "Les usines de guerre," pp. 36-8.

141. Strauss, "Le travail féminin dans les usines de guerre;" "La mère et l'enfant dans les usines de guerre," *Le Petit parisien*, 14 February 1917; Frois, *La santé et le travail des femmes*," pp. 120-4. Undoubtedly women's health deteriorated during the war, especially during 1917-1918. Catherine Rollet, "The 'Other War' I: Protecting Public Health," in Winter and Roberts (eds), *Capital Cities*, pp. 470-80 points to factory work as only one of several possible causes.

142. Diemer, "Les usines de guerre," pp. 36-8; Frois, *La santé et le travail des femmes*, pp. 42-3; Brincard, "L'armée féminine," p. 340.

143. Frois, *La santé et le travail des femmes,* p. 126.

144. Downs, *Manufacturing Inequality*, p. 173.

145. Cited in Dubesset *et al.*, "Female Munitions Workers," p. 195.

146. Roberts, *Civilization Without Sexes*, pp. 1-16.

147. Doléris and Bouscatel, *Néo-malthusianisme*, p. 22.

148. Brincard, "L'armée féminine, " p. 340; also Diemer, "Les usines de guerre."

149. Frois, *La santé et le travail des femmes,* p. 42.

150. Cova, *Maternité et droits des femmes*, p. 219.

151. Auguste Pawlowski, "La main-d'oeuvre féminine pendant la guerre," *Revue politique et parlementaire* (10 May 1917): 254-5, 250; also Raymond Thamin, "L'éducation des filles après la guerre," *Revue des deux mondes* 53 (1 October 1918): 521 and Abensour, *Les vaillantes*, pp. 118-19.

152. Dr V. Wallich, "Ce que feront les femmes après la guerre," *Revue philanthropique* 20 no. 38 (1917): 476; De Launay, "Problèmes économiques."

153. Cited in Cova, *Maternité et droits de femmes*, p. 203. De Witt-Schlumberger was not typical among feminists in her pronatalism. A member of the Conseil supérieur de la natalité and a militant of the league Pour la Vie, she published a pamphlet entitled *Mères de la patrie ou traîtres à la patrie.*

154. Alexandre Millerand, "Le devoir de demain," *La Revue bleue* 55 no. 8 (14-21 April 1917): 229.

155. Hodée, "La maternité;" Jeannine, "La femme au foyer," *La Bataille*, 16 November 1917; also A. Keufer in *L'avenir de la France, réformes nécessaires*, ed. Maurice Herbette (Paris: Félix Alcan, 1918), p. 400. Women socialists and labor activists like Capy, *Une voix de femme* and Hélène Brion, *La voie féministe* (1917) criticized this opinion as prejudiced and hypocritical.

156. Doléris and Bouscatel, *Néo-malthusianisme.*

157. Pawlowski, "La main-d'oeuvre féminine," p. 255 n.

158. Joly, "De l'extension du travail," p. 26; Jules Amar, "Reflexions d'un physiologiste sur la femme et le 'féminisme,'" *La Revue bleue* 56 no. 4 (February 1918): 116; Gabrielle Rosenthal, "Pour préparer les femmes de demain," *La Grande revue* 20 no. 2 (February 1916): 739-41. Adolphe Carnot in the inquiry, "La France d'après la guerre," *La Renaissance* 3 no 7 (1 May 1915): 1415-17 proposed that mothers of large families be granted a vote, but Henri Mazel, *La nouvelle cité de France* (Paris: Félix Alcan, 1917), p. 264, limited their proposed political status to a consultative assembly appointed by the legislature.

159. Toulouse, *La reforme sociale*, pp. 159-63.

160. Bazin, "Les fermes après la guerre," *L'Echo de Paris*, 15 December 1914; Amar, "Reflexions d'un physiologiste," p. 120; and Bazin, "Fermes vides," *L'Echo de Paris*, 10 January 1916.

161. Labat, "Le devoir paysan," p. 169.

162. Cited in Dubesset *et al.*, "Female Munitions Workers," p. 208.

163. André Citroèn, "La vie à l'usine," *Les annales conferencia; journal de l'Université des annales* (1918): 261-75; Downs, *Manufacturing Inequality*, pp. 188-9, 204; Joshua Cole, "The Transition to Peace, 1918-1919" in Winter and Roberts (eds), *Capital Cities*, pp. 209-11.

164. *La Vague*, 1 May 1919 cited in Dubesset *et al.*, "Female Munitions Workers," p. 208.

165. Such as Lt. Georges Grandjean, *De la dépravation . . . des femmes . . . des décadences* (Paris: La Maison d'art et d'édition, 1919).

166. Amar, "Reflexions d'un physiologiste," p. 119.

167. Downs, *Manufacturing Inequality*, pp. 188-9, 206.

168. Léon Abensour, "Le problème de la démobilisation féminine," *La Grande revue* 88 no. 1 (January 1919): 80-91.

169. De Launay, "Problèmes économiques," p. 166.
170. Ibid.; Toulouse, *La réforme sociale*, pp. 197–203.
171. Downs, *Manufacturing Inequality*, pp. 207–25.
172. Ibid., p. 210.
173. BMD dos 331 Receveuses tramways-bus, press clippings.

7

"I Want To Be Militarized"

In September 1915, a reporter from *Le Figaro* interviewed two women "young, discreetly elegant and as serious as bourgeois young ladies . . . One of them speaks in a hesitant, almost childish voice: 'Won't you speak for us, sir? What we ask is so simple. Like all women at this moment, we want to be of use.'"[1] This was a request that the French government had heard over and over since August 1914. But these were not young women "whose family, social position and studies have not prepared them for any particular occupation,"[2] as so many applicants were. Instead they were acclaimed aviatrices, whose exploits had contributed to France's world leadership in aviation. One of them, Marie Marvingt, was the first pilot to climb higher than 1,000 meters. The press had dubbed them modern Joans of Arc, demonstrating that in France, at least, bravura courage was not exclusively male.[3] Now they only wanted "to make our work useful. The aviators are warmly welcomed everywhere. Why rebuff the aviatrices?"[4]

Great Britain, Russia, the United States and Germany all authorized women's military auxiliary corps during the First World War;[5] but France did not. Although French women contributed mightily to the war effort, they did so only in private organizations or as individuals. The French government refused officially to mobilize or to militarize women. Why? First, the French government refused to recognize women as citizens with duties to the nation. As we have seen in Chapter 2, military service was tightly bound into French concepts of citizenship. If the state admitted women to military service, it would necessarily imply that women were full citizens. A major argument against women's suffrage and civic equality would be swept away. Despite the desperate shortage of military manpower, the French government resisted all efforts to obtain women's assistance with any such quid pro quo.

Second, the questions of whether and how women could and should contribute to the military raised in the most direct way all the dilemmas and anxieties about the relationship of women to the war. The possibility of militarizing women threatened the foundation of wartime gender construction. The military incarnated masculinity directed to the national cause. Besides reclaiming France's position in the world, the French army's exploits in war were supposed to restore masculine dominance in society, righting the wrongs that female emancipation and male decadence had done the gender system. To admit women to the military would undermine this project; either the army would masculinize the women or the women would feminize the army. The war's mission to restore virility to its proper role in French society would be betrayed.

To militarize women without further disrupting the gender system required a reconceptualizion of the relationship between gender and war; but this was rarely attempted. In the main, commentators and policy-makers sought to contain gender transgression by redefining the boundaries of masculine and feminine to keep men and women properly within them. This meant enlarging the feminine sphere and constricting the masculine by acknowledging that the war zone and the military contained within them outcroppings of the *arrière* and the civilian that could be appropriately assigned to women. The historians Margaret and Patrice Higonnet imagine the gender system as a double helix, a bifurcated spiral in which position on the feminine strand is always subordinate to position on the masculine strand. In wartime, they argue, women take on roles previously reserved for men, but this does not advance women's status relative to men, because the men vacating these roles have stepped up into the even more masculine role of soldier.[6] Opening certain jobs within the French military to women had the effect of advancing the gender relationship along this double helix; as women moved into formerly masculine territory in military administration, supply and support, now redefined as feminine, men were pushed up into the super-masculine preserves of command and combat. The gender construct would hold, although at a cost, most significantly paid in male lives in the trenches, but also in women's continued civic inequality.

Manpower and Citizenship

The decade of nationalist fervor that preceded the First World War had pushed the governments of both Britain and France hesitantly to recognize and organize an official, although strictly limited, role for women in the national defense: nursing. Besides creating small paid, professional army nursing corps of women, both countries included Red Cross nurses in their mobilization plans. In both cases, although recognized by the military and put under military authority in certain situations, these women remained unpaid volunteers, recruited and administered by private organizations and funded by their own resources and charitable contributions. As the historian Sharon Ouditt writes of the British case, but equally valid for the French, "if women were to contribute to their country's war effort they could do so, but at their own expense."[7] With the outbreak of the war, as we have seen, this hybrid form of private yet semi-official aid provided by women to military personnel spread quickly from nursing to many other services – canteens, hostels, clothing, food, entertainment, artificial limbs for the amputated, vocational training for the blinded, financial support to their widows and homes for their orphaned children. Many of these organizations sought and secured official recognition for their work. Indeed, the ministries of war in both France and England devoted a considerable amount of attention to their activities.

Most of these volunteer initiatives supported the war effort by trying to relieve the distress it caused. As Marie-Louise Le Verrier wrote in the feminist journal *La Française* in 1913, women's role in war was to "aid, to save, to console ... if possible we want to make our sons' and husbands' ultimate sacrifices less cruel by relieving the misery of our soldiers and alleviating their distress and by participating a little in the defense of our country."[8] And in this war, as we have seen, the French government was willing for women to provide these services.

Once the First World War became a war of attrition, however, feminine mobilization to alleviate suffering no longer sufficed. "Manpower," as it was termed in Britain, became the most pressing issue for the economy, but also for the military. As the shortage of male industrial workers led the Under-secretary for Artillery Albert Thomas to propose that munitions manufacturers hire women, a shortage of men in the trenches led military authorities in both England and France to consider using womanpower in non-combat jobs. The British military created the Women's Auxiliary Army Corps (WAAC) in 1917 and followed it shortly with naval and air force auxiliaries, the WRNS and the WRAF. By the end of the war, about 100,000 women had served in the British paramilitary and military auxiliary corps.[9] France chose a different solution: to recruit women as employees of the military. By 1917, the French army employed some 120,000 women as office staff, telephone operators, drivers, carpenters, and kitchen and laundry workers.[10] These French women did much of the same work as the British women's military corps; but they did it as civilians.

The British decision to militarize women and the French decision to employ them as civilians can be explained on purely practical, logistical grounds. The war was fought largely in France: thus the French military could recruit women from the local civilian population. The female staff could live at home and work for the military as they would for any other employer. By contrast, if the British army wanted to employ British women as telephone operators or laundresses in France, the army would have to take them along. The most practical solution was to take them as part of the military itself.

But practical concerns were not the whole story, and probably were not even the main story. As investigation of the French army's employment of women shows, the military was not comparable to civilian employers, and its efforts to employ women as civilians created many problems that militarization would have solved. Behind the two approaches emerge two different philosophies, engendered, for the most part, by differing political contexts. While it was important to the British government that women's work for the military be interpreted as an embodiment of national mobilization, in the French case, no such interpretation was necessary or desirable.

The first factor influencing the British decision to militarize women was the proven usefulness of women's private paramilitary groups, such as the Women's Convoy Corps and the Marchioness of Londonderry's Women's Legion. Women in these organizations wore uniforms and performed military-like duties, sometimes for the army itself; but they were not part of the military. They were recruited, organized and administered as private organizations with their own leadership, usually by notable women, in much the same way as benevolent organizations. The British army used services provided by some of these groups, especially nursing, cooking and transport, before considering creating its own female corps.[11]

The second factor was the "manpower" crisis, created, the British War Office was convinced, by men refusing to volunteer. As the historian Jenny Gould argues "if the [British] army could have gotten all the men it wanted without having to organize women, it probably would not have bothered to form the Women's Army Auxiliary Corps."[12] Desperate for more men, the British War Office demanded that Parliament institute conscription to flush out the "shirkers." To support this radical departure from the British tradition of a volunteer army, the War Office believed it had to demonstrate that the army was doing the utmost with all those who had volunteered. As a result, military and government officials began to consider seriously the formal use of women volunteers in the military. Conscription could then legitimately figure as a measure of last resort.[13] Thus women entered the British military as a consequence of the pressures of a shortage of men and the politics of conscription.

Because British women's admission into the military occurred within the context of a debate over conscription, it unavoidably played into the argument for female citizenship rights. Before the war, the militant wing of the British suffrage movement, the WSPU, had proclaimed British women's willingness to do military service on the same terms as men. The female paramilitary organizations claimed to be making good this commitment. Most British feminists in the mainstream suffrage movement, the NUWSS, and the WSPU made explicit the relationship between women's mobilization for war and their claim to political rights. Calling off their suffrage activities for the duration of the war and offering their services to the national defense, they demanded that the duties they were now performing must be repaid in short order with the franchise.[14] In creating women's military auxiliaries, the British government confirmed that, by volunteering to serve their country, British women were fulfilling the duties of citizenship.

By late 1915 the same shortage of men that was forcing the British to consider conscription also confronted the French army. The general solution – to use women in non-combat jobs to release men for the trenches – was the same as that contemplated in Britain. But because the political context was quite different, the policies the French government developed to mobilize women were markedly less favorable to women's claims to citizenship. In England, militarization of women was in part a public relations ploy to make male conscription palatable. In this context, women's voluntary status and civic commitment were nearly as important as the work they could do. For their action to demonstrate the need for male conscription, women had to be seen as female citizens, voluntarily rising to perform a service to the nation, a service that should be performed by men. In France, where universal male conscription already obtained, the initiative was couched in terms of simple efficiency, to free the men already conscripted for combat.

Grayzel?

Demonstrations of female citizenship were irrelevant. Thus, the French military had an option not available to the British government, to recruit women not as volunteers but as employees. The French military authorities chose to follow the precedent of industry and the civil service: they did not militarize women, they only employed them as individual civilians. In this way, they denied any suggestion that women, like men, were being called to national service, for which they should be recompensed with rights.

Like the British War Office, the French Minister of War made his decision within the context of the current discussions and demands, both of the army and of French women. Although France did not boast the number and strength of women's paramilitary groups that Britain did, nonetheless, over the course of the war some French women challenged the government, military authorities and public opinion to acknowledge that women, too, had a right and a duty to defend *la patrie*. They formed organizations, and some wore uniforms and even drilled in order to illustrate their claim. Most of the time, both the government and the press ignored them. But for a brief period, public opinion and policy-makers took up the issue of women's possible role in the military, and these women's initiatives achieved a certain prominence. For about eight months, from the spring to the fall of 1915, we find the efforts of women to be accorded military status publicized, discussed, and sometimes even applauded in the press, and considered seriously by the Ministry of War.

The discussion began in the spring of 1915 as a result of a changing understanding of the nature of the war and the evolution of women's volunteer war work. It was by then clear that France could not exist indefinitely in suspended animation; but neither could normal life return while the war raged. As the war of heroism became a war of attrition, a different relationship between the front and the *arrière*, and between masculine and feminine, had to be negotiated. While the chivalric knight required only that his lady weep at his fall or cheer at his triumph, the trench-fighter needed active assistance. Recognition that civilian society must aid the war effort if France was to be defended opened a greater terrain to women's initiatives.

Secondly, by the spring of 1915, women had seven months of experience in war work behind them. They had participated in both successful and unsuccessful volunteer efforts, and could now identify the needs to be met and the strategies most likely to succeed in meeting them. The first unfocused impulses to do *something* had been refined into programs and organizations. They had learned that even the war emergency did not obviate the need for lobbying and publicity in order to carry out their projects. The final factor was that throughout the spring and summer of 1915, although the government and the military were increasingly aware that women needed to be mobilized more effectively, the authorities were undecided about how best to use womanpower. The discussion was closed in the late fall of 1915 when the Ministry of War made its decision and launched its campaign to use women as civilian employees of the military.

Women's Paramilitary Organizations, 1915

When France's aviatrices made their plea in *Le Figaro* in September 1915, they were taking part in a reanimated public discussion about women's relationship to the military. Begun in 1913 by Mme Dieulafoy, the debate had languished in the first months of the war. As the Académician Maurice Donnay lectured approvingly, unlike British women, who immediately clamored to join regiments, French women had been content to enlist in humanitarian crusades.[15] However, by the time Donnay gave this speech, the issue had re-arisen. On 6 March 1915, *La Française* contemplated the prospect of "Women in the Army."[16]

In the following months, the discussion escalated over the potential benefits and risks of militarizing women, pushed by the personnel needs of the army and by some women's desire to act out their citizenship in military service. While many commentators continued to maintain that the nature of war and of women forbade women from playing any role in the military, others began to explore arguments in favor of their militarization. Initially, they presented the primary benefit as the solution to the military's shortage of combat soldiers, while the main risks appeared as threats to the gender order. In response to the latter, advocates of women's militarization devised a counter-argument; rather than masculinizing women, as their opponents claimed, women's entry into the military would remasculinize men – by removing them from "feminine" non-combat jobs and sending them into combat.

It was foreign examples rather than the proposals of French women that reopened the discussion of women's role in the military. Although Mme Dieulafoy's proposal for a female army reserve had received wide publicity in 1913, no one seemed to have remembered this until the French were confronted with the activities of Serbian women and Russian women, the alleged mobilization of German women and especially the presence of British paramilitary women in their midst. *Le Temps* raised the issue for the first time in July 1915 in response to a false report that Germany was going to conscript women. The article stated that although the issue had a vaudevillian ring, it had, in fact, originated with Mme Dieulafoy and "perhaps, all the same and pleasantry put aside," it was time for the French Ministry of War to consider it seriously. At the same time, the psychologist Dr Toulouse was waging a campaign in the pages of *Le Petit parisien* in favor of the French army following the British example. He also recalled Dieulafoy's proposal, but claimed that she and other feminists had gotten the idea from him![17]

The driving force of this discussion was a feared shortage of soldiers for the trenches, and the tone was rough-and-ready practicality that belittled concerns of gender disruption as trivial or pure prejudice. Dr Toulouse was the most voluble exponent of this argument. In a series of articles published in *Le Petit parisien* from July 1915 to January 1916, he defended the idea of admitting women to non-combat jobs in the military by citing examples of women's invaluable work replacing men in industry and civil administration. Pointing to the nurses under bombardment in the Dardenelles, he even justified using women in the war zone. And to those who intoned that "woman is weak, ignorant, undisciplined, indiscreet" and that to admit her into the business of war was to court "the end of all discipline . . . or the ruin of public morality," he replied that this was bunk. "The truth is that women in the armed forces will upset a few routines and here and there create some problems that will annoy our officials." This, he concluded, was a small price to pay for the inestimable contribution women could make. "No one has found anything better than women to help men in civilian life; we should try this system in the military."[18]

By identifying women's potential role in the military with their current replacement of men in civilian employment, Toulouse side-stepped the issue of the relationship between the feminine and war; but he slipped into it when he explained why he barred women from combat. At first he argued that this chivalry was based upon practicality; for the future of humanity, women's reproductive capacity had to be protected. "But our civilization rests on a law dear to all men's hearts: woman must not be exposed to violence or

236

brutal death. And, from a biological point of view, this law is perfectly justified. To ensure the perpetuation of the race, women's lives are infinitely more precious than ours."[19] This argument drew upon the traditional configuration of gender in wartime – men fighting to protect women – and implied its concomitant geographic segregation, man in the combat zone, women in the *arrière*. But Toulouse also argued that women be admitted to the war zone, especially as nurses. It was not risk of death that he denied women, but the right "to carry a gun. Women must not fire a shot, but they may expose themselves to danger."[20] His rationale for excluding women from combat was less "biological," then, than ideological, resting upon the polarity of life-giving and life-taking identified as feminine and masculine. Women could not engage in the real business of war, killing: that was the exclusive property, perhaps even the definition, of masculinity.

For those who opposed any relationship between women and the military, this gender ideology was the core of their argument. They did not deny that a manpower crisis existed; but they argued that to militarize women was not a viable solution. For them, Dr Toulouse's few problems and little annoyances became disabling catastrophes.[21] They drew upon a long tradition of iconography and discourse about French women in the military. One strand came from the music hall, with its play of cross-dressing and sex and gender transgression.[22] The other, carrying a similar but much more threatening message, came from images of women in France's revolutionary history, in 1793, 1848 and especially in 1871.[23] While the press smirked at the burlesque *femme-soldat* whose hour-glass figure burst out of her grenadier tunic (see Figure 7.1), she could not entirely banish the specter of gun-toting Louise Michel, the "red virgin" of the Commune. A woman in uniform was, paradoxically, an autonomous woman, not a wife, mother, sister or daughter – or mistress or prostitute. The uniform declared that her identity was not dependent upon a man but upon the state, which, in time of revolution, meant upon no authority at all. More than a transgression of the gender system, this was a denial of it, shaking civilization at its roots.

Such a scenario for disaster faced its own credibility problem, however, in the image of Joan of Arc. As Joan had loomed over pre-war discussion of French women's role in war, her presence also colored the wartime debate. Commentators who opposed the militarization of women had to explain why, if it was admirable for

Figure 7.1 Postcard of the music-hall image of the woman soldier. The caption at the top left reports: "Her presence will make a stay in the trenches more agreeable." © Musée d'histoire contemporaine – BDIC, reproduction by Archipel.

her to ride into battle, it was not appropriate for modern French women to follow her example. For most, it was because the female war heroines of the past were too masculine. In *Le Temps*, Jules Bertaut thanked God for Joan of Arc and the warrior princesses of the past, but nonetheless shook his head: "But you will notice that almost all the characteristics of these women are virile traits that have nothing to do with the feminine." France's modern civilization required a different version of heroism, and Bertaut pointed to the Invasion Heroine as a model:

> Which is the most beautiful role, that of the citizeness who throws herself into the action, the rebellious adventuress prancing at the head of the troops, or the humble woman standing stoically before the enemy, submitting . . . to the worst insults without her courage or her hope weakening? The latter has less drama but how much more human it is, how much better it conforms to feminine nature![24]

From this point of view, other nations' militarization of women was a sign of their lack of civilization. That Germany should intend "garrisoning of women" (not true in fact) attested to the savagery of German customs; some commentators implied this of Serbia and Russia as well.[25] As for the British "misses" in uniform, they were a symptom of the dangerous disorder of gender relations that infected British society, already evident in such pre-war phenomena as the aesthetes and the Suffragettes. In explaining why French women should not see in British women the reincarnation of Joan of Arc, Nadine, a columnist in the *Tribune de l'Aube*, stated that French women, fortunately, were not raised as tomboys; they did not play golf and tennis, they were "far from the intrepid English Suffragettes and too close to our bewigged grandmothers, too close to the old France!" This, she argued, was to the good, because, if the French woman did not have the strong hands of the British girl, she was blessed with a large heart – surely a more valuable attribute. In the typical calculation of gender as a scale balancing masculine and feminine, Nadine implied that, by gaining masculine hands, British girls had lost feminine hearts.[26]

Léon Absensour suggested an even more disturbing equation: as British women were gaining masculinity, British men were losing it. In admiring but fearful tones, Absensour described British paramilitary women as amazons, marching with a firm tread: "Some are beautiful, with the male beauty of young Londoners." In recent years, gender in Britain, he implied, had been in revolution; while there were now "some women made for battle, for violent action, adventures and fear," there were also "among the men the tranquil Sanchos."[27] Obviously this was not the model for France to follow.

Absensour's ambivalent reaction to the militarization of women represented French feminists as a group. As they had been disturbed in 1913 by Mme Dieulafoy's proposal for a women's volunteer auxiliary corps, French feminists were also hesitant in their response to the re-emergence of this idea in 1915. When Dr Toulouse accused them of not rallying to his campaign, the feminist journal *La Française* replied that feminists were abiding by the *Union sacrée*, and furthermore they had too many serious duties to consider such a "controversial subject."[28] Although in fact, some feminists did support Dr Toulouse's idea,[29] most held back. In a long article in *La Française* entitled "Women in the Army," Jane Misme concluded that French women were no less patriotic, courageous and competent than British women, and would gladly don uniforms if necessary; but in a country of universal male conscription, women's militarization, she hoped, was not needed. Marie de la Hire agreed, while Odette Bussard reiterated the definition of femininity as life-giving that excluded women from the military project of life-taking.[30]

Women who wanted to be militarized – including several committed feminists – took an active part in this discussion, which pitted the practical need for soldiers against gender ideology. Some, like the pilot Marie Marvingt, had individually offered their services when the war broke out, obviously expecting that they would be welcomed for their proven abilities. Instead, the French government summarily rejected such offers. For example, the new aeronautics department of the army requisitioned Marvingt's airplane, but refused her services, and the Service de Santé told women doctors, like Madeleine Pelletier, that if they insisted on serving, they might volunteer as Red Cross nurses.[31] Although sorely disappointed, they did not all give up and go home. Using the model of the benevolent societies, a few formed organizations to present their services to their country in a pre-packaged form, hoping that, if the military would not enroll them directly as individuals, it would contract for their groups' services.

Three such organizations were the Patriotic Union of Aviatrices of France,[32] the Women's Automobile Club For the Transport of the Wounded,[33] and the Volunteer Corps of French and Belgian Women for the National Defense, all founded in April 1915. Their founders, Marthe Richer, Jeanne Pallier and Mme Arnaud, lobbied the government and launched press campaigns to drum up support for their initiatives. They responded to the arguments over the militarization of women that emerged in the public discourse and tailored their proposals to make use of them. They also sounded notes of their own, stressing their talents, competence and patriotism. While the general debate focused upon the needs of the army and implications for the gender system, the women who wanted to be militarized tried to keep the issues of women's rights and national duties – in short, of feminine citizenship – integral to the discussion.

The Women's Automobile Club was the only one of these projects that achieved even partial success. Its president, Jeanne Pallier, was a pilot, who, like the other women pilots, had offered her services to the Ministry of War in August 1914 and been rejected. Shortly thereafter, she met Nelly Roussel and Marguerite Durand, leaders in the feminist movement, with whom she discussed how women like herself could best help the war effort. Her solution, supported by Durand, was to acquire a driver's license and found the Women's Automobile Club "to develop motoring for French women whether for sport or as a profession" and "to transport the wounded," in the words of its statutes. Although Pallier was the club's president, Durand was its chief financial support and political strategist. Pallier and Durand lobbied the Ministry of War and the Service de Santé, and members of the legislature and Durand orchestrated laudatory press coverage. In August, they persuaded Dr Dzieworiski, the director of the Service de Santé in Paris, to assign the club the task of transporting wounded within the Paris military district, a service the club performed for at least six months and perhaps longer. However, the club never received authorization to operate in the war zone, nor was it ever militarized. As far as the army was concerned, the club was a benevolent service, like the women who ran the Soldiers' Hostels or knitted winter clothes for prisoners of war.

Marthe Richer founded the Patriotic Union of Aviatrices with several other notable women pilots.[34] She, too, tirelessly lobbied the Ministry of War, the Undersecretary of State for Aeronautics and even the Service of Aeronautical Manufacture, and launched an astute press campaign in late September 1915, wrangling favorable interviews in *Le Figaro*, *Le Petit journal* and *Le Petit parisien* and comment in propaganda literature like Berthe Bontoux's book, *Les françaises et la grande guerre*.[35] However, she did not achieve even the partial success of the Women's Automobile Club. After the fall of 1915, when Richer's full-scale assault upon the military authorities failed, the club's members struck out on their own. Marie Marvingt, for example, managed to enroll briefly in the Italian air force and then set up a flying ambulance service there.[36] Marthe Richer would later claim to have been recruited as a spy.

We know much less about Mme Arnaud's Volunteer Corps of French and Belgian Women for the National Defense. According to press accounts, Mme Arnaud was the widow of a French army officer inspired by the British women's paramilitary organizations. She announced the formation of the Corps in an interview published by *Le Petit parisien* on 19 April 1915 and immediately drew noteworthy response from some of the paper's female readers.[37] Then the Corps dropped out of public sight until 11 January 1916, when it staged a demonstration in the Tuileries Gardens. About a hundred women, dressed in boy-scout-like uniforms, marched through the park to present a petition to General Gallieni, the Minister of War, at the Palais Bourbon. According to the report in *Le Petit journal*, they were not well received. In fact, they were not received at all. "They were forced to play hide-and-seek around the gardens. When they reached one door, they were driven around to another – while the onlookers jeered."[38] This was, presumably, the end of the Corps.

Pallier, Richer and Arnaud all based their organizations on the premise that they had special skills to offer that the military needed, and defined their goal as militarization. Marthe Richer explained the formation of the Patriotic Union of Aviatrices of France in this way: "I had wanted to enlist in military aviation. Not having succeeded on my own in achieving this, I had founded the Patriotic Union of Aviatrices of France. I hoped that grouped together we could overcome the resistance."[39] Jeanne Pallier founded the Women's Automobile Club as a step toward her ultimate goal; as she wrote to the feminist Marguerite Durand, "I want to be militarized." Rebuffed as a pilot, she acquired a driver's license because the army's need for ambulance drivers was apparent to all. Her club proposed to supply them, furthermore, "without costing any State agency any money, trouble or work at all." In return, Pallier wanted official sanction via militarization. The club's rule-book warned its members "since our medical units may be militarized, every active member must be willing to submit to military authority."[40] Mme Arnaud's bid for militarization was more direct. Like the British organizations, the Women's Legion and the Women's Volunteer Reserve, the Volunteer Corps was to be a paramilitary group. She declared that the women who joined would not "wage story-book war (*la guerre en dentelles*). The members will really be militarized, under the command of male officers . . . Equipped and fed, they will receive a khaki uniform and will learn to use a gun."[41]

In their interviews with the press and with government officials, Richer, Pallier and Arnaud supported their proposals by pointing to the shortage of fighting men. As Richer explained to the *Le Figaro* reporter, women pilots could take over the routine flight duties in the *arrière*, thereby freeing male pilots for combat. Mme Arnaud made a similar argument for her paramilitary corps: "For cooking, sewing on buttons, doing laundry, writing letters, no need for men, she told us; women will suffice." Besides taking the place of soldiers in housekeeping and office jobs, she claimed that this corps of women could escort convoys, guard prisoners of war and occupy captured towns, freeing men to do the actual fighting.[42]

All three also attempted to circumvent or deny the accusation that to militarize women would be to court gender chaos. In the course of lobbying for their projects, each of the women backed away from aspects of their initial proposals that most threatened the gender system. In particular, all three eventually denied that they planned to put women in the war zone. Arnaud, who, in April, had described her corps as armed and ready for defensive duty in the war zone, by January had retreated to petitioning only that her women replace soldiers "in the auxiliary services at the depot and in the rear" so that these men could be sent to the front to do the work that was "impossible for women."[43] The clubs of women pilots and women drivers had also proposed to fly or drive in the war zone, but later disclaimed such ambitions. In an interview published in *Le Petit parisien,* Richer denied that her pilots would transgress the barrier between front and *arrière,* masculine and feminine: "We don't ask to go to the front, because our situation as women does not permit us to play an active role. We think, however, that we can be useful in one of the services in the rear."[44] In a press release, Marguerite Durand made the same disclaimer about the Women's Automobile Club, but in fact, as Pallier admitted to *La Française,* her hope remained that "one day we will be authorized to cross the boundaries of the fortified zone [i. e. Paris] and carry out evacuations more to the front."[45]

Richer and Durand tried to create for their organizations images of respectable femininity. As we have seen, *Le Figaro* described the women pilots as the epitome of the feminine, elegant "little bourgeoises," with shy, childish voices. *Le Petit journal* illustrated its article on the Patriotic Union of Aviatrices with a photograph of Marthe Richer in a fashionable dress and large hat, looking like a society matron.[46] The press release that Durand wrote for the Women's Automobile Club presented its members as gracious, maternal lady-bountifuls and its services as conventionally benevolent and nurturing. "The wounded are astonished at the sight of the beautiful automobile that awaits them and the women who, with maternal gestures, help them inside, who cushion them with pillows, swaddle them in blankets – a cigarette? some chocolate? The offer is joyfully accepted and . . . away they go to the other hospital." Although they wore uniforms, these certainly weren't military uniforms; in fact, the uniform wasn't really a uniform at all, Durand claimed, just a simple blue suit.[47]

Mme Arnaud employed a different and more interesting argument about gender. Although she did discard the most masculine attributes of her corps, that it should be armed and operate in the war zone, she did not surround its image with shy voices, elaborate hats or maternal solicitude. Instead, she challenged the line of demarcation between the masculine and the feminine in wartime. Her corps, she argued, would expand the boundaries of the feminine in ways that were necessary in wartime in order to shame, or force, men into their masculine duties. She told *Le Petit parisien*: "What we especially want is to shake out the shirkers (*débusquer les embusqués*). And we are persuaded that, seeing women give such an example of patriotism, [men] will blush to remain any longer in the shadow of the desk, sheltered from all the risks that every day their comrades at the front accept with such heroic valor."[48] Where the British used women's paramilitary organizations to shame men into enlisting, Mme Arnaud believed her group would shame conscripts into fighting. Indeed, the Provisional Government in Russia in 1917 created women's battalions for precisely this purpose.[49]

Commentators in the press who believed that French women could or should be militarized developed this argument, stressing both the femininity of military women and their role in remasculinizing men. Articles on the British paramilitary and later the military auxiliary corps argued that despite the military appearance – uniforms, drilling, discipline – these British women were not really *femmes-soldats*, but housewives. In a series of articles published in *Le Petit parisien* in January 1918, Andrée Voillis depicted the new WAACs at work and in their barracks. Everywhere domesticity reigned supreme. Their barracks, decorated with flowers and curtains were "intimate and sweet, very feminine." Their officers were social workers who ruled via tact rather than stern command. Meanwhile, the WAACs cooked and cleaned for the soldiers; "the men fight, the women keep house for the soldiers." Nor had they lost their feminine charm. Unlike Abensour's depiction of the "male beauty" of the Women's Emergency Corps, Andrée Viollis's WAACs were femininely lovely, their uniforms "simple and practical," a "costume particularly suited to the supple and decided allure of svelte English women." They had "resolved the difficult problem of being virile without trying to become masculine, to do a man's work, all the while remaining, in the best sense, women."[50]

By remaining entirely womanly, military women impelled men into even more masculine identities. As recently as March 1915, the press had hailed the "soldiers of the rear," those in administration, supply and other non-combat jobs, as unsung heroes doing indispensable work.[51] In this new discourse, such men became sissies and shirkers. Dr Toulouse held up for derision such military postings as *lampiste*, the job of cleaning and filling lamps in the garrison, and pointed out that "housewives would know better how to buy codfish and other food, and seamstresses are better able to take care of clothing" than male conscripts assigned to these tasks.[52] He implied that any man doing such a job was shirking his masculine duty. To admit women into the military would relieve men from the degradation of doing feminine work and would force shirkers into combat to become the real men that nationalist rhetoric argued France so desperately needed. Thus, admitting women into the military, what at first glance seemed to threaten the gender order, in this argument became a powerful tool to confirm and strengthen it.

The rhetoric of womanly women and more manly men may have persuaded a few newspaper readers to view the potential militarization of women less skeptically; but it falsified in a disturbing way the experience of the few women who achieved military recognition, such as those of the Women's Automobile Club. On 23 August 1915, the Service de Santé accepted the club's services, assigning it the task of transporting wounded soldiers within the confines of the Parisian military district. The following day, the club's transport service was up and running, carrying out thirty-five transfers. By October Pallier claimed to have four automobiles and forty-nine drivers in constant use.[53] Pallier obviously reveled in her capacity as president of the club, and she and the members enjoyed the thrill of driving their big cars on official, military business. As they swung their Daimlers and Peugeots into the courtyard of Val-de-Grace and swept up to the steps, they swelled with pride in their competence and in the official recognition they received. In a letter to Durand, Pallier's emotions spilled over: "On a second trip . . . I found Director Dziewouski [*sic*], Major Sandral, etc. etc, all these authorities on the step waiting for Mr Justin Godart [Under-secretary of State in charge of the Service de Santé]. I was congratulated a bit and after turning around, like an old hand, I left. It is a little revolution in all the hospitals, where we get a very cordial welcome."[54] This was a far cry from the image of maternal solicitude cultivated in the Club's press releases.

The discourse that admitted women into the military in order to masculinize men redefined the boundaries of home and war, civilian and military, feminine and masculine without challenging their essential nature. It still positioned masculine and feminine as unequal opposites; women's duties, even when militarized, remained inferior to men's duties. Although necessary, they were naturally humble. *Le Petit journal* described the role Mme Arnaud's Volunteer Corps wanted to play as "evidently exempt from glory. But what of it? Darning warriors' socks and hemming their pants is still a way to serve their country."[55]

Although perhaps a clever riposte to the opponents of women's militarization, the emphasis upon the polarity and exclusivity of gender categories undermined women's efforts to define their patriotic service as emanating from citizenship duties shared by both sexes. When lisped in a childish voice and shaded by a frivolous hat, the question of why the army should welcome male pilots and rebuff female ones, for example, ceased to be serious. The answer was obvious: because men and women were different, so different that esoteric skills or patriotic fervor could not bridge the gap between them. Any argument based upon the similarity or even the equivalence of masculine and feminine was dead on arrival.

Nor did the reassertion of radical gender difference pay off in the short term: it did not achieve its immediate goal, the militarization of French women. While providing an excellent rationale to the military for exploiting female labor, it did not justify militarizing that labor. The argument was, in essence, that women should be admitted into the military in order to take over the feminine sphere that the military had inappropriately harbored and assigned to men. This raised an obvious alternative; rather than admit women into the military, why not expel this alien feminine sphere from the military by turning it over to civilians? In his series of articles pleading that the military make use of women, Dr Toulouse suggested this option. Rather than militarize women, he asked "Wouldn't it be simpler to demilitarize certain services?"[56] In the end, this is what the Minister of War, Joseph Gallieni, decided to do.

"The Replacement of Military Personnel by Women," 1916–1918

Appointed Minister of War on 30 October 1915, General Gallieni was immediately faced with a serious shortage of troops exacerbated by the disastrous campaign in the Dardenelles. Brief notes from his meetings throughout November and December indicate that "the troop crisis" was his top concern. He discussed strategies for weeding out "shirkers" from non-combat jobs and "malingerers" from the military hospitals, and immediately sought authorization from the legislature to conscript the recruits of 1917 ahead of their call-up date.[57] Thomas, who was beginning to replace men with women in the munitions industry, advocated a similar replacement in the military as a way of maximizing the number of combat troops. Gallieni was hesitant, however, well aware that this decision would not be popular with his regional commanders. In his initial circular sent to under-secretaries of the War Ministry, regional commanders and army administrators, he advised the use of women almost as an afterthought in a long recommendation about decentralizing decision-making, increasing efficiency and modernizing military administration. Women appeared in it as an efficient, modern innovation on a par with the telephone, the typewriter and carbon paper.

Gallieni further dampened hostile reaction by specifying that the women so employed should be "by preference, chosen from the wives, mothers, daughters or sisters of soldiers killed or wounded in the war." How could anyone object to this project for helping poor war widows and orphans by allowing them to use their special feminine skills at the typewriter keyboard in their country's hour of need? Only in the last sentence did Gallieni suggest the real reason for this efficient and charitable enterprise – a desperate shortage of manpower. "This supplementary feminine work force must result in the reduction of military and civilian personnel by at least an equal number."[58]

The War Ministry could not long disguise the true purpose of this initiative. Although Gallieni continued to link women primarily with typewriters, in a circular dated 26 January 1916 he instructed the same set of under-secretaries, commanders and administrators to study "the replacement of military personnel by women in all possible posts and employment," paying particular attention to supply depots and clothing production. Each was to send him a list of the jobs under his command suitable for female employment. This letter made no mention of modernization nor of benevolence to war orphans; the purpose of this action was clear: to reduce the number of soldiers in non-combatant posts.

Gallieni's circular of January 1916 was an order for a feasibility study rather than an instruction to employ women. The latter did not come until May and June. Six months later, most sectors and services had successfully recruited women to do domestic work like cooking and laundry; but many lagged in hiring women as office workers. But now there was a new War Minister, General Pierre Auguste Roques, who pushed the issue much more vigorously than Gallieni. On 2 December Roques declared the trial period over and ordered all sectors and services to fall in line promptly.[59] This produced a barrage of explanation, justification and complaint; but Roques and his successor General Lyautey refused to relent. After reviewing the criticism, Roques replied that instead of considering what jobs could be held by a woman, commanders and administrators must identify and justify those few garrison jobs that could only be held by a man – he suggested guards and a skeleton office staff for night duty – and employ women in all the rest. Over the next two years, the Ministry of War continued to send out numerous directives, hounding particularly recalcitrant services, like the military judiciary, and recommending ever greater utilization of women, for example as carpenters, bakers and drivers. Commanders who did not comply were threatened with replacement.

The press hailed the Minister of War's decision to employ women in terms fore-ordained by the discussion of the preceding year. *Le Petit parisien*, for example, preceded the news of Gallieni's January circular with a story about war widows working in the Ecole Militaire, complete with a picture of a bevy of women in black leaving the building (see Figure 7.2). The paper then framed the text of the circular with yet another article by Dr Toulouse, entitled "Féminisez." By implication, Toulouse claimed credit for Gallieni's decision, and berated the military for not moving faster and farther.[60] *L'Illustration* and other papers also covered the news in positive, even congratulatory, terms, while the feminist journal *La Française* swallowed its reservations and hailed the decision as a victory for women's rights. Even the natalist Gaston Rageot marveled: "The day when the colonel of a provincial regiment consented to open the gates to typists and orderlies in skirts has killed the last prejudice that still resisted the new spirit."[61]

The press stories about the army's employment of women emphasized pathos and domesticity. Most of the articles praised the army for hiring the female dependants of war heros and implied that the women were taking up the torch that had fallen from the hands of their men.[62] A common theme was the suitability of the women's work. A reporter touring a depot in Caen that had recently

Figure 7.2 The Ministry of War's first experiment in hiring women: war widows employed by the Ecole de guerre leaving work at lunchtime on 22 January 1916. © Musée d'histoire contemporaine – BDIC, reproduction by Archipel.

begun to hire women workers enthused that the place already showed "the woman's hand. What order and what activity . . . a state of impeccable cleanliness." An article in *Le Petit journal* said it all in its title: "Women in the Army; They Housekeep for France."[63]

In short, the press reassured their readers that these women had lost nothing of their femininity by working for the military. Even when they worked alongside soldiers, where military discipline reigned, they remained typical French women, docile, sweet, maternal and elegant. This was so because French women knew their place and their limitations, and had no ambition to usurp the prerogatives or duties of men.

> Women are proud enough to say that they can be good soldiers, not by seizing a rifle or a grenade but by tapping on a typewriter, stirring sauces, plying the needle, wielding brush and scouring powder, adding up columns of numbers, filing accounts, sorting rags, working with wood and with metal. There is no humble task when it comes to saving the Fatherland. Feminine patience and application will be precious auxiliaries to the superhuman valor of our soldiers.[64]

249

Instead of challenging masculine prerogatives, women's entrance into military employment affirmed them, by forcing men to take up their designated gender role in combat, as an article in *La Française* claimed. "Believe me, no once will find fault, except for the poor shirkers, forced to give up their places to the ladies."[65]

But everyone (shirkers excepted) was not as pleased as this response would have us believe. Once the Minister of War had made his decision, the spirit of the *Union sacrée* as well as censorship ensured such orchestrated optimism in the mainstream press. Feminists remained critical, and judged it too little and too late. Although *La Française* initially, although tepidly, hailed Gallieni's circular, Jane Misme later pointed to the Ministry of War's long hesitation to employ women, its positively obstructionist behavior toward volunteer efforts and its weak showing since finally taking the plunge. Now, she reported, the military did employ women in domestic tasks and routine office work; but what of the skilled women, with knowledge and superior abilities to offer? "Women doctors, drivers and flyers were welcomed less readily; we find only one woman doctor in a front-line hospital and only one woman in charge of a hospital in the rear." Compared to the British example, this was a sorry record indeed.[66]

The military press, by contrast, believed there was no need for such action at all. *La France militaire*, a magazine of the officer corps, reported Gallieni's November 1915 circular without accompanying comment; but in the following month it published two articles that made its opinion clear. An article entitled "Each Man in His Place" by the pseudonymous Sapiens did not mention women, but defended the employment of soldiers in non-combat roles.[67] After Gallieni ordered the employment of women, comments in *La France militaire* were carefully neutral, justifying caution without being openly critical. While the magazine occasionally ran stories suggesting how women could be better trained for military employment, it never indulged in the enthusiastic endorsement found in *Le Petit parisien*, for example.[68]

The lack of public enthusiasm in *La France militaire* was only a pale reflection of the private reactions of Gallieni's commanders. Most of them believed that women were not suited to work in the military nor was the military suited to accommodate women; and they did not hesitate to let the Ministry know their opinion. Their responses to Roques's circular in December 1916 chastising them for their inaction included considerable anti-feminine prejudice but also practical objections, some trivial but some serious.[69] These latter indicated that by opting to employ women without militarizing them, the War Ministry avoided one set of problems only to create another.

Few commanders were as forthrightly hostile as General Ruffeys of Nantes. He completely opposed the employment of women in any capacity in the military, but particularly in office work. His objections ranged from the difficulty of adapting civilian workers to military requirements to women's "periodic indispositions," "vapors," "indiscretion" and penchant for changing jobs, and, in his mind, guaranteed the failure of the experiment from the start. In Ruffeys's opinion, as in the minds of other generals, it was women's nature that was at fault, causing their frequent illnesses, whether real or imaginary, their indiscretion and unsatisfactory work, their conflicting domestic responsibilities and their disruptive sexuality. The recollections of Lucie Brun, who worked briefly at a regimental headquarters, lend some credence to the last point. According to her, most of the officers had *petites amies* among the office staff.[70] But femininity was not the only problem; it was the fact that they were civilians that limited women's work schedules and exempted them from the discipline and devotion to duty that could be exacted from soldiers.

General Dubois of Orléans presented women's civilian status as the heart of the problem, although the issue had two sides. Not only were women as civilians unsuited to military work; the military was not a suitable employer of civilians. In his mind, women's unfamiliarity with military procedure and terminology was hardly their own fault; the military had failed to adopt the standard business procedures practiced in the commercial and civilian administration for which women stenographers, typists and bookkeepers had trained. Other commanders protested that skilled office workers were impossible to find for the military installations that had been built in rural areas, while the danger from bombardment as well as the peripatetic nature of war-zone military posts prevented women from taking jobs there. General Drude of Rouen summed up the problem bluntly. Women could not be adequately disciplined, held to their work, made available day and night, and moved about as needed because "women are not bound by any enlistment." As civilian employees they retained the right to change jobs or quit work altogether if they were dissatisfied. Without militarization, the women were simply employees and the army simply an employer, subject to all the limitations and vagaries of the labor market. It was not a position to which the army was accustomed.

Minister of War Roques largely dismissed the objections that were based upon the defects of feminine nature; but he did concede that lack of preparation on the part of the military had made the hiring and retention of women difficult.[71] The initial instructions, for example, had insisted too much upon employing the relatives of war victims, leading some services to hire women unqualified for the work they were supposed to do. Salary scales had been set too low, and were insufficiently flexible to meet the needs of the market. Finally, women believed, mistakenly, he claimed, that they would be fired when the war was over, which had led to a large turnover. According to Roques, these problems were in the process of being rectified. He referred repeatedly to the experience of business and civilian administration as guides for women's employment, in effect denying that there was anything unique about the military.

But some issues were not so easily banished. One continuing perplexing problem was how to find qualified applicants for office work. Initially the Ministry of War did not foresee that recruiting women would require any effort at all. Unaware that the economy was picking up, and perhaps conditioned by conscription, throughout the first half of 1916 Ministry of War circulars assumed an unlimited pool of qualified applicants, and mainly focused upon prioritizing their claims. In fact, the problem that faced military employers was not how to choose among many qualified candidates, but how to find any at all. In its ignorance, the Ministry had not set up a recruiting office; it simply instructed commanders and administrators to advertise in the local press. As a result, not only did the military services compete with civilian employers for typists and telephone operators; they competed with each other. Eventually the military services created local recruiting offices; but with mixed results, due, according to General Valabrègue, to an unwillingness to consult local civilians, especially "ladies," as advisors. Valabrègue advocated enlisting Mme Avril de Sainte-Croix's National Council of French Women, already involved in Thomas's efforts to recruit women into war industries, in this task.[72] However, the Ministry of War refused to admit women, even in a consultative capacity, to its decision-making processes. In the end, it did turn to women's volunteer organizations, but only on an *ad hoc* basis and as a last resort. In the spring of 1917, the Ministry of War began to recommend that military administrators unable to fill jobs might perhaps consult the Association for French Women's Voluntary Enlistment in Service to the Fatherland, an organization directed by Mme Boutroux and Mme Borel.[73]

The army gradually adjusted itself to being a civilian employer in competition with other employers for a scarce labor supply, rather than an omnipotent authority that could order things as it wanted. Some commanders recognized that, unlike soldiers removed from domestic responsibilities, their women employees still had families to manage, food to buy and rent to pay. Their frequent absences were less due to vapors than to the conflicting demands of work and home. General Valabrègue, who was particularly sensitive to women's employment issues, recommended greater attention to "problems like those of children's day care, nurseries and canteens." Furthermore, as General Ruffeys reported, many women objected to the six-and-one-half-day work week mandated by the Ministry of War; they wanted "to devote all of Sunday to their housework and the care of their children."

Above all else, women's concerns were financial. They expected to be paid the going rate for their work, and had no compunction about changing jobs in order to earn more. As Roques admitted, the wage scale was set too low, a reason many commanders used to explain why they had hired so few women. Administrators asked for the right to pay what they deemed necessary, especially for skilled office staff, and also protested against the restrictions on pay raises and bonuses. How were they to keep experienced personnel when the cost of living was sky-rocketing if they could only increase salaries once a year, as the Ministry directed? One general warned that the army was risking "mass defections" and even strikes – this was the spring of 1917 – if it did not improve its pay policies.

Besides wages, women were concerned about expenses. Military bases tucked away in the countryside were the true white elephants as far as office staff were concerned. Although administrators had no trouble finding manual workers – peasant women were delighted to earn wages as cooks, laundresses and *femmes de peine*, loading and unloading material – there were no secretaries, bookkeepers or telephone operators to be had. Such skilled workers had to be imported from a city, and they had to be housed; as commanders of bases at Mamers, a village north of Le Mans, or Belley, a small town in the foothills of the Alps, pointed out, the Ministry of War's directives made no provision for this circumstance.

The issue became particularly acute with regard to telephone operators. As the Commander of the Army Automobile Service reported, the PTT paid between 7 and 9 francs a day and provided free lodging, subsidized meals and three weeks' paid annual vacation. He, by contrast, could only offer 6.50F to 7.50F, free lodging but no food allowance, and only seven days' paid leave a year.[74] Nor did the regulations allow for female employees to be issued travel orders or the use of the military postal frank. They were civilians, so they were supposed to pay their own way. But, as many commanders came to acknowledge, these women were also making considerable sacrifices in order to contribute to the military effort, and many of them were doing excellent work. General Valabrègue, always fertile with ideas, suggested that one way to offer some recompense would be to award loyal civilian employees a medal at the end of the war commemorating their services.

By hiring women as civilian employees, the Ministry of War hoped to acquire women's labor without weakening the gender order in ways that militarizing them seemed to threaten; military status with its privileges and its dangers would remain entirely masculine. By refusing women such privileges as travel orders, postal franking and free meals, the Ministry of War affirmed their civilian status. But, by keeping military service as a masculine preserve, the Ministry of War took on a new role, that of employer. This was a role for which the army was unsuited. Hierarchical and inflexible, the army was very poor at responding to market forces and at devising special solutions for special circumstances. The army had also built many facilities without considering the availability of a civilian labor force. When civilian administrations, like the PTT, had to entice trained people into backwaters, they did it with generous compensations and with promotion schedules that promised diligence would soon be rewarded with a better posting. The military was slow to follow suit, and in fact never did so entirely, largely because the sweeteners – housing, food allowances, paid travel and the like – were too close to the military privileges they insisted upon reserving for soldiers.

If we look at one example, the employment of women as drivers for the Army Automobile Service (Direction de Service Automobile, DSA), we see the fine line that the Ministry tried to draw between masculine and feminine, military and civilian, and the points at which it inevitably blurred. Using women as military drivers in the war zone raised all the issues into high relief.[75]

Women in Uniform in the Army Automobile Service

Driving for the DSA was the most adventurous job that the French military opened to women. Eventually, women drove army trucks, automobiles and motorcycles; in the war zone and the *arrière*, they delivered messages, chauffeured officers and transported wounded soldiers. Driving was also the best-paid of the military employments open to women. In 1918, while cooks could earn only 5F and typists about 6F, drivers were being paid 10F a day. However, there were never very many women drivers – less than 300 out of the approximately 120,000 women employed by the army.[76]

Unfortunately, we do not know very much about the women who drove for the army. None of them published memoirs, and the only names and personal information retained in the army's files relate either to women commended for their service or to those who caused a "scandal" and were fired. From this fragmentary evidence, however, it appears that most of the women that the army recruited as drivers were well-to-do – those most likely to know how to drive. A few, like the Marquise de Saint-Leger and Mme de Subligny, were aristocrats, known for their flamboyance and nerve. But the DSA also employed some working women, for example, Andrée Chaillot, a former seamstress who worked as a driver for the military depot in Vesoul.

Especially in comparison to the British, the French army was very slow to recruit women as drivers. At first, when Gallieni asked his commanders to assess what jobs could be done by women, Commander Doumenc, the Director of the DSA, mentioned clerical staff but refused to consider drivers. He routinely dismissed offers from women volunteers, such as the British First Aid Nursing Yeomanry Corps (FANY) or Jeanne Pallier's Women's Automobile Club. First, he cited the "toilet" excuse, so familiar to women trying to break into male preserves; women could not be admitted because there were no facilities for them. Secondly, they could not work in the war zone. Doumenc refused to acknowledge that the British army was already using FANY drivers very effectively in the war zone. Instead, he asserted his service's first priority was to "maintain manpower."

Under pressure of the Ministry of War,[77] the British example and the shortage of qualified men, however, the DSA did begin to employ women. In fact, at same time that Doumenc was rejecting women's services, several units had been using women, both as volunteers and as informal employees, for several months. If a woman had her own automobile and lived in the war zone, it was difficult for the army to turn her away when transport was so desperately needed. Finally, in the spring and summer of 1917, Lyautey ordered that male drivers be replaced with women, as the British had done, and appointed Captain Aujay as director of female personnel in the DSA. Aujay, as former head of the Office of Foreign First Aid (Sections Sanitaires Etrangères), had considerable experience dealing with British and American women volunteers. Several of the first women he recruited to drive for the DSA were American and British, while he was still looking for qualified French women drivers. One journalist thought that "gallantry" required that the first woman enrolled be Jeanne Pallier;[78] but the army made no such gesture. By this time, the Women's Automobile Club was inactive and Pallier was over fifty years old.

Having witnessed the British women drivers in action, some regional commanders welcomed and even applauded their new female employees whose "energy and nerve yields nothing to that of masculine personnel." General Pétain even recommended that the *Croix de guerre* be awarded to two drivers, Mme Albertine Gruel and Mme Georgina Ducreux, for "much devotion in often dangerous and painful circumstances." Such reactions were not universal, however. Some officers refused to give the women driving assignments, leaving them idle or giving them clerical work instead. In a letter to Doumenc, Mme Marguier protested that her commanding officer was trying to dismiss her and three other women on grounds of "lack of nerve" and incapacity when in fact they had rarely been allowed to drive in their six weeks of service. In another case, a battalion commander fired all the women drivers in his unit and replaced them with soldiers. In this case, he made no particular charges against the women, but simply stated that it was inconvenient to have to deal with women "in periods of active military operations" (this was during the German advance in the spring of 1918) and demanded that, throughout the DSA, women be "totally replaced by soldiers." His action was apparently supported by a circular from the head of the Service de Santé in the region, which had denounced the use of women drivers as dangerous. It was also, at least tacitly, supported by Commander Doumenc, who never approved of women drivers. Besides the evidence of his continuing carping letters to the Ministry of War on this issue, there are his memoirs. In this paean to DSA, he never once mentioned women drivers, and implied that the only women employed had been clerical staff.[79]

The only account we have of the Automobile Service from the perspective of a woman driver is Enid Bagnold's novel, *The Happy Foreigner*. It describes the work and romance of a British woman auxiliary attached to the French Automobile Service after the armistice. The heroine routinely encountered obstructionism and lewd comments from both officers and men, who expected women drivers to be incompetent and promiscuous. By contrast, Bagnold portrayed her heroine and other British and French women drivers as feisty, dedicated and conscientious, but often depressed and desperately lonely, "a loneliness beyond anything she had ever known,"[80] the effects of what we would today call a hostile work environment.

Much of the "inconvenience" of employing women drivers can be traced to their ambivalent position as civilians in the war zone. As civilian employees, they were expected to supply their own housing, food and transportation. However, this expectation was unrealistic in the war zone, particularly in a job whose main characteristic was mobility. Several commanders argued that militarization on the British model was the only practical solution.

Under pressure from field commanders, the Ministry of War eventually authorized the DSA to institute some policies that edged toward the militarization of its female personnel. Unlike other female employees, drivers were required to sign a three-month engagement and were not allowed to quit before their term was up. Other issues, such as the use of travel orders and postal franking, which could be regarded as perks of military service, proved to be stickier. Although Doumenc finally conceded that commanding officers could issue women travel orders, the Ministry of Armaments and War Materials then prohibited any women except nurses from riding in military vehicles. The issue was only resolved in October 1918, a month before the war ended, when Doumenc grudgingly concluded that "women drivers may be assimilated to soldiers in this regard." As for postal franking, housing and meals, however, he held firm, despite a barrage of complaints from commanders. Women drivers were civilian employees; the army was not to house, feed them or frank their letters even when they worked in the war zone.

The most controversial issue was clothing. In his initial instruction, Captain Aujay authorized volunteers to wear the uniform of their organization, if they had one, and also committed the army to providing work clothes.[81] In practice, this meant that women outfitted themselves as best they could. Since, unlike the case with nurses, there was no accepted costume for a *conductrice*, their outfits varied from the severely practical, which sometimes provoked the charge that they were aping the *poilus*, to what their commanders considered to be the fantastic. The British magazine, *Illustrated War News*, depicted "The Uniform Now Generally Worn" by women in the DSA as long high-heeled boots, breeches, a tight jacket, a cape and an out-sized beret.[82] Clothing like this, fulminated one inspector, was bringing discredit upon the Army.

The issue of dress raised the key factor that threatened the military employment of women, their sex. It was not only as civilians but as female civilians, a particularly dangerous category, that they caused problems. There were only two sorts of women permitted in the war zone, prostitutes and nurses. All other women were immediately suspect, subject to detention and removal from the war zone, and even interrogation and arrest as spies. Women drivers were obviously not nurses; no symbolic nun's veil covered their heads. Were they prostitutes or spies? Military authorities whom they met *en route* were liable to treat them as one or the other. As an inspector reported in summer of 1917, one of his drivers "experienced a regrettable incident with an agent of the *special morals police*, who misunderstood the real reason for her presence in Amiens." Other drivers, he reported, were hindered by repeatedly being stopped by military police along their route. Thus a major inconvenience to doing their job was – doing their job. As women they were presumed to have no right to be in, let alone drive around, the war zone. He asserted that women drivers needed to look official, they needed to look military: they needed uniforms.

By late 1917, the Ministry of War was finally convinced that uniforms were indeed necessary, and set about designing them – skirt, blazer, coat and beret. The DSA files contain several publicity photos of a woman in this uniform, posing against a variety of vehicles (see Figure 7.3). However, they remained very worried about the implications of this move, and hastened to reassure the public – and themselves – that the measure was a purely practical one without ideological import. In a press release run under the typical title of *Femmes soldats*, the DSA informed the public:

> For a little while our citizens have been seeing women wearing the uniform of our soldiers. Some have thought this was a masquerade, and

Figure 7.3 A much-reproduced publicity photo from January 1918 of an army driver in her new uniform, so new that it was still marked with the creases from the box! © Musée d'histoire contemporaine – BDIC, reproduction by Archipel.

they protested against what they thought was an improper disguise. It is nothing of the sort. The women who wear this uniform are volunteers incorporated into the Automobile Service, where they work as drivers. Regulations require them to wear military uniform.[83]

Putting the women drivers into uniform did not resolve the problem of their status in the military. Commanders were still unsure where and how to draw the line between civilian and military status, and they bedeviled Doumenc and the Ministry of War with numerous questions that the issue raised. In general, officers in the field favored extending military privileges to the women they employed, such as travel orders, postal franking and mess privileges, since to do so cost them little and made it much easier to deal with the women who worked for them. By contrast, the Ministry of War and the DSA headquarters reiterated the importance of maintaining women's civilian status by denying such privileges.

Of course it was not only women drivers' civilian status that troubled their commander-employers; it was also their sex. To many commanders, femininity encompassed a constellation of qualities inappropriate to military service – irresponsibility, irrationality, lack of discipline, indiscretion and especially sexuality. And it was to these supposedly feminine character traits, rather than to their incompetence as drivers, that commanders pointed when they dismissed women drivers. When called upon to justify his firing of Mme Marguier, Captain Meurisse lambasted "her conduct, her dress, her allure . . . all so extravagant." Apparently the "lack of nerve" and incompetence that he had cited in the letter dismissing her were for form's sake alone. Charges against the Marquise de Saint Leger united both aspects of the suspect female, the prostitute and the spy. "The Marquise de Saint Leger, of Polish–German origin, French by marriage, has become notorious for her eccentricities, the company she keeps with soldiers and the numerous intrigues she weaves." Most revealing was the case of Mlle Laurence Merino. In September 1918, the head of the military hospital in Compiègne wrote to her boss, suggesting she be recommended for the *Croix de guerre* for her energy, initiative, devotion to duty and bravery under fire. Unfortunately, her commander had fired her two weeks earlier for insubordination; she had taken two extra days of leave.

The French military successfully, if reluctantly, employed women in capacities that could be most easily redefined as feminine. First of all, this meant working in the *arrière*, where civilian status could most easily be maintained. It also meant jobs that were viewed as naturally domestic – keeping house for the soldiers – and the new clerical jobs of typist, stenographer and telephone operator, which had recently been designated as feminine. And it meant routine jobs, in which a worker could conform to an image of the feminine as docile, dependent and not very bright.

As we have seen, even in the *arrière* and even in secretarial work, it was not always simple to make the reality of the army's employment of women fit this ideal. As civilians and as feminine, women were an anomaly within the military, their status and their gender causing problems for their employers and hindering their work. This was most evident in the case of the women drivers employed by the DSA. Women drivers pushed against and crossed many of the boundaries between home and war, civilian and military, feminine and masculine. They operated in the war zone, wore uniforms and were accorded or acquired by common practice various military privileges. Their jobs could be routine; but, as Captain Le Lorrain had pointed out, the shifting fortunes of war, especially in 1918, created "unforeseen daily emergencies." They needed courage, resolution, enterprise and self-reliance to get their jobs done. Although the army occasionally praised and even rewarded these qualities, it more often found them problematic. Women who displayed them could just as easily be dismissed for causing a "scandal" as be commended for having gone beyond the call of duty. Mlle Merino may have been the only woman who was both simultaneously; yet her case is instructive. While bravery might pardon a multitude of masculine sins, it could not compensate for feminine insubmissiveness; Mlle Merino never received her *Croix de guerre*.

The military's ambivalence towards its female employees became more pronounced in late 1917 and 1918. Under Clemenceau, who was Minister of War as well as Prime Minister, the Ministry of War let up the pressure on regional commanders to weed out soldiers from non-combatant jobs. By late 1917, the number of women employed by the military was in decline, and the number of soldiers in non-combatant jobs leapt upward. The battalion commander who, in the spring of 1918, dismissed all his women drivers and replaced them with soldiers was responding to this wind-shift. One study found that in late 1917 the Ministry of War itself was employing nearly four hundred more soldiers and seventy-three less women than it had six months earlier.[84] After the débâcle of the Chemin des Dames offensive in the spring of 1917 and the mutinies it provoked, the army retired to the defensive to await the arrival of the Americans, which would solve the manpower shortage once and for all. Apparently, many French commanders also believed that the American *deus ex machina* relieved them of the need to hire women.

Once the war was over, it was immediately evident that the Ministry of War's experiment with "feminization" was over as well. Minister of War Roques had held out the prospect, but never the promise, of continued employment for women after the war.[85] However, three days after the armistice, army administrators were ordered to cease hiring women and to replace any who resigned with soldiers. The Ministry of War quickly drew up procedures for dismissing all female personnel and, by January, the dismissals were

261

under way, so hasty and so massive that the army was often unable to pay the small separation indemnities that the procedures mandated.[86] Only a small number of female steno-typists were kept on in the military administration.[87]

A few women, like Jeanne Pallier and Mme Arnaud, had hoped that the wartime crisis would open military service to women. Although even Mme Arnaud's Volunteer Corps did not propose identical military service for men and women, yet they hoped that, via some kind of military service, women's civic debt and thus their civic existence would be officially recognized. Instead, the Ministry of War chose to address the crisis by employing women as civilians, despite the problems this created for its commanders, and refused to accord them even auxiliary military status. Nonetheless, some commentators reacted to the army's employment of women as if this were equivalent to military service. Thérèse Casevitz-Rouff, in an article entitled "Women in the Service of the Army," claimed that Gallieni's decision "removed the last argument of those who refused women their political rights under the pretext that they haven't the same duties as men and are exempt from military service."[88] But of course, it did no such thing. Casevitz-Rouff acknowledged that the military employment of women "is no longer about feminism but is a measure of public safety," meaning that the military had not taken a partisan decision in favor of women but had acted in favor of the Nation as a whole. But the Ministry of War interpreted its action otherwise. It was indeed a measure of public safety, an emergency measure taken to meet a crisis rather than a reform intended to improve the army or to correct a civic injustice. Despite the press campaign justifying women's employment by the military, neither the Ministry of War, nor especially the army, had any intention of conceding a permanent feminine sphere within the military or of redefining the relationship between gender and war. And, to prevent any such interpretation, the Ministry of War carefully circumscribed the military's use of women to avoid anything that resembled the mobilization or militarization of women. As employees, women's only claim was to the wages they earned; they fulfilled no national duty, ran up no civic debt.

They also added no chapter to the story of French women at war. Unlike the "Khaki Girls" who figured in several popular British novels and memoirs,[89] no "Girls in Horizon Blue" entered French popular culture. Except for the middle months of 1915, the subject of women in the French military drew scant commentary in the press and, unlike nurses and munitions workers, did not claim the attention of propagandists. After the war, the fact that the French army had employed women and had even put some of them into uniform sank without a trace, helped into oblivion by commanders like Doumenc who had never approved in the first place. By employing women as civilians rather than militarizing them, the army had turned a potentially dramatic story into a banal employment history, stripped of any cultural and political significance. So the story of French women in the military was one that never happened.

Notes

1. Emile Bere, "Nos aviatrices s'ennuient," *Le Figaro*, 27 September 1915.
2. Alix, *La Croix-rouge française*, p. 8.
3. Georges Prade, "L'héroïsme féminin," *Le Journal*, 25 May 1914; Marie-Josèphe de Beauregard, *Femmes de l'air* (Paris: Editions France-Empire, 1993), pp. 75-86.
4. Bere, "Nos aviatrices s'ennuient."
5. Ursula von Gersdorff, *Frauen im Kriegsdienst 1914–1945* (Stuttgart: deutsche Verlagsanstalt, 1969). The German military authorized a Female Signals Corps in 1918 just before the war ended. I thank Sue Fisher for this reference.
6. Higonnet and Higonnet, "The Double Helix," in Higonnet *et al.* (eds), *Behind the Lines*, pp. 34–5.
7. Ouditt, *Fighting Forces, Writing Women*, p. 11.
8. Marie-Louise Le Verrier, "Les femmes et la défense du pays" *La Française*, 24 May 1913.
9. About 90,000 in the auxiliaries, 10,000–12,000 in the paramilitary corps. There was some cross-over between organizations; Krisztina Robert, "Gender, Class, and Patriotism: Women's Paramilitary Units in First World War Britain," *The International History Review* 19 no. 1 (February 1997): 52–3.
10. Abensour, "Le problème de la démobilisation," p. 80.
11. Jenny Gould, "Women's Military Services in First World War Britain," in Higonnet *et al.* (eds), *Behind the Lines*, pp. 114–25.
12. Ibid., p. 122.
13. Janet S. K. Watson, "Khaki Girls, VADs, and Tommy's Sisters: Gender and Class in First World War Britain," *The International History Review* 19 no. 1 (February 1997).

14. Robert, "Gender, Class, and Patriotism."
15. Speech given 20 March 1915, later published as *La parisienne et la guerre*, pp. 52–3.
16. Jane Misme, "Les femmes dans l'armée," *La Française*, 6 March 1915.
17. "La femme conscrit," *Le Temps*, 25 July 1915; Dr Toulouse, "Les femmes à l'armée," *Le Petit parisien*, 26 July 1915. He had suggested the military use women as early as 1905, but only as nurses in the medical service. This the government had adopted in 1907.
18. Dr Toulouse, "Les femmes et les auxiliaires," *Le Petit parisien*, 22 November 1915; and Toulouse, "Féminisez," *Le Petit parisien*, 27 January 1916.
19. Toulouse, "Les femmes à l'armée."
20. Toulouse, "Féminisez."
21. We find such opinions from all quarters, from the pro-governmental paper, *Le Temps*, in Jules Bertaut, "Les femmes de la guerre," 15 September 1915; from the socialist press, "Les femmes-soldats," *Voix des femmes*, 31 October 1917; and from military press, "Le problème des effectifs," *La France militaire*, 23 December 1915.
22. For example, the abundant drawings in *La Vie parisienne*, 53 (1915) from February through to April, and Rearick, "Madelon and the Men," pp. 1001–34.
23. Harriet B. Applewhite and Darline Gay Levy, "Gender and Militant Citizenship in Revolutionary Paris: A Study in Radicalisation and Repression 1791–93," in *Les femmes et la Revolution française: Actes du Colloque international, avril 1989*, 3 vols. (Toulouse: Presses universitaires du Mirail, 1989): I: pp. 63–9; Laura S. Strumingher, "The Vésuviennes: Images of Women Warriors in 1848 and Their Significance for French History," *History of European Ideas* 8 no. 4/5 (1987): 451–88; Gay Gullickson, *Unruly Women of Paris; Images of the Commune* (Ithaca: Cornell University Press, 1996).
24. Bertaut, "Les femmes de la guerre;" also La Hire, *La femme française*, pp. 16–17.
25. Michaux, *En marge du drame*, pp. 320–21; "La femme conscrit;" Abensour, *Les vaillantes*, pp. 137–9.
26. Nadine, *Rêves de guerre*, pp. 47–9; also Andrée Viollis,"La femme anglaise a conquis tous les droits pendant cette guerre," *Le Petit parisien*, 30 March 1917 and Donnay, *La parisienne*, p. 55.
27. Abensour, *Les vaillantes*, pp. 242–3.
28. Thérèse Casevitz-Rouff, "Les femmes aux services de l'armée," *La Française*, 4 March 1916.
29. For example, the society Suffrage des femmes; Bard, *Les filles de marianne*, p. 52.
30. Misme, "Les femmes dans l'armée;" La Hire, *La femme française*, pp. 16–17; Odette Bussard, "Lettre ouverte d'une féministe," *La Française*, 15 January 1916.

31. Beauregard, *Femmes de l'air*, pp. 75–86; Gordon, *The Integral Feminist*, pp. 141–2.

32. BMD dos 629 Femmes dans l'aviation.

33. BMD dos 367 Club féminin automobile.

34. Besides Richer and Marvingt, these included Hélène Dutrieu, Raymonde de Laroche, Mlle Damédoz, Mlle Picard and probably Jeanne Herveux. See BMD dos 629 aviatrices and dos Richard.

35. Bere, "Nos aviatrices s'ennuient;" "Les aviatrices veulent contribuer à la défense nationale," *Le Petit journal*, 28 September 1915; "Les aviatrices demandent à servir la patrie," *Le Petit parisien*, 30 September 1915; Bontoux, *Les françaises et la grande guerre*, p. 62.

36. Beauregard, *Femmes de l'air*, pp. 75–86.

37. "Un régiment de femmes est en formation à Paris," *Le Petit parisien*, 19 April 1915; "Les femmes qui veulent servir la France," *Le Petit journal*, 22 April 1915.

38. Jean Lecoq, "Les amazones parisiennes," *Le Petit journal*, 15 January 1916. "Les femmes dans les usines de guerres," *L'Illustration* 74 no. 3816 (22 April 1916): 380 judged that "l'accueil assez peu encourageant reçu par la délégation de dames en costumes militaires qui vinrent se presenter au général Gallieni, alors ministre de Guerre, ne laisse à cet égard que peu d'illusions."

39. Richer, *Ma vie d'espionne*, p. 5.

40. BMD dos 367 Club féminin automobile.

41. "Un régiment de femmes est en formation à Paris."

42. Bere, "Nos aviatrices s'ennuient;" "Les femmes qui veulent servir la France."

43. Lecoq, "Les amazones parisiennes."

44. " Les aviatrices demandent à servir la patrie."

45. BMD dos 367 Club féminin automobile; Thérèse Casevitz-Rouff, "Chez les automobilistes militaires," *La Française*, 30 October 1915.

46. Bere, "Nos aviatrices s'ennuient;" "Le grand chagrin des aviatrices, avoir des ailes et ne pas voler," *Le Petit journal*, 30 July 1915.

47. BMD dos 367 Club féminin automobile.

48. "Un régiment de femmes est en formation à Paris."

49. Laurie Stoff, "Russian Women in Combat: Female Soldiers of the First World War" (Master's thesis, University of Kansas, 1995).

50. Andrée Viollis, "Avec le corps d'armée des femmes anglaises," *Le Petit parisien*, 7 and 14 January 1918.

51. "Histoires des tranchées: Les poilus du front et les poilus de l'arrière," *Le Petit journal*, 29 March 1915.

52. Toulouse, "Les femmes et les auxiliaires." In 1917, the Théâtre du Palais-royal put on a comedy, "Madame et son filleul" by Maurice Hennequin, Pierre Veber and Henry de Gorsse, that ridiculed an *embusqué* whose job it was to chauffeur officers.

53. Casevitz-Rouff, "Chez les automobilistes militaires."

54. BMD dos 367 Club féminin automobile. Roberts, "Gender, Class, and Patriotism," p. 64, concluded that British women joined paramilitary organizations and the military auxiliaries from feelings of patriotism that called upon them to do something extraordinary, adventurous and significant. Being part of the military endowed them with "a part, however tiny, on the national stage."

55. Lecoq, "Les amazones parisiennes."

56. Toulouse, "Les femmes et les auxiliaires."

57. Marius-Ary Leblond, *Gallieni parle . . .* (Paris: Albin Michel, 1920), pp. 128–30, 153 and Joseph Simon Gallieni, *Les carnets de Gallieni* (Paris: Albin Michel, 1932), pp. 214–41.

58. The correspondence from the Ministry of War about the issue of female employment is contained in SHAT 7N 159 main d'oeuvre féminine. This circular is dated 10 November 1915.

59. General Faurie reported in April 1917 that, until this circular, commanders had not taken the employment of women seriously. See SHAT 7N 495 main d'oeuvre féminine, Rapport d'Ensemble sur l'utilisation de la main d'oeuvre féminine et observations sur les résultats obtenus, 24 April 1917.

60. "Les dames auxiliaires à l'Ecole Militaire," *Le Petit parisien*, 25 January 1916; Toulouse, "Féminisez."

61. "Des femmes dans les casernes," *L'Illustration* 74 no. 3817 (29 April 1916): 422; Casevitz-Rouff, "Les femmes aux services de l'armée;" Rageot, *La française dans la guerre*, p. 14.

62. "Les dames auxiliaires à l'Ecole Militaire;" "Les femmes 'cuistots' à Marseilles," *L'Echo de Paris*, 20 February 1916 .

63. BMD dos 940.3 Guerre 1914–18 press clippings, "Les femmes à la caserne," journal title missing, 7 April 1916; "Les femmes dans l'armée: Elles font le ménage de la France," *Le Petit journal*, 7 November 1916.

64. BMD dos 940.3 Guerre 1914–18 press clippings, "Les femmes au service du pays," journal title missing, 15 September 1916.

65. Casevitz-Rouff, "Les femmes aux services de l'armée." Similarly, "Les hommes combattent, les femmes travaillent," *Lectures pour tous* (15 January 1916): 604–12.

66. Jane Misme, "La guerre et le rôle des femmes," *La Revue de Paris* 6 (November 1916): 204–26.

67. "Nouvelles diverses," *La France militaire*, 13 November 1915; Sapiens, "Chacun à sa place," *La France militaire*, 13 December 1915.

68. "Main d'oeuvre féminine," *La France militaire*, 31 May 1916; "Les dames employés," *La France militaire*, 29 November 1916.

69. SHAT 7N 495 main d'oeuvre contains the correspondence of regional commanders to the War Ministry about this issue.

70. Bonnie G. Smith, *Confessions of a Concierge: Madame Lucie's History of Twentieth-Century France* (New Haven, CT: Yale University Press, 1985), p. 34.

71. The Ministry of War's responses are contained in SHAT 7N 159 main d'oeuvre féminine.

72. Valabrègue's and other commanders' recommendations are contained in SHAT 7N 495 main d'oeuvre féminine.

73. SHAT 16N 2440 main d'oeuvre féminine, 2 May 1917; Borel reports the organizations' efforts in glowing terms in *La mobilisation féminine*.

74. SHAT 16 N 2449 main d'oeuvre féminine.

75. Material about the female personnel of the Direction de Service Automobile is contained in SHAT 16N 2767 DSA personnel féminin.

76. SHAT 7N 495 main d'oeuvre féminine.

77. See memos from the Ministry of War to Doumenc, especially in 1917 in SHAT 7N 159 main d'oeuvre féminine.

78. Cited in Colin, *Ce n'est pas d'aujourd'hui*, p. 65.

79. Commandant Doumenc, *Les transports automobiles sur le front français 1914–1918* (Paris: Librairie Plon, 1920), p. 265.

80. Enid Bagnold, *The Happy Foreigner* (New York: The Century Co., 1920), p. 19.

81. SHAT 16N 2767 DSA-personnel féminin, 2 November, 1917.

82. *Illustrated War News*, ns 90 (27 February 1918): 40.

83. SHAT 16N 2767 DSA-personnel féminin, clipping from a newspaper in Chalons, no date..

84. SHAT 7N 159 main d'oeuvre féminine; Horne, "'L'impôt du sang,'" p. 203.

85. SHAT 7N 159 main d'oeuvre féminine.

86. SHAT 16N 2449 main d'oeuvre féminine. In response to a complaint by a former employee, Mme Martin, the commander of the motor pool at Saint-Dizier admitted his service owed about 50,000F in separation payments; SHAT 16N 2767 DSA-personnel féminin.

87. SHAT 7N 159 main d'oeuvre féminine.

88. Casevitz-Rouff, "Les femmes aux service de l'armée."

89. For example, Bagnold, *The Happy Foreigner*; Evadne Price, *"Not So Quiet"* . . . *Stepdaughters of War* (1930) and the Marchioness of Londonderry, *Retrospect* (1938).

8

The Enemy Was a Woman

In her memoirs, Marthe Richer told a typical story of the first days of the war. When her car broke down in the countryside, she walked to the nearest town in search of a mechanic and some gasoline. Without the mechanic but with a can of gas, she got a lift back on a hay wagon, to find a suspicious crowd surrounding her car. Her arrival caused a sensation: "My trip in the hay-cart – my Paris clothes – my presence in the war zone – all these facts must have seemed mysterious to those country folk," she mused. They immediately decided she was the ubiquitous spy, the Lady in the Hat, and demanded her arrest. "Death to the spy," Richer said they shouted as the police led her away.[1]

In August 1914, French people saw the mysterious Lady in the Hat everywhere, in the border areas but also in Brittany, in central France, even in the south. She wore fashionable clothes, a big hat concealing her face, and drove a powerful car. Ingenuously asking for directions, she "adroitly" turned conversation to local conditions, scrutinized railroad crossings and took lots of photographs. In the Lot-et-Garonne she tossed candy to children – candy that turned out to be poison! Elsewhere she poisoned wells. In the eastern border regions, she carried bullion to the enemy – like Louis XVI and Marie Antoinette in 1791.[2]

The outbreak of the war plunged both France and Germany into a spy scare.[3] All strangers, especially if they spoke with an accent, were tried and convicted in the court of public opinion. Since the war began during the height of the summer tourist season, France's seashore and countryside abounded in suspicious people. As Marcelle Capy wrote: "Were you traveling or strolling? Were you imprudent enough to ask directions? Were you in the South and did you have a northern accent? Were you in the North and did you have a southern accent? Spies!"[4] Incongruity, being out of place, was enough to spark accusations – an elegant lady in a village, a woman in the war zone or loitering at a garrison gate, or one who suggested gender transgression. The police stopped Madeleine Pelletier because her masculine appearance – her short hair and bicycle pants – caused people on the street to find her "not sympathetic;" they were disappointed when she wasn't arrested.[5] Not all such incidents ended benignly; the French army executed more than 250 people for spying during the war, and convicted and sentenced many more to lesser penalties. Very few of them were actually spies.[6]

The spy craze that swept France in August 1914 receded in 1915, only to surge again in 1917 and 1918. Interest continued high in the immediate post-war years, which saw the cultivation of the Mata Hari story and peaked in the mid-1930s, when several self-proclaimed spy-masters and master spies of the First World War published their memoirs. This pattern was not unique to France: the outbreak of war brought spy panics in England and Germany, too, and, later, the United States' entry into the war set off an American spy scare.[7] However, spy stories remained more integral to France's response to the war than to that of the other combatant countries. In the decades before 1914, spy stories were popular in France, as they were in England and Germany; but in France they were touted as more than adventure tales. For the Right, German espionage had become the favorite explanation of the French débâcle in 1870, creating an obsession with spying that came to a head, but was hardly laid to rest, in the Dreyfus Affair. So when, in the summer of 1914, France found itself suddenly invaded, its army driven back and Paris threatened once more, German espionage provided a ready-made explanation. French men had not lost on the battlefield; they were betrayed by the nefarious enemy within. And this scenario, in which German spies and sympathizers, pacifists, and "defeatists" stabbed the gallant French army in the back, cast women among the villains of choice.

French public opinion identified the archetypal spy who was to blame for all that threatened France within a few days of the declaration of war. Among the German spy's multiple personifications – priest, officer, waiter, traveling salesman, Jew – the Lady in the Hat stands out by her ubiquity, impartiality and credibility. While republicans suspected priests and the Right targeted Jews, everyone believed in the Lady in the Hat. Elegant, seductive, apparently rich, possibly foreign, she was mysterious and elusive; distance and frontiers meant nothing to her. She could get inside, coaxing out the secrets of the French heart and mind, sapping simultaneously French morals and morale; yet she moved freely outside, untrammeled by trenches or battle plans, passports or censorship. This phantasm of the emancipated woman, already branded in pre-war literature as the destroyer of the French family, was now out to destroy France itself. Three years before Mata Hari embodied her before the military court, public opinion had convicted her as France's most deadly enemy next to the Kaiser.

Against this secret feminine evil, the open, honest combat of soldiers was impotent. The French cause needed its own secret agents. The stories of Louise de Bettignies, Marthe Richer and especially the martyred English "miss," Edith Cavell, would seem to fill the bill; but they never did. The good woman could not triumph over the bad in the spy story. Many accounts confronted Mata Hari, the spy, with Miss Cavell, the saint; but never entirely successfully, because what made Cavell a saint and martyr was her innocence of the charges brought against her. Her advocates insisted that she was never a spy! On the other hand, the women who did admit, or even, like Richer, proclaim, their spying exploits in the French cause could only with difficulty be fashioned into heroines. There was something disingenuous about the notion of a good woman spying. Despite Lille's statue to Louise de Bettignies and a movie based upon Marthe Richer's adventures, the French public never took to any of these would-be spy heroines. In popular memory, Mata Hari easily upstaged them all.

Although miscast as a heroine, the female spy was a natural villain. She represented the dilemma that the First World War posed to French women in its most explicit form, the threat that women's willful involvement in this masculine national contest would imperil the war, the Nation and gender. Moreover, the female spy was a useful villain. She helped explain what was otherwise inexplicable: why French manhood had failed so singularly for four long years to achieve the victory that courage and sacrifice warranted. The fecundity and longevity of the female spy legend confirms how important the story was to French understanding of their experience in the war. A Mata Hari bibliography would surely rival that of Joan of Arc in the number of plays, films, novels, memoirs, histories and biographies devoted to her.

And yet Mata Hari did not have the last word. Although hers was the most potent image of Woman and the War to come out of the First World War in France, Mata Hari never encompassed the entire story of French women and the war. Public opinion, especially in

1917, was eager to convict her as the Enemy Within; but it hesitated to indict all women as her accomplices. As the trial of Hélène Brion in March 1918 showed, the ambiguous relationship of women to the war prevented even the label of traitor from sticking too closely.

The Lady in the Hat

France's obsession with spying predated August 1914. In seeking explanations for the outcome of the Franco-Prussian War, commentators had pointed to French weakness, especially the falling birth rate, and German strength, especially its industrial output. But for the nationalist Right, such above-the-board competition was inadequate to account for France's humiliating defeat; the Germans must have been up to something underhand, and that something was spying.[8] Léon Daudet was only the best-known author of many supposedly authentic accounts of Germany's massive secret penetration of a supine, naïve France. According to Daudet and his fellows, the Prussian Intelligence Service had blanketed France with agents, 30,000 according to the most frequently cited statistic.[9] By this means, the German army had complete knowledge of French transportation and communication systems and available resources, while moles inside the French government and the military, models, obviously, for Captain Dreyfus, provided advanced notice of French battle plans. Thus, it was little wonder that the French army was rolled up so ignominiously; the valiant French troops had marched into a dastardly German trap.

The supposedly factual accounts of what had happened in 1870 blended seamlessly into the turn-of-the-century spy fiction and fantasies of "the next war," like Captain Danrit's multivolumed *Tomorrow's War*.[10] Besides being adventure books with doses of science fiction, they were also what the historian Michael Miller has called "hate books," racist, anti-republican, anti-capitalist, anti-socialist, Anglophobe, Germanophobe, anti-Semitic and anti-feminist. Spies and sabotage were key in almost all of them; the invasions the heroes thwart were sneak attacks and secret infiltrations rather than "honest," man-to-man combat.[11]

These books established the conventions, characters and plots of the spy story that would shape French understanding of espionage and its relationship to war throughout the First World War and beyond; and, in them, the role of female spies grew. The supposedly factual accounts of German activities prior to the Franco-Prussian

War presented women in minor roles, as servants or occasionally as foreign-born or "false" Alsatian wives. After the turn of the century, however, in accounts like Edouard Rousseaux's *The Future Prussian Invasion and Espionage at the Frontier* (1905), and especially in Marcel Prévost's popular novel *Guardian Angels* (1913), the woman spy left the humble role of informant to become the *femme fatale* so popular in fiction in this period.[12] In *Guardian Angels*, the villains were foreign governesses, English and Italian as well as German, who used their positions in elite households not only to collect information but also to seduce and corrupt everyone who came within their orbit – husbands, sons, even daughters. Simultaneously they threatened the French family and the French state.

Julie Wheelwright points out that such stories suggested that any woman outside the confines of her family could be a spy – courtesans, of course, but also teachers, journalists, any working woman.[13] Rousseaux identified three types of women spies, the *mondaine*, the German governess, and "the innumerable chamber maids, cooks, waitresses, etc." who formed the "German feminine avant-guard." A real-life example, even though for "our" side, was Mme Bastian, the cleaning lady whose pilfering of the German embassy's trash at the behest of French military intelligence set off the Dreyfus affair. However, for these alarmist authors, it was not such women's ubiquity and invisibility that made them dangerous, but their femininity. Women were the "the most redoubtable squadron of German espionage" because they formed "a flying squadron, the squadron of music lessons and quadrilles, of flirts and slow waltzes under the soft light of chandeliers, in the heady scent of orchids and roses."[14] Cleaning lady, governess, and courtesan had collapsed into one phantasm of seduction and betrayal.

The belief that Germany had infiltrated France with a horde of spies prior to the Franco-Prussian War and the *femme fatale* of current spy novels merged in the Lady in the Hat in August 1914. Combining the ubiquity and mobility of the first with the mystery and sexual threat of the second, she was the incarnation of French fears at the outbreak of the war. The Right had preached that, despite the heroism of French masculinity, France was vulnerable from subversion, moral weakness and corruption within. In August 1914, these right-wing preoccupations became general, and the *mondaine* recast as master spy became the national enemy of choice.

The female spy was one piece of First World War lore shared by civilians on the home front and soldiers in the war zone. As we have seen, the DSA women drivers suffered from such suspicions. Even the presence of an officer did not provide an alibi. When the British General Allenby took his hostess, the Baronne de la Grange, with him on a tour of Ypres, sentries stopped them, convinced by the Baronne's presence (her hat?) that they were spies.[15]

Some soldiers and civilians also shared a suspicion of "strange" women who sought out soldiers. Captain Ladoux, head of the French counter-espionage service, suspected Marthe Richer of being a German spy because she frequented airfields; the fact that she herself owned a plane, had a pilot's license and energetically sought to persuade the Ministry of War to make use of her flying ability, was not, for him, an explanation, but further grounds for suspicion. Emile Massard, one of the earliest publicists of Mata Hari stories, claimed she had passed herself off as a volunteer nurse to pump wounded soldiers for information. This accusation drew upon the large stock of wartime stories of nurses roaming the war zone who turned out to be spies and saboteurs, like that of the mysterious Solange, who combined nursing with the seduction of officers in order to update a huge map of troop movements that hung over her luxurious bed.[16]

Even the *marraine* scheme could be a cloak for subversion. In September 1915 the *Petit parisien* reported the arrest of a German woman who, pretending to be a *marraine* innocuously named Suzanne, sold cocaine to French soldiers and extracted information from them. The paper admitted that correspondence with a *marraine* could be "very innocent," but it was wiser to proceed "with the greatest circumspection."[17] Emile Massard's post-war condemnation of *marraines* was more universal. In his influential book, *The Women Spies of Paris*, first published serially in *La Liberté* in 1921, Massard claimed that the *marraine* scheme was a national disaster.

> It was a magnificent opportunity for women spies to connect with soldiers at the front, to get the numbers of regiments, their sectors, and their morale.
>
> After having corresponded, on his next leave in "Panam" [i.e. Paris], the *filleul* would make this "*marraine*'s" acquaintance and then the effusions became more intimate and the exchange of information more complete . . . The beautiful *marraines* perhaps did some good for neurasthenic soldiers; they certainly did much harm to the army. These good ladies don't doubt that thanks to them, the enemy was easily able to locate units in the campaign and to estimate the number of troops facing them.[18]

Although the war zone and the home front shared these versions of the female spy, there were some that appeared only in one setting. In the war zone, farmhouses and village streets became strategic terrain to defend, occupy and attack, and any woman, even in her own home, was out of place and thus a potential spy. Soldiers told stories of women who hung out washing or stacked hay in coded patterns to pass information to the Germans. Refugees and women forced to billet soldiers could seem suspicious if they did not conform to soldiers' preconceived notions of feminine behavior. The Parisian press recounted some of these stories; Maurice Barrès was particularly credulous.[19]

The home front, too, had its particular versions of the woman spy, inherited directly from pre-war spy novels, such as the sinister German governess. André Avèze claimed that he had based his novel about an obsequious, enchanting German governess, Martha Steiner, upon true wartime incidents.[20] In this novel, in which the villainess's exploits served as a very loose plot upon which to string depictions of German atrocities and French derring-do, the governess not only seduced her employer and delivered the village to German pillage and rapine, she even had the German soldiers execute the little boy who had been her pupil. What more could treachery do?

Since the French government quickly interned or expelled enemy nationals, spy fantasies soon lost the German governess; but there remained a more invidious enemy, the foreign-born wife of a French citizen. In this suspicion, the pre-war attacks upon naturalization combined with distrust of femininity. Naturalized automatically at marriage, these women were not "really" French, warned alarmist columnists, so they would inevitably work against France from within. In an article entitled "No German Women in Wartime France,"[21] Maurice de Waleffe claimed to describe "the drama of all the French households in which the wife is a Boche (or an Austro-Boche), despite the legal fiction that bestows upon her, willy nilly, the nationality of her husband." Not only did this woman revolt her husband with her menus – prune compote and roast beef; she secretly hoped for a German victory. De Waleffe explained: "Woman, by her more precocious sensibility and her more restricted interior life, remains more a prisoner of the impressions of her earliest childhood than does man. Thus everywhere and always we see her the guardian of the traditions and the old cults of the race . . . Married or not, a German woman – during the war – stays a German."

The Right hammered at this thesis in the pages of *Libre parole* and *L'Action française*. In March 1916, Sylvain Gaudin de Villaine presented this argument in the Senate as an interpellation to the Minister of the Interior, Louis Malvy.[22] He claimed that governmental laxity permitted subversion to flourish in the rear that betrayed the French army. Among the pernicious "cosmopolitan vermin" were the "Boche," and Jewish, Turkish, Polish and Czech "Bochized" wives and mistresses of Frenchmen, "all these creatures protected at high levels, accommodated by a submissive police, connected to the Boche espionage offices hidden away everywhere."

Here, Gaudin de Villaine raised the third familiar version of the woman spy, the *mondaine* and courtesan. His speech was full of them, such as "a princess from a neutral country whose townhouse is one of the principal espionage centers in Paris," who corresponded directly with her ex-lover, the Kaiser, via diplomatic pouches and gained entrée into Parisian drawing-rooms via a Spanish courtesan and Comtesse X, a divorcée. In this mish-mash, the central accusations were clear; a fashionable, emancipated life-style, international connections and sexuality were the résumé of the female spy.

As in the war zone, where the soldiers' paranoia envisioned women's normal activities, such as hanging out laundry, as suspicious, in civilian society, too, the definition of espionage ballooned to include whole groups of women and categories of feminine behavior. Gaudin de Villaine accused all prostitutes of being a "network of feminine espionage that surrounds our officers and sons of good families on leave" and called upon the government to sweep up "all this vermin of female spies and their protectors." Sexual, moral and class contamination – lower-class women enticing upper-class, innocent, young men (sons of good families) into corruption – constituted espionage. As in Massard's attack upon *marraines* cited above, Gaudin de Villaine implied that indiscreet sexuality led to indiscreet communication, which in and of itself constituted espionage. The journalist Bory d'Arnex warned against another kind of promiscuous communication. Society ladies who ran charity workshops, she claimed, leaked news tidbits gleaned from official circles to "the working women, all ears, [who] hang on their words."[23] From them news spread to working-class neighborhoods, shopkeepers, bartenders, and then who knew where? Subversion, she implied, began when information crossed class and gender boundaries.

In August 1914, the woman spy had a definite form, *modus operandi*, and purpose. She was the Lady in the Hat, crisscrossing

France in her automobile, scouting information, spiriting away bullion and poisoning France's future, all at the Kaiser's behest. By 1916, however, her outline had blurred in every direction; her class, activities, even her purposes were no longer clear. She was Any Woman, and women's war service, whether as volunteer nurses, *marraines*, or workers, was no proof of patriotism. Even women whose intentions were honorable somehow aided the enemy through the indiscreet use of those peculiarly feminine attributes, bodies and tongues. Sufficient paranoia transformed expressions of feminine patriotism into their exact opposite, feminine subversion of the French war effort.

The Legacy of Miss Cavell

Edith Cavell was a middle-aged British woman who had founded a nursing school in Brussels in 1907 that in 1914 cared for wounded soldiers regardless of nationality. According to the propaganda that followed her execution in October 1915, the German Governor General von Bissing first suspected her of spying because of her non-partisan solicitude. When his surveillance yielded nothing, he resorted to deceit and seduction; a German spy disguised as a British officer seduced Cavell's maid, who promised to obtain Cavell's help in smuggling him to Holland. Upon receiving the spy's report, von Bissing ordered Cavell's arrest. On 5 August 1915, the story goes, German soldiers burst into Cavell's hospital, where they found her in a ward, dressing a soldier's wound. She asked to be permitted to complete her task but "at the signal of an officer hovering in the corridor, the corporal tore from her hand the bandage with which she was going to cover the wound and led the nurse away."[24] To add irony to brutality, some accounts claimed that the soldier whom she was tending was a German!

This vignette presented Miss Cavell as the antithesis of the Lady in the Hat. Rather than the enigmatic *femme fatale* who brought death and destruction, Miss Cavell was a healer, known and loved by all who knew her. Moreover, she was not a spy; it was she who was spied upon. All of the deceit, treachery and sexual intrigue came from her German persecutors. By creating Miss Cavell as an angel of mercy, the story denied her the role of spy heroine.

As Cavell readily admitted under German questioning, she was an important part of a resistance network extending from occupied France to the Dutch border that helped British, French and Belgian soldiers escape German-controlled territory. German authorities also arrested thirty other Belgians and French agents, including Philippe Baucq, editor of the clandestine journal, *La Libre Belgique*, and Louise Thuliez, a young woman from Lille, the network's most important courier, as well as the Comtesse de Belleville and Princesse Marie de Croÿ, whose big houses along the Franco-Belgian border, like Cavell's hospital in Brussels, served as hiding places for escaping soldiers. Baucq, Cavell, Thuliez, Belleville, and Louis Séverin, who was hiding men in his house when he was arrested, were condemned to death. Only Baucq and Cavell were executed, however; the international outcry over Cavell's death caused the others' sentences to be commuted to long prison terms.[25]

Both Marie de Croÿ and Louise Thuliez published accounts after the war detailing the workings of the escape line as well as their arrests, trial and imprisonment.[26] Thuliez was a recruiter for the organization, as well as being a courier and guide. Beginning in September 1914, she moved around the area over which the German invasion had swept, gathering up stranded French, British and Belgian soldiers and stashing them in hiding places like Croÿ's chateau at Bellignies, where a secret staircase provided just the right touch of cloak and dagger. Croÿ supplied them with clothes, food, money and false identity papers. From Bellignies, Thuliez guided the men to Cavell in Brussels or directly to the Dutch border. According to their memoirs and to Cavell's confession, the network helped over two hundred men to escape.

Although primarily an escape line, the network had engaged in subversion and espionage as well. Thuliez distributed clandestine journals such as *La Libre Belgique*, and smuggled in propaganda from the Netherlands. She admitted in her memoir that at least once she also carried out "an interesting piece of information [about] a munitions depot between Douai and Cambrai."[27] Although it is unlikely that Cavell herself engaged in espionage, she was in touch with agents of the British Intelligence Corps.[28] There were certainly enough elements in her experience as well as that of Thuliez and Croÿ to tell a tale of how courageously French, Belgian and English women had worked together against German domination, thus constructing a story of spy heroines. But this is not the story that was told.

The French propaganda about Miss Cavell stressed her healing, universal goodness and innocence rather than her intelligence, patriotism and courage. Rather than outwitting the Germans, like the Invasion Heroines, she outshone them with her virtue. A case in point was her ready and complete confession, which led to the arrest and conviction of several of her co-conspirators. This aspect of her story would have caused problems for casting Cavell as a spy heroine; however, as an innocent victim, such naïveté became proof of her transcendent virtue. Here is how Paul Painlevé dealt with this incident in his panegyric to her:

> Betrayed, arrested, was she to seek her salvation in silence, trickery or lies? This would have been to humiliate the ideal she served and, in order to live, to sacrifice all reason for living. No, she will speak: what she had done, she will tell without fear, with exactitude and simplicity. Like Antigone, she could have responded to the iniquitous judge who interrogated her: "I obey *The Law* but not *your* law. I obey the supreme law that is above all violence and whose triumph will avenge my death."[29]

Although she was a "daughter of intrepid England," her real cause was "above all violence," above partisanship, even patriotism. Her famous last words concluded every account: "I know now that patriotism is not enough; I must have no hatred and no bitterness toward anyone." Like the Invasion Heroine – Sister Julie, Mme Macherez – Miss Cavell became a symbol of civilization confronting barbarism, a martyr for humanity.

As befitted a martyr, the most important scene in the Miss Cavell story was that of her death. But here there was a stumbling block; unlike Mata Hari, who would go to her execution with style, it was believed that Cavell fainted as she was led on to the execution ground. If her confession prevented her from becoming a spy heroine, this swoon was a blemish on the story of Saint Edith. Some accounts claimed it was not fear that caused her to faint, but the horror of watching another person killed. In one version, the Germans, "with a refinement of cruelty," forced her to watch the execution of her colleague, Philippe Baucq. Another claimed: "They condemned her to death. She did not weaken. Without trembling, she stood at the stake. One of the soldiers of the execution squad refused to fire at this woman. With a shot from a revolver, the officer slaughtered him. Before this act of savagery, Miss Cavell swooned."[30] The most common story, of which the above was an elaboration, simply diverted attention from Cavell's weakness by focusing upon German brutality. It reported that the execution squad was unwilling to fire upon her recumbent body, so the officer in charged walked

Miss Edith Cavell

LA GRANDE ALLEMAGNE

Figure 8.1 The legend of Miss Cavell's execution. © Bibliothèque Nationale de France, Paris.

up to her and shot her in the head with his revolver[31] (Figure 8.1). With heavy sarcasm, propagandist Paul Gsell underlined the lesson already evident in the story of Cavell's arrest: "These simple soldiers had not profited from the teachings of *Kultur*. The officer had the superiority of education and, without doubt, birth."[32]

The story of Miss Cavell's death, which turned her execution into murder, made her a symbol of the suffering of occupied Belgium and France. A month after her death, the League of the Rights of Man sponsored a memorial evening in her honor at the Trocadero theater that included music, elegiac poetry and speeches by Ferdinand Buisson, president of the League, Paul Painlevé, who, at the time, was Minister of Public Education, and the feminist journalist Séverine. The keynote of each speech was that Cavell was a martyr, the reincarnation of Joan of Arc and the personification of all the "nations crucified" by Germany, which, like her transcendent soul, would inevitably triumph in the end.[33]

French Women and the First World War

As Julie Wheelwright has pointed out, the story of Cavell's death transformed an independent, active, authoritative personality into a passive victim. Her war work disappeared into the image of the unconscious innocent slaughtered by the brutal Hun.[34] Séverine declared Cavell had a "secret thirst" for martyrdom and argued that her end was predestined. "Edith Cavell could not have another [fate]: her memory would have been incomplete, even wasted by destiny if, around her nurse's cap, there was no trembling and resplendent halo of martyrdom."[35] Her death became her life's work.

A public subscription paid for a bas-relief commemorating Miss Cavell's martyrdom at the Place de la Concorde;[36] schools and hospitals were named in her honor, as was a mountain (in the Colorado Rockies) and a newly discovered star. A 1928 film, *Dawn*, retold her story, complete with her famous last words and the shot to the head. Anniversaries of her arrest and death saw the publication of commemorative articles and brochures.[37] The story of Miss Cavell, the martyr, had found a secure place in popular memories of the First World War.

The Miss Cavell story took shape in France and England while her colleagues Marie de Croÿ and Louise Thuliez were imprisoned in Germany. After they were released at the end of the war, both women took their stories to the French public, Thuliez in lectures and an article in the *Revue des Deux Mondes* in 1919 and Croÿ in a memoir published in 1933. Both stories are good yarns; yet neither woman became a popular national heroine. Thuliez remained well enough known in 1942 for the French Resistance to refer to her exploits in propaganda;[38] but she has disappeared from memory today. Marie de Croÿ's story disappeared even more quickly; except for a few articles that appeared at the time her book was published, she elicited no interest at all.

The main problem was that unlike Cavell, Thuliez and Croÿ had not died, and thus, no matter how much they had suffered, their stories were not about martyrdom. In fact, the core of the stories they told was not how the Germans had persecuted them, but how they had outwitted the Germans, hiding escaping soldiers, talking their way past checkpoints and eluding patrols. Despite Thuliez's title, "Condemned to Death by the Germans: The Story of a Companion of Miss Cavell," their stories did not fit into the mold of Miss Cavell's legend. When taken seriously, their stories could crack that mold; if Cavell was a member of the feisty team that Thuliez and Croÿ described, could she have been completely innocent of

why lack of women sources

the charges the Germans brought against her? In the end, the story of the martyred Miss Cavell not only prevented Cavell's incarnation as a spy heroine, it also prevented Croÿ or Thuliez from assuming the role either.

The one French woman spy who might have joined Cavell in the public memory as a heroine was Louise de Bettignies of Lille. Besides operating an escape line, Bettignies gathered information for both the British and French intelligence services. Of good family, religious and most important, killed (more or less) by the Germans, Louise de Bettignies could also appropriate many of the essential elements of Cavell's martyrdom. Furthermore, after the war, a team of relatives and former colleagues promoted her status as a heroine and martyr. Nonetheless, her story did not "take."

Although all the accounts conjured Louise de Bettignies as a sweet young girl, like Cavell she was a mature woman of proven independence and initiative when the First World War began. Daughter of a failed Lille industrialist, Bettignies had studied in England and had supported herself as a governess for several years. She was living at home when the war swept over Lille and began her career as a secret agent by volunteering to act as a courier for the Red Cross, taking letters to unoccupied France. Her success brought her to the attention of the British Intelligence Service. At their behest, Bettignies organized an information-gathering network, making good use of her Church connections to find trustworthy informants throughout the war zone. Marie-Léonie Vanhoutte of Roubaix became her principal assistant. Under the code names of Alice and Charlotte, the two women gathered reports from about two hundred agents in occupied France and delivered them weekly across the Dutch border. The information they collected was often very important: items such as the locations of artillery batteries, munitions depots and troop concentrations.

As told by her publicists after the war, the life "Alice" and "Charlotte" led was full of narrow escapes and audacious ruses. In order to cross the frontier unseen, Bettignies once swam an ice-filled canal and had several close calls with German patrols. On one occasion, as she loitered near a border crossing, she saw Prince Rupprecht of Bavaria drive up. She gaily accosted him, reminding him of when they had played bridge together at a spa; when he invited her to drive into Holland with him, she acquired an unconscious royal escort for her mission. In October 1915 the Germans captured both women; but, unlike Cavell, they did not provide much information to their interrogators and, although the network could not function without Bettignies's leadership, most of her agents avoided arrest. Owing to the international outcry over Cavell's execution, the German court martial commuted their death sentences to long prison terms. In prison, Bettignies continued to resist; citing the Hague Convention, she refused to do any work that might aid the German war effort, and encouraged fellow prisoners to do the same. Her recalcitrance earned her solitary confinement and later transfer to a prison in Germany, where privations and poor medical care led to her death in September 1918.

After the war, Bettignies's family and former colleagues campaigned to secure her a place in history. Both the French and British governments complied, awarding her four medals in all and ceremoniously returning her body to Lille for an impressive funeral in March 1920. Meanwhile, her family and friends promoted her reputation in publications and speeches. In 1924, Antoine Redier published the basic source for all later publicity, a volume entitled *The War of the Women* that recounted Bettignies's adventures and tragic death.[39] His main informant was Léonie Vanhoutte, who, unlike Bettignies, survived the war and became his wife. Vanhoutte also gave lectures and interviews extolling her friend. Later, Bettignies's niece, Hélène d'Argoeuves, published articles about her aunt and in 1956 a full-length book of her life and especially her death.

The effort that was supposed to concretize Bettignies's status as a national heroine was a monument in her honor in Lille, unveiled in a ceremony in 1927 that drew considerable press coverage (Figure 8.2). The statue depicts a kneeling French soldier kissing the chained wrists of a young woman who stands calmly above him, looking away at the horizon. Its base reads: "To Louise de Bettignies and to all the heroic women of the Invaded Country, A Grateful France, 1914–1918." Two bas-reliefs flank the inscription, one showing Bettignies guiding men to the border, the other Miss Cavell's execution. In 1938 she made another public appearance in the film *Sisters in Arms* by Léon Poirier.[40]

What is striking about this publicity is that in 1924, when Redier's book appeared, in 1927, and again in 1938, the press discovered Louise de Bettignies anew, each time extolling how much she had done for France and lamenting how she had been forgotten. They also often misspelled Léonie Vanhoutte's name (Van Hoste, Vanhouste, etc.), confused the women's *noms de guerre* with their real names and even sometimes spelled 'Bettignies' incorrectly.

Figure 8.2 The memorial to Louise de Bettignies in Lille. The inscription reads: "To Louise de Bettignies and all the heroic women of the Invaded Country, a grateful France."

Obviously neither the story nor the characters were implanted firmly in the public memory. Today, even in Lille, Bettignies's place in history is insecure. There is a Place Louise de Bettignies in the center of the city; but most *Lillois* whom I questioned thought she was a resistance fighter of the Second World War. The municipal tourist bureau had to consult a reference book to locate her monument, even though it is on one of the city's major boulevards.

Although Louise de Bettignies seemed to unify in one person the spy heroine and the martyr, her story demonstrates how antithetical these two themes were. In the main accounts by Redier and d'Argoeuves, her story fell into three parts, with martyrdom prepared in Part I and achieved in Part III, but separated by the spying adventures of Part II. Framed in this fashion, Bettignies's spying appeared not as a natural development of the story but as a detour from her path to sainthood. According to her publicists, Bettignies had two salient characteristics, her femininity and her piety; her decision to become a spy was something they had to explain – away. In their accounts, Bettignies did not choose to become a spy. Instead "a mysterious force" brought her to the attention of the British Intelligence Service, as one author asserted; then God compelled her to embrace espionage as a quasi-religious mission. "Joan of Arc, hesitating about her vocation, also had counselors. But higher than they, the *voices* spoke. Like Joan, Louise also heard these voices: 'Great-hearted daughter, you must go!'"[41] Bettignies's death confirmed the likeness: "As they did for Joan of Arc on the pyre, someone held out to her a large crucifix, which she kissed lovingly . . . What agony! She had given all, she had nothing to offer but this last sacrifice of dying alone, amid her enemies."[42]

Spy or martyr, it seemed that a woman could not be both; and, in the end, the temptation to turn Louise de Bettignies into a martyr, *à la* Cavell whose image shares her monument, was too great to resist. It was so compelling because, as the above quotations show, for a French audience especially, behind Cavell's story loomed an even more powerful master narrative of feminine wartime service, the story of Joan of Arc. And, despite her niece's purple prose, death from typhus and a botched operation could not compete with the firing squad or the stake. If the First World War's heroine was to be a martyr, that martyr would be Cavell.

The Legend of Mata Hari

Joan of Arc's legend prepared the way for Cavell's martyrdom; but the essential catalyst for her story was its usefulness. The French found in Cavell a potent symbol of civilization threatened by barbarism that explained the current suffering and promised the ultimate triumph of France. Similarly, pre-war spy fantasies predisposed the French public to believe in Mata Hari's guilt, but in 1917 it was the explanatory potential of her story that soldered it into the public memory.

Mata Hari was arrested on 13 February, tried on 24–25 July and executed on 15 October 1917; her drama coincided with the most important crisis that France experienced during the war since its outbreak. Its ally, Russia, was in Revolution, the Chemin des Dames offensive, begun in April, failed miserably, mutinies swept France's army and strikes its industry. Pedestrian explanations such as war weariness and poor leadership did not seem apocalyptic enough to encompass this disaster nor to exorcize the fears that it spawned. Into the breech steeped the publicists and politicians of the Right, who had long cried in the wilderness against foreign subversion, claiming that Republican laxity or complicity was selling France to the socialists, anarchists, Jews and Germans. What in 1910 and even in 1916 seemed to be ravings, in the summer of 1917 made sense. Unable to win in man-to-man combat on the battlefield, the Germans were undermining French resistance from within. German spies, German ideas, German gold, reaching into the government itself were responsible for France's desperate straits. In the summer of 1917, France succumbed to a spy scare that surpassed that of August 1914. The government expelled over one thousand foreigners and charged nearly five hundred people with spying, executing several of them, including, of course, Mata Hari.

In 1915 and 1916, the French public experienced a backlash against its initial credulity over the Lady in the Hat.[43] The spy stories that appeared in the press in this period were either pure adventure tales or were comical, like the many versions of the story of a border policeman who suspected a woman of carrying messages written on her body in invisible ink.[44] Those who warned of a German spy invasion shrank to the ranks of the Far Right, led by Léon Daudet, who continued to rail against Jewish, foreign and "Bochized" subversion in the pages of *L'Action Française* and in a new novel-cum-political tract, *Vermin of the World* (1916). His attacks had a clear political agenda, to tar Radicals as Germanophiles and traitors and drive them from power. Daudet's main targets were Joseph Caillaux, an influential Radical, although in 1917 not a member of the government, and his fellow Radical, Jean-Louis Malvy, Minister of the Interior. In 1917 Georges Clemenceau joined the campaign in the pages of his paper, *L'Homme enchaîné*, and in the Senate, scenting that here was a powerful weapon against Malvy, his long-time opponent. Daudet and Clemenceau claimed that Caillaux and Malvy were not only turning blind eyes to German espionage, but were actually selling France out. With their connivance, German agents had stirred up the strikes (and the mutinies, although these could not be mentioned publicly), and delivered French ships to German torpedoes and the plans for the Chemin de Dames offensive to the German High Command. More broadly, German money had bought off the press and the politicians to prevent the public from learning these ugly truths.

In the panicky climate of 1917, enough of this mud stuck to make a credible, if wildly distorted, image of French wartime politics. One of these charges was true; the Germans were trying to buy access to the French press. In the summer of 1917 two such cases became public, that of the anarchist paper, *Le Bonnet Rouge*, and, much more important, *Le Journal*, whose editor, Charles Humbert, was a senator with friends on the Left and the Right. These scandals appeared to substantiate the Right's view of governmental complicity in subversion. Malvy was forced out of the government at the end of August, and later both he and Caillaux were tried for treason.[45]

Where in this was the woman spy? According to the spy fiction and Gaudin de Villaine's scenario, she should have been at the center of the scene, spinning the seductive threads that entrapped all of France in a web of subversion. But, in fact, the *Bonnet Rouge* and the *Journal* affairs revealed no such feminine influence. Therefore she must have been lurking behind the scenes. In Mata Hari, she stepped on to the stage, flaunting every accoutrement of the spy of popular fantasy. She was a cosmopolitan of mysterious ethnicity, with a past as an exotic – i. e. nude – dancer, a peripatetic life-style and a reputation as a *demi-mondaine* with lovers in high places on both sides of the trenches. With her imperious manner, her extravagant wardrobe – and her hats! – she was a godsend to the French counter-espionage service; if she had not existed, they would probably have invented her, which is what they almost did.

All "true stories" of Mata Hari[46] begin with her real name, Margaretha Zelle, her nationality, Dutch, and her class; she was the daughter of a bankrupt haberdasher. At the age of nineteen, she married Rudolph MacLeod, a captain in the Dutch colonial army twenty-one years her senior, and went with him to the Dutch East Indies. The marriage did not prosper. Margaretha claimed Rudolph was a brutal bully; later she explained her refusal ever to appear without her breasts covered by the story that once in a rage he had torn off her nipples with his teeth. (Not true, said her prison doctor; she just had small breasts.)[47] Judging by her later life, Margaretha was probably extravagant and unfaithful. Once they returned to Amsterdam in 1901, Margaretha sued for divorce, and in 1904 came to Paris to make a name for herself as the exotic dancer Mata Hari (Eye of the Day, in Malay) and to live *la vie mondaine*, financed by wealthy lovers.

Mata Hari's act was an Oriental striptease; she shed multicolored veils while enacting a supposed Hindu temple dance, ending up wearing only her breast-plates, prostrate on the floor before an idol

(Figure 8.3). A popular and critical success, in 1905 she danced more than thirty times in exclusive Parisian salons and six times in the Trocadero Theater and other large theaters besides. At the time, she was only one of a number of exotic dancers – even more flourished in her wake – but what set her apart was that she kept up the act off-stage. As her celebrity grew, so did her story. She began by billing herself as Lady MacLeod, wife of a British lord, but soon developed a more authenticating background. She was the daughter of a Dutch officer and an Malay princess; she had been raised in a Hindu temple as a sacred dancer dedicated to Shiva. Her act and her ever-changing biography together played to Parisian fantasies of the erotic East; it conjured up vague hints of white slavery, lesbianism – Mata Hari performed at several of Natalie Barney's soirées – and of Salome, the *femme fatale* who hypnotized men and bent them to her will in order to betray them.

From Paris, which remained her main base and the locale of her greatest triumphs, Mata Hari went on to dance in Monte Carlo, Vienna, Milan and Berlin. But by the summer of 1914, both her careers, as a dancer and as a courtesan, were on the skids. She was thirty-eight: her dancing had been overtaken in artistry and daring by younger, more talented performers, and the spotlight of celebrity had moved on. She was living in Berlin not as the mistress of the *Kronprinz*, as she once boasted, nor the head of German Intelligence, as her accusers later would claim, but under the protection of an officer of the morals police. Germany's declaration of war led to her expulsion as a suspicious foreigner and the confiscation of her clothes and jewelry to pay her debts.

Here is where agreement among Mata Hari's serious biographers breaks down briefly. Did the Germans actually recruit and train her as a spy, as Léon Schirmann claims, or did she simply take their money and run, as Russell Warren Howe and Julie Wheelwright conclude? In any event, Mata Hari went to Paris, where she quickly came to the attention of Captain Georges Ladoux, head of the hastily-created French counter-intelligence service. A lady of such dubious ethnicity, morals, and connections was immediately suspected of espionage in the Paris of 1916. In his fantastical memoirs, Ladoux described her slinking into his office, attempting to seduce him with her hypnotic eyes and her husky "Oriental" voice and, so that we should be in no doubt as to her true nature, exhibiting a serpent tattooed on her wrist. Although he admitted that surveillance of her had led nowhere, he attributed this to her extreme cleverness

Figure 8.3 Mata Hari in her glory years. © Bibliothèque Nationale de France, Paris.

in deceit rather than to her innocence. Consequently, Ladoux immediately decided to try to "turn" her into a double agent, suggesting she could prove him wrong in his suspicions by playing the game for France instead of Germany. Seeing an opportunity to make some money – Ladoux says she requested a million francs – Mata Hari jumped at the chance, declaring she had once been the

German Crown Prince's mistress, that she had him at her feet; and more or less promising his head on a platter.[48]

However, her enactment of Salome in real life did not proceed so smoothly as it once had on stage. British Intelligence stopped her on her way back to the Netherlands. She promptly revealed she was a French spy; but when they applied to Ladoux for confirmation, he denied any knowledge of her. Mata Hari ended up in Spain, without money or contacts but still believing she was on a mission for France. She cultivated the German military attaché, Major Kalle, from whom she received enough money to get back to Paris to report to Ladoux. He, however, refused to see her; and shortly she was arrested as a German spy.

Although biographers disagree over whether she ever actually was a double agent, recent assessments conclude that, if she was, she was never a successful one. Such information as she possessed was rumor and society gossip. In her interrogations, she claimed to have strung along Kalle with tidbits she made up or had gleaned from the Paris papers, and this would seem to be the truth. In her eyes, she was a spy for France, and although she had not netted the *Kronprinz*, she thought Kalle a promising catch. She believed the accusations heaped upon her amounted to betrayal; given Ladoux's own account of his treatment of her, an impartial jury should have agreed.

But of course, Mata Hari did not have, had never had, an impartial jury. All the parties in her drama – the Germans, the British, the French, even the Dutch, found her instantly suspicious; she so resembled what they thought a spy should be. Ladoux's behavior is inexplicable unless viewed within the context of the all-enveloping espionage fantasy. Although immersed in the mundane work of intelligence gathering, surveillance and background checks, Ladoux believed firmly in the scenarios of Daudet and the spy novelists. The world of espionage constituted an alternative reality in which innocence and patriotism were cloaks for villainy and betrayal. Every unconventional person was suspect, every conventional life a cover story and every spy a double agent. Behind the scenes, directing the whole drama, the whole war, in fact, was the sinister spy-master. In Ladoux's post-war writing he filled this role with Fraulein Doktor, a steely-eyed tigress who ruled her spy empire with a pistol and a whip.[49] At the center of the stage, however, was the master spy. Ladoux was hardly the only member of the intelligence community to succumb to this scenario. It was shared by the British Intelligence chief, Sir Basil Thomson, and, most importantly for Mata Hari's fate, by Captain Pierre Bouchardon, the investigating officer of the military tribunal that tried her. He recalled her as "a tigress in the jungle . . . feline, supple, and cunning, accustomed to playing with everything and everyone without either scruples or pity, always ready to consume fortunes even if her ruined lovers then shot themselves; it was easy to see she was a born spy. She had all the qualities."[50]

The charges against Mata Hari were slender: that she had given the Germans information that dealt with "interior politics, the spring offensive, the discovery by the French of a secret of a German invisible ink, and the disclosure of the name of an agent in the service of England."[51] Evidence presented to support these accusations was nil, partly because the only real evidence against her was contained in a couple of decoded telegrams from the German embassy in Madrid. The French counter-intelligence service refused to divulge these, to prevent the Germans from learning that their code had been broken.[52] Nonetheless, the prosecuting attorney, Lieutenant André Mornet, whipped the molehill into a mountain, attributing to Mata-Hari all the evils that had befallen France since the beginning of the year.

Why did French military intelligence conspire against Mata Hari? Howe argued that so much of Ladoux's reputation rode on her case that he could not admit he had grasped a mere will-o'-the-wisp. Furthermore, according to Krop, Bouchardon was affiliated with the *Action Française*, and thus had a political ax to grind.[53] But after reading the post-war memoirs of Ladoux and Bouchardon, I think that their investment in Mata-Hari, master spy, went far deeper than careerism or politics. They believed in the witch who had put a hex upon France. To save France, it was their desperate duty to exorcize the demon by exposing Mata Hari and executing her.

At the time of her trial, the public was even less well informed than the military court of the exact nature of Mata Hari's crimes, except that they were "abominable" and that she had confessed to them. As Schirmann has shown, the government censors ensured that the press published the false report of her complete confession in order to nip in the bud any chivalric outburst against the execution of a woman such as the Cavell case had aroused.[54] Later reports added details: she had sold plans of allied tanks to the Germans, who then perfected the anti-tank shell that killed thousands at the battle of the Somme; she had betrayed the position of French ships to German submarines; and most damningly, it was she who gave the plans of the Chemin des Dames offensive to the German High Command. As if this were not enough, reporters implied that there were more deeds too dreadful to be revealed. One article claimed: "Later, when it is possible to tell the still secret story of German espionage in France during the war, the Hindu dancer will appear as one of the most odious figures and her punishment, the most deserved."[55] After the war, "the little mysteries of counter-espionage" continued to prevent complete revelation of how destructive Mata Hari's crimes had been. As Emile Massard said in his authoritative 1920 account, "To know them one has only to consult Mata's [sic] dossier. But we don't believe we are authorized to unveil them." Even in 1953, when Bouchardon published his memoirs, he explained that "professional secrecy" still prevented him from revealing all of her hideous crimes.[56]

In the summer and fall of 1917, Mata Hari was a convenient scapegoat, because she demonstrated that the source of France's disasters was foreign subversion – cosmopolitan vermin, in Daudet's term – rather than anything inherently wrong with France. This was comforting at a time when national morale definitely needed a boost; and the French readily accepted it. In an extensive survey of the French press, Schirmann found that only the *Bonnet Rouge* and, surprisingly, Clemenceau's *L'Homme enchaîné* expressed any skepticism. The garment worker Louise Delétang recorded the news of Mata Hari's execution in her diary, crediting her with torpedoing ships and "selling our soldiers."[57]

The legend of Mata Hari began to grow even before the end of the war. Particularly intriguing was the rumor of a Tosca-like attempt at a faked execution, with the part of Tosca played by a phantom lover, an aristocratic French officer who, when he failed to save her from the execution squad's bullets, withdrew from the world into a Spanish monastery.[58] Emile Massard claimed he wrote his account to set the record straight. In its introduction, Massard piled up his credentials of credibility – Legion of Honor, *Croix de guerre*, 1870 medal; but the most important one was that he had actually witnessed Mata Hari's trial. "This book," he asserted, "is not a novel, it is a document."[59] First published serially in the Right-wing journal *Liberté* in 1921, his version of Mata Hari's "true story" appeared in book form the following year and began an avalanche of "I Caught Mata Hari" memoirs. The British Intelligence chief, Sir Basil Thomson, published his account in 1922, Dr Bizard, who had attended Mata Hari in prison, weighed in in 1925, Ladoux in 1932 and Bouchardon, a late entry, in 1953. Meanwhile, Mata Hari began a second career as a character in fiction. She made her début in Charles-Henry Hirsch's novel, *La Chèvre aux pieds d'or* (1920), which was made into a play, *La Danceuse rouge*, the following year. Then she played a sinister bit part in Louis Dumur's controversial novel, *Les Défaitistes* (1923) and in many other works. Her film career began immediately too, in 1921. In later, better-known productions she was played by Marlene Dietrich (1931), Greta Garbo (1932), and Jeanne Moreau (1964). Even Mata Hari's daughter, who in reality died in 1919, went on to have a romantic afterlife in espionage in fiction and film.[60]

Mata Hari's posthumous career was due in part to her usefulness to the Right's efforts to keep French Germanophobia at a fever pitch and to continue their attack upon Malvy, who returned to public life after the war. For example, in *Les Défaitistes*, Dumur had his hero find Malvy's card in the boudoir of the mysterious lady spy whom he later caught in bed with, guess who? Mata Hari![61] But Mata Hari's drama had meaning beyond the crisis of 1917 and beyond right-wing politics. The story's staying power came from its apparent revelation of a fundamental truth about "Woman and War." Embodying the most monstrous incarnation of the Emancipated Woman, Mata Hari showed feminine independence and sexuality leading straight to the death of thousands of men and threatening the survival of the nation. This was the woman who transcended the firing squad – which, unlike Cavell, she met with head high in her best hat! – to secure the primary place in the French memory of women in the First World War.

Mata Hari's status as a best-seller after the war encouraged a few French women to audition for the part as her French equivalent. The music-hall singer, Mistinguett, entered the lists with the insinuation that she had done some high-class spying in Switzerland during the war. The press was skeptical, and Parisian society dismissed this as a bid for more celebrity.[62] A much stronger and more successful claim came from the *aviatrice* Marthe Richer, rebaptized Marthe Richard for her spying adventures. After the success of his memoir about Mata Hari, Ladoux published a second volume of revelations from the romantic world of espionage, purporting to recount the story of "The Skylark," France's foremost woman spy, Marthe Richard. Two years later, Richer published her own version of these fantastic exploits as a serial in *Paris-Soir* and later as a book.[63] Although her account did not entirely agree with Ladoux's, they followed the same outlines. Ladoux, suspicious of "Richard's" penchant for flyers and believing she was involved with the *Bonnet Rouge*, recruited her as a double agent and sent her to Spain, where she seduced the German naval attaché, von Krohn, rifled his files, visited a German submarine, unmasked German agents in Morocco and foiled a dastardly German plot to destroy Argentinian grain supplies with a thermos of weevils! In the end, prevented from carting off a whole trunk of German secrets by an inconvenient automobile accident, "Richard" exposed her lover's indiscretions to his embassy, thus ending his career. The story met with justified skepticism, even though Richer did receive a Legion of Honor.[64] And, in fact, Ladoux called his book about her "novelesque" and gave his heroine the slightly fictionalized name to suggest that the story was only "based on" reality rather than its faithful portrait. Richer, however, defended "Marthe Richard's" exploits as the unvarnished truth, and some accounts continue to credit her claims. In his biography of Mata Hari, Russell Warren Howe wrote that Richer was "the true courtesan-spy and double agent that Mata Hari was supposed by legend to have been."[65]

This was the conclusion for which Ladoux and Richer were aiming. The tale they concocted was intentionally modeled upon Ladoux's previous story about Mata Hari. Each, Ladoux claimed, was a natural spy, by which he meant a seductive woman with a little something disconcertingly masculine tucked away in her psyche. The plots of the two stories were also remarkably similar. Ladoux behaved in the same way to both; suspecting them of being German spies, he immediately tried to "turn" them into double agents. Each woman ended up in Spain; Richer claimed to have roomed next door to Mata Hari in a Madrid hotel. Each seduced a German military attaché who was head of German intelligence in Spain. Most readers missed this point where their parallel tales collided: Kalle and Krohn could not both have been head of German intelligence, but the similarity of their names allowed them to stand in for each other. Finally, Ladoux more or less abandoned "Richard" as he had Mata Hari; each woman had to plot her own course and run her own risks.

For Ladoux, the meaning of this doubling was that the story of "Marthe Richard" canceled out that of Mata Hari; "our" woman spy was better than "their" woman spy. The similarity of the two stories was to highlight the fundamental difference between the two women, and thus the two nations. "They were as different as a highly bred pedigree French racehorse and a Dutch half-breed. Several classes intervened between them, as would be said in the language of the track."[66] Several classes and a moral universe; for while Mata Hari was the dark demon, "Marthe Richard" was the Skylark.

Richer's version of the story raised a more troubling question. Unencumbered by Ladoux's desire to justify his treatment of Mata Hari and to show the French counter-espionage service to be a match for Germany's, Richer was more willing to flirt with the implications of her story's resemblance to Mata Hari's. Rather than opposites, she presented herself and Mata Hari as duplicates, sisters in espionage, working for opposite sides but nonetheless in sympathy. It was chance rather than virtue or patriotism that chose between them. As she remarked in an interview at the time her story appeared in *Paris-Soir*, "I got the Legion of Honor and [she] got the firing squad."[67] They were both heroines – or they were both whores.

Marthe Richer traded upon her certified status as a war heroine for the rest of her life, adopting the fictional "Richard" as her own name. Like those of Cavell, Bettignies and Mata Hari, her story was translated to celluloid – *Martha Richard in Service to France* (1937), starring Edwidge Feuillère and Eric von Stroheim. Yet the French public never took her to their hearts. After Ladoux's death in 1936, Richer repeatedly had to defend herself with threats and lawsuits against people who questioned her story.[68] Skepticism remained, however, because the public did not warm to her effort to recast the war heroine/martyr in the flamboyant mold of the *femme fatale*. In its obituary, *Le Monde* remarked that Marthe Richer was "the only woman decorated with the military Legion of Honor for heroic weakness before the enemy."[69]

Marthe Richer could parley her re-enactment of Mata Hari's story into personal celebrity, selling books, attracting interviewers and even, according to Romi, getting a fraud conviction quashed because of it;[70] but she could not reformulate France's notion of a heroine. The choice of war heroine and war villain came down to the trite opposition of virgin and whore. With Miss Cavell on one side and Mata Hari on the other, Richer's story made little mark. *polarized*

The Defeatist Bogeywoman, Hélène Brion

Mata Hari was the most famous villainess of the First World War; but she was not the last incarnation of Woman as enemy in France.

Under relentless pressure from the Right, the spy scare in 1917 broadened to target anyone who suggested a "premature," that is a negotiated, peace. Support for a complete victory, war *jusqu'au but* – to the bitter end – became the litmus test of patriotism. Malvy resigned in August in an effort to stem attacks upon the government; but in vain. The *Union sacrée* in the legislature shattered, and Clemenceau, who had led the pack against Malvy, became Prime Minister on 17 November 1917. He immediately declared war upon "defeatism" and its proponents: "No more pacifist campaigns, no more German intrigues. Neither treason, nor half treason, but war. Nothing but war. Our armies will not be caught between two fires."[71]

The most famous French pacifist was Romain Rolland, author of *Above the Mêlée* (1915); but he was in Switzerland and beyond Clemenceau's grasp. The government picked a closer and altogether more attractive target to demonstrate their tough resolve, the socialist feminist Hélène Brion. Brion was arrested for distributing anti-war pamphlets on 18 November 1917, the day after Clemenceau came to power. An orchestrated campaign in the press used the tropes of the female spy – seduction, sexual ambiguity, corruption, cosmopolitanism – to brand Brion, and with her anyone with doubts about the prosecution of the war, as desiring France's defeat. Pacifism became "defeatism," and its representative was a woman.

When the war began there was almost no organized opposition in France; and what little there was disappeared by late August, when the French learned that their country had been invaded. The war scares of the prior decade and the tide of nationalism they had helped to swell had already weakened commitment to pacifism. As we have seen in Chapter 2, feminists had begun to support a defensive war even before the outbreak of the First World War, and similar feelings had undermined syndicalist and socialist anti-militarism.[72] The socialist, syndicalist and feminist movements all immediately rallied to the *Union sacrée*, the major organizations, such as the Socialist Party (SFIO), the General Confederation of Labor (CGT), the National Council of French Women (CNFF), and the French Union for Women's Suffrage (UFSF), quickly endorsing the war effort as defending the nation and civilization.[73] Julie Siegfried and Adrienne Avril de Sainte-Croix, president and general secretary of the CNFF, wrote on 25 August: "Women of our land and our race, we will consent to all the sacrifices demanded of us with courage and absolute faith in the final victory."[74] Feminist internationalism was dead for the duration. When the CNFF refused to send a delegation to the international feminist peace conference at the Hague in April 1915, the press hailed this as a demonstration of French women's patriotic resolve.[75] There was little that separated this rhetoric from that of right-wing nationalists. As late as 1917, both Siegfried and Marguerite de Witt-Schlumberger of the UFSF still supported the war to victory at all costs. As Siegfried told an audience at the Trocadero, "If your hearts desire peace, our consciences prohibit it today."[76]

Although the *Union sacrée* was very real, especially in the first months of the war, it was never total. From the start, there were intellectuals and activists who refused to be mobilized. Roman Rolland was the most famous of these. His essay, *Above the Mêlée*, first appearing as articles in the *Journal de Genève* in 1914, was reprinted in France in June 1915 and became the touchstone for wartime pacifism.[77] There were also a few dissident socialists and syndicalists who eventually came together in the Zimmerwald movement. Gabrielle Duchêne and fifteen other French feminists sent a manifesto of support for the Hague conference that was published in *Jus Suffragii,* the journal of the international women's suffrage movement, in June 1915, although the letter was censored from the French edition of the publication. After the conference, Duchêne agreed to set up a French section of the International Committee of Women for Permanent Peace, the direct ancestor of the Women's International League for Peace and Freedom, at her office in the rue Fondary in Paris. Although rarely attracting more than twenty people to its meetings, the rue Fondary group, like Rolland's essay, gave pacifism a foothold in France during the war.[78]

The threads of feminist opposition to the war are one of the best-researched aspects of French women's history during the First World War.[79] However, although feminist historians can be pleased that some women stood firm against the war, the number was few, and the costs were very high. Women lost their friends, their institutional support and their jobs as a result of their doubts about the war's righteousness.[80] As Marcelle Capy reported in her pacifist tract, *A Woman's Voice in the Mêlée*, anyone who presumed to question the prosecution of the war was immediately accused of being a Germanophile and a traitor.[81]

During the crisis of 1917, this kind of thinking, and the repression to which it led, became more widespread at the same time as the anti-war movement itself began to grow beyond the ranks of a few beleaguered activists. In the summer, the strike wave began to exhibit anti-war overtones, and opposition to the war acquired a few more outlets, such as *La Voix des Femmes*, edited by Louise Bodin, a member of the rue Fondary group, which began publication in the fall of 1917, and a growing radical minority within the socialist and labor movements, now galvanized by the revolution in Russia.

From the beginning of the war, despite the universal adherence of feminist groups to the *Union sacrée*, the police suspiciously watched feminist organizations and publications. For example, they refused to allow Marguerite Durand to resume publication of *La Fronde* because its title seemed seditious. Informers filled the files of the police archives with reports on feminist meetings and even informal gatherings.[82] For the Right, feminism was dangerously cosmopolitan. Before the war, nationalists had condemned it as an Anglo-Saxon import; during the war, *Action française* pointed to the suspiciously "Boche" names of feminist leaders – Siegfried, Witt-Schlumberger, and the USFS's secretary general, Cécile Brunschvicg. The *Action Française* activist Emile Janvion, writing in 1918, summed up these fears: "During this war, it is feminism which, in its multiple ramifications, is the most active agent of avowed and camouflaged defeatism."[83] Thus the decision to prosecute Hélène Brion, a syndicalist leader and an outspoken feminist as well as a pacifist, was a deliberate one. It was meant to quash all these currents of opposition simultaneously, by convicting them of treason via the stereotype of the subversive woman.

Hélène Brion was a nursery school teacher in Pantin, a working-class suburb north-east of Paris; but her real love was politics. A friend of Marguerite Durand, Brion was a member of numerous feminist organizations such as the UFSF and the French League for Women's Rights. She was also an activist in the Socialist Party and in the syndicalist movement. As an officer in the National Federation of Teachers Unions and a member of the central committee of the CGT, her main goal was to bring feminism into the labor movement by demanding equal pay for women teachers and more broadly, women's right to work.[84]

When war broke out, mobilizing most male teachers, Brion found herself head of the Federation, along with Fernand Loriot, the organization's treasurer. Initially they supported the war, following the line of their parent organization, the CGT. In June 1915, another teacher, Marie Mayoux, persuaded the Federation's central committee to reaffirm the union's antimilitarism and to cease supporting the war. Brion did not agree with this policy, but went along with it, as party discipline required, eventually supporting the international socialist conference at Zimmerwald and, with her colleagues, joining the Committee for the Resumption of International Relations founded by the French Zimmerwaldians. As the war dragged on, the numbers of deaths climbed and the sacrifices demanded of working people mounted, Brion's commitment to her union's position became more genuine.

In the fall of 1917, the government began to crack down on pacifist teachers, and in October, it sentenced Marie Mayoux and her husband François to two years in prison for distributing an uncensored tract they had written. Entitled *Syndicalist Teachers and the War*, it explained their union's stance and called for an immediate negotiated peace without conquests or indemnities. According to the government, the pamphlet's purpose was "to demoralize everyone who reads it, to beat down their confidence, to discourage the soldiers who are fighting so gloriously for the *Patrie* and who are ready heroically to spill their blood for her."[85] Fear of renewed mutinies spoke loudly here. In fact, the Mayoux were the main advocates of pacifism within the teachers' union; their arrest and trial drew little comment.[86] No such reticence, however, surrounded Brion's case the following month.

At the time of her arrest on 18 November 1917, Brion had already been under investigation for several months as a prominent activist in an antimilitarist union, a feminist pacifist, and an associate of the Mayoux. The charges against her were essentially the same as those against Marie and François Mayoux: she had distributed their pamphlet and had posted up anti-war "papillons," that is, wall stickers with slogans like "Enough men killed! Peace!" However, the political climate had abruptly changed. Rather than wanting to downplay the existence of a pacifist opposition, Clemenceau's regime wanted to dramatize it, to demonize it, in order to win credit for crushing it. Michel Corday wrote in his diary on 19 November, "This arrest is a kind of present to celebrate the happy accession of His Majesty Clemenceau."[87]

At her trial, Brion argued forcefully that her pacifism was not defeatism; never had she called for peace at any price, and she always supported the soldiers.[88] In this, Brion mirrored the position of all but a small handful of French peace activists at the time. Although a few militant revolutionaries supported the Bolshevik belief that a military collapse would lead to a proletarian revolution, most were well aware that it would be more likely to bring German invasion. Instead, they advocated a negotiated peace that would end the killing immediately and produce neither victors nor vanquished. The heart of the government's campaign against Brion was to make the French public equate this position with defeatism and those who held it with traitors.

An article in *Le Matin* on the day of Brion's arrest detailed the specific charges against her and implicated all political opposition in defeatism. It claimed that, in her nursery school classroom, the police had found tracts that advised soldiers to desert. The police had also uncovered a "voluminous correspondence" with suspicious people, as well as copies of the proceedings of the socialist conferences at Zimmerwald and Kienthal. All of this "preached class hatred, resistance to military orders, peace at any price and the preparation of a general revolution." "Malthusianism, defeatism, anti-militarism, anarchy, such were the directing ideas that guided Hélène Brion."[89] Since Brion's friends quickly defended her in print, particularly denying that she had ever encouraged desertion or advocated peace at any price, *Le Matin* published a further demonstration that any sort of pacifism was treason. Citing Charles Seignobos, a Sorbonne professor, identified as "one of the principal theoreticians of pacifism" before the war, *Le Matin* asserted that in the current circumstances, pacifism was "nonsense" and that to desire peace by any means other than complete victory was defeatism.[90]

In order to construct and also to destroy defeatism via Hélène Brion, her pacifist ideas had to appear absurd. The press that attacked Brion rarely quoted her even in reporting on her trial, at which she spoke eloquently. Instead, journalists described her manner and the reactions of "sensible" people to her speeches. Brion was "a fanatical visionary, at once the victim of a mystical temperament and villainous suggestions."[91] Even in her own degenerate circles, "most of the time, her exaggerations put a smile on her auditors' lips." However, when patriotic people heard her, it was not with smirks but with anger. "In one meeting where she tried to expound her defeatist theories, some wounded soldiers took it badly and the speaker barely escaped getting one amputee's crutch over her head."[92]

Yet although her pacifist ideas were absurd, she herself had to be dangerous in order to appear worthy of prosecution and punishment. Brion's seriousness and her work as a nursery school teacher and labor leader, as well as her lack of sex appeal, made her an unlikely *femme fatale*. Nonetheless, the Right-wing press turned her into an intellectual "temptress" who "seduced" her fellow teachers, naive workers and innocent children. The *Nationale* compared Brion to a drug dealer handing out cocaine, and deplored the fact that she had been left so long in charge of impressionable children.[93]

Since her attackers could not turn the thirty-five-year-old teacher into a slinky siren, they played up the other side of the female spy's sexuality, its ambiguity. *Le Matin* called her "abnormal, at least" and cited as evidence the "fact" that she wore masculine attire, which several papers substantiated by printing a photograph of Brion in bicycle bloomers. At her trial, where pictures show her wearing a skirt and blouse with a floppy bow at the neck, reporters from the nationalist press insisted that her "blazer . . . strangely resembles a man's suit jacket, an outfit that is definitely a little masculine."[94]

This portrait of Brion as an unhinged visionary, seductive subversive and masculinized menace was intended to prepare readers to accept that Brion was not an honest if misguided idealist, but an active traitor, a spy. The nationalist press, such as *Le Matin*, *L'Echo de Paris* and Clemenceau's *L'Homme enchaîné,* now rebaptized *L'Homme libre*, dropped hints that most readers in 1917 could easily interpret. First, there was that "voluminous correspondence" with soldiers, munitions workers, German prisoners of war and Zimmerwaldian socialists. In addition, there were dubious visitors, such as the "two bizarre persons" hidden in her home for four days. One of them pretended to be a woman, but was obviously a man in disguise. Were they deserters? (Were they spies?) "After all, this is certainly possible."[95]

Finally, there was the claim that Brion had visited Russia, Zimmerwald and Kienthal. When it was publicly acknowledged that she had not, in fact, attended these socialist conferences, the right-wing press fell back upon the charge that she had *intended* to go, but had been stopped by the police at the border. Readers could conclude that Brion was "cosmopolitan vermin" and a Bolshevik revolutionary, and thus implicated in the summer's strikes and mutinies. The same papers also claimed that Brion was an anarchist, and insinuated that she was an associate of Almereyda and the *Bonnet Rouge.* To make the connection to the press scandals stronger, the *Petit Parisien* wondered where Brion had got the money to travel around making her anti-patriotic speeches and to print and distribute her despicable tracts. The reader was supposed to think "Aha, Germany, of course!" Only *Le Matin* actually mentioned the word "spy," but, as her friend Madeleine Vernet

300

angrily pointed out, readers primed with the summer's spy scandals and the Mata Hari case would easily read it between the lines.[96] But unlike Mata Hari, Hélène Brion was able to rally friends and colleagues publicly to her defense, even if they did not all agree with her opposition to the war. At her trial, fifty-seven people testified on her behalf; these character witnesses included not only other pacifists like Gabrielle Duchêne of the rue Fondary group, but also school directors, teachers, mothers of her students, and war widows, working women and neighbors from Pantin. The syndicalist movement and the women's movement, both of which the government branded as untrustworthy and subversive via its prosecution of Brion, kept aloof. However, individual leaders in both movements, such as Jules Bled of the CGT and the well-known feminists Nelly Roussel, Séverine and Marguerite Durand, spoke in her defense.[97]

The government intended Brion's arrest and trial to convince the French public that any opposition to its handling of the war was the equivalent of treason. This depended, however, upon publicity that, despite censorship and a cooperative right-wing press, the government could not completely control. In fact, the Right's obviously orchestrated vilification of Brion provoked an outpouring of support from friends, colleagues and political allies, who defended Brion in the press, in petitions to the government and at her trial.[98] The willingness of respected people to stand up for her, plus Brion's own defence at her trial, belied the deranged idealist, *femme fatale*, Amazon, subversive conjured up by nationalist journalists at the time of her arrest. Reports and illustrations of her trial in the mainstream press showed her to be a normal-looking schoolteacher and labor activist of demonstrable integrity and "a great heart," as even the prosecutor acknowledged.[99]

The trial gave wide publicity for the first time to principled opposition to the war. And, as constructed by Brion and reported in the press, this opposition was based upon Brion's status as a woman and her feminism. The prosecution had argued that Brion's feminism was a mere cloak for her defeatism; Brion firmly righted the terms of the relationship: "It is by feminism that I am the enemy of war," as it was by feminism that she opposed all brutal force that worked inevitably to woman's detriment. Pointing out that as a woman she was debarred from any political responsibility, she argued that propaganda was the only means women had of affecting society. Her intent, which was the special interest of all women, was to save children, present and future, from the horrors of war, to save the future of France as well as the justice and liberty for which France stood and that the war was eroding so frighteningly. "If you do not call upon women to help you, the loss will not be made up, and the new world you are pretending to found will be as unjust and chaotic as before the war!"[100]

Although the censors prevented the immediate publication of the text of Brion's defense, the government could not ban comment upon it. Left-wing papers in particular summarized Brion's argument as well as those made on her behalf by Nelly Roussel, Marguerite Durand and Séverine. *Le Pays* pointed out that they demonstrated that "'pacifism' and 'patriotism' are not contradictory," especially in women's mouths. The *Journal du Peuple* concluded that the trial posed the stark contrast of "the weak woman" and "man the warrior," and "yesterday the woman dared to speak of the ideal, of goodness, of justice, and finally of peace to men who, not wanting to understand, made armor plate of their office and resolved on denying this woman the right to think like a woman instead of like a soldier."[101] Such articles suggested that, in the current situation, to work for an immediate armistice and a negotiated peace was a brand of patriotism superior to the government's *jusqu'au butisme*, and particularly appropriate to women.

While Brion presented herself as a representative of all thinking, feeling women, her supporters declared her a war heroine, and for Madeleine Vernet, a martyr. In a brochure defending Brion published before her trial, Vernet evoked Miss Cavell and Jesus![102] In the end, the prosecution succeeded in getting a conviction, but the sentence – three years in prison, suspended – was hardly the endorsement the government had sought. The presiding judge later commented, "We are no longer in time of the Dreyfus affair," that is, when politics could dictate justice.[103] They also had no desire to crown Brion with a martyr's halo.

When Michel Corday learned of Brion's arrest, he remarked to Marcelle Capy that they should soon see "'Mankind Free' [an allusion to Clemenceau's paper] but 'Womankind in Chains.'"[104] To the extent that, in its campaign against Brion, the government succeeded in identifying "Womankind" as the Enemy Within that was preventing a masculine victory on the battlefield, this was the case. However, here the ambiguity of Woman's relationship to War intervened on Brion's behalf. Although the French public believed in Mata Hari and the incalculable evil she had done to the nation, they also

female patriotism

believed the story of Miss Cavell and the good she represented. And with her stood the many other heroines of wartime stories, the Invasion Heroines and the Heroines of the Harvest, the volunteer nurses, charity ladies and plucky *munitionettes*. In their stories, women's patriotism was often shadowed by a nagging doubt that feminine self-interest was inimical to the masculine war effort. This time, the tables were turned; the story of Hélène Brion as the war's, and therefore the nation's, enemy was undermined by a belief in the legitimacy of a different sort of feminine patriotism. Perhaps the Enemy Within was a woman; but not all women were enemies. Female patriotism was possible, even in women who opposed the war.

Notes

1. Marthe Richer, *I Spied For France*, trans. Gerald Griffin (London: John Long, Ltd., 1935), pp. 25-6.

2. Becker, *1914,* pp. 509-10; Pourcher, *Les jours de guerre,* pp. 49-57; Mme Louis Wachet, *La guerre en Champagne, en Argonne et dans les Ardennes: Heures tragiques, impressions et souvenirs* (Paris: Bloud & Gay, 1919), pp. 5-6; AN F⁷ 12938 Reports from Prefects, especially Lot, Lot et Garonne, and Lozère.

3. Becker, *1914,* pp. 497-513; Pourcher, *Les jours de guerre*, pp. 49-57.

4. Capy, *Une voix de femme*, pp. 87-8.

5. Gordon, *The Integral Feminist*, p. 144. In her *Mémoires: Clair de lune et taxi-auto*, p. 37, Elisabeth de Gramont reported that her big hat and mannish stride provoked similar suspicions.

6. In late 1915, an internal report of the German Intelligence Service found that very few of the people reported in the French press to be German spies worked for Germany: Schirmann, *L'affaire Mata Hari*, p. 153.

7. Gerd Krumeich, "L'entrée en guerre en Allemagne," in Becker and Audoin-Rouzeau (eds), *Les sociétées européennes et la guerre*, pp. 65-74; Wheelwright, *The Fatal Lover*; David French, "Spy Fever in Britain, 1900-1915," *Historical Journal* 21 (June 1978): 355-70.

8. Michael B. Miller, *Shanghai on the Métro: Spies, Intrigue and the French Between the Wars* (Berkeley, CA: University of California Press, 1994), pp. 22-6.

9. See Léon Daudet's articles in *L'Action française*, as well as his best-selling, supposedly documentary account, *L'avant-guerre: études et documents sur l'espionnage juif allemand en France depuis l'affaire Dreyfus* (Paris: Nouvelle Librairie Nationale, 1913); also Paul and Suzanne Lanoir, *L'espionnage allemand en France* (Paris: Albin Michel, 1908) and

Les grands espions; leur histoire; récits inédits de faits d'espionnage et de contre-espionnage de Frédéric Guillaume à nos jours (Paris: Librairie Gustave Ficker, 1911).

10. Capitaine Danrit [Emile Augustin Cyprien Driant], *La guerre de demain* (Paris: Ernest Flammarion, 1880s and 1890s). See also Paul d'Ivoi [Paul Deleutre], *La patrie en danger; Histoire de la guerre future* (Paris: H. Geffroy, 1905); Charles Malo, *La prochaine guerre* (Paris: Berger-Levrault, 1912).

11. Miller, *Shanghai on the Métro*, pp. 26–8.

12. Edouard Rousseaux, *La future invasion prussienne et l'espionnage à la frontière* (Mayenne: C. Colin, 1905), pp. 70–4; Marcel Prévost, *Les anges guardiens* (Paris: Librairie Alphonse Lemerre, 1913), reworked as a play in 1914 by Jean José Frappa and Henry Dupuy-Mazuel. Other *femme-fatale* spy novels include Ernest Daudet, *Espionne* (1905); Sollard, *L'espionne des Balkans* (1913); and André Cambon, *Courrier d'espionne* (1914).

13. Wheelwright, *The Fatal Lover*, p. 111.

14. Rousseaux, *La future invasion prussienne*, pp. 71–2.

15. La Grange, *Open House in Flanders*, p. 113; also see Lesage, *Journal de guerre*, p. 49.

16. Georges Ladoux, *Martha Richard, The Skylark, The Foremost Woman Spy of France*, ed. Warrington Dawson (London: Cassell, 1932), pp. 35–6; Emile Massard, *Les espionnes à Paris* (Paris: Albin Michel, 1922), pp. 35–8, 89; Wheelwright, *The Fatal Lover*, pp. 125–8; also the serial story by Jacques Brienne, "L'infirmière," *Le Petit parisien*, beginning 10 March 1916.

17. "La <<marraine>>," *Le Petit parisien*, 29 September 1915.

18. Massard, *Les espionnes*, pp. 217–18.

19. Wheelwright, *The Fatal Lover*, p. 104; Maurice Barrès, "Un côté ténébreux de cette guerre," *L'Echo de Paris*, 30 December 1914.

20. André Avèze, *Martha Steiner, gouvernante allemande* (Paris: Albin Michel, 1916).

21. Maurice de Waleff, "Pas d'allemandes en France pendant la guerre," *Le Petit journal*, 24 October 1916.

22. Eugen Weber, *Action Française: Royalism and Reaction in Twentieth-Century France* (Stanford, CA: Stanford University Press, 1962), pp. 94–5; Sylvain Gaudin de Villaine, *L'espionnage allemand en France 1914–1916* (Paris: Pierre Tequi, 1916).

23. Bory d'Arnex, *Parisiennes de guerre*, p. 35. Massard, *Les espionnes*, pp. 116–18 also linked charity work to spying.

24. *La vie et la mort de Miss Edith Cavell* (Paris: Fontemoing et cie., 1915), p. 70; Paul Gsell, *Edith Cavell* (Paris: Librairie Larousse, 1916); and BMD dos Cavell. In fact, it was a Frenchman, Gaston Quien, a member of her network, who betrayed Cavell.

25. A. A. Hoehling, *Edith Cavell* (London: Cassell, 1958).

26. Louise Thuliez, "Condamné à mort par les allemands: Récit d'une compagne de Miss Cavell," *Revue des deux mondes* 50 (1 April 1919): 648-81; Croÿ, *Souvenirs*.

27. Thuliez, "Condamné à mort," p. 668.

28. Wheelwright, *The Fatal Lover*, p. 124.

29. Paul Painlevé, introduction to *La vie et la mort de Miss Edith Cavell*, pp. x–xi (emphasis in text).

30. BMD dos Cavell.

31. *La vie et la mort de Miss Edith Cavell*, pp. 143, 211–13; BMD dos Cavell.

32. Gsell, *Edith Cavell*, p. 39.

33. Ligue des Droits de l'homme et citoyen, *Miss Edith Cavell, Eugène Jacquet* (Paris, 1916); also the Fédération des Eglises protestantes de France, *Service religieux célébré à l'Oratoire du Louvre en mémoire de Miss Edith Cavell* (Paris: Bureaux de Comité protestant de propagande française à l'étranger, 1915).

34. Wheelwright, *The Fatal Lover*, pp. 122–3.

35. Ligue des droits de l'homme, *Miss Edith Cavell, Eugène Jacquet*, p. 17.

36. The Germans removed it during the Second World War.

37. For example, articles in *Paris Soir*, *Le Petit parisien* and other papers on 13 October 1935, the thirtieth anniversary of her execution; a commemorative booklet published in 1965, the fiftieth anniversary, and a long article in *Le Monde* on 5 August 1994, the anniversary of her arrest, by the historian Annette Becker.

38. Becker, "D'une guerre à l'autre," p. 465; BMD dos Thuliez.

39. Antoine Redier, *La guerre des femmes* (Paris: Editions de la Vraie France, 1924) - first appeared in the *Revue française hebdomadaire* in October, November and December 1923; and "Comment Louise de Bettignies passait la frontière," *Revue des deux mondes* (1 November 1927): 105-16; Gem Moriaud, *Louise de Bettignies, une héroïne française, une vie romancée* (Paris: J. Tallandier, 1928); Hélène d'Argoeuves, "Louise de Bettignies, la <<Jeanne d'Arc du Nord>>" *Les Annales* (10 January 1938): 10-13 and *Louise de Bettignies* (Paris: La Colombe, 1956).

40. BMD dos Bettignies; Becker, "D'une guerre à l'autre," pp. 459-60.

41. Louis Madelin, "Fille au grand coeur, va" *L'Echo de Paris*, 5 May 1926.

42. Argoeuves, "Louise de Bettignies," p. 12. Also see Moriaud, *Louise de Bettignies*, p. 46.

43. Slater, *Defeatists*, pp. 28-9.

44. Hermant, *La vie à Paris*, 134; "Le journal d'une espionne," *La vie parisienne*, 53 no. 1 (2 January 1915); "On dit . . . on dit," *La vie parisienne*, 55 no. 4 (27 January 1917); Georges Ladoux, *Les chasseurs d'espions* (Paris: Librairie des Champs-Elysées, 1932), p. 174. In her memoirs, Mistinguett claimed this had happened to her. *Toute ma vie*, 2 vols (Paris: René Julliard, 1954), I: pp. 162-3.

45. Weber, *Action Française*, 104-10. For Daudet's own description of the campaign, see his *Le poignard dans le dos: notes sur l'affaire Malvy* (Paris: Nouvelle Librairie Nationale, 1918).

46. Biographies of Mata Hari are extremely numerous. The most recent are Russell Warren Howe, *Mata Hari, The True Story* (New York: Dodd, Mead & Company, 1986), Wheelwright, *The Fatal Lover* (1992) and Schirmann, *L'affaire Mata Hari* (1994).

47. Dr Léon Bizard, *Souvenirs d'un médecin de la Préfecture de police et des prisons de Paris (1914-1918)* (Paris: Bernard Grasset, 1925), pp. 83-4.

48. Ladoux, *Les chasseurs d'espions*, pp. 231-52.

49. Ladoux, *Les chasseurs d'espions*. Historians differ on whether Fraulein Doktor ever existed. Of course, she did publish her memoirs in *Paris-Midi* in 1933, but that is hardly proof. Schirmann insisted she existed (*L'affaire Mata Hari*, p. 25), while Pascal Krop, *Les secrets de l'espionnage français de 1870 à nos jours* (Paris: Editions Jean-Claude Lattès, 1993), p. 220, called her mythic.

50. Basil Thomson, *Queer People* (London: Hodder and Stoughton, 1922); Pierre Bouchardon, *Souvenirs* (Paris: Albin Michel, 1953), p. 309. Like Ladoux, Bouchardon was a romancer, with numerous novels with titles like *L'énigme du cimetière de Saint-Aubin* and *La malle mystérieuse* to his credit.

51. Judgement of 25 July 1917 cited in Wheelwright, *The Fatal Lover*, p. 91.

52. Howe, *Mata Hari*, argues that the Germans deliberately sent the revealing messages in a code they knew the French had broken in order to "burn" Mata Hari for her clumsy spying efforts in Spain.

53. Howe, *Mata Hari*, p. 196; Krop, *Les secrets*, pp. 229-30.

54. Schirmann, *L'affaire Mata Hari*, pp. 164-6.

55. BMD dos Mata Hari, "Mata Hari a été fusillée," s.l. 16 October 1917.

56. Massard, *Les espionnes*, p. 57; Bouchardon, *Souvenirs*, p. 314. In fact, Mata Hari's dossier remained closed to researchers until recently.

57. Schirmann, *L'affaire Mata Hari*, pp. 160-1; Delétang, *Journal d'une ouvrière*, p. 360.

58. Wheelwright, *The Fatal Lover*, pp. 129-30.

59. Massard, *Les espionnes*, p. 7.

60. Schirmann, *L'affaire Mata Hari*, pp. 201-3; Wheelwright, *The Fatal Lover*, pp. 129-44.

61. Louis Dumur, *Les défaitistes* (Paris: Albin Michel, 1923), pp. 176, 232.

62. "Mistinguett détective," *Le Petit parisien*, 23 July 1918 and Mistinguett's rebuttal on 26 July; Masson, *Les espionnes*, pp. 179-85. Une actrice, *La vie frivole*, p. 255. In her memoirs, *Toute ma vie* I: pp. 164-7, Mistinguett claimed that she had carried out some secret missions but that she was not really a spy, although Malvy had accused her of spying. Krop, *Les secrets*,

pp. 218–19 believed that she was recruited to dig up dirt about Caillaux and Malvy.

63. Ladoux, *Martha Richard*; Marthe Richer, "Ma vie d'espionne au service de la France," *Paris soir*, 20 September–23 October 1934, published as a book in 1935 and translated as *I Spied for France*.

64. Romi, "Enfin la verité sur Marthe Richard," *Paris-Villages* no. 9 (1985): 29–39 concluded the medal was actually awarded to her in lieu of her late husband, an official in the Rockefeller Foundation.

65. Howe, *Mata Hari*, p. 121.

66. Ladoux, *Martha Richard*, p. 40.

67. Cited in Wheelwright, *The Fatal Lover*, p. 63.

68. Romi, "Enfin la verité."

69. "La mort de Marthe Richard," *Le Monde*, 10 February 1982.

70. Romi, "Enfin la verité."

71. Cited in Jere Clemens King, *Generals and Politicians: Conflict Between France's High Command, Parliament and Government, 1914–1918* (Berkeley, CA: University of California Press, 1951), p. 193.

72. Becker, *1914*, pp. 84–119.

73. On socialists, see Alfred Rosmer, *Le mouvement ouvrier pendant la guerre*, Vol. I, *De l'Union sacrée à Zimmerwald* (Paris: Librairie du Travail, 1936) and Annie Kriegel, *Aux origines du communisme francaise (1914–1920)* 2 vols (Paris: Mouton, 1964); on the labor movement, see Annie Kriegel and Jean-Jacques Becker, *La guerre et le mouvement ouvrier français* (Paris: Kiosque A. Colin, 1964) and Horne, *Labour at War*. On feminists, Bard, *Les filles de marianne:* and Françoise Thébaud, "Le féminisme à l'épreuve de la guerre," in Thalman (ed.), *La tentation nationaliste*, pp. 17–46.

74. BMD dos 396 Conseil national des femmes françaises.

75. For example, "Féminisme et pacifisme," *Le Temps*, 25 August 1915; Louise Compain, "Les femmes et l'action internationale," *Grande revue*, 19 no. 10 (December 1915): 327–36.

76. Cited in Thébaud, *La femme au temps de la guerre de 14*, p. 247; Bard, *Les filles de marianne*, pp. 17–18.

77. Becker, *The Great War*, pp. 85–93; Prochasson and Rasmussen, *Au nom de la patrie*, pp. 142–56.

78. Bard, *Les filles de marianne*, pp. 94–102; Thébaud, *La femme au temps de la guerre de 14*, pp. 252–3.

79. Besides Bard and Thébaud, also see Judith Wishnia, "Feminism and Pacifism: The French Connection," in *Women and Peace: Theoretical, Historical and Practical Perspectives*, ed. Ruth Roach Pierson (London: Croom Helm, 1987), pp. 103–13 and Sandi Cooper, "Pacifism in France, 1889–1914: International Peace as a Human Right," *French Historical Studies* 17 no. 2 (Fall 1991): 359–86.

80. Huguette Bouchardeau, preface to Hélène Brion, *La voie féministe* (Paris: Editions Syros, 1978), p. 38; Bard, *Les filles de marianne*, pp. 90–4

and BMD dos Colliard.
81. Capy, *Voix de femme*, pp. 90–1.
82. Bard, *Les filles de marianne*, pp. 58–9.
83. Emile Janvion, "Le féminisme défaitiste," *L'Effort*, 2 November 1918.
84. Bouchardeau, preface to Brion, *La voie féministe*; Bard, *Les filles de marianne*, pp. 102–7; Wishnia, "Feminism and Pacifism," pp. 103–47.
85. "Le procès Hélène Brion et Mouflard devant le Premier Conseil de Guerre: Le défaitisme et les défaitistes," *Revue des causes célèbres politiques et criminelles* (2 May 1918): 130.
86. BMD dos Mayoux.
87. Corday, *The Paris Front*, p. 294.
88. "Déclaration d'Hélène Brion lors de son procès, le 29 mars 1918" in Brion, *La voie féministe*, p. 112.
89. "Une institutrice arrêtée à Pantin," *Le Matin*, 18 November 1917.
90. BMD dos Brion, "Unanime réprobation du monde de l'enseignement," *Le Matin*, s. d. but obviously in November 1917.
91. "La morale du procès Brion," *La Nationale*, March 1918.
92. "Unanime réprobation du monde de l'enseignement."
93. BMD dos Brion, "Le cas de Mlle Brion," *Le Petit journal*, s. d.; "La morale du procès Brion."
94. N. Sant'Andrea, "Le procès d'Hélène Brion devant le 3e conseil de guerre," *La Voix nationale*, 25 March 1918.
95. BMD dos Brion, "L'institutrice arrêtée," s. l. s. d., probably November 1917.
96. "Une institutrice arrêtée à Pantin;" Madeleine Vernet, *Hélène Brion, une belle conscience et une sombre affaire* (Epône: Société d'Edition et de Librairie de "L'Avenir Social," November 1917), p. 8. For the ensemble of newspaper accounts of her arrest, see BMD dos Brion.
97. Bard, *Les filles de marianne*, pp. 104–5; Madeleine Vernet, Henriette Izambard, Lucie Colliard, "L'affaire d'Hélène Brion," *La Bataille*, 21 November 1917; Thébaud, "Le féminisme à l'épreuve de la guerre," p. 36; "Le procès Hélène Brion et Mouflard."
98. BMD dos Brion, "L'institutrice de Pantin et la propagande défaitiste: Les amies de Mlle Brion la défendent," s. l., 20 November 1917; Becker, *The Great War*, pp. 308–9.
99. BMD dos Brion press clippings; "Procès Hélène Brion et Mouflard," p. 154.
100. "Déclaration d'Hélène Brion lors de son procès."
101. Alfred Dominique, "Le procès de Hélène Brion: Vers l'acquittement," *Le Pays*, 26 March 1918; "Hélène Brion devant le Conseil de guerre," *Journal du peuple*, 25 March 1918; also Georges Yvetot, "Un beau procès," *La Voix des femmes*, 17 April 1918.
102. Vernet, *Hélène Brion*, p. 4.
103. Bard, *Les filles de marianne*, p. 105.
104. Corday, *The Paris Front*, p. 294.

Conclusion

For many French women in the countryside, the war ended as unexpectedly as it had begun. Marie-Cat Santerre recalled that when the church bells rang on 11 November 1918, at first the villagers did not know what they meant. People in the cities, especially Paris, had more warning; on 6 October, the seamstress Louise Delétang heard the rumor that the Germans were seeking an armistice. Her diary entries for the following month recorded the rumors of the Kaiser's abdication and the revolution in Berlin, her hopes rising in consequence. On 10 November, a Sunday, she and many other Parisians swarmed the boulevards, hoping to hear the signal that the armistice had been signed. Yet, on Monday, when the cannon sounded, Delétang initially felt stunned. People on the street questioned each other – Was it really over? As Marguerite Lesage recorded in her diary: "Oh! The divine moment in which we had not dared believe." But then France erupted into wild rejoicing. Santerre recalled: "Joy spread through the streets of the village. Women went out on their doorsteps, children ran by yelling and old people wept in the streets like kids." In Paris, at the Place de la République where a crowd danced, at the Place de la Concorde "black with people" paying tribute to the statue of Strasbourg, and on the Champs Elysées, where Delétang joined the throng, "from hour to hour, the crowd grows, surges up, then down, the young people shout, sing, gambol; the *midinettes*, tricolor ribbons in their hair, the workers, the soldiers come down toward the center of Paris, waving their flags and shouting: 'Long live the poilus!'"[1]

Accounts from both the city and the countryside described the celebration as undifferentiated, "the crowd" or "the villages" or "the people," or explicitly inclusive: young and old, men and women, soldiers and working girls. The community was united in age and gender; and it was united in emotion as well. As Geneviève Aimée reported, "everyone hugged, laughing and crying at the same time." In this way, they presented the scene of the armistice as the counterpart and resolution to the scenes of the war's outbreak. War had divided France, sending men off with cheers while women stayed behind in tears; peace reunited the nation. Accounts from the countryside emphasized the parallel by pointing out that the bells that had rung the alarm on 1 August 1914 now on 11 November 1918 rang in joy. The novelist Lucie Delarue-Mardrus wrote: "It was Resurrection Day. The war was over . . . I thought that life would pick up where we had left it, after the parenthesis of four years of abominations."[2]

War meant rupture; peace meant return. Return of the men, first of all. "They are coming home!" Aimée recalled her neighbors shouting. But she also recalled that some people ran home weeping, "those for whom 'they' would not be coming home." And, of those who did, as Santerre recalled, many were wounded or crippled and, even when whole, were "serious, sad, unsmiling." At the other end of the social spectrum, Elisabeth de Gramont suffered the same disillusionment. "They don't want anything more to do with heroism! and no one on the homefront can understand them."[3]

The influenza epidemic added to the uncertainty. Already in October the *grippe* had rivaled the rumors of approaching peace for public attention. On 20 October, Delétang noted in her diary that the flu was claiming more victims in Paris than German shells or bombs. On 5 January 1919 she sadly wrote: "We desired the Era of Peace as if all suffering would disappear with its arrival; however, we still have some very hard times" – high prices, "the disappearance of all foodstuffs as if by enchantment," the task of rebuilding the devastated North – and the influenza, which had already claimed 100,000 lives.[4] The war cast a long shadow.

Could "life" pick up from where it had been left off? Could the gap between front and home front be closed, and gender relations snap back into place? Would peace close the parenthesis of abominations, but also of opportunities, that war had created; or would it open a new chapter? What had the war done to gender? And what had women's mobilization done to war? From the first days of the war, social commentators argued over the meaning of women's warwork for the future of France, especially for post-war relations between the sexes. While some believed that the gender system, as illuminated in the war's glare, had held firm, many warned that it was in the process of modification, for better or for worse.

In the first years of the war, permeated with belief in the *Union sacrée*, most commentators agreed that women's wartime patriotism would lead to greater post-war harmony between the sexes. For feminists, this meant greater gender equality. For example, Julie Siegfried, president of the CNFF, argued in January 1915 that men, by asking for women's help, and women, by giving it, were taking the irreversible first step. "Man and woman are two to work together and, according to the old words of humanity's bibles, the woman begins to be for man the helpmate who is his like."[5] Throughout the war, feminists like Siegfried and Léon Abensour argued that, women's war service having demonstrated their civic equality to men, the vote must surely follow.[6]

At the same time, feminists emphasized that civic equality did not mean the end of gender differentiation. Wartime mobilization had confirmed the equal but complementary status of the sexes. The post-war harmony would be one of collaboration of difference in mutual respect best exemplified in marriage. While predicting the advent of women's suffrage, Abensour assured his readers that this inevitable consequence of the war would not bring about an upheaval of gender. "Let's be reassured that every woman will give up without regret the masculine soul that of tragic necessity and with miraculous energy she has filled for a few days. Replacement workers, heroines will not be less good wives."[7]

Greater gender equality was not the only definition of gender harmony, however. Conservatives also predicted a restoration of the couple and the family; but rather than an equal partnership, they argued that the war demonstrated the validity of male superiority and female subordination. In September 1915, Pierre Mille in *Le Temps* reprinted a letter supposedly from a young woman who had sent her "baby" brother off to war. She confessed that by this act, her view of him had undergone a sudden rectification. "I bow very low before this child who has suddenly become my senior. I blush now at my blindness." Hortense Cloquié agreed, predicting in 1915 that women's experience in the war, far from leading to feminism, would rightly cause women to make heroes of their men. "He will always keep the superiority over the woman of having been a soldier in the Great War."[8]

Commentators writing in 1915 and 1916 were virtually unanimous that the parallel mobilization of the genders for war would result in a better, stronger, gender system even though they disagreed about what "better" meant. By 1917 doubt and anxiety began to infuse the discussion; perhaps the war's impact upon gender would not be so benign. An inquiry published in *La Renaissance* in the spring of 1917 began a national discussion of women's post-war destiny. Extending over five numbers of the magazine, the series printed commentary from Academicians, women's rights advocates, politicians, physicians, professors and novelists.[9]

This survey and the many articles and books on the topic that followed raised fears that instead of restoring, correcting and strengthening the gender system and thus the foundations of France, the war was wounding it, perhaps fatally. Rather than victory's automatically opening a door to harmony and peace, these publications morosely predicted or anxiously denied that victory would precipitate a sex war. Raymond Thamin, in a 1918 article, pondered what might happen in the workforce: "For, let's imagine the men, the day after their brutal combat, reclaiming their place in careers invaded by women if these latter no longer want to see themselves as provisional substitutes. Will a sex war follow the other war?" The novelist J. H. Rosny *aîné* expressed his skepticism about the future of gender harmony in the family:

> On the question of the fate of couples in which the husband, upon return from the trenches, finds a wife who has learned during his absence to direct his business and take initiatives and carry responsibilities, and who no longer is willing to be kept aside, you see me a little hesitant and a little skeptical about the perfect agreement of such couples.[10]

Who was at fault? Whose behavior and attitudes must change so that gender harmony could be restored? Judiciously avoiding blaming either sex, Rosny argued that the war had separated the genders, thus distorting the way that both men and women naturally adjusted to each other. Both Séverine and Marcel Prévost blamed the effects of war on men alone, Séverine finding the war had brutalized them, while Prévost worried that it had increased "male arrogance."[11] Most commentators, however, saw the root of the problem in women's wartime mobilization, which had lured them away, however necessarily, from their feminine duties to home and motherhood. The debate over work and maternity that had arisen from women's replacement work merged seamlessly into this discussion of post-war gender relations. Like Eugène Brieux, of the Académie Française, most commentators concluded: "The solution to the problems rests, in my opinion, especially on women. They must go toward work. They should embrace it! . . . Nor should they forget that France needs babies!" Somehow women's work and perhaps even civil rights had

Conclusion *Roberts*

to be reconciled to wifely submission, housewifely duties and, especially, motherhood. Rather than assuming that victory would automatically restore a balance, they gloomily agreed that women would have to be helped, encouraged and even forced to fulfill their primary duty of maternity.[12]

The debate over how to re-establish gender harmony, the family and motherhood continued to percolate until the end of the war and beyond, as the historian Mary Louise Roberts has demonstrated in *Civilization Without Sexes*. As the men came home in the winter of 1918–1919, French women met them joyfully but also anxiously. Since the discussion had produced no consensus on what had happened to gender in the war, they had no model for making reunion work. Each couple had to come to their own *modus vivendi*. Some, indeed, seemed to pick up where they had left off. Elisabeth de Gramont wrote of one such prisoner of war: "After lunch Monsieur X gets up. 'Where are you going?' 'To the Post Office,' the old conjugal response taken up like the rest." You would have thought, she concluded, that he'd only been away over night.[13] But there were many women, like Marguerite Lesage, who worried that changes the war had wrought would weigh down upon their marriages. The pictures that her prisoner-of-war husband sent her revealed "an even harder look, a look I don't recognize" – too much sadness, suffering and hatred, she thought. She herself had become assertive and, she feared, unfeminine. How would they rebuild their union?[14]

The question of the war's impact upon gender was not resolved; but it was raised and debated. The same cannot be said for the question of women's impact upon war. Their massive mobilization in support of the war seemed to have made hardly a dent in the assumption that war was a masculine preserve, outside and even opposed to women's domain. A few commentators paralleled men's and women's war service, but they never equated them. The war was man's responsibility; woman's war work was to be man's helpmate, as Julie Siegfried had said.[15] The fact that, by contrast with what happened in Russia, Great Britain and the United States, the French government had refused to militarize any women strengthened war's gender division. A debate over civilian mobilization in 1927 essentially recapitulated the debate of 1917, demonstrating how little opinions had changed. As in 1917, the proposed law would have made "all native born and naturalized French citizens, regardless of age or sex" liable to conscription in the national defense. However, parliamentary debate focused upon the provisions for requisitioning property and labor, and women slipped out of consideration, as they had in 1917. In 1927, feminists were as torn between the civil equality the proposal proclaimed and their rejection of militarism as they had been ten years earlier. The young Simone de Beauvoir recalled that when she was presented with a petition denouncing the proposal: "I was in a quandary. I was all for the equality of the sexes; and in case of danger, wasn't it one's duty to do all one could to defend the country?" However, she signed, because she was told the law would mean the end of freedom of thought and conscience and a general militarization of society – which, of course, she opposed. A meeting of the CNFF on the issue ended in an uproar, with shouts of "War upon War!" drowning out the speakers.[16]

Although the war had put gender relations in doubt, this doubt had not led to a re-evaluation of the relationship of gender to war. War was masculine, and woman's connection to it remained ambiguous, sometime helper, but also sometime opponent, and it was as war's natural enemy that woman seemed most salient in the post-war years. Among the many optimistic predictions of the good women's wartime mobilization would bequeath to the post-war world was the claim that women would prevent another such war. The surge of women's pacifist activity after the war seemed to confirm this prediction.[17] However, the 1920s and 1930s saw the ascent in popularity of another image of woman as war's enemy – that of Mata Hari. Where feminist pacifism proclaimed the feminine's triumph over war, the Mata Hari story depicted war's triumph over the feminine. There was fascination in her exotic life and spying exploits; but the essential truth of her story was played out at the execution wall. The war won and woman lost. As Klaus Theweleit has argued, this is the ultimate message of all war stories.[18] Perhaps that is why Mata Hari is still with us, one of *People* magazine's *Unforgettable Women of the Century*, while all the First World War heroines have slipped into oblivion.[19]

The story of Mata Hari has survived; but not as a First World War story. Instead, she embodies the seductive Feminine in eternal opposition to War, rather than women's experience in that particular war. The male story of the trench-fighter also conveys universal truths about the meaning of war as male suffering and sacrifice beyond all bounds of reason and the slaughter of masculine innocence on the altar of nationalism; but at the same time it is firmly rooted in the memory of the First World War. There is no such story that expresses the meaning of French women's experience in this war, but instead a multiplicity of stories, each with a double meaning. One is a story of true self-sacrifice and patriotic devotion similar, but never equal, to men's; and the other, a tale of falsity and feminine self-interest that undermined the male war effort. The second, dark meaning did not emerge from a simple exercise in misogyny, although, of course, this was seldom lacking. Rather it was a way in which the French public, including women, sought to understand and explain the experience of the war, an innocent France invaded, its heroic troops stalemated and massacred. It was impossible to look to the army to explain the invasion and occupation, the food shortages and strikes. As embodiments of French honor and sacrifice, the soldiers' story *had* to end in victory, however painfully and irrationally bought. So to understand disaster and contemplate the possibility of defeat, the French turned to stories about women. Mata Hari filled this role most dramatically; but she did not stand alone. Ranged in her shadow were a host of ambiguous women: the volunteer nurse – angel of the battlefield or ambitious husband-hunter? the peasant woman – heroine of the harvest or deserter? the *marraine* – the soldier's support or his betrayer? Invasion heroine or Occupation collaborator? . . .

Although Mata Hari and Miss Cavell, too, linger on, the ambivalent stories of French women in the First World War have now faded almost entirely from the public's memory. But as Roberts's work demonstrates, they played important roles in post-war France, both helping and hindering French society in assimilating the changes the war had wrought. Although her study concludes in 1927, French suspicions of feminine patriotism did not dissipate so quickly. The belief that the feminine was sapping France from within, confirmed over and over in First World War stories, made a dramatic comeback in the Vichy regime. On 20 June 1940, Marshal Pétain explained to the French people that their defeat was due, in large part, to feminine selfishness and lack of patriotism, which had produced "too few children" to defend the Nation.[20] French women would need to "prove" their patriotism all over again.

Notes

1. Grafteaux, *Mémé Santerre*, p. 83; Lesage, *Journal de guerre*, p. 222; Becker, *The Great War*, p. 321; Delétang, *Journal d'une ouvrière*, p. 445.

315

2. Geneviève Aimée, *Ma vie n'est qu'un seul jour* (Etrépilly: Presses du Village, 1986), p. 22; Delarue-Mardrus, *Mes memoirs* , p. 235; also Pourcher, *Les jours de guerre*, p. 499.

3. Aimée, *Ma vie*, p. 22; Grafteaux, *Mémé Santerre*, p. 83; Gramont, *Mémoires*, p. 232.

4. Delétang, *Journal d'une ouvrière*, pp. 440, 458; Becker, *The Great War*, p. 319; Catherine Rollet, "The 'Other War' II: Setbacks in Public Health," in Winter and Roberts (eds), *Capital Cities*, pp. 480–5.

5. Siegfried, *La guerre et le rôle de la femme*, pp. 7–8.

6. "Les femmes pendant et après la guerre," *Le Petit journal*, 17 April 1916; "La femme française glorifiée à la Sorbonne," *Le Petit parisien*, 20 April 1917; Abensour, "Les femmes et l'action nationale;" Juliette Adam, "La valeur sociale et nationale de la femme," *La Revue hebdomadaire* 26 no. 15 (14 April 1917): 195–202. Even conservatives like Louise Amélie Gayraud, "L'oeuvre féminine et le féminisme," *La Revue hebdomadaire* 25 no. 30 (22 July 1916): 525–40; and Maurice de Waleff, "La guerre et le féminisme," *Je sais tout* 13 no. 143 (15 October 1917): 384–92 assumed that suffrage was in the cards.

7. Abensour, *Les vaillantes*; p. 307; also Frédéric Masson, "Les femmes pendant et après la guerre," *Lectures pour tous* 26 no. 9 (3 March 1917): 24–5.

8. Pierre Mille, "Les femmes," *Le Temps*, 22 September 1915; Hortense Cloquié, *La femme après la guerre; ses droits, son rôle, son devoir* (Paris: Maloine, 1915).

9. J. Gabelle, "La place de la femme française après guerre," *La Renaissance* 5 no. 4 (17 February 1917); Suzanne Grinberg, "Le role de la femme française après la guerre," *La Renaissance* 5 no. 5 (3 March 1917), no. 6 (17 March 1917), no. 7 (31 March 1917), and no. 8 (14 April 1917). See Roberts, *Civilization Without Sexes,* 12.

10. J. H. Rosny, *aîné*, "Le rôle de la femme française après la guerre," *La Renaissance* 5 no. 6 (17 March 1917): 8–9; Thamin, "L'éducation des filles," p. 151.

11. Rosny, *aîné*, "Le rôle de la femme française," 8–9; Séverine, "Le rôle de la femme française après la guerre," *La Renaissance* 5 no. 8 (14 April 1917): 9; Marcel Prévost, "Le rôle de la femme française après la guerre," *La Renaissance* 5 no. 7 (31 March 1917): 9–10.

12. Eugène Brieux, "Le rôle de la femme française après la guerre," *La Renaissance* 5 no. 7 (31 March 1917): 7, 10; also Alfred Musigny, *Les femmes et l'avenir de la France* (Paris: Editions de la *Revue contemporaine*, s.d.); Auguste Keufer, "Les ouvriers" in *L'avenir de la France, réformes néces-saires* ed. Maurice Herbette (Paris: Félix Alcan, 1918), pp. 395–418; Joly, "De l'extension du travail;" Louis Narquet, "La femme dans la France de demain," *Mercure de France* (16 July 1917): 250–74; Georges Renard, "La crise de main-d'oeuvre," *Revue bleue* 56 nos. 11–12 (June 1918): 336–9, 368–71.

13. Gramont, *Mémoires*, p. 234.
14. Lesage, *Journal de guerre*, pp. 86, 139, 151, 169.
15. Among many examples, see Barthou, *L'effort de la femme française,* p. 1; La Hire, *La femme française,* pp. 9-10; Abensour, *Les vaillantes,* pp. 12-17 and Pitrois, *Les femmes de 1914-1915,* p. 2.
16. Challener, *The French Theory of the Nation in Arms,* pp. 184-214; Simone de Beauvoir, *Memoires of a Dutiful Daughter,* trans. James Kirkup (New York: Harper Colophon Books, 1959), pp. 237-8; Bard, *Les filles de marianne,* pp. 145-6.
17. Bard, *Les filles de marianne,* pp. 129-44; Sandi Cooper, "Pacifism, Feminism and Fascism in Inter-War France," *The International History Review* 19 no. 1 (February 1997): 103-114.
18. Theweleit, "The Bomb's Womb," in Cooke and Woollacott (eds), *Gendering War Talk,* p. 285.
19. *Unforgettable Women of the Century,* People Books, (New York: Time Inc. Home Entertainment, 1998), p. 52.
20. Cited in Margaret Collins Weitz, *Sisters in the Resistance: How Women Fought to Free France 1940-1945* (John Wiley & Sons, Inc., 1995), pp. 44-5.

Select Bibliography

1. Archives

Archives de la Préfecture de Police, Paris (APP).
Archives Nationales, Paris (AN).
Bibliothèque Marguerite Durand, Paris (BMD).
Service Historique de l'Armée de Terre, Château de Vincennes (SHAT).

2. Contemporary Periodicals

L'Action féminine: Bulletin officiel du Conseil national des femmes françaises
L'Action social de la femme
L'Automobile aux armées
La Bataille syndicaliste
Le Correspondant
L'Echo de Paris
La Femme de l'avenir
Le Féminisme chrétien
La Française
France militaire
La Fronde
La Grande revue
Lectures pour tous
Le Petit Journal
Le Petit Parisien
Renaissance politique
La Revue bleue
La Revue des deux mondes
La Revue hebdomadaire
La Revue philanthropique
La Suffragiste

Bibliography

Le Temps
La Vie féminine; union littéraire, artisique et sociale
La Vie parisienne
La Voix des femmes, politique, sociale, scientifique, artistique

3. Contemporary Publications and Memoirs

Abensour, Léon. "Les femmes et l'action nationale." *La Grande Revue.* (December 1915): 39–54.

— *Les vaillantes: Héroïnes, martyres et remplaçantes.* Paris: Librairie Chapelot, 1917.

— "Le problème de la démobilisation féminine." *La Grande Revue.* (January 1919): 80–91.

Aimée, Geneviève. *Ma vie n'est qu'un seul jour.* Etrépilly: Presses du Village, 1986.

Alix, Andrée d'. *La Croix-rouge française. Le rôle patriotique de femmes.* Préface de Georges Goyau. Paris: Perrin et cie., 1914.

Antelme, Jeanne. *Avec l'armée d'orient. Notes d'une infirmière à Moudros.* Paris: Emile-Paul *frères*, 1916.

Argoeuves, Hélène d'. *Louise de Bettignies.* Paris: La Colombe, 1956.

Arguibert, Maïten d'. *Journal d'une famille française pendant la guerre.* Paris: Perrin et cie., 1916.

Aurel [Mme Alfred Mortier]. "Moeurs de guerre," *La Grande revue* 19 no. 9 (November 1915): 20-38.

Avèze, André. *Martha Steiner, Gouvernante allemande.* Paris: Albin Michel, 1916.

Avril de Sainte Croix, Adrienne, ed. *Dixième congrès international des femmes, Paris le 2 juin 1913; Compte rendu des travaux.* Paris: V. Giard et E. Brière, 1914.

Bagnold, Enid. *The Happy Foreigner.* New York: The Century Co., 1920.

Baraduc, Jeanne [Jeanne Galzy, pseud.]. *La femme chez les garçons.* Paris: Payot et cie., 1919.

Barbusse, Henri. *Under Fire*, trans. W. Fitzwater Wray. London: Dent, 1926.

Barrès, Maurice. *L'appel au soldat.* Paris: Félix Joven, éditeur, 1899.

— *Autour de Jeanne d'Arc.* Paris: Librairie Ancienne Edouard Champion, 1916.

— *Le coeur des femmes de France: Extraits de la Chronique de la grande guerre (1914–1920).* Paris: Librairie Plon, 1928.

Barthou, Louis. *L'effort de la femme française.* Paris: Bloud et Gay, 1917.

Bazin, Réné. *La campagne française et la guerre.* Edition de *l'Echo de Paris.* Paris: Ch. Eggimann, 1916.

Benoit, Martine. "Les femmes et la guerre de 14-18: Témoignages." *Le Peuple français* (July-September, 1978): 27-31.

Bérard-Camourtères, Léa, ed. *Au service de la France: Les décorées de la grande guerre.* s.l.: Gravure et Impression SADAG, s.d.

Bizard, Dr Léon. *Les maisons de prostitution de Paris pendant la guerre.* Poitiers: Société Française d'Imprimerie, 1922.

—— *Souvenirs d'un médecin de la Préfecture de police et des prisons de Paris (1914-1918).* Paris: Bernard Grasset, 1925.

Bontoux, Berthe M. [Berthem-Bontoux, pseud.]. *Les françaises et la grande guerre.* Paris: Bloud et Gay, 1917.

Borel, Mme Emile. *La mobilisation féminine en France (1914-1919).* Paris: Imprimerie "Union", 1919.

Bory d'Arnex, Angèle [Jacques Vincent, pseud.]. *Parisiennes de guerre (1915-1917).* Paris: Editions de la France, 1918.

Bosc, Pierre. *Les allemands à Lille.* Paris: Editions de Foi et Vie, 1919.

Bouchardon, Pierre. *Souvenirs.* Paris: Albin Michel, 1953.

Boulenger, Marcel. *Charlotte en guerre ou le Front de Paris.* Paris: La Renaissance du livre, 1917.

Bouvier, Jeanne. *Mes mémoires ou 59 années d'activité industrielle, sociale et intellectuelle d'une ouvrière 1876-1935,* ed. Daniel Armogathe with the collaboration of Maïté Albistur. Paris: La Découverte/Maspero, 1983.

Brion, Hélène. *La voie féministe,* ed. and Preface by Huguette Bouchardeau. Paris: Editions Syros, 1978.

Bussy, Jack de [Jacqueline Liscoät]. *Refugiée et infirmière de guerre.* Paris: Eugène Figuière, 1915.

Capy, Marcelle. *Une voix de femme dans la mêlée.* Paris: Librairie Paul Ollendorff, 1917.

Carles, Emilie. *A Life of Her Own: A Countrywoman in Twentieth-Century France,* as told to Robert Destanque, trans. Avriel H. Goldberger. New Brunswick, NJ: Rutgers University Press, 1991.

Celarié, Henriette. *Emmenées en esclavage.* Paris. Bloud et Gay, 1918.

—— *Les jeunes filles déportées par les allemands.* Paris: Bloud et Gay, 1918.

Citroën, André. "La vie à l'usine." *Les annales conferencia; journal de l'Université des annales.* 1918: 261-75.

Clermont, Camille. *Souvenirs de parisiennes en temps de guerre.* Paris: Berger-Levrault, 1918.

Cloquié, Hortense. *La femme après la guerre; ses droits, son rôle, son devoir.* Paris: Maloine, 1915.

Coetzee, Frans and Marilyn Shevin-Coetzee, eds. *World War I & European Society: A Source Book.* Lexington, MA: D. C. Heath and Company, 1995.

Colette. *Les heures longues.* Paris: Arthème Fayard, 1917.

Colombel, Mme Emmanuel. *Journal d'une infirmière d'Arras: août–septembre–octobre 1914.* Paris: Publications Bloud et Gay, 1916.

Combarieu, Jules. *Les jeunes filles françaises et la guerre.* Paris: Librairie Armand Colin, 1916.

Congrès national des droits civils et du suffrage des femmes, Paris, 1908, ed. Mme Oddo Deflou. Paris: 1910.

Corday, Michel. *The Paris Front: An Unpublished Diary: 1914–1918.* New York: E. P. Dutton & Co., 1934.

Coubé, Abbé Stéphen. *Le patriotisme de la femme française.* Paris: P. Lethielleux, 1916.

Courson, Comtesse Roger de. *La femme française pendant la guerre.* Paris: P. Lethielleux, s.d.

Crémieux, Julie. *Croquis d'heures vécues, 1914–1919.* Fourmies: Imprimerie Bachy, 1934.

Croÿ, Marie de. *Souvenirs de la princesse Marie de Croÿ.* Paris: Librairie Plon, 1933.

Daudet, Julie Rosalie Céleste. *Journal de famille et de guerre 1914–1919.* Paris: Bibliothèque-Charpentier, 1920.

Delarue-Mardrus, Lucie. *Mes mémoires.* Paris: Gallimard, 1938.

Delécraz, Antoine. *1914: Paris pendant le mobilisation: Notes d'un immobilisé.* Geneva: Editions du journal *La Suisse,* [1915].

Delétang, Louise. *Journal d'une ouvrière parisienne pendant la guerre.* Paris: Eugène Figuière, 1935.

Deleutre, Paul [Paul d'Ivoi, pseud.]. *1914–1915: Femmes et gosses héroïques.* Paris: Ernest Flammarion, 1915.

Descaves, Lucien. *La maison anxieuse.* Paris: Georges Crès & cie., 1916.

Doléris, Dr Jacques Amédée and Jean Bouscatel. *Néo-malthusianisme: Maternité et féminisme: Education sexuelle.* Paris: Masson et cie., 1918.

Donnay, Maurice. *La parisienne et la guerre.* Paris: Georges Crès et cie., 1916.

—— *Lettres à une dame blanche.* Paris: Société littéraire de France, 1917.

Dorgelès, Roland. *Les Croix de bois.* Paris: Albin Michel, 1919.

Dromart, Marie Louise. *Sur le chemin du calvaire.* Paris: La Maison Française, 1920.

Drumont, Mme Edouard. *Le journal d'une mère pendant la guerre.* Paris: Attinger *frères*, [1916].

Duhamelet, Geneviève. *Ces dames de l'hôpital 336.* Preface by Georges Docquois. Paris: Albin Michel, 1917.

Dumur, Louis. *Les défaitistes.* Paris: Albin Michel, 1923.

Duplessis de Pouzilhac, Paul. *Les mouettes aux croix-rouges: contes médicaux de guerre.* Paris: A. Maloine *et fils*, 1917.

Eydoux-Démians, M. *Notes d'une infirmière 1914.* Paris: Librairie Plon, 1915.

Foley, Charles. *Sylvette et son blessé.* Paris: E. Flammarion, 1917.

Formont, Maxime. *La dame blanche.* Paris: A. Lemerre, 1917.

[Foucault, André]. *Cahiers d'une femme de la zone.* Paris: Ernest Flammarion, 1918.

Foucault, Marquise de. *A Château at the Front*, trans. Georges B. Ives. Boston: Houghton Mifflin Company, 1931.

France. Ministère des affaires étrangères. *The Deportation of Women and Girls from Lille.* New York: George H. Doran Company, 1916.

Gaubert, Ernest. *Voix de femmes.* Paris: Georges Crès et cie., 1916.

Gaudin de Villaine, Sylvain. *L'espionnage allemand en France 1914–1916.* Paris: Pierre Tequi, éditeur, 1916.

Gayraud, Amélie. *Les jeunes filles d'aujourd'hui.* Paris: Chez G. Oudin, [1914].

[Geraldy, Paul.] *La Guerre, madame . . .* Paris: Georges Crès et cie., 1916.

Godfroy, Léonie. *Souvenirs d'ambulance et de captivité (Noyon à Holzminden).* Paris: Librairie de "L'Eclair," [1917].

Grafteaux, Serge. *Mémé Santerre, A French Woman of the People*, trans. Louise A. Tilly and Kathryn L. Tilly, ed. Louise A. Tilly. New York: Schocken Books, 1985.

Gramont, Elisabeth de. *Mémoires: Clair de lune et taxi-auto.* Paris: Grasset, 1932.

Gromaire, Georges. *L'occupation allemande en France (1914–1918).* Paris: Payot, 1925.

Gsell, Paul. *Edith Cavell.* Paris: Librairie Larousse, 1916.

Havard de la Montagne, Madeleine. *La vie agonisante des pays occupés; Lille et la Belgique: Notes d'un témoin, octobre 1914–juillet 1916.* Paris: Perrin et cie., 1918.

Hélias, Pierre-Jakez. *The Horse of Pride: Life in a Breton Village,* trans. and ed. June Guicharnaud. New Haven, CT: Yale University Press, 1978.

Hermant, Abel. *La vie à Paris (1916)*. Paris: E. Flammarion, [1917].

Jacquemaire, Madeleine Clemenceau. *Les hommes de bonne volonté*. Paris: Calman-Lévy, 1919.

Jacquet, Victor. *Lettres à une marraine: Notes d'un fantassin*. Paris: La Maison Française d'Art et d'Edition, 1920.

Klotz, L. L. "La femmes française pendant la guerre." *La Renaissance politique économique, littéraire et artistique*. 5 no. 3 (3 February 1917): 2564-6.

La Boulaye, M. de. *Croix et cocarde*. Paris: Librairie Plon, 1919.

Ladoux, Georges. *Les chasseurs d'espions*. Paris: Librairie des Champs-Elysées, 1932.

— *Martha Richard, The Skylark, The Foremost Woman Spy of France*, trans. Warrington Dawson. London: Cassell, 1932.

La Grange, Clémentine de. *Open House in Flanders 1914-1918*, trans. Mélanie Lind. London: John Murray, 1929.

La Hire, Marie de. *La femme française: son activité pendant la guerre*. Paris: Librairie Jules Tallandier, 1917.

Landre, Jeanne. *L'école des marraines*. Paris: Albin Michel, 1917.

Lechartier, Georges-Clément. *La confession d'une femme du monde*. Paris: Plon-Nourrit, 1914.

— *La charité et la guerre*. Paris: Bloud et Gay, 1915.

Legrand, Dr César. *L'assistance féminine en temps de guerre*. Paris: Librairie universelle, 1907.

Lejars, Dr Félix. *Un hôpital militaire à Paris pendant la guerre: Villemin, 1914-1919*. Paris: Masson et cie., 1923.

Léra, Maria [Marc Hélys, pseud.]. *Cantinière de la Croix-rouge 1914-1916*. Paris: Perrin et cie., 1917.

— *Les provinces françaises pendant la guerre*. Paris: Perrin et cie., 1918.

Lesage, Marguerite. *Journal de guerre d'une française*. Paris: Editions de la diffusion du livre, 1938.

Lespine, Louis. *Les hôpitaux de la Croix-rouge française en temps de guerre: Comment les organiser et les faire classer*. Paris: Berger-Levrault, éditeurs, 1914.

Leune, Hélène. *Tel qu'ils sont: Notes d'une infirmière de la Croix-rouge*. Paris: Librairie Larousse, 1915.

Ligue des Droits de l'homme et citoyen. *Miss Edith Cavell, Eugène Jacquet*. Paris 1916.

Martineau, Juliette. *Journal d'une infirmière*. Angers: Imprimerie G. Grassin, 1916.

Massard, Emile. *Les espionnes à Paris*. Paris: Albin Michel, 1922.

Massis, Henri and Alfred de Tarde [Agathon, pseud.]. *Les jeunes gens d'aujourd'hui*. Paris: Librairie Plon, 12th edition, 1919.

Masson, Frédéric. *Les femmes et la guerre de 1914*. Paris: Bloud et Gay. 1915.

Mellor, Mme Paul Alexander. *Pages inédites sur la femme et la guerre: Livre d'or*. Preface by Maurice Donnay. Paris: Devambez, 1916.

Michaux, Baronne Jane. *En marge du drame: journal d'une parisienne pendant la guerre, 1914-1915*. Paris: Perrin et cie., 1916.

Mignon, Dr Alfred. *Le Service de santé pendant la guerre 1914-1918*. 4 vols. Paris: Masson et cie., 1926-7.

Misme, Jane. "La guerre et le rôle des femmes." *La Revue de Paris*. 6 (November 1916): 204-26.

Mistinguett. *Toute ma vie*, 2 vols. Paris: René Julliard, 1954.

Mitchell, Hary. *La marraine: comédie en un acte*. Paris: Librairie Théâtrale, Artistique et Littéraire, 1916.

Moriaud, Gem. *Louise de Bettignies, une héroïne française, une vie romancée*. Paris: J. Tallandier, 1928.

Musigny, Alfred. *Les femmes et l'avenir de la France*. Paris: Editions de la *Revue contemporaine*, s.d.

Nadine. *Rêves de guerre: Une femme de France à ses soeurs françaises*. Ligugé (Vienne): Imprimerie E. Aubin, 1916.

Narsy, Raoul. *La France au-dessous de tout: Lettres de combattants rassemblées*. Paris: Bloud et Gay, 1915.

Office central des oeuvres de bienfaisance, Paris. *Paris charitable pendant la guerre*. Paris: Librairie Plon, 1915.

Pau, Marie-Edmée. *Histoire de notre petite soeur Jeanne d'Arc, dédiée aux enfants de la Lorraine*. Paris: E. Plon et cie., 1874.

Pawlowski, Auguste, "La main-d'oeuvre féminine pendant la guerre." *Revue politique et parlementaire* (10 May 1917): 248-55.

Pelletier, Madeleine. *La femme en lutte pour ses droits*. Paris: V. Giard & E. Brière, 1908.

Pitrois, Yvonne. *Les femmes de 1914-1915*. Geneva: J.-H. Jeheber, [1915].

Prévost, Marcel. *Les anges gardiens*. Paris: Librairie Alphonse Lemerre, 1913.

Provins, Michel. *Ceux d'hier, ceux d'aujourd'hui*. Paris: La Renaissance du livre, 1916.

Rabut, Marie. *Les étincelles*. Dijon: Imprimerie Jobard, 1917.

Rageot, Gaston. *La française dans la guerre*. Paris: Attinger *frères*, 1918.

Redier, Antoine. *La guerre des femmes.* Paris: Editions de la Vraie France, 1924.

Renoult, Abbé Joseph. *Le coeur de la française.* Evreux: Imprimerie Ch. Hérissy, 1916.

Riche, Daniel. *L'amour pendant la guerre.* Paris: Editions J. Ferenczi, 1917.

Richer, Marthe. *Ma vie d'espionne au service de la France.* Paris: Editions de la France, 1935. (In English: *I Spied for France,* trans. Gerald Griffin. London: John Long, 1935.)

Rimbaud, Isabelle. *Dans les remous de la bataille – Charleroi et la Marne – Reims.* Paris: Librairie Chapelot, 1917.

Robert, Henri. "La femme et la guerre." *La Revue mondiale* (May 1917): 243–57.

Roger, Noëlle [Hélène Pittard]. *Les carnets d'une infirmière.* Paris: Attinger *frères,* 1915.

—— *Le feu sur la montagne: journal d'une mère: 1914–1915.* Paris: Attinger *frères,* 1915.

Rossignol, Elisa. *Une enfance en Alsace, 1907–1918.* Paris: Editions Sand, 1990.

Roussel-Lépine, José. "Une ambulance de gare." *Revue des deux mondes* (1 and 15 June 1916): 665–84; 910–34.

Sarcey, Yvonne. "La visite des universitaires des annales aux usines Citroën." *Les annales conferencia; journal de l'Université des annales* 1918: 275–7.

Shéridan [Gaston Edenger]. *Une grande blessée: pages de guerre d'une amoureuse.* Paris: La Renaissance du livre, 1917.

Siegfried, Julie. *La guerre et le rôle de la femme.* Cahors: Imprimerie Coueslant, 1915.

Smith, Bonnie G. *Confessions of a Concierge: Madame Lucie's History of Twentieth-Century France.* New Haven, CT: Yale University Press, 1985.

Spont, Henry. *La femme et la guerre,* 2nd edition. Paris: Perrin, 1916.

Strauss, Paul. "Le travail féminin dans les usines de guerre." *Revue philanthropique* 19 (1917): 113–21.

Taudière, Mme Henry. *En pensant aux absents: Histoire de l'ambulance de l'Absie (de septembre 1914 à mai 1915).* Paris: Plon-Nourrit et cie., 1915.

Tinayre, Marcelle. *La veillée des armes – Le Départ: Août 1914.* Paris: Calmann-Lévy, 1915.

Toulouse, Dr Edouard. *La réforme sociale: Question sexuelle et la femme.* Paris: Bibliothèque-Charpentier, 1918.

Ulmès, Renée d'. *Auprès des blessés*. Paris: Librairie Alphonse Lemerre, 1916.

Valrose, Pierre de. *Une âme d'amante pendant la guerre 1914*. Paris: Perrin et cie., 1916.

Vernet, Madeleine. *Hélène Brion; Une belle conscience et une sombre affaire*. Epône (Seine et Oise): Société d'Edition et de Librairie de "L'Avenir Social" à Epône, 1917.

La vie et la mort de Miss Edith Cavell. Preface by Paul Painlevé. Paris: Fontemoing et cie., 1915.

Vismes, Henriette de. *Histoire authentique et touchante des marraines et des filleuls de guerre*. Paris: Perrin et cie., 1918.

Vitry, Françoise. *Journal d'une veuve de la guerre*. Paris: Maison française d'art et d'édition, 1919.

Wachet, Mme Louis. *La guerre en Champagne, en Argonne et dans les Ardennes: Heures tragiques, impressions et souvenirs*. Paris: Bloud et Gay, 1919.

Weiss, Louise. *Mémoires d'une européenne. I: 1893–1919*. Paris: Payot, 1968.

Witt-Guizot, François de. *La femme et la guerre: Comment une femme peut-elle servir la France en temps de guerre?* Autun: Imprimerie Pernot, 1913.

Zeys, Louise. "Les femmes et la guerre." *Revue des deux mondes* 257 (September–October 1916): 175–204.

4. Secondary Sources

Audoin-Rouzeau, Stéphane. *Men at War 1914–1918: National Sentiment and Trench Journalism in France during the First World War*, trans. Helen McPhail. Providence, RI: Berg, 1992.

—— *La guerre des enfants 1914–1918: essai d'histoire culturelle*. Paris: Armand Colin, 1993.

—— *L'enfant de l'ennemi (1914–1918): Viol, avortement, infanticide pendant la Grande Guerre*. Paris: Aubier, 1995.

Augé-Laribé, Michel. *L'agriculture pendant la guerre*. Carnegie Endowment for International Peace, Division of Economics and History. Histoire économique et sociale de la guerre mondiale, no. 7. Paris: Presses universitaires de France, [192?].

Bard, Christine. *Les filles de marianne: Histoire des féminismes 1914–1940*. Paris: Librairie Arthème Fayard, 1995.

Beauregard, Marie-Josèphe de. *Femmes de l'air*. Paris: Editions France-Empire, 1993.

Bibliography

Becker, Annette. *Les monuments aux morts; Patrimoine et mémoire de la grande guerre.* Paris: Errance, 1989.

—— "D'une guerre à l'autre: mémoire de l'occupation et de la résistance: 1914–1940." *Revue du Nord* 76 no. 306 (July–September, 1994): 453–65.

—— *Oubliés de la Grande Guerre: Humanitaire et culture de guerre 1914–1918: Populations occupées, déportés civils, prisonniers de guerre.* Paris: Editions Noêsis, 1998.

Becker, Jean-Jacques. *1914: Comment les français sont entrés dans la guerre.* Paris: Presses de la fondation nationale des sciences politiques, 1977.

—— *The Great War and the French People,* trans. Arnold Pomerans. New York: St Martin's Press, 1986.

—— and Stéphane Audoin-Rouzeau, eds. *Les sociétés européennes et la guerre de 1914–1918.* Paris: Publications de l'Université de Paris X-Nanterre, 1990.

Berenson, Edward. *The Trial of Madame Caillaux.* Berkeley, CA: University of California Press, 1992.

Blancpain, Marc. *La vie quotidienne dans la France du Nord sous les occupations (1814–1944).* Paris: Hachette, 1983.

Bonneau, Monique. "Luttes ouvrières: Les grèves de 1917 et 1918." *Le Peuple français* (April–June 1979): 24–9.

—— "Les femmes et la guerre de 1914–1918: Les ouvrières et l'industrie de guerre." *Le Peuple français* (July–September 1979): 17–20.

Boulin, Pierre. *L'organisation du travail dans la région envahie de la France pendant l'occupation.* Carnegie Endowment for International Peace, Division of Economics and History. Histoire économique et sociale de la guerre mondiale, no. 29. Paris: Presses universitaires de France, 1927.

Buffton, Deborah Darlene. "The Ritual of Surrender: Northern France Under Two Occupations, 1914–1918, 1940–1944." Ph.D. dissertation, University of Wisconsin, 1987.

Cadogan, Mary and Patricia Craig. *Women and Children First: The Fiction of Two World Wars.* London: Victor Gollancz, 1978.

Challener, Richard D. *The French Theory of the Nation in Arms, 1866–1939.* New York: Columbia University Press, 1955.

Cobb, Richard. *French and Germans, Germans and French: A Personal Interpretation of France Under Two Occupations 1914–1918/1940–1944.* Hanover, NH: University Press of New England, 1983.

Bibliography

Cochet, Annick. "L'opinion et le moral des soldats en 1916 d'après les archives du contrôle postal," 2 Vols. Thèse pour le doctorat. Paris X-Nanterre, 1986.

Cooke, Miriam and Angela Woollacott, eds. *Gendering War Talk.* Princeton, NJ: Princeton University Press, 1993.

Cooper, Sandi E. "Pacifism in France, 1889–1914: International Peace as a Human Right." *French Historical Studies* 17 no. 2 (Fall 1991): 359–86.

—— "Pacifism, Feminism and Fascism in Inter-War France," *The International History Review* 19 no. 1 (February 1997): 103–14.

Cova, Anne. *Maternité et droits des femmes en France (XIXᵉ–XXᵉ siècles).* Anthropos. Paris: Economica, 1997.

Créhange, André. *Chômage et placement.* Carnegie Endowment for International Peace, Division of Economics and History. Histoire économique et sociale de la guerre mondiale, no. 27. Paris: Presses universitaires de France, 1933.

Crofton, Eileen. *Women of Royaumont: A Scottish Women's Hospital on the Western Front.* East Linton, Scotland: Tuckwell Press, 1996.

Cruickshank, John. *Variations on Catastrophe: Some French Responses to the Great War.* Oxford: Clarendon Press, 1982.

Daniel, Ute. *The War From Within: German Working-Class Women in the First World War,* trans. Margaret Ries. Oxford: Berg, 1997.

Darrow, Margaret H. "French Volunteer Nursing and the Myth of War Experience in World War I." *American Historical Review* 101 no. 1 (February 1996): 80–106.

Dottin-Orsini, Mireille. *Cette femme qu'ils disent fatale: Textes et images de la misogynie fin-de-siècle.* Paris: Bernard Grasset, 1993.

Downs, Laura Lee. *Manufacturing Inequality: Gender Division in the French and British Metalworking Industries, 1914–1939.* Ithaca, NY: Cornell University Press, 1995.

Ducasse, André, Jacques Meyer and Gabriel Perreux. *Vie et mort des français, 1914–1918.* Paris: Hachette, 1959.

Ehrenreich, Barbara. *Blood Rites: Origins and History of the Passions of War.* New York: Metropolitan Books/Henry Holt and Company, 1997.

Eksteins, Modris. *Rites of Spring: The Great War and the Birth of the Modern Age.* Boston: Houghton Mifflin Company, 1989.

Elshtain, Jean Bethke. *Women and War.* New York: Basic Books, 1987.

—— and Sheila Tobias, eds. *Women, Militarism and War: Essays in History, Politics, and Social Theory.* Savage, MD: Rowman & Littlefield Publishers, 1990.

Fayet-Scribe, Sylvie. *Associations féminines et catholicisme XIXᵉ– XXᵉ siècle.* Paris: Les Editions Ouvrières, 1990.

Flood, P. J. *France 1914–18: Public Opinion and the War Effort.* New York: St Martin's Press, 1990.

Fournier, Jean Pierre. "Evolution du Service de santé militaire française pendant la guerre de 1914–1918." Thèse, Montpellier III, 1996.

Fridenson, Patrick, ed. *The French Home Front, 1914–1918,* trans. Bruce Little. Providence, RI: Berg, 1992.

Frois, Marcel. *La santé et le travail des femmes pendant la guerre.* Carnegie Endowment for International Peace, Division of Economics and History. Histoire économique et sociale de la guerre mondiale, no. 23. Paris: Presses universitaires de France, 1926.

Gervais, Michel, Marcel Jollivet and Yves Tavernier. *Histoire de la France rurale* Vol. 4: *La fin da la France paysanne de 1914 à nos jours,* Georges Duby and Armand Wallon, general editors. Paris: Editions du Seuil, 1976.

Gillis, John R., ed. *Commemorations: The Politics of National Identity.* Princeton, NJ: Princeton University Press, 1994.

Gordon, Felicia. *The Integral Feminist: Madeleine Pelletier, 1874– 1939.* Minneapolis, MN: University of Minnesota Press, 1990.

Gran-Aymeric, Eve and Jean. *Jane Dieulafoy, une vie d'homme.* Paris: Perrin, 1991.

Grayzel, Susan. "Mothers, *Marraines* and Prostitutes: Morale and Morality in First World War France." *The International History Review* 19 no. 1 (February 1997): 66–82.

Hanna, Martha. "Iconology and Ideology: Images of Joan of Arc in the Idiom of the Action Française, 1908–1931." *French Historical Studies* 14 no. 2 (Fall 1985): 215–39.

—— *The Mobilization of Intellect: French Scholars and Writers during the Great War.* Cambridge, MA: Harvard University Press, 1996.

Harris, Ruth. "The 'Child of the Barbarian': Rape, Race and Nationalism in France During the First World War." *Past & Present* no. 141 (November 1993): 170–206.

Hause, Steven C. *Hubertine Auclert, the French Suffragette.* New Haven, CT: Yale University Press, 1987.

—— with Anne R. Kenney. *Women's Suffrage and Social Politics in the French Third Republic.* Princeton, NJ: Princeton University Press, 1984.

Higonnet, Margaret Randolph, Jane Jenson, Sonya Michel, and Margaret Collins Weitz, eds. *Behind the Lines: Gender and the Two World Wars.* New Haven, CT: Yale University Press, 1987.

Hoehling, A. A. *Edith Cavell.* London: Cassell, 1958.

Horne, John. "'L'impôt du sang': Republican Rhetoric and Industrial Warfare in France, 1914–1918." *Social History* 14 no. 2 (May 1989): 201–23.

—— *Labour at War, France and Britain 1914–1918.* Oxford: Clarendon Press, 1991.

—— "Les mains coupées: <<atrocités allemandes>> et opinion française en 1914." *Guerres mondiales et conflits contemporains* 43 no. 171 (July 1993): 29–45.

Howe, Russell Warren. *Mata Hari, The True Story.* New York: Dodd, Mead & Company, 1986.

Huston, Nancy. "Tales of War and Tears of Women." *Women's Studies International Forum* 5 no. 3/4 (1982): 271–82.

—— "The Matrix of War: Mothers and Heroes." In *The Female Body in Western Culture,* ed. Susan Rubin Suleiman. Cambridge, MA: Harvard University Press, 1986.

Hynes, Samuel. *A War Imagined: The First World War and English Culture.* London: The Bodley Head, 1990.

Jeffords, Susan. *The Remasculinization of America: Gender and the Vietnam War.* Bloomington, IN: Indiana University Press, 1989.

King, Jere Clemens. *Generals and Politicians: Conflict Between France's High Command, Parliament and Government, 1914–1918.* Berkeley, CA: University of California Press, 1951.

Knibiehler, Yvonne, Véronique Leroux-Hugon, Odile Dupont-Hess, and Yolande Tastayre. *Cornettes et blouses blanches: Les infirmières dans la société française (1880–1980).* Paris: Hachette, 1984.

Krop, Pascal. *Les secrets de l'espionnage français de 1870 à nos jours.* Paris: Editions Jean-Claude Lattès, 1993.

Krumeich, Gerd. *Armaments and Politics in France on the Eve of the First World War: The Introduction of Three-Year Conscription, 1913–1914,* trans. Stephen Conn. Dover, NH: Berg Publishers, 1984.

Laouénan, Roger. *La moisson rouge; Les bretons dans la grande guerre.* Paris: Editions France-Empire, 1987.

Bibliography

Leroux-Hugon, Véronique. "L'infirmière au début du XXᵉ siècle: nouveau métier et tâches traditionnelles." *Le Mouvement social* no. 140 (July–September 1987): 55–68.

Lorentzen, Lois Ann and Jennifer Turpin, eds. *The Women and War Reader.* New York: New York University Press, 1998.

Margadant, Jo Burr. *Madame le Professeur: Women Educators in the Third Republic.* Princeton, NJ: Princeton University Press, 1990.

Margolis, Nadia. *Joan of Arc in History, Literature and Film: A Select, Annotated Bibliography.* New York: Garland Publishing, 1990.

Marwick, Arthur. *Women at War, 1914–1918.* London: Croom Helm, 1977.

Maugue, Annelise. *L'identité masculine en crise au tournant du siècle, 1871–1914.* Paris: Editions Rivages, 1987.

McMillan, James F. *Housewife or Harlot: The Place of Women in French Society 1870–1940.* New York: St Martin's Press, 1981.

Meyer, Jacques. *La vie quotidienne des soldats pendant la grande guerre.* Paris: Hachette, 1966.

Miller, Michael B. *Shanghai on the Métro: Spies, Intrigue and the French Between the Wars.* Berkeley, CA: University of California Press, 1994.

Moses, Claire Goldberg. *French Feminism in the 19th Century.* Albany, NY: State University of New York Press, 1984.

Mosse, George L. *Nationalism and Sexuality: Respectability and Abnormal Sexuality in Modern Europe.* New York: Howard Fertig, 1985.

—— *Fallen Soldiers: Reshaping the Memory of the World Wars.* Oxford: Oxford University Press, 1990.

Nye, Robert A. *Masculinity and Male Codes of Honor in Modern France.* Oxford: Oxford University Press, 1993.

Offen, Karen. "Depopulation, Nationalism, and Feminism in Fin-de-Siècle France." *American Historical Review* 89 no. 3 (June 1984): 648–76.

—— "Defining Feminism: A Comparative Historical Analysis." *Signs* 14 no. 1 (Fall 1988): 119–57.

Oualid, William and Charles Picquenard. *Salaires et tarifs: Conventions collectives et grèves.* Carnegie Endowment for International Peace, Division of Economics and History. Histoire économique et sociale de la guerre mondiale, no. 32. Paris: Presses universitaires de France, 1928.

Ouditt, Sharon. *Fighting Forces, Writing Women: Identity and Ideology in the First World War.* London: Routledge, 1994.

Perreux, Gabriel. *La vie quotidienne des civils en France pendant la grande guerre.* Paris: Hachette, 1966.

Pierson, Ruth Roach, ed. *Women and Peace: Theoretical, Historical and Practical Perspectives.* London: Croom Helm, 1987.

Pourcher, Yves. *Les jours de guerre: La vie des français au jour le jour entre 1914 et 1918.* Paris: Plon, 1994.

Prochasson, Christophe and Anne Rasmussen. *Au nom de la patrie: Les intellectuels et la première guerre mondiale (1910-1919).* Paris: Editions La Découverte, 1996.

Rearick, Charles. "Madelon and the Men - in War and Memory." *French Historical Studies* 17 no. 4 (Fall 1992): 1001-34.

—— *The French in Love and War: Popular Culture in the Era of the World Wars.* New Haven, CT: Yale University Press, 1997.

Reynaud, Emmanuel. *Les femmes, la violence et l'armée: Essai sur la féminisation des armées.* Paris: Fondation pour les études de défense nationale, 1988.

Robert, Jean-Louis. "La CGT et la famille ouvrière 1914-1918: première approche." *Le Mouvement social* no. 116 (July-September 1981): 47-66.

Robert, Krisztina. "Gender, Class, and Patriotism: Women's Paramilitary Units in First World War Britain."*The International History Review* 19 no. 1 (February 1997): 52-65.

Roberts, Mary Louise. *Civilization Without Sexes: Reconstructing Gender in Postwar France, 1917-1927.* Chicago: University of Chicago Press, 1994.

Romi. "Enfin la verité sur Marthe Richard." *Paris-Villages* no. 9 (1985): 29-39.

[Ruault, L.] *Cent ans de Croix-rouge française au service de l'humanité.* Paris: Hachette, 1964.

Sarti, Odile. *The Ligue Patriotique des Françaises, 1902-1933.* New York: Garland Publishing, 1992.

Schirmann, Léon. *L'affaire Mata Hari: Enquête sur une machination.* Paris: Editions Tallandier, 1994.

Schultheiss, Katrin. *Bodies and Souls: Politics, Gender and the Professionalization of Nursing in France, 1880-1922.* Cambridge, MA: Harvard University Press, forthcoming.

Shevin-Coetzee, Marilyn and Frans Coetzee, eds. *Authority, Identity and the Social History of the Great War.* Providence, RI; Berghahn Books, 1995.

Slater, Catherine. *Defeatists and Their Enemies: Political Invective in France 1914-1918.* Oxford: Oxford University Press, 1981.

Stewart, Mary Lynn. *Women, Work, and the French State: Labour Protection and Social Patriarchy 1879-1919*. Montreal: McGill-Queen's University Press, 1989.

Thalmann, Rita, ed. *La tentation nationaliste: Entre émancipation et nationalisme, la presse féminine d'Europe, 1914-1945*. Paris: Editions Deuxtemps Tierce, 1990.

Thébaud, Françoise. *La femme au temps de la guerre de 14*. Paris: Editions Stock, 1986.

Theweleit, Klaus. *Male Fantasies*, 2 vols, trans. Stephan Conway in collaboration with Erica Carter and Chris Turner. Minneapolis, MN: Minnesota University Press, 1987.

Tombs, Robert, ed. *Nationhood and Nationalism in France From Boulangism to the Great War, 1889-1918*. London: Harper-Collins, 1991.

Tylee, Claire M. *The Great War and Women's Consciousness: Images of Militarism and Womanhood in Women's Writing, 1914-64*. Iowa City, IA: University of Iowa Press, 1990.

Wall, Richard and Jay M. Winter, eds. *The Upheaval of War: Family, Work and Welfare in Europe 1914-1918*. Cambridge: Cambridge University Press, 1988.

Warner, Marina. *Joan of Arc: The Image of Female Heroism*. New York: Alfred A. Knopf, 1981.

—— *Monuments and Maidens: The Allegory of the Female Form*. New York: Atheneum, 1985.

Watson, Janet S. K. "Khaki Girls, VADs, and Tommy's Sisters: Gender and Class in First World War Britain." *The International History Review* 19 no. 1 (February 1997): 32-51.

Weber, Eugen. *The Nationalist Revival in France, 1905-1914*. Berkeley, CA: University of California Press, 1959.

—— *Action Française: Royalism and Reaction in Twentieth-Century France*. Stanford, CA: Stanford University Press, 1962.

Wheeler, Bonnie and Charles T. Wood, eds. *Fresh Verdicts on Joan of Arc*. Garland Publishing, 1996.

Wheelwright, Julie. *The Fatal Lover: Mata Hari and the Myth of Women in Espionage*. London: Collins & Brown, 1992.

Winock, Michel. "Jeanne d'Arc." In *Les Lieux de Mémoire* Vol. III Part 2. *De l'archive à emblème*, Pierre Nora, general editor. Paris: Gallimard, 1992.

Winter, Jay and Jean-Louis Robert, eds. *Capital Cities at War: Paris, London, Berlin, 1914-1919*. Cambridge: Cambridge University Press, 1997.

Winter, Jay and Emmanuel Sivan, eds. *War and Remembrance in the Twentieth Century*. Cambridge: Cambridge University Press, 1999.

Wishnia, Judith. "Natalisme et nationalisme pendant la première guerre mondiale." *Vingtième siècle* 45 (January–March 1995): 30–9.

Woollacott, Angela. *On Her Their Lives Depend: Munitions Workers in the Great War*. Berkeley, CA: University of California Press, 1994.

Zeiger, Susan. "She Didn't Raise Her Boy to Be a Slacker: Motherhood, Conscription and the Culture of the First World War." *Feminist Studies* 22 no. 1 (Spring 1996): 7–40.

Index

Index

Index

Index